EDUCATION AND RURAL DEVELOPMENT

EDUCATION AND RURAL DEVELOPMENT

Edited by

PHILIP FOSTER and JAMES R. SHEFFIELD

Routledge
Taylor & Francis Group

LONDON AND NEW YORK

First published in 1972

2 Park Square, Milton Park, Abingdon, Oxon, OX14 4RN
711 Third Avenue, New York, NY 10017

Routledge is an imprint of Taylor & Francis Group

British Library Cataloguing in Publication Data
A CIP catalogue record for this book
is available from the British Library

ISBN13: 978-0-415-39294-5 (hbk)
ISBN13: 978-0-415-50245-0 (pbk)

World Yearbook of Education

The World Year Book of Education 1974

Education and Rural Development

Joint Editors:

Philip Foster, B.Sc. (Econ.), Ph.D.
Director, Comparative Education Center
University of Chicago

James R. Sheffield, Ed.D., B.A.
Associate Professor
Teachers College, Columbia University

Published in association with
the University of London Institute of Education
and Teachers College, Columbia University, New York, by
Evans Brothers Limited, London

Published by

Evans Brothers Limited

Montague House

Russell Square

London, WC1B 5BX

© Evans Brothers Limited 1973

First published 1973

Printed in 11/12 Bembo (270) in Great Britain by
Western Printing Services Ltd, Bristol
Bound by the Pitman Press, Bath

ISBN 0 44457 7 PRA 3507

The World Year Book of Education 1974

Editorial Board

Contents

List of Contributors

Anderson, C. Arnold, Ph.D., Professor of Education and Sociology, University of Chicago; Director Emeritus, Comparative Education Center, University of Chicago, U.S.A.

Anderson, John E., B.Soc.Sc., M.A., Principal, College of St. Mark and St. John, Plymouth, England; formerly Lecturer in Education and Sociology, University of Sussex, England

Castillo, Gelia T., Professor of Rural Sociology, Department of Agricultural Education, University of the Philippines, Philippines

Chaudhri, D.P., M.A., Ph.D., Senior Lecturer, University of New England, Australia; formerly Lecturer, University of Delhi, India

Evenson, Robert, Ph.D., Associate Professor of Economics, Yale University, U.S.A.; formerly Visiting Associate Professor of Economics, University of Chicago, U.S.A., and Assistant Professor of Economics and Agricultural Economics, University of Minnesota, U.S.A.

Forni, Nadia, 'Laurea' Political Sciences, M.Sc., Officer, Human Resources and Institutions Planning Unit, FAO, Rome, Italy

Foster, Philip, B.Sc.(Econ.)., Ph.D., Professor of Education and Sociology, University of Chicago; Director of the Comparative Center, University of Chicago, U.S.A.

Green, Donald G, Ph.D., Associate Researcher, Food Institute, East-West Center, University of Hawaii, U.S.A.

Harker, Bruce R., M.A., Ph.D., Assistant Professor, Oakland University, Michigan, U.S.A.; post-doctoral Fellow, University of Chicago, U.S.A.

Holmes, B., Ph.D., Reader in Comparative Education, University of London Institute of Education, London, England.

Hornik, Robert C., M.A., Data Analyst, El Salvador ETV Project Evaluation, Institute for Communication Research, Stanford University, California, U.S.A.

Hunter, Guy, M.A., Programme Director, Overseas Development Institute, University of Reading, England

Lee, H. P., Ph. D., Lecturer in Chinese, Cornell University, Iowa, U.S.A., formerly Researcher, International Council for Educational Development

McAnany, Emile G., B.A., M.A., Ph.D., Acting Assistant Professor, Stanford University, California, U.S.A.; formerly field director, research, ETV El Salvador, consultant to Unesco in Africa

Mayo, John K., A.B., M.A., Ph.D., Lecturer, Department of Communications and Research Associate, Institute for Communication Research, Stanford University, California, U.S.A.

Nash, Manning, B.S., A.M., Ph.D., Professor of Anthropology, University of Chicago, U.S.A.

Odia, Solomon, Employment and Manpower Planning Department, ILO, Geneva; formerly Deputy Director, ILO Area Office, Dar es Salaam, Tanzania

Paulston, Rolland G., B.A., M.So.Sc., Ph.D., Professor of International and Development Education, University of Pittsburgh, U.S.A.; formerly consultant to Unesco, U.S. AID, Ford Foundation, *et al.*

Schultz, Theodore W., Honorary LL.D., Ph.D., Professor (Charles L. Hutchinson Distinguished Service Professor), University of Chicago, U.S.A.; formerly Chairman, Department of Economics, University of Chicago, U.S.A.

Sheffield, James R., B.A., Ed.D., Associate Professor of Education at Teachers College and Director of the Center for Education in Africa at Teachers College, Columbia University, U.S.A.

Singleton, John E., Ph.D., Professor of Education and Anthropology, University of Pittsburgh, U.S.A.; formerly Chairman, International and Development Education Program, University of Pittsburgh, and Associate Director, International Development Fellowships Program, East-West Center, University of Hawaii, U.S.A.

Voisin, André, B.Sc., formerly Technical Counsellor to the Minister of Agriculture, Government of Gabon, and Agricultural Education Officer, FAO, Rome, Italy

Watts, Ronald, B.Sc., free-lance journalist, and consultant; formerly Principal, Embu Institute of Agriculture, Kenya, and Lecturer in Agricultural Extension, Makerere University, Uganda

Wilson, Fergus B., C.B.E., M.A., formerly Chief, Agricultural Education, Extension and Rural Youth Service, FAO, Rome, Italy, and Professor of Agriculture and Dean of the Faculty of Agriculture, Makerere University, Uganda

Wood, A. W., M.A., M.Phil., Ph.D., Chief, Divisions of Programme Development and Liaison, Bernard van Leer Foundation, The Hague, Netherlands

Preface

It is very appropriate that this edition of the *World Year Book of Education* should concern itself with rural development. Since the end of the Second World War, a vast amount of scholarly ink and practical action has been devoted to the problems of the less developed areas of the world and however currently preoccupied we might be with some of the immediate educational 'crises' of the developed nations, we should do well to remember that about two-thirds of the world's population still lives in countries with an average per capita income of less than $250.00 per year. Of these, the vast majority are rural dwellers who continue to depend upon agriculture for their livelihood, and there can be little doubt that in the less developed nations rural people have often been shortchanged in the allocation of social and economic benefits. Although it can be argued that the distinction between urban and rural is not always so clear cut as we believe, it is still true that in most areas the gap between urban and rural levels of welfare continues to widen and may ultimately lead to forms of extreme political reaction to what are increasingly seen as intolerable circumstances. If for no other reason than the recognition that some of these extreme imbalances must be rectified, we feel that this volume is timely and perhaps overdue.

Upon considering the format to be adopted for this edition of the *World Year Book*, we finally rejected the notion of trying to provide a 'world wide' coverage of the theme. Our feeling was that any attempt to include materials on the relationships between education and rural development in all major geographic regions might lead to the production of a descriptive catalogue with little analytic content. We therefore decided to invite a limited number of authors whom we believed could make substantial conceptual or empirical contributions to the discussion of education and rural development either from the standpoint of a particular discipline or as a result of their substantial direct experience in field situations. We make, therefore, no apology for not having provided a universal coverage of problems and areas, but trust that the essays will provide a series of complementary insights to the reader. Moreover, in our introductory section to the *Year Book*, we have felt constrained to present some of our own views on crucial issues in education for rural development. Certainly, these summary observations by no means reflect the opinions of a number of individual contributors, but neither of us felt comfortable with the constraints of a purely passive editorial role.

Finally, we announce with regret that this is the final edition of the *World Year Book of Education*. The decision not to continue with its publication was only made after long and earnest discussion by the editorial board and was prompted by several considerations. When it was first conceived, the *Year Book* performed a vital function in what was then a limited universe of scholarship and provided a valuable medium for the discussion of significant issues among a relatively small group of scholars and practitioners. Within the last decade or more, however, there has been a major proliferation of educational research journals and the field of comparative studies has itself become more specialized and infinitely more complex. In line with what we believe to be an almost inevitable trend in most disciplines, it has become clear that scholars now increasingly prefer to publish their research and findings within more specialized periodicals with the result that the pool of potential contributors to the *Year Book* has declined. Moreover, there are hard logistical problems connected with the continuous publication of an annual volume on a multiplicity of themes: given the sheer explosion of knowledge in the last twenty years, it has become virtually impossible for any general editor or group of editors to keep abreast of developments in such a way as to feel they have relative mastery of all aspects of the field of study. Two decades ago, it might have been possible to point to one or two scholars who could claim 'omnicompetence' in the field of comparative education— anyone who made such a claim now could hardly expect to be taken seriously! Thus the editorial burden has continued to increase while it has not been found practical to continue with the *Year Book* on the basis of continuously recruiting special advisory editors for the publication of each specific volume. For these reasons alone, therefore, it has become increasingly difficult to publish the *Year Book* on an annual basis.

Dr. Brian Holmes was therefore invited by the editorial board to prepare a 'valedictory' chapter to be included in the present volume. This is a particularly appropriate choice, since his connexion with the *Year Book* has lasted for many years, and it is to his efforts that much of the continued high standard of the annual productions is due.

Philip Foster
University of Chicago

James R. Sheffield
Teachers College,
Columbia University

General Introduction

Philip Foster and James R. Sheffield

It is not surprising that educational planners in less developed countries enter the 70s in a somewhat chastened mood. Over the last decade or more the formidable expansion of educational facilities that has taken place in most of these nations rested upon rather tenuous evidence concerning the role that education plays in the general development process. The notion that schools were *the* primary vehicle of development was rather an act of faith than a result of solid empirical evidence and in the light of recent events, one can only conclude that in many respects the consequences of educational planning have fallen short of initial expectations and hopes. Indeed, we are all a good deal more cautious now about what we can expect from the schools and we increasingly recognize that the problems of national development are a good deal more intractable than we had initially supposed.

In consequence, there has been much greater hesitancy in recommending massive increases in educational expenditures in the developing nations and the orthodoxies of the 60s have far less currency than they did; there is less talk about the overwhelming need for the production of high and middle-level manpower as if this, in itself, guaranteed development and few writers now speak in terms of 'global educational planning linked to general social and economic priorities'. Above all, we are far more conscious of the severe political constraints within which planning must occur and it is not by chance that in the last two or three years we have increasingly begun to speak of the 'political economy' of educational planning—a better way of describing perhaps what planning *really* involves.

It is unlikely therefore that we shall see another 'Ashby Report', for example, with its plea for the generation of 'massive, expensive and un-conventional plans' for educational development and its suggestion that 'every available penny' be invested in education.[1] There is certainly room for 'unconventionality' in educational planning but there is an increasing reluctance to give education an almost unqualified priority over develop-ment in other sectors. Basically, the major deficiency in so many of the national education plans of the 1960s was the sheer impossibility of evaluating their economic and social outcomes. But it is the evaluation of outcomes that lies at the very heart of the planning process and a belated recognition of this fact has led to a far more pragmatic orientation and a greater will to carefully assess the consequences of *specific* educational changes. Rather than view educational development as resulting from an overall 'master plan' there is a willingness to try a series of educational alternatives and to see which 'experiments' seem to work and, just as significantly, to see what innovations can be diffused widely and at low cost. As some cynics have noted, virtually any scheme can be made to work providing enough money is poured into it, but the real problem is to see which of them are really self-sustaining and can be effectively replicated.

Current scepticism does not imply that educational planning is a dead issue; it merely means that our definition of the process has changed and we now realize that planning is not a science but an art – an art which may, indeed, rely upon the gathering of hard empirical data concerning the consequences of educational development but which ultimately involves the formulation of policy in the light of conflicting ends, some of which are not primarily economic in nature. Along with this recognition has gone a greater appreciation of the fact that much education is not confined to the formal schools and that the bulk of effective training in any society occurs in far less structured situations. A few years ago it was unusual to hear any discussion of the extent to which 'informal' education agencies could be harnessed to the development process. As later pages will testify, there is plenty of room for the greater utilization of educational institutions and processes that lie outside the school system, but at the outset a warning is necessary: informal education is only under certain circumstances a *substitute* for schooling – more often than not it is likely to be complementary to it, and there is a very real danger that current enthusiasm for informal education will ignore this point. There is some risk that in the same way that manpower planning was the fad of the 60s that informal education will become the fashion of the 70s. Neither constitutes a panacea, however, and as one of the present writers argued some years ago, the real task is 'to identify potential situations in which other agencies can with adequate inducements take over a large number of educational functions; and . . . to indicate what are the comparative advantages and limitations of various types of educational programmes, in the schools and outside of them, in economic growth.'[2] This task will involve careful, comparative research – not the proclamation of new educational orthodoxies.

Coincident with this sceptical trend has been a greater concern with rural development and some speculation concerning the role that education might be expected to play in the process. To be sure, over the last decade, voices were raised pointing to the relative neglect of rural areas in the less developed nations but much of this comment was ignored for two principal reasons. First, local elites were initially dazzled by the prospects of future industrial growth and it has taken some time for them to recognize that their countries will continue to be heavily dependent upon agriculture for the foreseeable future. Even where the development of agriculture was formally accorded high priority, development was frequently conceived of in terms of large-scale, mechanized agriculture. It has taken time (and sometimes disastrous experience) to convince governments that development in most areas is likely to be dependent upon the stimulation of a transformed peasant agriculture based upon relatively small holdings.

Second, although urban centres generally account for only a small proportion of the population of most less developed countries, it is clear that town dwellers constitute a powerful constituency to which political elites are peculiarly sensitive. It was in the towns that the demand for education initially developed most rapidly, and the relatively greater concentration of schooling in urban centres reflected, therefore, a response to immediate political pressures. Thus, although it is usually true that rural areas command a greater *aggregate* share of resources than the towns (obviously, since in most less developed countries the overwhelming bulk of the population lives in the rural hinterland) it is nonetheless the case that urban centres tend frequently to obtain a *disproportionate* share of benefits.

However, even where it can be assumed that the rural areas are achieving some sort of 'parity' in terms of the allocation of educational resources, the point can still be made that the kind of education provided is ill-adapted to rural 'needs'. Of course, it is in one sense true that schools were initially an urban phenomenon in most developing nations and their curricula and activities reflect, in some measure, the immediate exigencies and demands of the urban environment. But the extent to which urban and rural schools can be allowed to substantially diverge from each other in terms of their curriculum and organization is an issue that has been debated with a variable degree of intensity for well over a century. In both British and French colonial territories, for example, there was a substantial concern over the development of educational organizations and content geared specifically to the needs of village life. As the records shows most efforts in this direction were lamentable failures and retrospectively the reasons for failure are clear enough.

The majority of schemes for a 'rurally biased' educational system rest upon the not unreasonable assumption that the bulk of the population in less developed countries will continue to reside in rural areas for the foreseeable future and will depend upon agriculture for its livelihood. What is a much more questionable issue is to what extent the formal educational system taken alone can contribute *directly* to rural development and by so doing check the 'flight from the land' that so many observers seem to be concerned about.

Historically, there can be little doubt that rural populations have resisted attempts to provide specifically rural or agricultural curricula in the schools. With much justification they have recognized that to accept such a situation would condemn them to a relatively disadvantaged position vis-a-vis urban populations in terms of opportunities for geographical, social and economic mobility. Quite simply, 'separate is not equal' and rural dwellers have long known it. No amount of juggling with the curriculum of the schools for example is likely to alter the legitimate aspirations of rural children and their parents or in some way tie them to the land.

Indeed, we believe that in the educational context much of the debate concerning rural as against urban development is spurious. For many years, by far the majority of children in the less developed areas will not proceed beyond primary school even if they complete it at all. Do we under these circumstances expect these schools to do much more than provide those rudiments of literary and numeracy that in fact underpin development in *both* rural and urban areas? Anyone sufficiently acquainted with the realities of primary schooling in less developed countries will recognize that the schools have a hard enough task to convey these skills without expecting them to perform as spurious agricultural vocational institutions.

Further, this whole line of thought stems from an assumption that one can easily separate out the factors that promote rural as opposed to urban development and keep the two areas distinct. It is this oversimplified model of development that has led some observers, for example, to speak of a 'modern' and 'traditional' economic sector as if these were quite independent entities that hardly influenced each other. In practice, we now discern that there is a whole area of economic activity which does not fall comfortably into either category and in which a large proportion of the working population in the less developed countries is actively engaged. Failure to realize the existence of this 'murky' sector has in fact led some scholars to speak of widespread unemployment among educated school leavers when, in fact, their definition of 'unemployment' is all too inadequate. Doubtless in many less developed countries school leavers find it difficult to find full-time paid wage employment with modern enterprises, but this does not suggest that they are economically inactive or totally unemployed.

In similar fashion then, it sometimes makes little sense to talk of clearly defined urban and rural sectors without recognizing that there is an extensive shadow land between them within which people and resources actively move. In fact, rural and urban development is essentially inter-twined; the boundaries between town and country are relatively fluid with a constant pattern of migration between city and countryside. Individuals may migrate to the towns for a period and return to the home village to acquire agricultural land often with capital derived from urban employment. Alternatively, resources are constantly siphoned back from the towns to rural districts and indirectly, therefore, urban prosperity contributes to rural growth. Conversely, kinship networks often enable the rural migrant to obtain support during periods of temporary urban residence and even where these migrants are residents in towns for substantial periods it is not unusual for them to maintain agricultural enterprises in the countryside that are maintained and im-proved through the use of urban-derived income.

Under such conditions it is not very useful to talk of clearly separable urban and rural educational enterprises. Undoubtedly, in many nations the products of rural schools not infrequently visit the towns in the hope of finding employment but there is now some evidence that if they are unsuccessful in their search, they ultimately return home and do not necessarily swell the ranks of an urban, unemployed *lumpen proletariat*.[3] So long as this kind of mobile situation persists and, surely, it is an inev-itable consequence of the development process itself, it makes little sense to speak of a 'dualistic' system of education catering specifically to the presumed needs of the urban and rural masses. The only societies in which such a system would seem likely to work would be essentially static or those where government was prepared to use some measure of coercion by obliging sub-groups to enter the kinds of educational institution deemed most appropriate for the overall developmental needs of the state irrespective of whether these groups desired this particular form of education or not. We are all of us only too familiar with some current examples where the development of forms of education 'specific to the needs and traditions of minorities' turn out to be no more than rationaliza-tions for sustained inequality.

In summary, therefore, although it is reasonable to assume that formal schooling plays some role in rural and agricultural development, it is quite apparent that schooling *alone* is not likely to effect any major rural transformation. Whatever the role that education plays, it is not likely to be a powerful agency of change if all that we mean by education is the development of specialized vocational or proto-vocational education in agriculture in lower level schools. In fact, education is but one element that contributes to rural development and at certain stages is conceivably far from being the most important.

Obviously, agricultural development presupposes the existence of adequate markets for products and a minimal transportation system.

Supplies of new types of seed and other factor inputs are essential (most of the new 'miracle strains', for example, achieve little unless their use is combined with the extensive employment of fertilizers and irrigation), and this underlines the overwhelming importance of continuous agricultural research. But at the heart of the issue, we believe, lies the question of incentives. If we consider the problems of agricultural development and innovation (a narrower theme than that of rural development) it seems fairly clear that many farmers in the developing nations are far from being 'conservative' in their orientiations and are willing to adopt new agricultural techniques and practices providing there is adequate incentive for them to do so. The truth is that in many cases this simply does not exist; no amount of agricultural education in the schools or extension work among farmers will lead to agricultural development if, for example, irrational pricing policies or regressive taxes on export crops deprive the farmer of any real motivation to transform his methods of production. Likewise, in many areas the constraints of traditional land tenure systems or demands stemming from the network of kinship obligations may operate as serious checks upon the willingness of farmers to invest in the improvement of other land and resources. One can think, therefore, of a number of impediments to agricultural growth that are not likely to be influenced by changes in educational policy and our task becomes, therefore, to assess on the basis of the limited empirical evidence now available what realistic contribution educational development might be expected to make in the general process of rural transformation.

To be sure, the authors of the essays in the ensuing pages of this volume are by no means agreed upon the educational strategies that would seem to be most conducive to rural development. Indeed, their observations range from essentially 'transformationist' viewpoints which suggest that substantial improvement in rural conditions can only take place in the context of more general revolutionary change, to more 'gradualist' orientations wherein development is seen in terms of a multiplicity of small scale changes which in themselves do not presuppose a massive and traumatic restructuring of the entire social order. We are not sure to what extent these polarities are at all reconcileable since they stem, in the last resort, from a set of very different ideological assumptions about the nature of social change. It is most important, however, that we recognize that such profound differences exist and to this end we have included materials on rural development and education in the People's Republic of China, Cuba and Tanzania since it seems to us that these societies exemplify an essentially transformationist approach to rural problems. Indeed, we suspect that some of the articles that appear in this volume would be conceived as largely irrelevant to those who see China, Cuba and

Tanzania as constituting exciting new models for rural development in the third world.

However, one cannot continue a discussion at a purely rhetorical level for, in the last resort, both transformationist and gradualist approaches to development will be judged in terms of the tangible contribution they make to the quality of life in rural areas. In the main, this resolves itself into seeing to what extent these alternative policies lead to a rise in the actual standard of living of the rural masses and at what cost. As one Tanzanian farmer observed 'You can't eat *ujamaa*' and this seems to express to us the essence of the rural problem shorn of its ideological overtones. To return to an earlier remark it is virtually impossible to undertake any substantive judgment of educational strategies for rural development unless we have some techniques of empirically measuring their outcomes. At this stage, however, it does seem to us that a sufficient body of empirical evidence does exist to warrant us reaching some tentative conclusions as to the lines of educational action that would seem to be most viable.

First, education is associated with agricultural modernization insofar as farmers in less developed countries who have acquired some schooling appear more willing to adopt new methods and techniques than their less educated peers. This is not to suggest that uneducated farmers are un-receptive to change, but that the 'propensity to innovate' seems greater among those with more schooling (although, parenthetically, the advantages stemming from this may be partially offset by the increased private and social costs of education). Although the evidence is not unambiguous, it would appear that the principal impact of schooling occurs indirectly through the diffusion of literacy which, in turn, leads to a rise in the general level of communication skills among farmers rather than through the acquisition of specific agricultural expertise within the context of the formal educational system. It is also notable that recent studies indicate that, in general, rates of private and social return to primary education are higher than returns to the secondary or tertiary sectors in most developing areas.

Taken together these two kinds of findings would suggest that investment in a general primary education that concentrates upon the basic acquisition of literacy and numeracy should be accorded a relatively higher priority at early stages of development than all-out concentration upon the production of vocationally trained people at the post-primary level since a 'critical mass' of basic literacy seems to be a necessary, if not sufficient condition for both urban and rural development. This is not to suggest that rural schools should not teach, for example, a form of science that is substantially based upon the study of the local rural environment (surely this is no more than sound pedagogy). However, rural curricula, predicated on the assumption that lower level schools can' effectively teach agricultural techniques or generate enthusiasm and commitment to farming, are largely non-viable. In effect, the major 'target' population for agricultural or rural education is not children but adults who are already more or less committed to an agricultural or rural future. It is the farmer – not the pupil – who must be the main object of specific agricultural training, although this training itself is likely to be more effective when it is extended to an already more or less literate population.

Educational work among farmers can generally take two forms. First, knowledge of new types of input and technique can be diffused through the use of the mass media using both the printed word and radio. However, it is now clear that the effectiveness of such media is extremely limited where a large proportion of the rural population is unschooled. Illiterate farmers cannot read agricultural pamphlets but neither, for that matter, are they particularly responsive to the radio even where this form of communication is already widely diffused. At early stages of development the use of mass media is circumscribed and information is most effective when it is diffused on a substantially face-to-face basis. In other words, effective agricultural training largely takes place through the mediating influence of particular individuals.

This implies that a second strategy based upon *direct* extension work among farmers is likely to be more productive in both the long and short run, and countries committed to both 'gradualist' or 'transformationist' policies seem to be increasingly concentrating upon various forms of extension programmes. It is nonetheless still true that even where rural development is accorded high formal priority in government plans that the proportion of educational resources devoted to the direct education of farmers is usually minuscule; this in spite of the fact that even badly planned extension work can have a high pay-off as opposed to other forms of investment.

At present, the education of farmers takes several alternative forms. Most commonly, agricultural demonstrators and technicians are given responsibility for dealing with all farmers in a general district or region. As later pages will show, such a distribution of resource personnel can seriously lower the effectiveness of farmer education where trained workers are in short supply. As opposed to this 'shotgun' approach some nations have concentrated upon working with specific subgroups within the farming population: these are frequently 'master farmers' who have already demonstrated innovatory capacities and who seem to be most receptive to the diffusion of new techniques and practices. In effect, master farmer programmes depend ultimately on the assumption that there will be a substantial 'trickle down' effect from the immediate beneficiaries of agricultural programmes to the majority of less effective agriculturalist within the region. Finally, it has become increasingly common in some areas to provide agricultural training in short-term residential courses where farmers from a given area can receive a more intensive instruction on a given topic, under more qualified staff, than most extension programmes can muster.

All these alternative types of programme have their specific logistical problems and it would be premature to conclude what particular forms of curriculum and organization together, or in combination, are most useful. Once again, therefore, the need for careful evaluation of specific types of training project is imperative. However, one thing seems to be true of all forms of extension and farmer training: their effectiveness is lowered if these efforts are not paralleled by a substantial research input. It is in this area that the nexus between higher level educational institutions and field efforts is so vital: there is such variability in local agricultural conditions and potentialities that no extension scheme is likely to be highly successful unless it is backed by agricultural research substantially geared to the needs of particular sub-regions. It would be unrealistic to expect tertiary institutions to produce farmers in large numbers: their major role lies in the preparation of research personnel, the generation of research and, in part, the training of agricultural technologists. Training alone is certainly not enough since such inputs must be paralleled by a willingness to invest large sums in research enterprises. The Philippines seem a classic case where the proliferation of agricultural training colleges and universities and the ensuing substantial production of agricultural scientists and technologists has seemed to have little effect on development. Quite apart from multiple 'institutional' impediments to rural change in the Philippines, it would seem plausible that training efforts have had limited effect since they have not been supplemented by any substantial research inputs applicable to local variant situations.

In short, rural development is very much a 'seamless web': technology, research, education, and organization are inextricably intertwined in the process and mutually reinforce each other. Under these circumstances, it is difficult to point to clear priorities in planning although the editors subscribe to the view that *any* kind of planning is effective only insofar as a framework is created in which rural dwellers are able to make some of their *own* decisions concerning the allocation of their resources. Thus far, a great number of rural programmes have been predicated on the basis that the planners know what is best for other people. Such an approach ultimately involves a degree of coercion of farmers and it is small wonder that results have been so meagre in many areas. After a half century of Soviet agricultural planning, for example, the Soviets still suffer endemic agricultural crises and rural productivity remains low in spite of substantial technological inputs. This kind of experience argues for a massive decentralization of decision making processes and an effort to generate relatively pragmatic forms of 'incentive planning' and responsiveness to market conditions in rural development.

Yet it must be conceded that such flexible strategies involving the decentralization of planning procedures and the devolution of responsibilities to more locally based agencies pose serious political risks in the less developed nations. Most governments are committed to policies that would facilitate rural development but they are, at the same time, committed to the notion that economic and social differentials between regions should be minimized. These considerations based upon notions of social equity frequently turn out to be the most powerful determinants of educational policies in the new states; no one acquainted with the African scene, for example, can fail to be impressed by the fact that most major decisions are made in the light of the competing claims of numerous ethnic and regional minorities and in this kind of context, viable strategies conducive to speeding up rates of rural development run afoul of political pressures for parity in the allocation of resources. No communities or groups like to feel that they are being left behind in the development process, and it is possible that decentralized patterns of planning may, indeed, exacerbate differentials between regions; in the short run, at least, areas with greater agricultural potential and more educated innovatory rural populations are bound to pull ahead of more 'backward' areas.

An example of this classic developmental dilemma is to be found in Tanzania. Perhaps no country has committed itself so resolutely to a programme of rural transformation and certainly no less developed nation had consciously attempted to accord such a central role to the schools in this process. At the same time, it has been made very explicit that the pace of development will have to be slowed down if growth is to be achieved only alongside a widening of the economic differentials between regions and ethnic minorities. The paradoxical result has been that where 'progressive' farmers are beginning to emerge and where agriculture is showing signs of growth, the government is apt to regard such developments with suspicion as being contrary to the fundamentally socialist ethos of the new Tanzania.

Egalitarian ideology can, therefore, come into direct conflict with those policies designed to maximize rates of economic development in the rural areas but the equity/efficiency dilemma exists in one form or another in all less developed nations where resources are limited. The present editors believe (though some authors in this volume do not subscribe to the view) that development is only likely to occur where differentials in regional rates of progress are not only tolerated but accepted as an inevitable corollary of the growth process. Planning can achieve a great deal in developing the kind of infrastructure and network of communications necessary for rural development, but in the last resort, many crucial decisions have to be made by rural dwellers themselves. Given the incentives and the information, we have little reason to doubt that the farmers in the less developed nations will respond to new opportunities but transformation in the first instance, at least, might require the emergence of an agricultural 'kulak' class that can provide direct leadership and reference group functions in rural communities. If we believe that this kind of cadre is a prerequisite for development, then our educational and agricultural policies can be geared to facilitating its creation. If, however, we regard the emergence of this kind of group with suspicion (and many less developed countries do) then planning procedures must, of necessity, be based on a far more centralized and perhaps more coercive set of orientations. However, while coercion has apparently produced impressive results in China, for example, there are few if any less developed nations whose elites have a comparable degree of commitment or the political capacity to force change in this manner. In most circumstances if market incentives are suppressed, a heavy burden is placed on the administrative machinery to direct the course of rural development. Regardless of one's political orientation, it is clear that the centralized planning apparatus in most countries simply cannot develop effective programmes for diverse rural populations. We are hopeful, therefore, that rural communities will be increasingly responsible for shaping some of their own educational programmes and will be allowed to play a greater role in helping to make these decisions that are vital to their future.

REFERENCES

1. *Investment in Education*. Report of the Commission on Post-School Certificate Higher Education in Nigeria (Lagos: Federal Ministry of Education, 1960).
2. Philip Foster, 'The Vocational School Fallacy in Development Planning' in C. Arnold Anderson and Mary Jean Bowman (eds.) *Education and Economic Development* (Chicago: Aldine Press, 1965) p. 162.
3. For some observations along these lines see, for example, Lewis Brownstein, *Education and Development in Rural Kenya: a Study of Primary School Graduates* (New York: Frederick Praeger, 1972); and Tina Wallace, *Working in Rural Buganda: A Study of the Occupational Activities of Young People in Rural Villages and Young and Unemployed – Who is and What Does it Mean* (Department of Sociology, Makerere University) mimeographed.

General Issues

Philip Foster and James R. Sheffield

With a topic as diffuse as 'Education and Rural Development' it becomes a formidable task to organize an edited volume in terms of any clearcut classificatory scheme. The articles that follow are either based upon a disciplinary stance and indicate what kinds of contribution to contemporary discussion can be expected from the various social sciences or, alternatively, they stem from prolonged practical experience in different types of action-oriented programme with which various writers have been associated. To this extent the eclectic field experience of some contributors provides a useful counterpoint to the more systematically oriented approach of the social scientist: an exercise, perhaps, in the relation between theoretical and practical wisdom. Moreover, the authors can also be distinguished in the degree to which they have oriented themselves to a broad discussion of general themes in an essentially comparative perspective or have rather concentrated their discussion upon the problems of particular regions or countries. It is upon this principle that we decided to divide the present volume into two sections. The first treats a number of general issues whether viewed from the perspective of distinct social sciences or more diffuse experience while the second concerns itself more directly with what are in effect 'case histories' in development.

Part I begins with a general discussion by Fergus Wilson who views the problem from the vantage point of long experience in agricultural education in East Africa and then later with FAO in Rome. Wilson's field perspective is then balanced by C. Arnold Anderson's more sociologically oriented overview that examines the appropriate loci for different types of rural education within the framework of a typology of needs. The economists make their first contribution in Theodore Schultz's critical examination of the state of current knowledge as to the role that farmer education can play in the process of agricultural development and in doing so he dispels many current myths concerning farmer behaviour and 'mentality'.

From a rather different perspective Hornik, Mayo and McAnany also emphasize the complex interplay between technology, the 'message', the target, the audience and existing incentive structures. While they note the possibility of stimulating rural community activities through the use of the mass media, they are also acutely conscious of the limitations of such an approach and certainly do not see the development of media technology as constituting any panacea for rural problems.

Donald Green links two salient current orientations by developing a broad conceptual framework for viewing non-formal education in the context of systems analysis. In many ways, his essay is in sharp contrast to the microcosmic orientation of the anthropologist: John Singleton in his overview of the relationships between school and local community does well to remind us of the basic social and cultural realities that may facilitate or hinder the implementation of broadly conceived strategies for change.

Perhaps one of the most vexing problems of the less developed countries is the considerable underutilization of the talents of rural youth and E. W. Wood describes some of the more promising efforts to develop effective out-of-school programmes for youth in rural areas. By contrast, E. R. Watts, drawing upon his extensive field experience in East Africa examines some general strategies to meet the educational needs of adults who are already committed to the farm life. Watts has some important things to say concerning the use of extension services but his paper is particularly useful when read in conjunction with Robert Evenson's more analytic discussion of the relation between research, extension and schooling in agricultural development. In effect, the latter argues that both formal and informal education will only have limited impact if climatic sub-regions are not prepared to invest in high quality and fundamental research.

Finally, Nadia Forni's broad overview of a variety of recent developments in rural education serves as a useful bridge to the case studies in Part II.

Education for Rural Development

Fergus B. Wilson

The first UN Development Decade opened with high hopes and widespread expectations, more particularly on the part of newly independent nations, that through concerted planning and an expansion of technical assistance of many kinds some, at least, of the more serious economic and social problems facing the developing countries of the world would be solved or greatly alleviated. In the field of education, the decade was, in many areas, characterized by an unprecedented expansion of education and training. New universities, technical colleges and a wide range of other educational institutions were established. At the international level, Unesco, along with other specialist agencies of the United Nations – FAO, ILO and WHO – greatly expanded their services to general education as well as to vocational, technical and professional training in many fields. Educational planning also received an important stimulus under the aegis of the International Institute for Educational Planning (Unesco) inaugurated in 1963. Under a wide variety of programmes of international and bi-lateral technical assistance, together with the work of foundations and non-government organizations, support was given for the expansion and improvement of institutions of education and training throughout the developing world. Finance to support the capital implications of many of these programmes has been made available through the World Bank (IBRD) and its associated regional organizations as well as through other technical assistance bodies.

It might reasonably be claimed, therefore, that in terms of financial investment, technical assistance, and other forms of support, the 1960s should have resulted in highly significant advances in meeting urgent national needs for trained manpower as well as in the broader fields of rural and national development. In most of the countries concerned, education costs represent one of the largest single items of the national budget and governments are entitled to expect a steadily increasing return in respect of what is essentially a long-term investment. In practical terms, it must be seen not merely as satisfying a basic human right but also as making direct and specific contributions to the achievement of national development policies and plans. Judged by some of these criteria it could hardly be claimed, except in a relatively few instances, that as a result of the very substantial 'input' of educational investment throughout the decade, the major problems of national development have been brought markedly nearer solution. Indeed, it might very reasonably be observed that for many governments their economic and social problems are at least as grave and considerably more urgent than they were ten years or so ago. Massive unemployment and underemployment, both in urban and rural areas, are widespread phenomena. Very substantial numbers of school leavers are unable to find any paid employment in which they can begin to develop the skills they have learned in school or elsewhere. National wealth has not expanded at rates which would really stimulate the expansion of local industry or trade and commerce and thus open up job opportunities for young people. Agriculture, the sheet anchor of the economies of so many of these countries, has failed to expand and intensify its production at a sufficient rate to fully meet the food needs of rapidly increasing populations or to generate much needed rural wealth. It would, of course, be incorrect to attribute this lack of adequate progress to the failure of education, for many other factors have contributed. Nevertheless, these disappointments must be a matter of vital concern to educationists if they are to claim, as is the purport of this chapter, that education is a 'key' element in the whole of rural and national development.

Within education systems themselves there are many factors which are giving grave concern not only to governments but also to those directly responsible for the implementation of national educational policies. Statistics show, for example, an alarming dropout rate in many primary school systems and, in spite of all the educational effort, increasing numbers of illiterate people in not a few countries. Perhaps more serious than this is a widespread feeling in many of the developing nations that the kinds of education which have been introduced and fostered over the past few decades have very limited relevance to their situation, problems and immediate needs. So far as rural development is concerned it might even be claimed that much formal education is counter-productive in the sense that it has tended to alienate children from agriculture and the social traditions of the rural environment and created in them the desire for clerical types of employment which, in present circumstances, only a very small proportion of school leavers can hope to achieve. There is, in fact, evidence of a deep questioning of the validity of many kinds of education and a growing desire to evolve new policies more attuned to national situations, aspirations and needs. Many of the systems currently in force have had their origin in countries which are highly industrialized with urban-based populations. It is hardly surprising that they have not proved to be well suited for countries where a large proportion of the population is rural and which have only fairly recently embarked upon the complex process of modernization. In the past there have been many attempts, through adding agriculture and school gardening to the curriculum, to give educational systems a 'rural bias'. In general these efforts have been far from successful and it is now realized that nothing short of a general and continuing reform of entire systems of education and technical training is necessary if they are to be effective instruments of progress. The primary concern of this paper is the contribution of education to rural development but since national systems must broadly conform to a general pattern and since also urban and rural development are essentially complementary it is considered necessary to offer the foregoing generalizations as a background.

Rural Areas and National Development

It is now widely accepted that rural areas and rural people have an exceptionally important role to play in the future progress and prosperity of most of the developing countries. In the first place the great majority of the people of these countries are rural dwellers who derive their livelihood from agriculture and related occupations. Statistics for the countries of Africa, for example, show that at present more than 80 per cent of the total population are rural (in a few countries it is somewhat less and in others it is up to 90 per cent or more). Projections of population growth and distribution made in connection with FAO's Indicative World Plan for Agricultural Development – 1965/85 – show that this proportion of rural dwellers is unlikely to fall by more than 5 to 10 per cent during the period under review whilst the total number of rural people is, in fact, likely to increase due to population growth. Secondly, most of the countries concerned are basically agricultural – the land and its potential for development are their most important single asset. Indeed it might be said, in many instances, that the steady and sustained improvement of agricultural productivity represents the essential basis of many other forms of development including that of local industries and commerce. Traditionally in many parts of the world the rural areas have been and still are a continuing source of skilled manpower for the growing towns and cities and their expanding commercial and industrial enterprises. In many of the developing countries, however, the rural areas have a new kind of role to play. They have, somehow or other, to provide occupations and livelihood for very large numbers of young people who, in present circumstances, cannot be absorbed into urban life and employment. It might therefore be claimed that in addition to a vital economic function the rural areas also have an extremely important social contribution to make in present difficult circumstances. Thus rural development is beginning to assume a far more important place in many national policies than was the case ten to twenty years ago. Rural development is also attracting considerable support under technical assistance programmes in which, more and more, the basic problems as well as their solution are seen to be essentially human. Indeed, the human resources of the rural areas are seen as their greatest potential asset and education as one of the key elements in their motivation and training for the service of development.

In a situation where future progress and prosperity are so dependent upon the improvement of agriculture and the development of related rural crafts and industries, it is somewhat paradoxical that agriculture as a professional career and farming as a vocation hold so little attraction for young people and enjoy so poor an image in the public esteem. Indeed, for the more intelligent and ambitious rural children, education for many years has been looked upon as providing the major escape route from the drudgery and miserable financial returns of subsistence or near-subsistence agriculture to the better prospects and greater amenities of urban life and employment. Farming is seen as the occupation which young people may be obliged to follow if they are unsuccessful in ascending the educational ladder or finding part employment elsewhere. Agriculture is the low-choice option for prospective students whose academic attainment at school has failed to qualify them for entry to medicine, engineering or other prestige subjects at college or university. There are, of course, exceptions to this dismal state of affairs and public opinion is slowly changing but all too frequently agriculture is still the 'poor relation' of other professions.

It is not difficult to discern the main reasons for this state of affairs. In relatively few of the developing countries has the application of science and technology significantly changed the basic patterns of peasant sub-sistence agriculture. Almost all operations from land preparation to harvest are still by hand labour using primitive tools and implements. Crop as well as livestock production is subject to the hazards of climate and pests and diseases, on soils and pasture land which are often impoverished. Invest-ment in land improvement, the use of fertilizer, more productive strains of seed, better tools and equipment are often minimal for the majority of farmers do not have access to the necessary resources for their purchase. Levels of production are low and what seasonal surpluses may be available for cash sale are subject to unpredictable fluctuations in the local market. Often there is no properly organized system of marketing. In some countries the incongruous spectacle is seen of well developed and highly profitable estate enterprises alongside large numbers of small peasant holdings still operating at subsistence level. It is the general condition and lack of prospects of these numerous small underdeveloped and under-financed family farms which have helped to give to agriculture its poor image in so many countries. The urgent need for rural development, the need to create far more worthwhile job opportunities for young people in rural areas, and the need to expand and diversify agricultural production all imply a far greater investment in the rural community and in the creation of an institutional structure to support a growing, modern agricultural industry.

The establishment of a satisfactory basis upon which to build new and far more productive systems of farming is a lengthy, complex and difficult business. Each country, and often the different regions within countries, pose their special problems which call for careful study and the trial and evaluation of new methods before a general advance is possible. In many instances basic reforms in land tenure may be required before new and viable systems of modern farming can be established. In many of the developing countries the cash earning elements superimposed upon traditional systems of subsistence agriculture have consisted principally of crops grown for export. Whilst it is true that many of these cash export crops have been important sources of foreign exchange for the countries which produce them, they have certainly not provided a broad base for a sustained rise in the productivity of peasant agriculture. The unit value of most of these primary products of tropical agriculture has not risen proportionately with the cost of imported manufactured goods in the post-war period. Thus, although production for export must continue to be an important source of revenue in many of the tropical countries of peasant agriculture, the search for new strategies to ensure a more permanent and satisfactory basis for agricultural growth and prosperity continues. The future emphasis must surely be, in many instances, upon production geared to the expanding needs of the industries and urban populations of the countries and regions themselves. To an ever increasing extent prosperity in local agricultural systems will depend in the main upon their ability to produce efficiently those crops, livestock and horticultural products required by urban and industrial populations and new industrial processes within individual countries or common market regions. In such ways it is possible to see the complementary roles of agriculture and other industries; of rural and urban interests. In an expanding and prosperous agriculture there will be a growing demand for the supplies, services and facilities essential to a modern industry. Likewise such services will inevitably imply the establishment of rural-based industries, banks, workshops, cooperative organizations and the like. Not only will such developments generate employment opportunities outside farming itself, but they also will depend very greatly upon education and technical training in a wide range of skills. Finally, and perhaps most important of all, such fundamental changes in agriculture and in rural society are only likely to be achieved as attitudes are changed and people – individuals, families and communities – can be drawn into new aspirations and endeavour. Herein lies both the challenge and the opportunity for all those responsible for the planning and implementation of educational policy and programmes in the future.

Education as a Component of Rural Development

It will be clear from this brief survey of the agricultural situation and some of the problems associated with change and development in rural areas that if education is to make its most effective contribution it will itself need to undergo major changes both in content and application. Whole systems of education will need to be geared to meeting the needs of a dynamic situation. Not only do the planners of specific rural development projects need to give far more attention to their educational implications, but also it is essential for educators to envisage their function as partners in the development team. Experience in many countries has shown how complex is the whole process of rural development and that attention to certain aspects and neglect of others can lead to the waste of resources and ultimate failure and disappointment. The 'package deal' involving the combined use of irrigation, fertilizers, improved husbandry practices and new techniques along with high yielding strains of seed in the programme of the 'green revolution' is but a single example in the field of agricultural improvement. Individual components of this package could not, by themselves, have achieved a break-through in productivity. The major factors involved in rural development are much more complex for they concern different government ministries, local and central authorities, and all the problems of priorities when available resources are exceedingly limited. Education and vocational training in agriculture can achieve little in support of agricultural development in the absence of a strong government policy, backed by financial support, for developing the agricultural resources of the nation. It is no good encouraging young people to choose farming as a career and providing them with technical training if, in fact, farming as it exists offers almost no opportunities of a better life and a reasonable cash income. Young people are simply not satisfied to bind themselves to the kind of life which their parents in the rural areas have been obliged to follow. Thus education and training in the context of rural development need to be linked to a vigorous and effective policy for the development of agriculture, rural crafts and local industries. In the same manner, ministries responsible for agriculture, public health, labour, community development and the like are themselves greatly dependent upon education in all its aspects for the success of their development programmes.

Few would disagree with the need for more effective coordination of the work of the different government departments and non-governmental agencies involved in rural development. The problem really assumes formidable proportions when it comes to the practical implications of implementing such a policy. And yet this must be done if real and lasting progress is to be achieved. Many governments already have machinery in the shape of ministries of economic planning or national development councils which provide a basis for coordination and cooperation between the work of the various bodies directly involved in rural development. To be fully effective such cooperation must clearly exist at all levels and, in particular, at the community level. It is not too much to expect that under enlightened leadership the village school, the rural training centre and any other educational institution at this level should provide a focal point and forum where extension workers and others can find a congenial meeting ground where they can gain an understanding of the aims and work of other members of the development team and explain their own. Circumstances vary greatly and the manner in which effective cooperation can be achieved will also differ from country to country and even within different areas of the same country.

This vital need for teamwork can be met in many different ways. Perhaps one of the most important is at the stage when those who are to be trained for work in rural areas – teachers, agricultural extension workers, public health personnel, cooperative staff and others – are undergoing their professional training. Even if the separate 'schools' in which these people are trained need to be distinct there is surely a very strong case for siting them in close proximity so that certain basic courses can be common to all and students can share a common social life. This is the broad function of universities and of many polytechnics where separate faculties enjoy a measure of independence and autonomy but also derive the great advantages of many common services (libraries, residential facilities, etc.) and integration within a single institutional structure. There is scope for much greater consultation and cooperation in the modification of course structures and individual syllabi in all aspects of education connected with rural development. Since the system of general education provides the essential foundations upon which subsequent technical and vocational training are based it is clear that this, too, will call for much modification in the light of changing needs and circumstances.

One of the major themes of International Education Year (1970) was that of life-long education – a process which starts in the pre-school life of the child, is developed throughout formal schooling, and continued in one form or another in adult life. Education is thus conceived as a steady and continuing process in which literature, the mass media, and further education courses of many kinds all have important contributions to make. The development of work-oriented literacy programmes provides further evidence of the recognition that education, especially in rural areas, must embrace those who have not had the benefit of formal schooling as well as others who may have had some schooling but who, without further help, will lapse into illiteracy. Thus both in formal education as well as the growing extent of informal education there is a clear recognition of its enormous importance to the whole process of rural and national development. Regular in-service training courses for those who often work in relative isolation – village school teachers, agricultural extension workers, and others – not only provide an essential opportunity to enable them to keep abreast of developments important for their work but also a most useful 'feed-back' of experience of those who operate at the field level in rural programmes.

Thus if education is to become a key element in the whole process of rural change and development, present systems in many countries will need to undergo much modification. Both primary and secondary schooling need to relate their structure and curricula far more realistically to both the urban and rural environment. They need to lay sound foundations not so much for higher education of an academic type as for the development of skills and initiative in the whole range of vocational, technical and professional training. The extraordinary notion that university education is so greatly superior to other kinds of technical and vocational training has somehow to be overcome for it is at these other levels that skilled people are required in very considerable numbers for all the essential processes of development. Universities can themselves make important contributions in overcoming this problem through their extra-mural activities, and in-service training courses for those who have not previously attended university and through special support and help for teachers and trainees at all levels. Unless a better balance is achieved between the different kinds and levels of technical education and training and better career prospects established for skilled technicians, education will fail to make its proper contribution to the real needs of development. The establishment of more efficient and productive systems of farming certainly calls for the services of highly trained scientists, engineers, economists and others but it cannot be achieved in practice without the support of very considerable numbers of people skilled in the many aspects of new management practices of crop and livestock production. In many cases very large numbers of small scale farmers need to be convinced of the advantages of adopting new practices and given detailed technical instruction in their use. This is a task calling for a high degree of skill and ingenuity on the part of field extension staff. The efficient functioning of cooperative marketing, credit and farm supplies organizations is again dependent upon sound basic training and regular in-service courses for technical and administrative staff. Once again it is necessary to invoke the concept of a harmonious and well balanced team approach to agricultural and rural development in which the central figures are the farmer, the farm family and the rural community.

Agriculture and the School System

Reference has already been made to attempts in many parts of the developing world to give to education a 'rural bias' through the addition of agriculture as a school subject and in many instances through the development of school gardens. There have also been many attempts through the provision of 'farm schools' to provide a practically based vocational training for primary school leavers who, it was hoped, would enter farming as a career and by putting into practice the improved methods they had been taught, would induce others to follow. More recently a number of governments have adopted the policy of including agricultural science or vocational agriculture as specific subjects in the secondary school curriculum and substantial numbers of agriculturists are being trained as teachers. At the less formal level there have been developments on a large scale of Young Farmers Clubs, 4-H type clubs and other activities of this kind. Many of the more recent developments have not been in operation for a sufficient length of time to form an objective judgment as to their influence in effecting a real change of attitude towards farming as a career or making a significant contribution to agricultural development. It may still be true to state that the majority of those who take agricultural subjects in secondary school do so in the hope that it will ultimately lead to paid employment rather than to a career in farming. At the present low level of peasant farming in many countries and the shortage of available good land and essential services such an attitude is understandable. It underlines the proposition that training for work in agriculture must essentially be complemented by a vigorous policy of agricultural and rural development.

If agriculture and its development are so vital to the life and progress of so many countries it certainly seems reasonable that it should feature in the general school curriculum. Whether it should best take the form of a specific subject-matter field or be taught there indirectly through the use of agricultural examples in a number of the subjects taught (as, for example, in biology, geography or mathematics) will be dictated by circumstances. Many believe that the school system itself is best used as a preparation for subsequent vocational or technical training which are most effectively provided by the institutions which are organized in close association with farming and other rural occupations and industries. Within the primary school system children are often too young to be taught the manual skills associated with farming. School gardens have all too often been the means of alienating children for life from the desirability of farming as a career. Somehow or other they tend to be associated with laborious and rather unrewarding manual tasks. Only in exceptional instances are they places which excite the interest and pride of children. Ideally they should provide the most interesting and relevant laboratory in the school, but this is rarely achieved since very few of the teachers concerned have had the kind of training whereby they are able to make effective use of a well-planned garden as well as of the countryside around in their teaching.

It would certainly seem appropriate that from an early age children in both urban and rural areas should be made aware of the place of agriculture in the life and progress of their nation. There is much that could be taught of the manner in which different patterns of land use have evolved in relation to major factors of the environment. Appropriately, the production of crops and livestock may be linked to the teaching upon nutrition and diet now being developed in many education systems. For schools in rural areas there is the fascinating study of the changing seasons and the agricultural operations with which they are associated. There must be few areas of the world where it is not now possible to explain to children how through the application of science and technology, human skill and endeavour, traditional systems of agriculture can be transformed into a modern farming industry with all the benefits to rural society and the national interest which this implies. These then are, perhaps, some of the ways in which an informed interest in agriculture and rural development may be gradually built into the whole system of education. They do not necessarily imply that agriculture, as a separate vocational subject, should be taught. Indeed, the approach through well organized voluntary activities of the 4-H type whereby groups of children have their own specific projects involving crops, poultry, rabbits and perhaps small farm livestock which they rear and care for may be an extremely effective way of teaching the basic skills of crop cultivation and animal husbandry. Such programmes, however, can only hope to be successful when supported by well-trained leadership and some financial and technical help.

The inclusion of vocational agriculture in the programmes of secondary schools involves not only the training of teachers but also a considerable financial outlay if the practical aspects are to include provision of a farm-workshop and land for certain aspects of crop and livestock production. Such farmland and the enterprises associated with it need to be very well managed professionally if they are not to deteriorate into poor and un-productive holdings of no educational value and of no credit to the institutions concerned. Some residential secondary schools have succeeded in developing outstandingly successful commercial farms on land at their disposal. The Gayaza Girls High School Farm/Diet project in Uganda and the Navuso Agricultural Secondary School in Fiji are two examples known to the author. Doubtless there are others elsewhere but it must be remembered that a great deal of careful thought and planning, together with initial and continuing financial support, went into their development. They have also had the benefit of well-qualified farm managers. These farms have exercised a profound influence upon the whole life and teaching work of these schools although in neither case has the primary aim been to produce practical farmers. Rather has it been to show how agricultural land can be developed and managed so that it is highly productive, contributing to a far better and more varied diet for the children and enabling them to participate in all kinds of technical skills associated with the use of machinery and much more productive livestock and crops. They see farming in a totally new light; the tractor becomes to them a symbol of the emancipation from hand hoe subsistence agriculture. In the case of Navuso Agricultural School there has, for a long time, been specific training in agriculture (theoretical and practical) as an important part of the curriculum. The aim of this has been to prepare boys for employment in agriculture as skilled workers, field extension staff and in other capacities. There has also been a 3-year pupil farmer scheme designed to prepare a small number of selected boys who have completed their secondary education for careers in farming itself. Thus recognition has been given to the fact that specific vocational training for a career in farming logically follows *after* general education has been completed.

Many farm school projects have failed to achieve the primary purpose for which they were established: the training of prospective farmers. Records for many such schools indicate that the proportion of those who have been trained and subsequently enter practical farming is very low. In fact, most of those who enter such schools do so as the only means available to them to continue their education. Their hope is to make use of this opportunity as a means of obtaining some kind of qualification with which to seek paid employment mostly outside agriculture. It is, in fact, expecting a very great deal that a young unmarried man with primary education and one or two years training at a farm school will succeed in establishing himself as a successful independent farmer. If he is able to work on the family farm with the prospect of achieving his own farm in due course, that is an entirely different matter. But it has to be appreciated that farming is a complex and risky business. Far more is required than a knowledge of the techniques of producing certain crops or raising livestock. The aquisition of management skills involved in the use of very limited resources is largely a matter of time and experience. Those who are going to farm on their own account need, in addition to their technical training, a period of apprenticeship. This they undergo in many countries through working for other farmers until they have the knowledge, skills, resources and confidence to launch out on their own. Almost certainly they could not succeed single handed: they would need the support and help of a wife, and perhaps of others at critical periods in the farming year. It is, therefore, not difficult to understand why so many farm schools have not been very successful in producing significant numbers of progressive young farmers in areas of peasant agriculture.

The problem of how educational systems may best be adapted to cater to the needs of agricultural and rural development is complex and difficult. It involves ministries and interests outside education for the education programme and, if it is to be an instrument of change and progress, must itself be dovetailed into an overall pattern of integrated development. In the long period of transition from subsistence land use to the establishment of a modern agricultural industry, education and training becomes increasingly vital to success. Small farmers must possess the basic skills of literacy and numeracy if they are to avail themselves of technical change and better management of their resources. As farming becomes more sophisticated and involves greater investment the skills of business management become at least as important as a knowledge of husbandry practices. Perhaps the most fundamental incentive for improvement in peasant agriculture is the prospect of a better home and better future for the children of the family farm. Thus, all measures which may contribute to better family living must be regarded as equally important with those associated with technical improvements in agriculture. All these things have deep implications in the shaping of educational policies to meet present needs and the changing situation in rural areas and amongst rural communities.

A New Strategy for Agricultural Education

If the development of the agricultural, forestry and other natural resources of the rural areas is of critical importance to the future progress of the peoples of many developing countries, then it is reasonable to postulate that agricultural education (using this expression in its broadest sense) has a vital role to play in the whole development complex. Agricultural research, teaching and the whole process of conveying the results of research and technological improvement to the farmer through extension and other services, are all dependent upon well trained scientists, technicians and skilled operators. Furthermore, the farming community itself must undergo certain educational processes if its members are to respond to the opportunities as they become available. It is, therefore, not surprising that the 1960s witnessed a very rapid expansion of institutions of agricultural education and training, at all levels, in many areas of the developing world. Had this accelerated programme not been undertaken, the agricultural, veterinary or forestry services of many of the developing countries, now independent, would have required very large numbers of expatriate staff to maintain them. In fact, the majority of senior professional posts in many of these countries are now held by well-trained local staff although, owing to expanding needs, there are still shortages. At the intermediate or technician level and in spite of the expansion of agricultural colleges and technical training institutes there still seems to be a chronic shortage of skilled technicians of many kinds. In some countries, for example, a single agricultural extension worker is endeavouring to serve a farm family population of several thousand. Likewise many specific projects in such specialized areas as irrigation, range management, horticultural crops, dairying and others are still hampered through shortage of trained and experienced staff. At the farmer training level all that can reasonably be claimed is that a start has been made in various and interesting ways but a very great deal remains to be learned and undertaken before it can be claimed that the farmer and the rural community are effectively served.

Many systems of agricultural education, and even larger numbers of institutions, have not been in existence for a sufficient length of time for an initial assessment of their usefulness in development to be made. Are the attitudes and professional skills of those who graduate proving adequate in meeting the peculiarly difficult problems with which so many countries are currently faced in agricultural and rural development? Is the balance of output of university graduates to trained technicians well matched to actual needs? Are the length and content of courses satisfactory or is there a case for shorter basic training followed, in appropriate cases, by in-service courses after practical experience has been gained in employment? These are but a few of the many issues which face those in developing countries endeavouring to improve agricultural education in a situation of urgent demands and limited resources.

Many of the problems which confront agricultural education are basically similar to those of education systems in general. There is wide recognition that the introduction of systems from one country to another, without modification, has seldom produced results which are satisfactory. However, the whole process of adaptation involving as it does changes in course structures, curricula, new textbooks and teaching materials and, indeed, the training of teachers, takes a very considerable time and many processes of trial and error. Perhaps one of the most important needs today is to initiate some systematic study of needs and the planning of a strategy to meet them. At present in many countries the elements of agricultural education and training are fragmented among institutions of different kinds controlled by separate ministries, not necessarily in competition with each other, but by no means fully and effectively coordinated within the framework of an overall plan. It is notoriously difficult in the context of the changing situations of developing countries to achieve any reliable assessment of the requirements for trained manpower at different levels and in the wide range of skills essential for balanced development. And yet some such process must be initiated if the systems of technical training are to be effectively geared to meeting needs for trained manpower. Within many courses themselves there is still a great tendency to adhere to conventional models without due regard to the kind of situations and responsibilities with which students will be faced when they have completed their studies. Thus, it is essential that those responsible for the design and teaching of courses should be in close and regular contact with the services and industry for which their students are being trained. Technology is expanding fast and as a result both the structure and content of courses need to be flexible. The sciences and technology associated with agriculture cover a very broad spectrum and great skill and discrimination are required if the overloading of courses and failure to adhere to sound principles of education are to be avoided. Thus, there is a very important need for research and planning at the national level and within institutions themselves in order to achieve a balanced and integrated system of agricultural education geared to meeting carefully studied needs. It may well be that certain university departments could play an important part in aspects of research connected with the whole planning process.

Closely connected with planning is the whole notion of coordination. This would not be difficult if all the institutions concerned were the responsibility of a single ministry or government department, but this is seldom the case. Universities are usually autonomous although, since their finances are principally or wholly dependent upon government, certain pressures can be brought to bear upon their policies. At the technical and vocational levels training institutions may be the responsibility of ministries of education, of agriculture, of animal production or natural resources, according to the country in which they are situated. In all these circumstances it is highly desirable that some mechanism be established whereby those responsible for the administration of these institutions be brought together, at regular intervals, for consultation with a view to achieving a team approach to what is clearly an area of common concern. National councils of agricultural education on which all major interests are represented could, under good leadership, perform a valuable service not only to the system itself, but also to the wide range of technical and commercial interests which it serves. The East African Council for Agricultural Education inaugurated in 1963 under the aegis of the University of East Africa has been the means of bringing together representatives of all levels and types of agricultural education along with those of the agricultural services, research, and commerce with a view to better coordination and understanding. During the course of its existence it has initiated surveys of trained manpower requirements, a university sponsored diploma award at the technical level common to all the agricultural colleges of East Africa, and provided a forum at which innovations of various kinds can be discussed. Each country will wish to decide for itself how to work towards effective coordination of agricultural education and training once there is a realization of its importance and a willingness on the part of the ministries concerned to collaborate.

It is understandable that in the early phases of development the resources available for agricultural education have been mainly devoted to the training of agricultural scientists, teachers, administrators and other professionals at the university level and a range of technicians, principally those required so urgently for the extension services, at other institutions. It is, in fact, essential that this work be continued and there is every indication that it should be greatly strengthened at the technical level in many countries. However, it has always to be remembered that agricultural progress is ultimately dependent upon the farmer, the farm family and the rural community in which they live. Is it possible that there may, in some cases, have been too much emphasis upon the training of scientists and civil servants and far too little on the education of the rural community whose full cooperation in the whole process of development is so vital? Much has been said in recent years on the topic of ways and means through which the human resources of rural development may be mobilized for progress. Here is an area of unlimited potential which in many countries has hardly begun to be effectively served. Attitudes have to be changed, new values created and a general climate conducive to progress established. Both the school system and various kinds of technical training have immensely important roles to play. Farmer training institutions, rural training centres, village polytechnics or whatever they may be designated are essentially institutions of the people established in their midst. The task of those who staff them calls for rare qualities of character and technical skill. This type of work together with those of the village primary school and the extension workers of various kinds is deserving of far greater attention and support than has been the case in the past. This is the front-line where the battle for rural progress is to be won or lost. Rural people through the influence of education of many kinds, formal and informal, must be enabled to become active partners in development instead of, as so often heretofore, the passive recipients of good advice.

There is one area in which investment should produce dividends out of all proportion to the expenditure: an expansion in the educational and employment opportunities for girls and women. It is well known that in many of the developing countries not only do women cultivate most, if not all, of the food crops but they also exercise a very important influence in decision-making relative to the family farm. And yet the field extension services have been staffed almost exclusively by men. At the subsistence level and on the small family farm it is almost impossible to separate the functions of crop growing, feeding and providing for the family, marketing of produce and purchase of the necessities of life for they are all calls upon the extremely limited resources of labour and cash within which millions of rural people have to operate. In these circumstances the economy of the home is the economy of the farm and vice versa. Improvements in the feeding of the family and in the management of the home go hand in hand with better farming. Thus the education of girls and women, the opening of opportunities to professional and technical training, and their employment in the agricultural, community development education and public health services in rural areas could then represent the most fundamental of all contributions to rural progress. There are already indications in many parts of the world of a rapidly changing attitude and girls are to be found in faculties of agriculture, agricultural colleges, home economics departments of universities and technical training institutions. It will be a considerable time before the influence of these relatively new developments can be fully experienced but there can be no doubt of their potential importance as stabilizing and progressive influences in the whole field of education for development.

Conclusion

Rural development is an immensely broad subject embracing a range of situations, problems and potential in different parts of the world. An attempt has been made in this article to draw attention to the great importance of rural areas and rural people to national progress in the developing countries. Education clearly has an immensely important role to play in the whole complex of rural development. It can only achieve its full potential if it is in spirit as much as in practice a fully integrated component of the development 'team'. This team approach to rural development implies a willingness on the part of government, universities, heads of educational and other institutions, and others to sacrifice some degree of their autonomy in return for the satisfaction of knowing that, in such a context, their work is likely to be of far greater usefulness in the great task of rural and national progress.

GENERAL REFERENCES

1. United Nations Economic and Social Council – Report of the Secretary General to the 43rd Session on Development and Utilization of Human Resources in Developing Countries. May 1967.
2. International Institute for Educational Planning – 1963–67 Progress Report. UNESCO/IIEP, 1967.
3. Provisional Indicative World Plan for Agricultural Development 1965–85. FAO 1969.
4. World Conference on Agricultural Education and Training. Report Vols. I and II – FAO/UNESCO/ILO, 1970.
5. Education in Rural Areas. Commonwealth Secretariat, London 1970.

Effective Education for Agriculture

C. Arnold Anderson

Controversies and proposals relating to rural education make up a substantial part of all the literature about agricultural development on the one hand, and about education for development more generally on the other. The key points in this literature exemplify all the basic conflicts of viewpoint about optimal strategies for development policy. In one article it is impossible to present a balanced assessment of so wide-ranging a set of topics and issues. Instead one must select while maintaining sufficient breadth of view to see each topic in perspective.[1] Associated risks of imbalance are inescapable.

There are distinct though cross-cutting dimensions of education for agriculture that must command attention. Among the many complications is the fact that provision must be made for education of both those who farm and of those who will help in one way or another to educate farmers or to generate new information for them. One must inevitably give attention to the general education of rural children, some of whom will become farmers while others will find jobs in town. Among the programmes, formal or informal, for those who will deal in various ways with farmers we must include training of the researchers who will bring new opportunities for production in agriculture. There also are questions as to where the teaching and learning will take place, who will take the responsibility for providing opportunities to learn, and how much of the education will be informal (even almost invisibly so), how much formalized, both in and out of schools. And we must ask further what sorts of things will be taught, what learned in these various contexts, noting that what is taught and what learned are by no means coterminous. Given so complex a network, any one starting point must quickly lead into other topics. Nevertheless, the central foci of the two main parts of this chapter are quite different. Part I (The Content and Loci of Education) is built around a typology of curricula and around general issues and debates concerning adaptive education and training appropriate to particular settings. Part II (Education for Agricultural Transformation) is focused upon the dynamics of agricultural progress and on what this implies in education for innovation and for diffusion of new practices.

I

The Content and Loci of Education

The oldest and most persistent debates concerning education in developing countries, particularly in the rural village, have centred on the broad issue of adaptation of education to the local situation, specifically on the merits of vocational courses, respectively for elementary and for secondary schools. (Agricultural education at post-secondary levels is quite another matter.) Back of these arguments are some conflicting pedagogical postulates about what 'practical' lessons in primary schools do to student knowledge of and attitudes toward farming, sharp disagreements as to why individuals migrate to cities, contrasting values with respect to the distribution of opportunities among the population, and diverse views or confused perceptions of what adaptation to the local situation may mean. These debates relate to every aspect of education, and are inseparable from basic issues of policy in education for agriculture. First, I present an abstract typology of curricula, noting some of its applications to education for agriculture, whether that education is formal or non-formal and whatever the various roles relating to agriculture in which the learners are or will be acting. Second, I make some brief preliminary remarks on 'where who may best learn what'. Third, I shall take up some points at which I see an emerging consensus concerning 'adapted education', and discuss the relevance of this convergence to education for agricultural progress.

A Typology of Curriculum Content

A scheme that embraces both explicit and 'hidden' curricula in diverse learning and teaching situations, both formal and non-formal, is laid out below. I submit that all these types of learning and teaching material can be empirically identified, though the mixtures vary with the locus of the teaching or learning and with the characteristics of the learners.

		Local	
	Universal	*Non-Parochial*	*Parochial*
Cognitive			
Technical-manipulative	1*a*	1*b*	1*c*
Verbal-mathematical	2*a*	2*b*	2*c*
Social-institutional	3*a*	3*b*	3*c*
Affective			
Technical-manipulative	4*a*	4*b*	4*c*
Verbal-mathematical	5*a*	5*b*	5*c*
Social-institutional	6*a*	6*bc*	

The 'universal' category includes basic materials that have relevance across many cultures and societies; I include scientific method here, despite assertions by some writers in LDCs that it is merely a form of western parochialism. The most unambiguous cells in this column are 1a and 2a; their relevance for productivity of agriculture, as of other sectors, is indisputable. At simple levels 1a would be exemplified by the principle of the lever, 2a by literacy and competence in the four operations of arithmetic. Cognitive sorts of social-institutional learning (how to get around in life) in some variant are worldwide, with content ranging from an international cosmopolitan culture to local features important to quite small groups. Affectively, attachment to the land is so commonly a trait of peasant societies as to justify its inclusion in cell 6a. Presumably there are some universal rules for obtaining aesthetic effects (type 4a) and some recurrent modes of ritual behaviour (type 5a).

The second column refers to what is in essence universal but locally adapted; e.g. features of local soils or flora and fauna that are important for agriculture (types 1b and 2b) and knowledge about local traditions for sharing the duty to pay rent on tilled land. The existence of this knowledge that is so vital for successful tillage in a particular district is not, however, any argument for giving primary pupils lessons on farming or practice in school gardens. The strictly parochial learning usually will be traditional. It may either foster or retard agricultural progress; an example of type 1c would be theories of genetics that are counterproductive in animal husbandry. The distinction between the two sorts of non-universalistic material, the parochial and local non-parochial, is important for all aspects of cognitive learning and the affective commitments to technical-manipulative or verbal-mathematical modes. Type 5c includes the many sorts of xenophobic history lessons, and 4c would be illustrated by senti-mental attachment to local dances to bring rain. Admittedly it is difficult to distinguish the three variants of the social-institutional modes, but ability to distinguish the three aspects of rules for the conduct of leaders can make or break a programme for community development.

Controversies about the most suitable instruction tend to narrow down to debates over (a) 'practical' and local versus general cognitive training in the rural schools (types 1b and 2b as against 1a and 2a), or (b) a parochial as against a universalistic cognitive and affective emphasis. Yet, to repeat, the importance of knowledge about local soils or plants adds no weight to proposals for farming lessons in primary schools, while the fact that thousand-year-old Japanese techniques of joinery and norms of loyalty to a working team and its patron support complex folkways of production gives us no guidance on what kinds of instruction should be vocationa-lized. All sorts of material belong in a well-rounded curriculum for any society; the task for pedagogical strategists is to parcel out the different materials by category of pupils and level of school and to decide which learning should be left to out-of-school situations.

Loci and Modes and Learning

Peasants around the world have displayed scepticism about much of the advice received from agriculturalists; the reluctance to give up tried ways for unknown ones has often manifested disenchantment with advisers' ignorance in adapting new crops or new techniques to an unfamiliar combination of soils and weather. On the other hand, in few countries can skills of cultivating food plants today be confined to replication of hereditary lore and habits. Malthusian population pressures, new markets for food among burgeoning town populations, and competition in supplies that reflect adoption of the 'green revolution' elsewhere are forcing peasants to consciously modify their production practices. Moreover, this is an ongoing process; each cohort of youth learns many ways of life borrowed from 'more advanced' societies, ways that embody both new opportunities and new pressures for change. The range of competencies expands constantly in both variety and in level. This is true for peasants who just begin to realize that traditional ways of gaining subsistence will no longer suffice; it is even more true for soil chemists or meteorologists or for the tax experts who design new ways to raise the revenues from agriculture without 'killing the goose'.

Among the many unhelpful residues from the now-waning vogue for manpower planning is an encouragement to think of individuals as bundles of skills suitable for the practice of particular occupations. It would seem more useful to take a broader perspective: individuals are rounded persons possessing diverse motivations and capabilities and it is unimaginative to think of them mainly in terms of requirements for a pre-defined occupation. The most important skills may be those that change the profile of the occupation. But whatever skills we consider, their inculcation can go on in diverse places: the family, under a tutor or a master of apprentices, in a full-time or part-time school, as a participant observer at work, or simply by one's own experience. Where the learning commonly does, or may best, take place will depend both on technical-economic factors and on determinants of motivation to learn and to apply what is learned.

The most generally applicable basic skills that facilitate future information gathering and learning tend to be taught in schools. However, the know-how that enables a man to adjust promptly to new situations, to work with others, or to have assurance in making effective decisions – these skills usually can be developed only in a work and decision situation. A society's total system for the formation of human resources is much more than its schools; it includes the learning facets of the operation of every institution though always there is interaction between education in schools and elsewhere. Indeed, where particular skills will be learned, if at all, depends partly upon a society's prescriptions as to how much formal instruction must be certified in order that individuals may enter upon a career path of greater or less standing, each path including more or less future training and learning. The impact of either educational or agricultural policies upon learning for agriculture may be quite different for the farmer and for the extension agent or researcher. But the application of education in farming comes about through an interactive network among all of these people and others.

The more widespread is the demand for a skill and the slower its obsolescence, the more practicable it is to formalize the training. But when the conditions under which training occurs appreciably affect the perceptions of relevance and associated motivations to learn, less formal situations appear more attractive. As the cost of training (measured in foregone working time) rises, non-formal procedures multiply, but if there is too much interference with the work of production pressures arise to shift back toward in-school training. However, if schools must use expensive equipment that quickly becomes obsolete, the in-school arrangement loses its attraction, as occurs also whenever it becomes difficult to obtain instructors who possess up to date knowledge. 'Universal' material will more often be purveyed in formal schools, but their work in most societies is heavily qualified by out of school learning of the more parochial material. At the same time the motives that enhance effectiveness in use of the more formal lessons – whether at work or in non-formal acquisition of further skills – are nourished mainly by rather casual sorts of instruction, including learning the 'hidden' curriculum. Efforts to plan the non-formal learning opportunities, it should be emphasized, rarely can be counted on. The aim, rather, should be to arrange so that needs or demands for different skills can be signalled to potential suppliers of the training – a system that can be very effective even though no one can itemize in advance the kinds of training that will prove to be most suitable for a given economic sector or type of worker.

A New Consensus Regarding Adapted Education in the Schools

Among writers on 'development education' a few years ago, there were few dissenters from the view that the schools being transplanted into developing countries were unsuited to local needs and most especially to the needs of rural people. The borrowed schools were accused of being academic, bookish, urban oriented, and ineffective for knitting a new nation together. Schools were expected rather to stimulate national loyalty without arousing corrosive nationalism, to orient youth to planners' notions of suitable occupations, to instill appreciation of manual skills and of agriculture, to arouse commitment to development goals, and meanwhile to weaken inequalities in economic conditions or distinctions in power and privilege. In short, the schools were supposed to connect borrowed aspirations for modernization with surviving traditions from local pre-modern ways of life.

Two decades of wrestling with these tasks (whether as national officials or as representatives of outside assistance agencies) has deepened our appreciation of how rarely new institutions fulfil expectations. Today we are more aware that each society will follow its own route to development,[2] and we are beginning to understand how idiomatic motivations always are intermingled with generic processes of social change. The themes of modernity are woven in distinctive ways into the warp of local custom. But we also are coming to acknowledge that individuals must become estranged in some degree from tradition if they are going to participate in bringing a new society to birth. Basic general education must become the cornerstone of the curriculum in rural as in urban lower schools, and despite its inherent challenge to parochial traditions. Where, as in most LDCs, the population are mainly peasants, large minorities in rural areas must become literate if the society is to adapt the more productive foreign techniques into practices that can support and diffuse modernization. The transformation of traditional agriculture[3] is inseparable from this modernization of rural society.

Increasingly it has come to be recognized also that an exclusively practical or technical education would be neither economically sound nor socially and politically acceptable. But when we seek an optimum proportion of cognitive, normative, and 'practical' material in the school lessons, all criteria of a 'balanced' programme prove illusory. A balance clearly must be found in a larger context than any particular segment of the school system or even of the whole system. Balance always includes the non-school ways in which men learn and are taught and the ways in which they build upon experience to apply and extend their skills.

Once this larger view is accepted, several things follow. The argument for practical agricultural education in schools withers, but we come to a new appreciation of what literacy contributes to development in agriculture. Also the thorny problem of rural-urban migration begins to take on a different colouration; certainly the case for using practical education in village schools as a deterrent to migration loses support. Some interpret the flow of migrants to towns as proof that rural schools are failing in their task – or that they are doing the wrong job too well. But today we possess much evidence that peasants do not disdain farming when they have a tangible likelihood of gaining a satisfactory income from it. Indeed, rural pupils are less venturesome than urban pupils in setting their occupational aspirations.[4] Nor is schooling a condition of rural-urban migration. We need only recall that ignorance of industrial skills did not deter African peasants from migrating a long distance to industrial jobs,[5] and in many African countries a large proportion of the rural labour force are foreign hired labourers.[6] A buoyant rural economy appears to be accompanied by rising demands for hired farm labour rather than by surplus labour.[7] At the same time, in at least some countries rural-urban migrants are more likely to find employment than do those rural youth who remain behind.[8] Some evidence suggests that migrants out of rural areas tend to be both the least and the best schooled.[9] The heart of the migration problem appears to lie in the terms of trade between rural and urban sectors,[10] and present-day educational practices have only a loose link with policies that set the terms of trade.

It is futile to seek an educational solution to a non-educational problem, as a growing number of writers acknowledge. Giving youth an inferior quality of schooling hardly keeps them out of the towns. Schooling designed deliberately to discourage their migration puts rural youth in a still more disadvantaged position in finding work than had their schooling been better.[11] To avoid myopic conclusions one needs to keep in mind that many educated young people are 'unemployed' precisely because they have the holding power to engage in job search – especially in the more distant places where search takes more effort – until they get a comparatively good job, with promise for the future. Meanwhile, second-rate schooling for rural youth, if it has any direct effect, discourages the very transformations of rural life that would enlarge opportunities in the villages and market towns, a transformation that would draw informed youth into that growth instead of locking them into a stagnant agriculture by ignorance.[12]

II

Education for Agricultural Transformation

An education that will fit in with other movements toward an improved agriculture must be multi-pronged. But before sketching rough outlines of such an educational programme, it may be well to notice two sorts of question that can be basic in devising a useful educational strategy. (1) What are the non-human as well as the human imperatives for agricultural development? (2) What sorts of responses in production can we expect from peasants if opportunity knocks?

Farmers as Rational Economic Men

Analysts of agricultural development have tended to take opposed views of peasant farmers. One group assumes farmers to be essentially rational economic men who will take advantage of opportunities to better themselves economically. In this view, farmers respond to clear and dependable evidence of new market opportunities by increasing or diversifying production.[13] The other group contends that peasants must first be reoriented in their outlook on life so that they become 'development minded'. I line up with the first viewpoint,[14] namely, that in education emphasis need not be put explicitly upon efforts to remould attitudes or values. The emphasis rather would be on information and on training men to decode information and to interpret its implications for managerial decisions in their farming enterprise. Obviously incentives to raise productivity will more quickly be turned into motives for doing so if the terms of trade between agriculture and the non-farm sectors are not disadvantageous to peasants.

The necessity of having markets to actualize the potentials of education was pointed out by Bidwell in his analysis of the agricultural transformation in southern New England around the opening of the nineteenth century.[15] 'Inefficiency of agriculture was not due to ignorance,' runs one of his subheads; indeed those farmers were avid readers of books and newspapers and they were extraordinarily innovative as craftsmen. But 'a market for increased agricultural produce was not at hand, therefore progress along that line was not remunerative' and 'the campaign of "agricultural" education of the latter half of the eighteenth century was without results.' Even the less educated or illiterate farmers in the LDCs respond readily to changed opportunities to get good prices for commercial crops. Education becomes important when information is comparatively difficult to obtain and to interpret, whether that information refers to markets or to production methods and inputs. The peasant does have some reliable knowledge of his own, and if education is to be effective it must build on that knowledge while taking into account the risks that the peasant faces and the external constraints on his options.

In contrast to the often-demonstrated responsiveness of peasant producers to clear opportunities, massive reorganizations of agricultural management and installation of state-sponsored settlement projects designed to force progress and quasi-rationality upon the peasants run into unanticipated problems by their disregard of both individual incentives and peasant knowledge. Without elaborating these imprudent public policies,[16] I accept Berg's view[17] that reliance upon market incentives protects poor countries against massive misallocation of resources. It would follow also that suspicions of traders and accusations of inflated marketing margins are used to support policies that depress the aspirations of peasants. And so we come directly to the question as to what are the imperatives for agricultural development.

Some Imperatives for Agricultural Progress

Arthur Mosher lists five essentials for agricultural advancement:[18]

(1) transportation facilities, (2) a dependable marketing system, (3) a flow of new production techniques from research, (4) supplies of production factors at suitable prices, and (5) economic incentives for increasing production. He also specifies three 'accelerators': (1) educational programmes at several levels, (2) suitable credit facilities, and (3) farmers' associations of various kinds. Hayami and Ruttan[19] give a more compact list: (1) a non-farm sector able to turn out the products for use in farm production at encouraging prices, (2) technical innovations that will increase the demand for non-farm inputs into agriculture, (3) general and specific education for farmers, and (4) transformations of institutions affecting farming (such as tenure practices). A key element in both lists is an emphasis on research and innovation. Research generates opportunities for an agricultural transformation and at the same time it both draws upon educational resources for the research itself and increases the potential pay-off from education among farmers and among the agents who in one way or another diffuse information among peasants.

As agricultural economists have been saying, what is needed among farmers is not just improved proficiency in routine skills of tillage but a capability that will permit the introduction of new and more complex combinations of non-human inputs into the production process.[20] The strategic question is: what kinds of improved human capital, distributed over what proportion of the peasants, and in what distributional pattern, are needed to make use of new seeds, cheaper fertilizer, more precise schedules of weeding, and so on?

Education and Research for Agriculture

Appropriate techniques for farming are extremely locality-specific. Few plants or techniques can be borrowed from other economies without adaptation to very localized circumstances.[21] It does not suffice to think only in terms of the broad categories of labour-poor or land-poor agrarian systems or even of such categories as rice areas or pastoral areas.[22]

The test of effectiveness is tighter for agriculture than for most other activities by which men gain a living. One can carry textbooks and methods of teaching arithmetic across the world; while for a few decades of adjustment, learning will be lower than in the original country, teachers nevertheless can depend upon the native wit of pupils to compensate so that fair proportions of pupils will perform acceptably. Mining equipment can easily be put into operation on the other side of the world. But one cannot just carry some maize seed or a rule of thumb for fertilizer dosages to another locality – often not even within the same region of one country.

In order to borrow agricultural techniques that will be suitable for local application and to keep up with the pace of potential improvement, a country must also be active in carrying out the necessary adaptive research. And in order to conduct this research successfully the country must develop the capability to do basic research in agriculture and in the underlying sciences.[23]

Research that will pay off in higher agricultural production – and especially knowledge of how to design such research – is a comparative newcomer on the technological scene.[24] For the US it is estimated that total agricultural research plus extension costs are shared about equally by public and private funds. Most of the biological research takes place in public establishments; a larger part of the development of machinery is by private persons or firms, for they can recoup such research costs through patents.[25] Seemingly, few major breakthroughs in agricultural techniques occur, rather there is a steady cumulation of smaller adaptative innovations, suited to particular situations. But to discern and to push through the most promising of such innovations requires a diversified establishment of specialists for each of the world's many agrarian systems. The widely popularized picture of scientists making big discoveries (such as 'new rice') that are then disseminated to peasants by zealous extension workers conceals and misleads more than it reveals. A fresh look at the diffusion of farming information and practices is called for.

Diffusion of Agricultural Information and Innovation

'It would be a salutory, and perhaps rather shattering, exercise to close down the extension services in some parts of Africa' and then contrast agricultural growth in those areas with that in areas in which extension work had been continued.[26] As often has been observed, the 'market incentive' approach to rural transformation tends to emphasize the importance of research while the 'diffusion model' of technical change emphasizes the utility of extension education. But scepticism about the effectiveness of agricultural extension agencies has been rising, along with respect for the economic intelligence of peasants. Unfortunately, there are almost no data by which to compare the pay-off from extension with that from research, for few studies include both data about the economic incentive for farmers to modify their practices and data about communication channels or farmers' personal traits. One would expect that returns to extension and to research would be complementary; returns to investments in extension (and similar activities) will be higher the greater the practical importance of what there is to extend, which brings us back to the contributions of adaptive research.

The benefits from research will be higher if innovations are taken up rapidly by peasants. Given relevant adaptive research and new opportunities for profit, what determines the rate of adoption of new practices? Specifically, how far will education of peasants increase their capability quickly to adopt promising innovations? To what extent are education of peasants and an effective extension service substitutive or complementary in this process of technical change?

The debate over the merits of adult literacy programmes has sharpened of late.[27] Meanwhile, more economists have been stressing the role of schooling in improving decision making by farmers: allocative efficiency in the determination of input combinations in production and the mix of outputs of the farm.[28] Obviously, an economic assessment of programmes for adult literacy must consider what this literacy costs in relation to what it contributes when measured in terms of capability for managing a farm and as compared to other methods for obtaining the same capability. On the other hand, one cannot interpret a wide dispersion of innovations among farmers as evidence for the effectiveness of a literacy campaign; equal or greater diversity in productivity may be observed among the farmers in a developed country.[29] A few attempts at better specification of the nature of these relationships are appearing in the literature of agricultural economics and in that relating to human capital.

For the US there is some evidence that intensive extension assistance is useful, especially for those farmers who are the less schooled; extension agents provide for such farmers the information–decoding and allocative guidance that better-schooled farmers can carry out for themselves.[30] On the other hand, it is well known that the extension workers in many countries tend to disdain the technical skill of peasants,[31] and that those specialists are chronically unable to work out effective ways to assist the less adept farmers. These journeys in futility have sometimes reflected, among other things, the colonial service traditions of using extension agents to enforce marketing rules and cultivation practices that actually were less suited than the ones chosen by the peasants without help. But it is clear, also, that when innovations entail complex interdependent elements in a new scheme of production, some minimum of peasant literacy or schooling may become a precondition of effective learning from most extension agents. In part because crops are so locality–specific, in part because some innovations entail relatively simple, some more fundamental or complex adjustments in farming practices, and in part because of other localized ways of behaving, the amount of extension-agent time needed by peasants to effect a rise in productivity will vary with the locality being examined. In some situations illiterate farmers will learn only (after some lag) by following their neighbours, while somewhat better educated peasants can effectively absorb intensive extension help. Still further up the scale of capability, the lead farmers may decode most of the information for themselves. Their role as unofficial extension agents is a significant spill-over or 'externality' effect of their prior education and abilities.

This view of the interrelationships between education or schooling and innovation fits into the overview of Yudelman.[32] Provided for all farmers would be 'additive investments that reduce losses' to farmers: provision of roads, water supply, crop storage, locust control. For the best educated and most innovative and change-prone peasants there would be special arrangements for credit and pinpointed technical information, but they will be able to get most of the information they need from the various mass media. The less informed farmers would be helped by receiving a basic education without special attention to agriculture: thereby those farmers would become more ready for extension help in 'processing knowledge from research for application'.[33] Since in most countries the private firms that deal in fertilizer or machinery can supply a growing share of all extension work, societies that limit such enterprises out of a 'socialist' ideology are throttling a major channel of effective communication and practical education.[34]

In addition to work by agricultural economists and by practitioners in agricultural sciences, there is a mounting sociological literature on the relationships between literacy or schooling of peasants and the diffusion among them of technical innovations.[35] As Rogers indicates (p. 70), the utility of literacy lies in its opening of access to printed media, enabling individuals to control the rate at which they take in messages and to store information for use when wanted, and generally facilitating skill in the more complex analytic and decision capabilities. How literacy fosters impersonal and less provincial contacts has been explored by many other writers.[36] The role of schools as purveyors of universalistic values and of the core idea in modernization is often mentioned;[37] indeed Armer finds that modernity is correlated strongly with formal schooling even independently of the effect of educated parents, mass media, and similar influences.[38]

Yet the association between literacy or schooling and the technical progressiveness of peasants is less marked than one might expect after pondering such generalizations. In most situations[39] the association is very modest and varies erratically from one setting to another. Rahudkar's study of a decade ago in India[40] illustrates the dilemma. He found, as have others, that peasants who made no adoptions have little if any schooling; but those who made several adoptions were not solely the well-schooled and included many unschooled. The illiterate quarter of his sample make a seventh and the least-educated two-thirds of peasants made half the total adoptions in the village. Such attenuated correlations between schooling and innovation do not support an inference that the presence of schooled men in the village is unimportant, however. In fact, the more effectively the literate farmers transmit information and examples to less-educated ones, the lower will be these within-village correlations. While the more intensive the contacts of extension agents with farmers the more does extension education foster efficient and progressive decision making, intensive contacts are expensive. Wide diffusion of new practices in LDC villages must depend upon face-to-face contacts and demonstrations – an informal extension system among neighbouring peasants. Schooling alone will not make a peasant into an effective informal extension agent, but usually it will be a condition of such leadership.

'Vocational' Education for Agriculture

In a search for promising strategies of education for agricultural develop-ment (whether broadly or narrowly defined), many vague and indis-criminate proposals have been set forth by individuals and by international agencies.[41] One can share Dumont's indignation at the inertia and self-serving activities of officials in developing countries, yet realize that his ruralized schools would not be favoured by peasants who see schools mainly as a way out of agriculture for their children. Proposals to double-deck rural schools so that only a few pupils are given a course that will qualify them for secondary education would be rejected by parents in most countries. Neither would it be practicable 'to bend over backwards to make the content in urban as well as rural schools relevant to the rural milieu of the nation'.[42]

Perhaps some of the anxieties about the deficiencies of rural schools deal with imagined problems, arising from misconceptions of what sorts of learning take place and are relevant both in schools and in other agencies of education, formal and non-formal. If primary schools were ruralized, they are the more likely to function poorly in preparing farmers for innovative leadership. At the same time, those schools will become inefficient circuitous routes to the main path of general education. Once we abandon the search for a way to make primary pupils practice farming, we can turn to the main task. Which sets of individuals need training focused explicitly on agriculture and in what forms? Four target groups can be distinguished:[43] (1) farmers and members of their families, (2) those who directly serve farmers (extension agents, community development workers, agricultural research personnel), (3) indirect servers of farmers (key persons in firms buying from and selling to farmers), (4) policy makers for agriculture (including both political farmers' leaders and key policy makers with broader interests and powers).

Beginning with the fourth category, it is obvious that ultimately the welfare of farmers is affected more by policies on taxation, social security, or treatment of private enterprise (in both farming and farm-serving activities) than by most educational efforts explicitly for farm people. It follows that education of potential elite persons about the place of agriculture in the total economy or about the incidence of taxes and subsidies can be crucial in determining the welfare of farmers and of their livelihood. This sort of education will go on mainly in upper-secondary schools and colleges. If the distinctive technological features of a dynamic farming system are not appreciated, there can hardly be a vigorous service sector to farming (category 3) and the extension system will be incapable of substituting for the missing middlemen. An information system explicitly for the managers of non-farm businesses dealing with farmers has never been designed, though a few enterprisers will receive higher education at the side of men intending to do agricultural extension work or research. There is the prod of profit to induce those middlemen (and manufacturers of farm inputs) to keep up with agricultural research, drawing directly upon the sources of innovation or even participating in development of new devices. No one yet has seriously tried to meld agricultural and manager education to improve the effectiveness of these indirect servers of agriculture.

The principal task of formal education for agriculture lies in preparing individuals to be direct servers of farmers (category 2). Since research must be locality-specific in order to make agriculture progressive, the research station (possibly also with branches) must reach a critical mass in order to be effective.[44] Moreover, that research staff must largely be at world levels of competence.[45] But this set of stipulations can present a major dilemma in policy making for higher education. In most countries academic custom upholds a practice of 'horse-trading' in sharing funds among departments in universities. A brief for expanding the programme in geology is followed by a plea to strengthen the work in mathematics. Since academic prestige is won by launching postgraduate programmes, pressures to match expansion with expansion starts the ratchet escalation of university costs. In the abstract, every field of study can be made to seem essential for development. Unfortunately, no solid case can be made out in many countries for giving all these sorts of training in the local university when demands on scarce education funds are so large. In addition, in much of the world, agriculture is put with the 'second class' academic subjects outside the university, thus further reducing its bargaining power for resources. Without elaborating further, the truly basic research in agriculture must be done just in order to facilitate the assimilation of new crops or techniques from abroad *without* tolerating a matching expansion in support of other kinds of instruction or research.

In numbers of direct-serving personnel, secondary schools train more than do universities; only a handful of extension specialists in the LDCs need university training. This is the area in which justification lies for a small number of strong secondary technical schools and post-secondary institutes with specialization in agriculture.[46] Such schools would also enrol a rather small number of pupils who intend to become farmers. In many countries these schools can function also as centres for localized extension programmes and dissemination of information (as in newspapers published by students for farmers) and in some cases they could be combined with field branches of the experiment station. This arrangement may modify but rarely will dispose of one of the problems that faces most attempts to develop vocational or technical programmes – reluctance of youth to take such courses in the face of the high returns and large subsidies to individuals who pursue academic curricula and continue into university. Furthermore, field workers in agricultural programmes often are paid less than their educational peers in other ministries. A perennial problem is the shortfall of science students in both secondary schools and teacher training colleges.[47] Finally, these agricultural secondary schools are all too likely to offer a programme that stresses skills in the narrow sense, neglecting the instruction in information processing and resource management that constitutes the vital core of decision-making in progressive farming.[48]

Conclusions

Let me now try to pull together the diverse perspectives presented in preceding pages. It has been argued that basic general education contributes strongly to innovative leadership among practising peasants, but agricultural development does not presuppose such education to be widespread within each community. Without compromise, I accept the view that direct instruction about farming is a poor use of the time of all elementary and most secondary pupils. By contrast, there is strong evidence that short courses in farmer training centres can improve peasants' skills, the skills of their wives (who often are actually the tillers), and prepare the offspring who plan to become farmers. By contrast, evidence mounts that conventional extension work (which rarely includes intensive face-to-face guidance in decision making) will alone make little impact upon agricultural productivity. In any case, extension work is effective only when experiment stations have produced something that farmers can profitably use. This means that there must be a base in local adaptive research which the extension agent then can put into terms comprehensible to the ordinary peasant. The means for following such advice must be at hand, and it must be clear that the venture is well worth the risk of trying the new.

One can hardly overemphasize the importance for rural people of having multiple sources of out-of-school learning available. When those opportunities are rich, innovations will normally spread rapidly and farmers themselves will become a growing source of improvements. Agents of firms selling to or buying from peasants and the innovative farmers themselves become important sources of new ideas. Especially in view of the suspicion among farmers about exhortations from strangers, whatever expands the informal channels of communication – while also linking those to research centres – will help to make agriculture more productive.

Finally, education of the children of peasants is education for whatever those children will do in life. Farm families are the source of much of the non-farm labour force. It is fortunate, though not accidental, that the best curriculum in basic education is much the same, whether for rural or urban living, for farming or for virtually any other non-routine occupation. Meanwhile, an enriched environment of non-formal but specialized agricultural education among the peasant parents of these youth will have its general spillover in the form of an enhanced confidence with which young people approach the problems of their careers and a readiness to take on decision-making tasks and responsibilities.

REFERENCES

1. Previous papers by me bearing upon the present topic include: 'Education in the Transition from Subsistence Agriculture' (International Social Science Council, 1965, processed); 'Technical and Vocational Education in the New Nations.' pp. 174–89 in A. Kazamias and E. H. Epstein (eds.), *Schools in Transition* (Rocklyn, N.J.: Allyn & Bacon, 1967); 'Reflections upon the Planning of Out-of-School Education,' for a December, 1971 conference at the International Institute of Educational Planning (and earlier versions of the article). An illustrative inventory of out-of-school programmes can be found in J. R. Sheffield and V. P. Diejomaoh, *Non-Formal Education in African Development* (New York: African-American Institute, 1972).

2. David L. Szanton, *Estancia in Transition* (1971) p. 84.

3. T. W. Schultz, *Transforming Traditional Agriculture*, 1964. The positive role of tradition is excellently demonstrated in M. Singer, 'Beyond Tradition and Modernity in Madras,' *Comparative Studies in Society and History* 13(2): 160–95, 1971. It has been found that the best qualified teachers, while often zealous to strengthen national unity, have the least interest in or acquaintance with local life.

4. P. J. Foster, 'Secondary Education: Objectives and Differentiation,' in *Educational Problems in Developing Countries* (1971) p. 86.

5. O. Falae, 'Unemployment,' *Manpower and Unemployment Research in Africa*, 5(1): 19, 1972.

6. P. Hill, 'The Occupations of Migrants in Ghana,' University of Michigan Museum of Anthropology, *Anthropological Papers*, 42, 1970; E. J. Berg, 'Economics of the Migrant Labour System,' in H. Kuper (ed.), *Urbanization*

and *Migration in West Africa* (Berkeley, California: University of California Press, 1965), p. 163.

7. E. S. Clayton, *Agrarian Development in Peasant Economies* (Long Island City, N.Y.: Pergamon, 1964), p. 95; Hill, *op. cit.* It should be recalled that the farm population of the US, for example, did not begin to decline in absolute numbers until after World War I.

8. M. Peil, 'Ghanaian Middle School Leavers: A Follow-up Study,' *Manpower and Unemployment Research in Africa* 3(2): 18, 1970.

9. P. Hill, 'Notes on the Occupations of Former Schoolboys: the Case of a Hausa Village,' *Nigerian Journal of Economic and Social Studies* 11:243, 1969; J. Gugler, 'On the Theory of Rural-Urban Migration: the Case of Sub-Saharan Africa,' ch. 6 in J. A. Jackson (ed.), *Migration*, 1969; R. E. Beals, *et al.*, 'Rationality and Migration in Ghana,' *Review of Economics and Statistics*, 49:480–6, 1967.

10. C. K. Eicher, 'African Agricultural Economics: Research Direction' in N. N. Miller (ed.), *Research in Rural Africa* (1968) pp. 152–62.

11. There was a similar dispute about the gains and losses from educating peasants in late eighteenth century Prussia that included virtually every argument heard today; see J. G. Gagliardo, *From Pariah to Patriot*, 1969, pp. 96–7; D. B. Abernethy, *The Political Dilemma of Popular Education* (1969) p. 90.

12. But these points do not constitute an argument for endlessly extending elementary education in disregard of claims from other sectors.

13. There is impressive evidence that farmers in different countries have responded appropriately to the contrasting relative shortages of land and of manpower; see Y. Hayami, *et al.*, 'An International Comparison of Agricultural Production and Productivities,' University of Minnesota Agricultural Experiment Station, *Technical Bulletin* 277, 1971; mechanization is the more appropriate response to the latter shortage while for the former improved biological elements that call for labour-intensive practices should be found.

14. I. Adelman and G. Dalton, 'A Factor Analysis of Modernization in Village India,' *Economic Journal*, 81:563–79, 1971; for industrial workers see the evidence in P. Kilby, *Industrialization in an Open Economy: Nigeria 1945–66*, (1969) p. 216; Eicher, *op. cit.*, p. 154.

15. P. W. Bidwell, 'Rural Economy in New England at the Beginning of the Nineteenth Century,' *Transactions Connecticut Academy of Arts and Sciences*, 20: ch. 5, 1916.

16. J. LaPalombera, 'Political Science and the Engineering of National Development,' in M. Palmer and L. Stern (eds.), *Political Development in Changing Societies* (1971) pp. 42f.

17. E. J. Berg, 'Structural Transformation versus Gradualism: Recent Economic Development in Ghana and the Ivory Coast, in P. J. Foster and A. R. Zolberg, *Ghana and the Ivory Coast: Perspectives on Modernization* (1971) p. 219.

18. A. T. Mosher, 'The Development Problems of Subsistence Farmers,' in C. R. Wharton, Jr. (ed.), *Subsistence Agriculture and Economic Development* (1969), ch. 1.

19. Y. Hayami and V. W. Ruttan, *Agricultural Development: an International Perspective* (Baltimore: John Hopkins Press, 1971), ch. 11.

20. J. M. Stam, 'Resource Limitation, the Demand for Education and Economic Growth – a Macroeconomic View,' Michigan State University, *Agricultural Economic Report*, No. 147, 1969, pp. 6, 12; for a discussion of the complements needed to make effective use of new rice varieties, see R. Barker, 'The Evolutional Nature of the New Rice Technology,' Stanford Food Research Institution *Studies* 10(2): 121, 1971.

21. Barker, *op. cit.*, p. 125; R. E. Evenson and Y. Kislev, 'Investment in Agricultural Research and Extension: a Survey of International Data,' Yale University, Economic Growth Center, *Discussion Paper* No. 124, 1971.

22. Hayami, *op. cit.*, pp. 5, 9; one does not speak just of 'rice areas' but of more delimited situations.

23. Evenson and Kislev, *op. cit.*, p. 14; support for scepticism about global research installations is expressed by Evenson in 'Notes on the International Agricultural Research System' (1972 processed).

24. T. W. Schultz, 'The Allocation of Resources to Research,' in W. L. Fischel, *Resource Allocation in Agricultural Research*, (1971) pp. 90–120, discusses the belated payoff from this research in the US.

25. Hayami and Ruttan, *op. cit.*, pp. 145f.

26. S. Carr, 'Agricultural Research or Extension Services: Which Has Failed?', *Rural Africana*, No. 16. 1971, p. 3; Eicher, *op. cit.*, pp. 165–6.

27. P. J. Foster, 'Problems of Literacy in Sub-Saharan Africa,' in T. A. Sebeok, *et al.* (eds.), *Current Trends in Linguistics*, v. 7:588–617.

28. F. Welch, 'Formal Education and the Distributional Effects of Agricultural Research and Extension,' in Fischel, *op. cit.*, pp. 183–194; D. P. Chaudhri, 'Education and Agricultural Production in India,' University of Delhi doctoral dissertation, 1968; B. R. Harker, 'Education, Communication, and Agricultural Change: a Study of Japanese Farmers,' University of Chicago doctoral dissertation, 1971; see also Harker's chapter in the present volume.

29. Hayami and Ruttan, *op. cit.*, pp. 276–7.

30. W. E. Huffman, 'The Contribution of Education and Extension to Different Rates of Change,' University of Chicago doctoral dissertation, 1972, pp. 31–38.

31. G. Castillo, 'A Critical View of a Subculture of Peasantry,' in Wharton, *op. cit.*, pp. 136–41; J. G. Liebenow, 'Agriculture, Education, and Rural Transformation: with Particular Reference to East Africa,' Indiana University Carnegie Seminar, 1969.

32. M. Yudelman, 'Problems of Raising African Agricultural Productivity,' Duke University Seminar, 1962, processed, pp. 56–7.

33. D. R. Kaldor, 'Social Returns to Research and the Objectives of Public Research, in Fischel, *op. cit.*, pp. 62–79.

34. G. L. Brinkman, 'Reconciling Proposed Investments in Agricultural Education, Infrastructure and Production in Nigeria, 1969–1985,' Michigan State University, *CSNRD Publication* No. 32, pp. 63f.

35. E. M. Rogers and L. Svenning, *Modernization among Peasants: the Impact of Communication* (1969).

36. J. Goody, 'Literacy and the Non-Literate,' London: *Times Literary Supplement*, May 12, 1972, p. 540; see also J. Goody (ed.), *Literacy in Traditional Societies*,

1968, editorial introduction and cross references to particular chapters; V. R. Dorjahn, 'The Extent and Nature of Political Knowledge in a Sierra Leone Town,' *Journal of Asian and African Studies* 3(3–4):203–15, 1968.

37. For example, J. W. Hanson, 'Enhancing the Contribution of Formal Education in Africa,' American Council on Education, Overseas Liaison Committee, *Papers on Priority Research Topics*, No. 2, 1971, p. 10.

38. M. Armer and R. Youtz, 'Formal Education and Individual Modernity in an African Society,' *American Journal of Sociology* 76(4): 604–26, 1971.

39. As shown by Rogers and Svenning, *op. cit.*, pp. 76–91, 108–19.

40. W. B. Rahudkar, 'Farmer Characteristics Associated with the Adoption and Diffusion of Improved Farm Practices,' *Indian Journal of Agricultural Economics*, 17(2):82–5, 1962.

41. Unesco, International Advisory Committee on Agricultural Education and Science, *Final Report*, 1967, p. 4; Unesco and other agencies, *World Conference on Agricultural Education and Training*, Report, 1970, v. I, pp. 45–62; J. Ader, 'The "ruralization" of primary education,' *Prospects in Education* No. 2, 1969; R. Dumont, 'Agricultural Development, Particularly in Tropical Regions, Necessitates a Completely Revised System of Education,' Unesco Conference on the Methodology of Human Resource Formation in Development Programmes, 1963 (processed).

42. Unesco, 'Adaptation of Education to the Needs of the Modern World in Rural Areas,' Unesco International Education Year, Report No. 9, 1970, p. 4.

43. C. R. Wharton, Jr., 'Education and Agricultural Growth: the Role of Education in Early-Stage Agriculture,' in C. A. Anderson and M. J. Bowman (eds.), *Education and Economic Development* (Chicago: Aldine Press, 1965), ch. 10, specifically p. 204.

44. Hayami and Ruttan, *op. cit.*, pp. 289–93.

45. R. Evenson, paper cited for 1972 in footnote 23; how easily otherwise incisive analysis can wander into obsolete ways of thinking is illustrated by the factitious manpower calculations for farm-serving personnel given in Brinkman, *op. cit.*, pp. 84f.

46. J. Moris, 'Farming Training as a Strategy of Rural Development,' in J. R. Sheffield (ed.), *Education, Employment and Rural Development*, 1967, pp. 322–65.

47. Center for the Study of Education in Changing Societies, *Primary Education in Sukumaland (Tanzania)*, 1969, p. 18; P. B. Renes, *Teacher Training at Butimba*, 1970, p. 89; S. Pratt, 'Report on the Supply of Secondary Level Teachers in English-Speaking Africa: Tanzania,' Michigan State University, *Country Studies*, No. 8, 1969. The World Bank's *Sector Working Paper* (1971) on Education is quite superficial – though uneven in quality – and has little contribution for understanding the intricacies of an education for agriculture.

48. K. Schaedler, *Crafts, Small-scale Industries, and Industrial Education in Tanzania*, 1968, pp. 56–98; A. Callaway, 'Training Young People within Indigenous Small-Scale Enterprises: the Nigerian Example,' prepared for the same conference cited in f.n. 1, pp. 6, 10; D. Wardle, *Education and Society in Nineteenth-Century Nottingham*, 1971, at p. 124 and 147ff demonstrates the salient role of private-venture education in England in the early years of the century.

3

The Education of Farm People: An Economic Perspective[*]

Theodore W. Schultz

Since the studies of the economic value of schooling and higher education are generally restricted to non-farm males, it may seem that education as a form of human capital is sex-specific, and that it is of value only to males who are not engaged in farm work. Then, too, the abundant crop of economic growth models with few exceptions leave agriculture out, and thus seemingly, the formation of capital and the employment of labour matters only when it occurs in sectors other than in agriculture. It is, of course, a fact that farm people are a tiny fraction of the population of the United Kingdom and the United States. It is also a fact that the literature in both education and economics is mainly produced by urban oriented scholars. Poets, however, continue to cherish the virtues of rural living and some ecology minded urban youth are rich enough to afford communes and organic gardens. But the people for whom agriculture is a way of life, upwards of half of the population of the world, are not rich. Nor do they have illusions about nature; for they know its harshness.

Economic growth and education are both necessary in improving the standard of living of farm people. Growth shapes the demand for schooling and higher education, and education is a source of the supply of useful acquired abilities. The economic growth of any country is a complex dynamic process and the gains in agricultural productivity are an important part of it in most of the less developed countries. The education of farm people, as the modernization of agriculture proceeds, in turn contributes to the gains in agricultural productivity, and to the improvement of farm life via the non-market activities of the members of the farm household.[1] My approach in determining the economic value of these contributions of education is to distinguish between the factors and processes that account for the demand for education and the supply of it. Education in this context consists of those 'teaching' and 'learning' activities that contribute to the acquisition of *useful* producer and con-

[*] I am indebted to Emery Castle, Lee Martin, Jacob Mincer, Vernon Ruttan, Edward Schuh, Anthony Tang and Delane Welsch for their useful comments on an early draft of this paper.

sumer abilities. Being useful implies that these acquired abilities have some social value and since scarce resources are required to acquire them they have some economic value. It follows that education has, for the purpose at hand, the attributes of an investment because people make *current* sacrifices in order to acquire *future* satisfactions and earnings. Parents sacrifice by foregoing some current consumption or investment in other forms of capital in order to provide schooling for their children. So does a community or a country because it too foregoes some alternative investment or consumption whenever it allocates resources to education.

The burden of this paper is to analyse the economic conditions that explain in large measure the differences in demand for and supply of education. It is in two parts. I shall first present four different economic types of agriculture and indicate the educational implications of each type. I shall then consider various opportunities to invest in schooling and education and the priorities among them with special reference to the less developed countries.

I

To guide this part of the analysis I shall adopt two highly simplified economic models: one designed to treat an economy that is in long run equilibrium; and the other to treat an economy that is dynamic for reasons that it is in the process of modernization and it, therefore, is not in a state of equilibrium. Both of these models will be applied in turn to agricultural sectors where the economic circumstances are such that people, in general, are very poor, and then to sectors where people are rich.

Farm people over the world produce and consume under widely different economic circumstances. In thinking about the actual and possible diversity that accounts for the different 'states of the agricultural economy' four different types are here postulated, namely: (1) traditional agriculture, (2) modernizing, but poor, (3) rich and continuing to modernize, and (4) rich with the modernization of agriculture completed.

What types (1) and (4) have in common in terms of economic theory is that production and consumption activities are at long run equilibrium. Although the difference between them in family income is very large, both (1) and (4) are here treated as stationary economic states. Types (2) and (3), however, are dynamic processes that have not arrived at a long run equilibrium. The agricultural sector of India exemplifies type (2), and that of the United States type (3). Although there is no empirical counterpart of class (4), it is an instructive model in thinking about what would happen should this dynamic process terminate to see what it might imply with respect to the education of farm people. Then, too, while it would be hard to identify agricultural sectors that are today strictly traditional in terms of economic theory, historically there have been long periods when agriculture over large areas was, for all practical purposes, at such a long run equilibrium.[2]

Turning to some of the educational implications of these four economic states, the following sketches will serve to indicate the underlying economics from which they are derived.

Traditional Agriculture

As already noted, traditional agriculture production activities and farm household consumption activities are assumed to be in long run equilibrium. For this economic state to occur several critical conditions must be satisfied, namely: (1) the state of the arts must remain constant both with respect to production and to consumption, (2) the state of the population must be stationary, (3) the state of preference and motives for holding and acquiring sources of income and of preference with respect to consumption must remain constant, and (4) all three of these states must remain constant long enough for the marginal preferences and motives for acquiring agricultural factors as sources of income and the preferences underlying consumption, to arrive at an equilibrium both with respect to the marginal productivity of the factors and to the marginal utility of the services of goods and time of farm people entering into consumption.[3]

Whenever these conditions are satisfied it means that farmers have been doing the same things for generations. Changes in inputs and techniques of production have not been crowding in on them. Neither in consumption nor in production would farm people be endeavouring to decode new information with a view to deciding whether or not to use a new input or a new consumption item. They would know from long experience the quality of the factors that they employ, the productivity of the crops that they grow, and the utility of what they consume. The value of none of these would have been altered appreciably by changes in the state of the arts. Traditional farmers, accordingly, would continue year after year to cultivate the same type of land, sow the same crops, use the same techniques of production, bring the same skills to bear, and consume as they have for generations. All of this information both with respect to production and consumption is passed on from father to son and from mother to daughter by word of mouth and by demonstration. The economic routine of production and consumption would go on in a strictly traditional manner.

The educational implications of this economic conception of traditional agriculture are that farm people acquire the information that is useful to them in production and in consumption informally, by passing it on from one generation to the next, and that the economic value of formal schooling is small. There is little or no economic incentive to make current sacrifices to acquire schooling because the future returns from it do not warrant the sacrifice. There is also another implication, namely, schooling *per se* cannot bring about the transformation of traditional agriculture.[4]

Modernizing, but Poor

Economic theory is still an incomplete guide in analysing this class of countries, partly because growth models have been developed without sufficient involvement in the facts and partly because the economic dynamics of this process are exceedingly complex. In poor countries where agriculture is of the traditional type, modernization begins when farm people can improve their economic lot by acquiring, adopting, and learning how to use efficiently new inputs that are superior in economic productivity compared to traditional inputs. These superior inputs come predominantly from advances in the sciences to the extent that they provide new useful knowledge that is applicable in production or consumption.

There is, however, much confusion in identifying the sources of additional income streams from modernization. The necessary inputs and incentives to begin the modernization process are not to be had by using the following means: (1) Expert advice provided by extension services organized and staffed on the presumption that farm people who are poor are inefficient in their production and consumption activities. Economic theory and an impressive body of evidence both indicate that they are comparatively efficient in using the sources at their disposal. It is one of the wrong roads on which many have embarked.[5] (2) Making more capital available by providing credit on better terms will induce farmers to invest in additional traditional factors but not in the superior inputs unless arrangements have been made to supply them. Here, too, both theory and evidence show that whereas agricultural production is increased somewhat by this means, it is not the mainspring of the green revolution. (3) Rich countries making their farm surpluses available to poor countries on concessional terms over a period of years is also one of the well-travelled wrong roads; it tends to impair farm incentives within the receiving country and to induce the country to neglect the modernization of its agriculture and it becomes worse off with respect to producing its own food than it would be without such food aid. In each and all of these, what really matters, are there new, additional income streams to be had?

In building the road that leads to an abundance of food, agricultural inputs that are better than the traditional ones must be at hand, and there must be efficient economic incentives to induce farmers to acquire, adopt, and learn how to use them effectively. It cannot be stressed too strongly that the modernization of agriculture would be impossible were it not for advances in scientific knowledge. It is the accumulation of this knowledge and its applications that is presently the most important factor of production in modern agriculture.[6] In retrospect, it is evident that during the long history of pre-science agriculture, there were some innovations, discoveries and some learning from trial and error. But pre-science agriculture, then and now, for it still prevails in many parts of the world, was and still is at the mercy of the vicissitudes and niggardliness of nature. Raw land and brute labour cannot dispel the ancient fear of starvation, out of which arose the age-old prayer, 'Give us this day our daily bread'. Surpluses of food grains are a recent development; Mexico now has a 'surplus' of wheat and even Japan has a 'surplus' of rice. Thus, abundance replaces the niggardliness of nature and the contributions of the sciences are a necessary part of this achievement.

But what is often overlooked in featuring the high yielding wheat and rice varieties is that the gains in agricultural productivity are dependent upon a wide array of scientific knowledge – physics, chemistry, and biology and also upon engineering for irrigation, transport facilities and agricultural machinery. There is, however, a strong tendency, which is all very human, to claim too much for that bit of new knowledge about which the particular scientist or engineer is an expert. Then, too, the large gains to be had from these better production possibilities in agriculture depend in large measure upon the combinations of technical factors and the gains from the *interactions among them*.

Norman Borlaug would be the first to agree that the new dwarf wheat varieties developed by the Rockefeller–Mexican enterprise require fertilizer, water management, control of pests and *a lot of dry-season sunshine*. Similarly, fertilizer by itself is not a panacea no matter how cheap it may become or how abundant the supply. Thus, neither the highly productive new varieties nor the cheap fertilizers are by themselves sufficient, although the plant breeders and the engineers who developed the high compressor processes to produce cheap nitrogenous fertilizer have both been necessary parts of the process. So are the irrigation engineers, although engineers have had a built-in bias for large systems while neglecting small projects and tube wells. When it comes to pesticides (which are also necessary) the types of pest control that will be required in conjunction with the new agricultural input in the developing countries are as yet in large part not known.

The popular urban view is that modern, science-oriented agriculture spoils the soil as a biological habitat and reduces the effective supply of agricultural land. But in general it is not so. The 'interaction' between farmers and soils is usually beneficial; the goodness of the earth as agricultural soil is in substantial part man-made. The renowned soils of Iowa, for example, are presently better than they were, say, four decades ago as measured by output (average corn yields since then have risen from around 35 to 100 bushels an acre).[7] Closely related is the marked increase in the effective supply of agricultural land. It is not true that the *supply* of agricultural land is fixed once and for all by the surface of the earth. On the contrary, the supply of it is a fairly elastic economic variable over time depending on the interactions between new knowledge, additions of complementary forms of capital and the value of farm products. The supply can be augmented in many different ways, but mainly by increasing its capacity per acre in much the same way as the airplane now carries several times as many passengers as it did in earlier years. Thus, for example in the United States, the increases in crop production per acre have been so large that over 50 million acres have been taken *out* of crops during the last several decades. A similar development is underway in parts of western Europe. When the agriculture of India has become fully modernized, it also will require less crop land than the acreage presently under cultivation provided the population growth is checked.

The necessary economic requirements consist of efficient economic incentives, suppliers of information, and arrangements for learning the new farming skills. Throughout much of the world in both rich and poor countries, farm people are thwarted by distortions in economic incentives, by high cost information and by less than an optimum amount of schooling. The process of modernization is delayed because of the time that is required to learn the new farming skills mainly as a consequence of the low level of formal education.

It is unfortunately true that the dominant elite view, both in capitalistic and socialistic countries, has long been that farmers are dullards, inherently backward, strongly inclined to farm in accordance with tradition and fundamentally indifferent to any new and better economic opportunities. Thus, they have long been maligned. One of the main purposes of my book, *Transforming Traditional Agriculture*,[8] was to lay to rest this widely held, mistaken view about farm people. The green revolution has undoubtedly accomplished more than my book did in establishing the fact that farmers, however poor they may be, they are not indifferent to real opportunities to improve their economic lot.

The gains in agricultural productivity from modernization in the less developed countries have five far reaching economic implications that call for a comment. (1) The increasing dependence on imported food grains of some of the major densely, long settled, poor countries that occurred during the early post World War II period is being reduced markedly by the increases in their agricultural production. The OECD view, expressed as late as the mid-sixties, is no longer tenable. A few of these less developed countries are now prepared to export some farm products to the European Economic Community countries, but the barriers that the EEC has erected to keep such imports out make it very difficult. (2) In coping with the complex issue of excessively high human fertility in most less developed countries, the increases in production of food grains give the less developed countries some additional much needed time in which to cope with the growth problems and population. (3) The entire economy of these countries is much more dependent upon the gains in agricultural production than is the case in the rich countries. The possibility of attaining general economic growth in the less developed countries is measurably enhanced by these agricultural gains. (4) Although in many less developed countries the ratio of farm workers to the area of land under cultivation is still rising, it would be an error to infer from this that the modernization of agriculture cannot proceed. The new, superior, agricultural inputs are, in general, highly divisible: a bushel of high yielding dwarf wheat, a bag of fertilizer, and a few pounds of pesticides. Similarly, small farm machinery and garden tractors can be had and they can be efficient as the farmers of Japan and Taiwan have demonstrated. (5) Last but not least is the important implication that the agricultural productivity accruing from advances in knowledge means cheaper food, and a rise in the real income of consumers because in a well managed economy,[9] these gains result in lower food prices and as this occurs they enhance the well-being of consumers.

By way of a digression, in analysing the role and behaviour of organized agricultural research, the study by Hayami and Ruttan[10] is a major advance. They have extended economic theory to explain the behaviour of this research enterprise as an endogenous sector in modern economic growth. Thus, guided by theory, they have developed an 'induced development model' for analysing the differences in the responses over time of this research sector to the differences in factor endowments and associated differences in factor prices. They derive from this model a series of testable hypotheses. The empirical part of their study concentrates on the agricultural experience of Japan and the United States since 1880. Their findings support over a wide range of differences in economic circumstances (i.e. in factor endowments, associated factor prices, and in product prices), their hypothesis of the interdependence of the research sector and the other endogenous parts of the economy. They also identify the key problems that await solution in transferring scientific knowledge through the development of the capacity of experimental stations.

Returning to poor farm people who are beginning to modernize and to the educational implications of this we have already noted that the demand for schooling increases. Farm people in the developing countries as a rule enter upon this process with very little formal schooling. Though they are illiterate, it does not imply that they fail to respond to better economic opportunities. What is implied is that in order to cope efficiently with the new inputs in production and with the better possibilities in consumption the abilities acquired from schooling become valuable. Elementary schooling becomes rewarding, especially so after the completion of the fifth, sixth, and through the last elementary school year during which the ability to read and write becomes firmly established. Here we have the key to the demand for schooling under these circumstances. The attributes of this demand will be examined in some detail later in this chapter.

Rich and Continuing to Modernize

The advanced countries qualify. Farm family incomes are high by world standards. The agricultural sector in these countries has become highly productive. Even so, all manner of technical and economic changes are crowding in on farm people. The dynamic pace is such that a new input becomes 'obsolete before its productivity can be fully explored'.[11] Equilibrium is neither at hand nor in sight. Both the farm-firm and the farm household are in this dynamic state. In managing their farms and households, farm people are continually reaching for new things, trying them, learning about them, and deciding whether they are worthwhile. They are adjusting their household activities no less than their farming activities to changing technical and economic conditions. Farm people in some of these countries have made extraordinary adjustments during recent decades in trying to stay abreast of changing circumstances. The farm population has declined dramatically and the number of farms has dropped sharply. But more of the same is in prospect.

The educational implications of this type of economic development have been investigated by Welch.[12] His findings are that in a technical dynamic agriculture of this type the explanation of education's productivity is mainly in the difference in the *allocative abilities* associated with the difference in the level of education. The hypothesis is that more educated farm people 'are more adept at critically evaluating new and reportedly improved inputs'. They 'can distinguish more quickly between the systematic and random elements' as they seek to take advantage of the new inputs whether it be in production or in consumption. Welch's empirical analysis supports this hypothesis in the domain of production to which he limited his test. His results show that this 'allocative ability plays a key role in determining education's productivity in agriculture and is most relevant in a dynamic setting'.[13]

Clearly, in the United States, as modernization continues at this rapid pace, where farm people have in general high levels of income, the economic value of education is such that the optimum level is not attained by elementary schooling. More education than this is required to satisfy the demand for education of farm people. Farm people with 12 years of schooling are winning out in competition with those who have 8 and less years of schooling. Furthermore, those with 16 years of education have been gaining relative to other levels over time.[14]

Rich and Modernization Completed

It is a theoretical assumed type that is nowhere in sight; for there is no agricultural sector in any of the advanced countries that qualifies. It is nevertheless a useful model in thinking about the economic value of education and the demand for it on the part of farm people. Suppose that an advanced agricultural sector were to arrive at a long run equilibrium, exemplified by a stationary economic state. Under such circumstances, the economic activities of farm people would become repetitive, doing year after year essentially the same things except as each family made accommodation to meet its life cycle requirements. There would be no new inputs to upset this routine. The information required pertaining to production and consumption would have been learned and it would be passed on from one generation to the next. The economic value of the allocative ability associated with education would decline. The optimum level of education would become less than it is where farm people have attained a high level of productivity and modernization is continuing at a rapid pace. Relatively high work skills would still be needed but not the entrepreneural allocative ability. Farm people with 12 years of schooling would no doubt do about as well as those with more education.[15] Even less than 12 years might suffice, that is, would become the optimum under such circumstances.

II

The costs of education can be reckoned fairly accurately provided the students' earnings foregone are not omitted. But, the benefits that accrue to students and to society from education are much harder to get at. There is no programme planning model that will tell a country what it should do in allocating resources to education. The computer with all its capacity cannot print the instructions that investors in education require. In the developing countries, on which I shall concentrate in this part, data are in poor repair and the future demands for the wide array of acquired skills, which are a function of the dynamics of the economy, are shrouded in uncertainty including the substitution possibilities among skills under changing economic circumstances.

In looking for evidence on the economic value of education, it is obviously necessary to examine both the costs and benefits of education. These costs and benefits are, in large measure, determined by the rate of economic growth. Thus, much depends on the state of the economy. It should be clear from the first part of this paper that economic growth is not an equilibrium state, but a dynamic process. For the purpose in this part, growth implies responses to investment opportunities in acquiring additional income streams at a price lower than the equilibrium price. In terms of investment decisions, whether in physical capital or in human capital including education, economic growth is a consequence of the allocation of investment resources in accordance with the priorities set by the relative rates of return to alternative investment opportunities. Formally, the reciprocal of the highest rate of return option is, in theory and in fact, the lowest price of additional growth.

Accordingly, as investment in human capital in the form of education occurs, it is here treated as a response with due allowance with respect to the cost of education, to the demand derived from growth, measured in terms of its contributions to producer and consumer productivity. In this context the economics of education directs attention to the interactions between economic growth and education. As developing countries succeed in improving their economic lot, three important interactions have been identified and substantially quantified.[16]

1. The accumulation of human capital represented by education occurs at a higher rate than that of nonhuman capital.
2. Although the difference in the relative earnings between workers with little and those with much education decreases, it is the absolute difference in earnings that determines whether additional education is warranted.
3. As economic growth proceeds, the inequality in the distribution of personal income appears to show some signs of decreasing. Increases in education and in on the job training may be among the explanatory factors.

Investors tend to prefer industries, the growth of which exceeds that of the economy. Education qualifies. Most societies prefer both higher earnings and less inequality in personal incomes; they are both associated with investments in education. Yet, despite these favourable interactions between economic growth and education, the costs and returns (benefits) that are specific to education must be taken into account. But here a serious difficulty arises because those who have a special interest in education are inclined to underestimate the real costs and to mis-specify the benefits.

With respect to costs, *earnings forgone* while attending school are conveniently omitted both in the rich and in the poor countries. Whereas in rich countries earnings foregone are important at the higher levels of education, in the poor countries they are as a rule also significant at the upper part of elementary schooling,[17] all of the talk of chronic unemployment notwithstanding. They are real costs that are borne by the families with children because already at the tender age of 10 to 14, children are called upon for useful work in agriculture which is the dominant sector in most developing countries. Moreover, in the context of economic growth, the value of time rises and as this occurs the earnings foregone by students rise as a consequence. Nor are earnings forgone a trivial part of the costs of education. The available evidence suggests that they are half or more of the total *real* cost of higher education, upwards of half of the real cost of secondary schooling, and in developing countries, earnings foregone may account for a third or more of the total real cost once children reach the fifth grade in their elementary school.

In accounting for the benefits from education, it is not sufficient to look only at the higher earnings associated with more education. There are also private satisfactions associated with education. It is appropriate to think of these as cultural satisfactions that accrue to the student over his lifetime. Although they are non-pecuniary rewards that defy estimation, they must nevertheless be kept in mind. Meanwhile, much is made these days especially so by the proponents of more higher education on behalf of the long list of social benefits of such education. It is increasingly clear that most of the social benefits on this list are unsubstantiated. The real benefits that come from higher education accrue predominantly to the students. There are, however, two exceptions, neither of which appears on the list of these proponents. The first consists of the social benefits that are associated with the education of females. It is revealed in what children acquire from their mother's education; this particular social benefit also enhances the educability of subsequent generations. The other social benefit that is not on the list, as noted earlier, is the benefit from the allocative ability based on the observed increases in this ability associated with the rise in education in decoding and in interpreting new technical and economic information pertaining to production and consumption. As a consequence the more educated adjust their behaviour more rapidly (with a shorter lag) than do the less educated. In production, under competition, it follows that the productivity gains from new inputs are transferred to consumers more rapidly than would otherwise be the case.

Where farm people are 'poor but modernizing', the supply of capital is meagre and the demand for it increases because of the many alternative investment opportunities. The rate of return under these circumstances is generally higher than it is in rich countries. Thus, in competing for funds, the rate of return to investment in education in this class of poor countries 'must' also be higher than in the rich countries. There are two key issues: What is the ranking of schooling and higher education as an investment? What are the priorities among the educational options? The 'answers' are of necessity in very general terms, and even at best, only approximate; and in view of the scattered evidence, they are tentative although plausible in terms of theory. They are contained in the following four propositions.

1. Among the educational options, the highest private rates of return in most of these countries are to be had from additional investments in elementary schooling, mainly from completing the fifth to the last elementary year.
2. When account is taken of the benefits bestowed on the next generation the highest social rates of return are to be had from investments in the education of females.
3. The efficiency of the schooling investment process tends to be the highest where there is a general framework of public rules concerning school attendance and granting equal treatment in receiving public funds, designed to maximize the domain of family and local community decision-making.
4. Given 1, 2 and 3 above and given a *successful modernization process*, the rates of return to schooling tend to be fully as high as they are on the better half of the investments in nonhuman capital.

The supporting evidence and the implications of each of these propositions call for elaboration. Each will be considered briefly in turn.

The available evidence is most telling with respect to the *first* proposition. In terms of rates of return, higher education ranks below elementary schooling.[18] The rate of return on completing the fifth, sixth and on to the last elementary year is as a rule the highest. The reasons for this result appear to be as follows:

(1) For a person to remain literate over his lifetime, presumably more than four years of schooling is usually required.

(2) The economic value of having the ability to read and write is much enhanced by the opportunities which are forthcoming in a dynamic economy; this is once again the ability to decode, interpret, and act efficiently in taking advantage of technical change and new economic information. While it is true that this allocative ability continues to increase with more education, when the total real costs of the additional education are reckoned, the rate of return tends to be highest for the fifth and subsequent elementary years in these developing countries.

(3) Among the educational options, there is in most countries a long standing bias in favour of higher education. Educators tend to nurture thi bias. Universities like steel mills are symbols that enhance national prestige. The influential classes want their children to acquire a university education preferably at public expense. Thus the stage is set in favour of higher education relative to the lower levels of schooling for the rank and file of the population. Moreover, this bias is evident not only in Colombia, Mexico and other developing countries, but also in the United States and in other rich countries. Leaving the economic value of university research associated with graduate work aside, the rate of return to

undergraduate instruction is substantially below that for the lower levels of education.

The support for the *second* proposition comes largely from recent studies made possible by the extension of economic theory in analysing the non-market activities of the household. Seeing the earnings foregone that enter into the formation of human capital, the stage was set for development of the 'allocation of time'.[19] Becker's paper represents an important new development in economic thinking; it treats time as the fundamental unit of cost in individual allocative decisions with respect to both labour and consumption. Analytically, it provides economists with a major new economic approach to the non-market household activities, especially so in accounting, for the economic value of the time of women. We now see that each consumer commodity has two prices attached to it – a money price, as in traditional consumer choice, and a time cost in acquiring, processing and consuming the commodity. The bearing and rearing of children are also an integral part of this new economics of the household.

For the purpose at hand, it is the wide array of effects of the education of females that the investors in education in the developing countries can ill afford to overlook. The organizational efficiency of the household and its contribution to family consumption appears to depend in substantial part on the level of the schooling of the woman. Most women in the developing countries are poorly equipped in terms of the schooling that is required to manage their households skilfully in taking advantage of new technical information with respect to nutrition, health and child care. Another favourable effect of the schooling of women is the improvement in their ability to decode, interpret and successfully adopt the new, superior contraceptive techniques. The acquisition of more schooling by females tends to raise the age of marriage, a strong factor in reducing fertility. Thus, the implications of compulsory school attendance for more years than has been traditional (many females presently attend school not at all) is strong and clear with respect to reducing fertility. The most important effect of the schooling of females may well be the social benefit that arises out of the marked advantage that children derive from being reared in homes where the mothers have this schooling. There is a growing body of evidence in support of the inference that the level of schooling of mothers is most important in accounting for the quality of the inputs they provide for their children. It is this class of social benefits that argues strongly for more public investment in the schooling of girls. Whereas in the case of males, the gains in productivity from more schooling accrue predominantly to those who acquire the schooling; in the case of females, there are substantial benefits from more schooling that accrue to society. It is this particular social benefit that accounts for the relatively high social rates of return to the investment in the education of women featured in the second proposition.[20]

Turning to the *third* proposition, thinking continues to be confused and clarifying evidence is hard to come by. The long standing controversy on the role of the private self-interest of families in the schooling of their children versus the role of public and professional bodies in deciding the content and the amount of schooling, is still with us as it was when the classical economists divided on this issue. It is a difficult issue because each of its three inter-related parts, i.e. standards, information and incentives, requires fine tuning in order to approach an optimum allocation and utilization of resources devoted to schooling and higher education.

Standards In providing funds for education, public bodies must establish standards that are to govern the utilization of such funds. A government or any public agency would be irresponsible if it did not do so. The un-solved problem, however, is twofold: (1) These standards have to be acceptable politically, and (2) for the resources to be used efficiently, they must combine a minimum of central control of schools consistent with a maximum of family and community involvement in decision-making with respect to the schooling. Most countries and especially the developing countries tend toward over-centralization of their educational systems. Thus, the standards that are established thwart local involvement, and private self-interest and initiative is blunted. The recent US 'revenue-sharing' controversy reveals how difficult it is for Congress to agree upon standards that are politically acceptable. In turn, the controversy about the merits of 'school vouchers' suggests how hard it is to get acceptance of the allocative role of the private self-interest of students (families) in matters pertaining to education.

Information With respect to earnings foregone, students (families) are well informed. But with regard to the benefits that will accrue to them from schooling, the state of information is far from optimum. How much more are they likely to benefit from more schooling? Will they be less subject to unemployment? (In the US, lifetime unemployment is sub-stantially less for the more educated. But what are the facts on this point in the developing countries?) The normal life span is increasing. But there is a long lag before the importance of this favourable development for investment in education becomes known to most families. But worse still is the lack of information on the value of the different components of education and on the differences in the quality of the instruction.

Incentives It is not difficult to specify formally the desired properties of these incentives; but it is very hard to achieve them in practice. Formally, they should be efficient both socially and privately; they should also be clear and strong in order to mobilize the private self-interest of students (families). A major difficulty arises out of the fact that they tend to be inefficient because they fail to provide students (families) with socially appropriate scarcity signals so that students (families) can make socially efficient choices. The key argument in favour of student vouchers is that when public funds for education are thus allocated they would become efficient incentives both privately and socially. There are, of course, all manner of compromises each with its price, and the price is relatively high in developing countries where capital is very scarce.

My *fourth* proposition rings a bell that is pleasing to the ear of investors in education. It announces that there are investment opportunities in education that will enhance the future economic well-being of a developing country fully as much as the better half of the investment opportunities in nonhuman capital, that is, in structures, equipment, inventories and in land improvements. But, the conditions set forth in presenting this proposition must not be overlooked. They are that the fifth and subsequent years of schooling rank very high. From a social point of view looking to subsequent generations the education of females also ranks high. The proper organization of public provision for and private utilization of funds, including the earnings foregone and other resources of students (families), is important. But there is still another essential condition and that is *successful modernization*. If the country is not embarked on modernization, if it is not acquiring and adopting new superior techniques and other inputs, but it is coasting along in a traditional manner – *there will be little or no pay-off on additional investments in education*. If the development is sluggish and sporadic, the rewards from more schooling will be low and subject to much uncertainty. But as the dynamics of development become strong and continuous, the additional skills and abilities associated with more schooling are in demand and the rates of return to the investment in them become high and as favourable as the best alternative investment opportunities.

In conclusion, the implications of the four propositions that have been featured are applicable in determining the opportunities to invest in the education of farm people in poor countries where farm-firms and farm households are benefiting from modernization.

REFERENCES

1. In a larger context, the value of an education will vary depending upon economic and social conditions. It has a value when farm people migrate to take a better job, when they enter upon off-farm employment while maintaining residence on the farm, when they search for technical and economic information in making more nearly optimum lifetime consumption-savings plans, and when they invest both in physical and human capital.

2. See B. H. Slicher Van Bath, *The Agrarian History of Western Europe, A.D. 500 to 1850* (New York: St. Martin's Press, 1963).

3. See my *Transforming Traditional Agriculture* (New Haven: Yale University Press, 1964) pp. 29–54 for a systematic presentation of this economic conception of agriculture.

4. There is an argument for two apparent qualifications to this statement. (1) If well educated people were to replace illiterate farmers, as occurred in Israel and modern agricultural inputs are at hand, the transformation of traditional agriculture takes place rapidly. (2) Schooling of farm youth in low level traditional agriculture, for example, in Northeast Brazil, leads to out-migration and this migration may be viewed as setting the stage for agricultural modernization.

5. This statement does not imply, however, that organized agricultural extension services are not worthwhile once new superior inputs from research are at hand and the economic requirements are favourable for their adoption. On the contrary, it is at this juncture that the benefits relative to the costs of extension activities, reveal a high rate of return.

6. The part that follows on the interactions between science and agriculture is drawn in the main from my paper prepared for the 21st Pugwash Conference, Sinaia, Romania, August 1971.

7. Obviously, other major factors also contribute to these increases in corn yields.

8. Schultz, *op. cit.*

9. Unfortunately there are few such economies.

10. Yujiro Hayami and Vernon Ruttan, *Agricultural Development: An International Perspective* (Baltimore: Johns Hopkins Press, 1971).

11. Finis Welch, 'Education in Production', *Journal of Political Economy.* 78, 1970, 35–59.

12. Welch, already cited.

13. Welch, p. 47.

14. See below

14. In March, 1970, 10·8 per cent of the employed males in agriculture had one or more years of college (7·6 per cent, 1 to 3 years; 3·2 per cent, 4 or more years). Of the employed females in agriculture, 12·5 per cent had one or more years of college (9·8 per cent with 1 to 3 years; and 2·7 per cent with 4 or more years). The proportion of all farmers and farm managers with one or more years of college appears to have doubled between 1952 and 1970 in US agriculture. From data in Special Labor Reports 125 and 65 of the Bureau of Labor Statistics on *Educational Attainment of Workers.*

    G. S. Tolley, in his study 'Management Entry Into US Agriculture',

American Journal of Agricultural Economics, 52, November, 1970, shows that agriculture is undergoing replacement of one kind of human capital by another because high level management farms experience favourable cost curve shifts, which explains the replacement of many low management by fewer high management farms.

15. Welch, already cited, p. 55, notes that agricultural research expenditures in the US per farm were $4·30 in 1940 and $28·40 in 1959 (in constant 1959 dollars). His estimates indicate that 'if research were to fall from $28·40 to $4·30 . . . the relative wage of college to high school graduates would fall from 1·62 to 1·43, indicating that one-third of the wage differential would disappear.'

16. These three interactions are examined in some detail in my 'Optimal Investment in College Education: Equity and Efficiency', in the May/June Supplement to the *Journal of Political Economy*, Vol. 79.

17. Edward Schuh's comment on this point is a useful elaboration. '. . . the opportunity costs of education to the poor are even more important then they are to the well-to-do. . . (for) a very poor farmer in Northeast Brazil . . . the marginal productivity of the son is much, much lower than that of the son of a well-to-do rancher. But the *relative* importance of that sacrificed output to the (poor) family is much greater. Hence, in poor agriculture, there is a doubled edge sword. Not only does the education have little value, but the sacrificed output of a son attending school is relatively more important in terms of the family income.'

18. This statement is supported by studies of annual earnings; when 'wage rates' are used these rates of return appear to be more nearly equal.

19. Gary S. Becker, 'A Theory of the Allocation of Time', *Economic Journal*, LXXV, 1965, pp. 493–517.

20. The present state of knowledge pertaining to this proposition is summarized in my 'Woman's New Economic Commandments', *Bulletin of Atomic Scientists*, February 1972.

BIBLIOGRAPHY

Gary S. Becker, *Human Capital: A Theoretical and Empirical Analysis, with Special Reference to Education* (New York: NBER, 1964).

— 'A Theory of the Allocation of Time.' *Economic Journal* 75 (September 1965): 493–517.

Gary S. Becker, and Barry R. Chiswick, 'Education and the Distribution of Earnings', *American Economic Review* 56 (May 1966): 358–69.

Lee Benham, 'The Returns to Education of Women.' Workshop paper, University of Chicago, May 1971.

Yoram Ben-Porath, 'The Production of Human Capital and the Life Cycle of Earnings.' *Journal of Political Economy* 75 (August 1957): 352–65.

Mary Jean Bowman, 'The Costing of Human Resource Development.' In *The Economics of Education*, E. A. G. Robinson and John E. Vaizey (eds.) (New York: St Martin's Press, 1966), pp. 421–50

— 'The Human Investment Revolution in Economic Thought.' *Sociology of Education* 39 (Spring 1966): 111–37.

Mary Jean Bowman, and C. Arnold Anderson, 'Distributional Effects of Educational Programmes.' In *Income Distribution Analysis*, Series 23 (Raleigh: North Carolina State University, 1966).

D. P. Chaudhri, 'Education and Agricultural Productivity in India.' PhD dissertation, University of Delhi, 1968.

— 'Farmers' Education and Productivity: Some Empirical Results from Indian Agriculture.' Human Capital Paper 69:04, University of Chicago, 1969.

Barry R. Chiswick, 'The Average Level of Schooling and the Personal Distribution of Income by Regions: A Clarification.' *American Economic Review* 58 (June 1968): 495–500.

— 'Earnings Inequality and Economic Development.' *Quarterly Journal of Economics* 85 (February 1971): 21–39.

Albert Fishlow, 'Levels of Nineteenth Century American Investment in Education', *Journal of Economic History* 26 (December 1966): 418–36.

Bruce L. Gardner, 'An Analysis of US Farm Family Income Inequality, 1950–1960.' PhD dissertation, University of Chicago, 1968.

Zvi Griliches, 'Research Expenditures, Education, and the Aggregate Agricultural Production Function.' *American Economic Review* 54 (December 1964): 961–74.

— 'Notes on the Role of Education in Production Functions and Growth Accounting.' In *Education, Income, and Human Capital*, W. Lee Hansen (ed.), Studies in Income and Wealth, Vol. 35, (New York: NBER, 1970) pp. 71–115.

— 'Education, Income, and Ability.' *Journal of Political Economy* 80 (May/June 1972 supplement).

Giora Hanoch, 'An Economic Analysis of Earnings and Schooling.' *Journal of Human Resources* 2 (Summer 1967): 335–40.

W. Lee Hansen, and Burton A. Weisbrod, *Benefits, Costs, and Finance of Public Higher Education* (Chicago: Markham, 1969).

F. K. Hines, Luther Tweeten, and J. Martin Redfern, 'Social and Private Rates of Return to Investment in Schooling, by Race-Sex Groups and Regions.' *Journal of Human Resources* 5 (Summer 1970): 318–40.

Harry G. Johnson, 'The Economic Approach to Social Questions.' *Economica* 36 (February 1969): 1–21.

Thomas Johnson, 'Returns from Investment in Schooling and On-the-Job Training.' PhD dissertation, North Carolina State University, Raleigh, 1969.

Anne O. Krueger, 'Factor Endowments and Per Capita Income Differences among Countries.' *Economic Journal* 78 (September 1968): 641–59.

Simon Kuznets, *Modern Economic Growth* (New Haven: Yale University Press, 1966).

Robert T. Michael, *Effects of Education on Efficiency in Consumption* (New York: NBER, forthcoming).

Jacob Mincer, 'On-the-Job Training: Costs, Returns, and Some Implications.' *Journal of Political Economy* 70 (October 1962, supplement): 50–79.

Jacob Mincer, 'The Distribution of Labour Incomes: A Survey with Special Reference to the Human Capital Approach.' *Journal of Economic Literature* 8 (March 1970): 1–26.

— 'Schooling, Age, and Earnings.' Preliminary typescript, NBER, 1969.

June O'Neill, 'The Effects of Income and Education on Inter-Regional Migration.' PhD dissertation, Columbia University, 1969.

Paul T. Schultz, 'Secular Trends and Cyclical Behaviour of Income Distribution in the United States: 1944–1965.' In *Six Papers on the Size Distribution of Wealth and Income*, Lee Soltow (ed.) (New York: NBER, 1969).

Theodore W. Schultz, 'Reflections on Agricultural Production, Output, and Supply,' *Journal of Farm Economics* 38 (August 1958): 748–62.

— 'Our Welfare State and the Welfare of Farm People.' *Social Service Review* 38 (June 1964): 123–29.

— 'Education and Economic Opportunities in Depressed Areas: Implications for Research.' In *Problems of Chronically Depressed Rural Areas* Raleigh: Agricultural Policy Institute, North Carolina State University, 1965). pp. 45–53

— *Investment in Human Capital: The Role of Education and of Research* (New York: Free Press, 1971).

— 'The Optimal Investment in College Instruction: Equity and Efficiency.' *Journal of Political Economy* 80 (May/June 1972 supplement).

Aba Schwartz, 'Migration and Lifetime Earnings in the US' PhD dissertation, University of Chicago, 1968.

Lewis C. Solmon, 'Capital Formation by Expenditures on Formal Education, 1880 and 1890.' PhD dissertation, University of Chicago, 1968.

S. G. Strumlin, 'The Economic Significance of National Education' (1925). Translated from the Russian and reprinted in E. A. G. Robinson and J. E. Vaizey (eds.), *The Economics of Education* (New York: St Martin's Press, 1966), pp. 276–323.

Finis Welch, 'Determinants of the Return to Schooling in Rural Farm Areas, 1959.' PhD dissertation, University of Chicago, 1968.

— 'Measurement of the Quality of Schooling.' *American Economic Review* 56 (May 1966): 379–92.

— 'Education in Production.' *Journal of Political Economy* 78 (January/February 1970): 35–59.

E. G. West, 'Private Versus Public Education.' *Journal of Political Economy* 72 (October 1964): 465–75.

4

The Mass Media in Rural Education

Robert Hornik, John K. Mayo and Emile G. McAnany

Our focus in this discussion is upon the developing nations of Africa, Asia and Latin America for it is here that the need for rural education is most urgent and here that a broader use of the mass media is being most vigorously advocated.[1]

Educators in the developing countries are turning their attention to the problems of rural education as a matter of social justice as well as political necessity. They realize that the neglect of rural people is no longer tolerable. As investments in education have grown, it has become obvious that schooling, like most social institutions, remains essentially an urban phenomenon, particularly at the secondary and university levels. In most developing countries, the vast majority of rural youth are still denied the opportunity to study beyond the second or third grade, while a significantly larger number of their counterparts in the urban areas are able to progress through more advanced academic levels. Such educational imbalances help attract the ablest young people to the cities and make the development of the rural, agricultural economy much more difficult. To promote a more balanced growth between the urban and rural sectors, educators have advocated not only the extension of educational oppor-tunities, but also the establishment of different kinds of educational services for rural areas.

Formal and Informal Education

In the rural areas of most developing countries, the school is the only means of formal instruction currently available. It is an expensive process encompassing different subjects and different levels of instruction all requiring a large number of trained teaching and supervisory personnel to run efficiently. School is also a cumulative process; students are generally required to master the skills of one level before proceeding to another.

The poor conditions found in the rural schools of most developing countries are well known: antiquated and irrelevant curricula, ill-prepared and overworked teachers, and a dearth of learning materials and teaching aids such as libraries, science laboratories, or even enough desks or textbooks for all the students. If the school is physically distant from the city, its instruction tends to be culturally isolated from the particular community in which it is located. Because most teachers, curricula, and learning materials come from outside, the skills and information taught rarely meet the needs of rural children. Furthermore, many rural primary schools have only one or two teachers and they are located in areas where children are poor, undernourished, and consequently achieve less than their counterparts in urban areas. All these problems tend to discourage rural teachers and drive them toward the cities. Indeed, assignment to a rural school often comes as a punishment or because a particular teacher does not have enough seniority or political leverage to obtain a favoured assignment in an urban area.

Primary school dropout rates are generally high throughout developing countries, but when the urban-rural breakdown is made, it often reveals a disastrous situation in rural schools, with dropout rates before the sixth grade often in excess of 80 per cent of first grade entrants. Schools are simply not providing a basic education for the vast majority of rural youth.

Even if major improvements are achieved in the quality of schooling and in the numbers of children being educated through the kinds of educational reforms presently being enacted in El Salvador, Mexico, Peru, and the Ivory Coast, the employment problem facing growing numbers of rural graduates is likely to remain. Unless rural areas can become self-developing centres of economic growth and opportunity, graduates, whether well trained or not, will continue to leave a stagnant situation for an unknown but more appealing life in the city.

Reversing these failures of rural education while working within the existing formal school structure has its own special difficulties. An entrenched bureaucracy, such as a ministry of education, is by nature slow to change or accept innovation. Convincing officials at all levels to implement even the best designed reforms is no easy task. In addition, teachers may not understand or accept a new role and, as gatekeepers, they may try to transform a new instructional programme into what they have always taught.

Given the immense problems and the difficulty of changing the existing system, a growing number of critics such as Ivan Illich have recommended that all schools be abandoned, and that new educational strategies be adopted. At a minimum, development planners are looking beyond formal schooling to more informal educational strategies for extending education and ultimately for improving rural life.

Informal education is not easily defined. It can be an extension of the formal school system, as in the correspondence or 'open' schools; it can be a parallel instructional system where differently focused school equivalency work is carried on; it can be a skills training course in agriculture, literacy or mechanics; or it can be a radical departure from the formal school system, as in the kind of 'cultural action' programmes devised by the Brazilian educator, Paulo Freire.[2] Later in the discussion, we will elaborate further upon the different kinds of informal education projects being developed for the rural areas and try to explain why the mass media have come to play an increasingly important part in such projects.

Introducing any informal educational system may present new difficulties, however. If the formal system suffers in part because of the immovability of its bureaucracy, at least it has a bureaucracy. No planner should underestimate the difficulty of recruiting, training, housing and establishing communication links within a new bureaucracy. Even in countries that have instituted profound educational and social changes in recent years, such as Cuba and China, schools have not disappeared.

Secondly, the formal school system has an established call on a government's budget whereas an informal system may have support for a brief time, but then may lose its backing with a change of government leadership or priorities. Furthermore, a formal school system generally can count on the allegiance and support of most people within a society. Thus, if change is to be introduced within the formal system, administrators are assured of at least tacit approval from the general public.

Finally, while informal education is able to generate initial enthusiasm, most programmes have not maintained themselves for long periods of time. One is tempted to predict such a waning of enthusiasm for all such projects. For some campaigns with specific short term goals (like vaccination drives or even a literacy campaign like Cuba's in 1961) a concentrated period of high enthusiasm is sufficient. For teaching general learning skills, however, a longer period of education is necessary. Unless there exists an ongoing structure that will function not only during periods of high enthusiasm but during slack periods as well, the failure of all but relatively brief campaigns is likely.

Given these disadvantages, it is clear why most educators (themselves products of a traditional schooling) have opted to reform education within the formal school structure.

The Mass Media in Rural Development and Education: An Overview

As educators and politicians have become aware of the need to provide more educational opportunities to the rural areas, the mass media have loomed ever larger in their thinking. At this point it is useful to examine why development planners have expressed so much interest in the media and what specific roles they have assigned to them.

Looking back over the past two decades, we find that as concern for rural development intensified, different educational and social change strategies were articulated. The potential use of the mass media for a wide variety of tasks was given a thrust forward by Daniel Lerner whose book, *The Passing of Traditional Society* (1958), heralded the vital role of mass communications in the diffusion of information as well as modern social values. Wilbur Schramm in his book, *Mass Media and National Development* (1964), summarized previous experience in this area and outlined more completely the specific roles that the mass media might play in rural development. The growing advocacy of the media's role by communication theorists coupled with the results of some interesting media-assisted rural education projects, such as Colombia's Radio Sutatenza, interested development planners everywhere and prompted them to rely more on the mass media in their projects.

A concurrent technological breakthrough was also important in enhancing the role of the mass media in rural education. Until the late 1950s, broadcast technology was prohibitively expensive for most developing countries and its reception in rural areas depended largely on the availability of electricity. The invention of the transistor and its rapid commercialization in the manufacture of inexpensive, battery operated radios meant that, for the first time, radio broadcasts could be beamed at rural areas far removed from existing power sources.

Radio health campaigns, farm forum discussion groups, and literacy projects blossomed in the first decade of the transistor. Most of these projects operated on the fallacious notion that messages conveyed by the mass media would automatically have a direct and powerful impact on rural audiences. Such optimism was unfounded, and in retrospect it seems clear that the early concentration on the new technology was at the expense of content development and a proper regard for programme utilization techniques. To the planners' dismay, early experiences with the mass media in rural education revealed that rural people preferred popular music to new agricultural programmes and soap operas to health information. It was discovered that simply reaching rural audiences with information was not in itself a sufficient means to foster social change.

It became clear by the middle of the last decade that neither advocacy of the mass media nor hardware oriented trial and error projects were enough to meet the needs of rural areas. A period of reassessment began, therefore, with planners asking how effective the media really were in solving rural problems. Unesco, having assisted many mass media projects, undertook a series of brief case studies to review the status of some thirty projects.[3] Although no thorough study of the media's effectiveness was undertaken at that time, a number of common problems were identified: the emphasis on hardware at the expense of content development, the lack of clear project objectives, the reliance on foreign technicians and the lack of adequate training provisions for local personnel, and the fact that virtually no feedback systems or serious evaluations had been undertaken by the projects themselves.

In addition to the internal problems identified by the Unesco study, another problem has recently been raised by social critics who are aware that the media, besides transmitting practical information of one sort or another, are also highly susceptible to control by vested commercial and political interests, both from within the countries and abroad. Many have feared that the mass media campaigns will be transformed into instruments of propaganda and repression instead of development.[4]

All of these factors make serious evaluation and criticism of existing mass media projects a mandatory task. A few studies are under way and others will undoubtedly follow. Careful analysis and discussion of the results should help guide planners toward a better use of the media in rural education. In the meantime, we will attempt to summarize in the remaining portion of this chapter what lessons seem to have been learned so far from the application of the media in formal and informal educational settings.

The Mass Media within Formal Educational Settings

It is easier to identify the projects using one or another of the mass media for formal school instruction than those engaged in informal education. School based projects tend to be more visible; they are generally bigger, more costly, and national in scope. Informal education projects, on the other hand, are often locally initiated efforts operating on a much smaller scale with far lower capital and operating costs. The Unesco volumes provided a comprehensive summary of the major formal school projects in 1967. Six years after publication of the Unesco cases, most of the major formal school projects are still in operation, while others have been inaugurated in the meantime.

The major uses of television as an instructional medium in developing countries are found in Colombia, Niger, Samoa, Mexico, El Salvador, and the Ivory Coast. Colombia began its ETV system for primary schools in 1964 and broadcasting continues to approximately 350,000 students in grades one through six. Although a comprehensive study of the Peace Corps' role in the first three years of the project was completed in 1966,[5] no serious evaluation of the project has been undertaken since that year.

Niger began its project in 1964 with an attempt by a team of French experts to provide a modern education to rural primary students. Working with classroom monitors instead of formally trained teachers, the project consisted of only twenty pilot classes through its first five years (1968–72). The project will expand in 1973 to a much wider national audience and it is hoped that the research results of the long experimental period will soon be published.

In contrast to Niger, Samoa began its ETV system on a large scale in 1964, serving over 7,000 students in all twelve grades. There have been a number of problems with the Samoan project, stemming largely from its precipitous beginning, but until the 1971–72 school year no systematic evaluation of learning results had been carried out.[6]

El Salvador inaugurated its ETV system for grades 7–9 in 1969. The El Salvadoran ETV system is but one component of a major educational reform and it is the first truly nation-wide project to be undertaken by a developing country, albeit a very small one. The El Salvador project is also the first to have a serious evaluation unit built into it from the start.[7] As one of the youngest members of the ETV fraternity, El Salvador learned from the experiences of other countries and so far has been able to avoid duplicating many of their mistakes.

The inauguration of a national ETV system in the Ivory Coast in 1971 completes the list of major projects using television in formal school settings. The Ivorian government's main objective is to provide universal primary education by the year 1980. Although classroom reception is currently concentrated in the southern two-thirds of the country, the project will soon expand through a nation-wide network. A great many planning documents for this project have been published by the Ivorian and French governments as well as by Unesco, but evaluation of the project's effectiveness is just getting under way.

When we turn from television to the older medium of radio, we find far fewer projects serving rural schools. This is unfortunate because radio offers a technically less complex and cheaper means for reaching large rural areas. Costs for radio systems are generally estimated to be one-fifth to one-eighth those of television. Radio systems have been installed and maintained without the large reliance on foreign experts that television technology usually implies and, at least for the next five to ten years, radio will be able to penetrate many remote rural areas which are not reached by television signals.

Examples of projects using radio within formal school settings are neither as numerous nor as well publicized as those using television. Since the early 1960s, Thailand has used radio extensively in its rural schools. The Unesco case studies report on this project and an update on recent results may be undertaken this year.

Mexico has used radio in several experiments. A government sponsored project in the rural state of San Luis Potosi utilizes radio as a supplementary instructional medium for grades 4–6 in primary schools where a single teacher must often handle the three grades simultaneously.[8] Up until 1972 radio was also used in schools serving the Tarahumara Indian population of Northern Mexico. After an evaluation revealed that the radio schools were, in fact, not meeting the needs of the Tarahumara people, but rather those of other racial groups, the schools were phased out. A new plan was devised whereby radio will be used to provide informal, community education to the Tarahumara.[9]

On the African continent, a small radio station in Bunia, Eastern Zaire has had some success broadcasting lessons to both primary and secondary students in its neighbouring region. Although this work has been underway for almost three years, no evaluation of its effectiveness has been made. Senegal has found the teaching of French by radio so well received that government planners have decided to use television as well. However, radio will remain the chief medium of instruction for the rural students, at least for the forseeable future. Finally, Tanzania has made a considerable commitment to radio instruction for its rural areas, although unlike most other countries, its use of radio is integrated within a broad rural development plan that aims to transform Tanzania's countryside into the foremost sector of economic growth.

Television and radio are being used to reach large numbers of rural students at various academic levels within many developing countries. And as cost-conscious politicians are putting pressure on educators to provide new solutions to the vast qualitative and quantitative problems endemic to rural schools, the media are being turned to almost as a panacea for educating future generations of students. This turning to the mass media has not been well received by some critics.

To summarize, the following arguments against the use of the mass media in formal schooling have been advanced in the past:

1. A media project inevitably attracts a lot of attention and therefore is more likely to be used as an instrument of propaganda than as a means for solving deep-rooted educational problems;
2. Even if the media can provide educational opportunities to more rural students, there is little cost-effectiveness evidence to justify the large expenditures demanded by most media systems. It is better to spend limited resources on other needs, such as raising teachers' salaries;
3. Media systems save no money and almost always end up costing more than was originally projected;
4. The mass media have a centralizing tendency which unavoidably reinforces the *status quo*, thereby strengthening existing institutions like the school system and making real change impossible.

These arguments have been directed more at television and less at the lower cost media such as radio, radio-vision, or print.

The following counter-arguments in favour of expanding the uses of the mass media in formal rural education are customarily advanced:

1. The media can increase educational opportunity by allowing a system

to reach many more students and, at the same time, improve the quality of instruction by distributing the best possible teaching;

2. Media instruction can be a powerful instrument for educational innovation because it reaches all classes simultaneously, breaks old traditions of teaching, and demands new roles and responses from classroom instructors;

3. Rural teachers not only receive help in organizing their own work from the media teachers, but by working with the media their sense of isolation is reduced;

4. A commitment to the full utilization of the media can act as a catalytic agent for changes in other parts of the educational system such as curriculum, teacher training, etc.;

5. Once established for teaching rural students, a media system can be used for a wide variety of other purposes at the village level: in-service teacher training, adult literacy, health and birth control campaigns, to name a few.

The validity of arguments for and against the media can be tested only in the experience of various projects. Up until the present time, these arguments have been largely theoretical and highly speculative. And while it is clear that existing projects are not performing as well as they might, research is badly needed to determine where the media have seemed to work well in formal school systems and where they have not.

The Mass Media within Informal Education Settings

Advocates of informal educational strategies often point out that the crucial need of rural people is for more practical information; information that will help them upgrade the productivity of their land, improve the quality of their diet, and allow them to reduce the incidence of disease by adopting better health practices in the home. Such information has customarily been provided in the course of formal schooling and through extension programmes of one sort or another. Yet, extension agencies, like the school system, reach only a small fraction of the rural population of most developing countries. There has simply not been enough trained manpower nor enough money nor enough commitment to extend basic social services to the entire countryside. Barring a radical reorganization of the priorities of the developing countries or a financial commitment to their rural areas which would have to far surpass current spending levels, it is clear that existing extension efforts can have only a slight impact on the conditions of rural life. Critics of the existing situation insist new ways must be found to diffuse the information that is vitally needed in rural communities.

The mass media as well as lower cost communication technologies (i.e., film loops, slides, and newsprint) are an obvious means for channelling such information on a much wider basis than is currently done. And, indeed, the media have come to play an increasingly important part in the thinking of development planners. They point out that newspapers, radio, and increasingly television, reach rural communities whose size and/or remoteness have prevented the building of schools or the attention of other social agencies. There is a growing faith that the mass media can provide many of the same kinds of information and services as do the traditional agencies and do so just as effectively and at far less cost.

Given the fact that modern communications technology, notably radio, has now achieved virtual saturation coverage in almost all developing countries, what evidence is there to justify the high hopes development planners have for its wider applications in the service of rural education and social change? Unfortunately, the evidence is by no means clear. What Philip Coombs viewed as a 'bewildering assortment' of nonformal education projects and training activities in 1968 is as bewildering today as it was then,[10] and as applicable to media-assisted projects as for those which have proceeded along more traditional lines. Nevertheless, a review of the available case materials suggests that the effectiveness of the communication media in development programmes – here called informal education – seems to vary according to three basic criteria:

1. The composition and motivation of the intended audience or client group.
2. The particular goals set forth by the projects and the relation of those goals to the content of the messages transmitted by the media.
3. The administrative competence and flexibility of the organizations which are responsible for the media-assisted campaigns.

In this section we shall examine these criteria in light of the limited amount of research that has been done on informal education projects that have relied to some extent on the mass media.

There has been a considerable diversity among the audiences of informal education programmes. Such diversity is exhibited in the wide range of ages, occupations, previous educational experiences, and motivations of the people who have been attracted to one type of programme or another. Generally, the audiences have been self-selected and they can be categorized according to their common informational needs or educational interests. Among the most common audiences served by informal educational programmes are:

(a) Farmers seeking advice on how to improve the yields of their crops and the general quality of village life (examples: the rural radio forums of India, Ghana, Togo, Dahomey, Jordan and Upper Volta)

(b) Mothers seeking information on how to safeguard the health of their children and advice on how to plan the size of their families (examples: Taiwan's mothers' clubs, Zaire's Radio Star health programme, as well as a large number of private and government sponsored birth control campaigns throughout the developing world)[11]

(c) Students continuing their studies by correspondence and with radio or television in the absence of an alternative opportunity to continue their education in school (examples: the 'open' schools of Japan, Germany, Australia, Kenya, etc.)

(d) People of all ages learning to read and write (example: Radio Sutatenza, Colombia's literacy and rural development programme)

(e) Teachers, extension agents, and other professionals working in the field and in need of continuing guidance and support.

To single out the above groups is in no way to deny that much information is obtained by individuals who have no specific interests or purpose in mind other than relaxation when they use the mass media. Communication scholars such as Lerner claim, in fact, that it is people's attention to the media *per se*, and not their exposure to any particular kind of programme which helps to determine their modernity and willingness to adopt innovations.[12] Nevertheless, our concern here is not the incidental learning that results from media exposure or the psychological determinants of increased exposure on the part of rural people to the mass media, but rather the evidence supporting the plea from within developing countries and elsewhere that the media be assigned a more important role within informal education projects. To evaluate the media's effectiveness in informal education projects to date, it is necessary to specify the goals that different projects have worked toward as well as the nature of the content or messages that the media were assigned to carry in each instance.

Change in some attitude, behaviour, or community condition is usually behind the drive to organize an informal education project, but judging from the existing evidence on informal education projects, the absence of any more specific change objectives has hampered the definition of coherent working strategies and has led to the assignment of a rather inefficient and traditional pedagogical role to the media. By the same token, the lack of concrete objectives has greatly complicated the task of project evaluation. Nevertheless, a review of existing case studies reveals that informal education programmes usually have applied the media to accomplish one or more of the following four objectives.

1. *Extend the formal school by providing instruction in traditional academic*

subjects Such programmes allow formerly isolated students with little hope of continuing their education in formal school settings to pursue their education via radio or television. Radio instruction techniques were pioneered in the remote rural regions of Australia and New Zealand where the children of farm families generally received instruction via short-wave broadcasts. Although as orginally devised, these systems allowed pupils to communicate directly with their teachers via the same medium, this aspect has since been dropped in settings where two-way communication is not possible. To maintain the two-way flow of communications between teacher and pupil, however, new methods of feedback and control have been developed. The most noteworthy of these is the correspondence format whereby students periodically send examples of their work to teachers at the broadcasting centres. There teachers review students' progress and make suggestions either directly to the students on the air or by returning tests and other written work through the mail. This pattern has proved so successful that many countries are inaugurating such 'open schools' instead of making new investments in costly campus facilities.

Although the 'open school' model has spread rapidly in recent years, it is not clear how such programmes contribute to the improvement of rural life, other than in the most general sort of way. The spread of 'open schools' at the primary and secondary levels may, in fact, have a boomerang effect in the rural areas of developing countries by increasing the appetite of students for higher levels of academic training. This tendency, already under way in most developing nations, accelerates the exodus of competent and enterprising young people from the countryside and tends to swell the ranks of the urban unemployed with recent rural graduates unable to market their new skills in the city, yet unwilling to return to the countryside.

2. *Upgrade the competence of rural people by providing basic skills training* This category encompasses the literacy projects that have been undertaken in virtually all countries in recent years. The mass media have played a large part in these campaigns and the programmes have been customarily directed at the rural areas. The most highly publicized project of this kind is Radio Sutatenza, a church financed network of radio stations that is based in Bogotá, Colombia. At last count, Radio Sutatenza had over 260,000 regular listeners and 4,000 village leaders. The village leaders play an essential role in this system for they are responsible for organizing the reception of the programmes at the community level, and for channelling progress reports back to the teachers in the studio. In recent years, Radio Sutatenza has evolved into a broader community action programme with new goals reflecting the growing awareness that literacy,

in and of itself, is perhaps not too crucial a factor in the development of rural life.

Up until quite recently, literacy was regarded as the fundamental human skill without which modern knowledge could not spread; without literacy, it was feared, rural communities would remain isolated and underdeveloped. Literacy is still considered a vital factor in building self-esteem and in motivating rural people to adopt other 'modern' behaviours and attitudes, but most development experts seem to agree that substantial progress can be made by rural people even if they remain illiterate.

A concomitant problem with literacy projects is that reading and writing skills tend to deteriorate unless they are practiced continually. In practical terms, this means that the newly literate person must be supplied materials that will allow him to practice and maintain his new skill. Most literacy projects have experienced difficulties producing and distributing materials of this kind and as a result many people have slipped back into functional illiteracy.

It must also be pointed out that the diffusion of the mass media into the rural areas of most developing countries has itself undermined the once unchallengeable priority of literacy training in the minds of many development planners. It is clear that the mass media can transmit much of the information and advice that rural people seek; information that up until a few years ago was only available through direct contact with extension agents or through the printed word.

3. *Provide practical information and advice on a continuing basis* Within informal education projects that stress this goal, the media have customarily acted as surrogate extension agents. They have relayed the identical messages that human extension agents have been carrying to the rural areas for years. Of course, the media cannot adequately fulfil all the roles of the traditional agent – they cannot interact with the rural farmer to clarify the latter's doubts, for instance – but they can reach thousands of farmers simultaneously while a large team of extension agents might spend their entire careers carrying the same message to an equivalent number of people.[13]

The success of the media in stimulating lasting change in rural areas seems to rest on two basic factors: the motivation and willingness of the rural audiences to integrate new information into their everyday patterns of life, and the ability of a particular sponsoring agency to anticipate the need for and provide the supplementary services and materials (fertilizers, new seeds, vitamins, birth control devices, etc.) whose adoption might be encouraged in the media campaigns. The more successful community development projects, such as those undertaken in the Comilla region of

East Pakistan and in the Andean region of Vicos, Peru, have met both of these requirements. The leaders of these projects anticipated the need to provide additional services once the change process got under way, and they were able to keep abreast of the requests of their rural clients. In both instances, the projects' leaders had specified their change objectives beforehand and had developed mechanisms for determining whether or not those objectives were being met.

4. *Stimulate community development through the encouragement of self-reliance and self-help projects* The lexicon of development has for some time included the concepts of self-reliance and self-help, but they have generally not been effectively promoted in most rural education programmes. At the planning level, an undue emphasis has been placed on the mobilization of external resources and the building of increasingly complex media delivery systems to reach rural people. While such systems are indeed important and deserve the continuing concern of development specialists, their high cost and complexity may be self-defeating in terms of their relevance to rural life or the ability of rural people to utilize them.

Increasingly, rural development has come to be viewed not only in terms of filling informational and skill gaps, but as the strengthening of people's critical abilities which, presumably, enhance their capacity and will to diagnose their own needs, assert their own rights, and demand greater control over the decisions that affect their lives. In this conception of development, the ability to think critically arouses greater political consciousness in people which, in turn, leads them to concerted action on behalf of their communities. What was once development *for* rural people becomes development *by* rural people themselves.

Experience in Brazil and Bolivia has shown that once traditionally oppressed rural people liberate themselves through a development process that Paulo Freire has designated 'cultural action for freedom,' the pressure for change is increased on traditional institutions and leaders. For this reason, educational projects that have used the media for sensitizing rural people to their social situation and vulnerability have been highly political in tone and intent. Within revolutionary societies such as Cuba, China, and Tanzania, for example, education programmes directed at rural audiences have been carefully designed to stress a particular political ideology and its relation to development, while similar programmes within conservative military regimes such as Bolivia and Brazil have been abruptly terminated when they began to have some effect.

Within informal education projects we find very little research available on what patterns of organization and control seem to offer the highest probability of success. One reason the administrative lessons of informal education projects have not been widely diffused is that numerous projects have been started only to be abandoned, and no one has taken the time to analyse just what went wrong.

One clear impression that does emerge from existing case studies of informal education projects is that the media can rarely, if ever, be relied upon exclusively. To work effectively, they must be integrated into existing patterns of communication at the local level. This is not to say that persuasive messages aimed, for example, at individual farmers will not succeed in convincing some of them to try an innovation, but that such messages reinforced by other social mechanisms and pressures are likely to have a more powerful impact. It is for this reason that most extension agencies encourage the formation of discussion clubs to provide a filter for the reception of information and advice pertaining to new agricultural practices. Such projects can be found in most developing countries, but in Upper Volta, Dahomey, and the Central African Republic, to name but a few, radio has been used primarily to supplement the work of rural extension agents.

A second impression is that very few agencies involved in informal education projects have paid enough attention to the problems of training their staffs in the proper techniques for utilizing the mass media. Tradition, it turns out, has proved to be an obstinate enemy even within agencies whose function it is to promote innovations of one kind or another. Also, because broadcasters and politicians are often the most aggressive parties in encouraging the wider use of the mass media for rural development, there is a sad history of conflicting jurisdictions and rivalry for control over the projects. Informal education projects frequently must draw together planners from a variety of government agencies such as education, agriculture, public health, information, transport, etc., and these groups do not necessarily agree on what an education programme for the rural areas should be. Where this situation has not resulted in complete paralysis, there has often been fuzzy planning and a poor use of the media.

At the local level where the programmes are received a different set of administrative problems have emerged. Here the issue has not been conflicting claims to authority, but rather a lack of leadership and organization. One of the priority tasks of media-assisted development campaigns is the identification and support of local leadership; leadership capable of sustaining interest in the educational programmes. In reviewing the achievements of the radio farm forum model that was pioneered in Canada in the 1940s and replicated in India, Ghana, Togo, Malawi, and many other countries in the following decades, a Unesco study concluded that local organization and the position of the local discussion leader were crucial to the programme's effectiveness.[14] It is clear, however, that no matter how highly motivated the local leaders, they cannot be expected to do the job alone. They must be supported by appropriate materials and advice. Once having been persuaded to adopt a new fertilizer, farmers will naturally become apathetic toward the innovation if they are unable to obtain it. Likewise, as we stated earlier, villages on the threshold of literacy are apt to become frustrated if they are unable to obtain reading material suitable to their level of comprehension and related to their needs. Continuing material support and feedback play an essential role in reinforcing newly acquired attitudes and skills and in keeping up the morale of the programme's local leaders.

The problems of unclear administrative arrangements, unsteady local interest and organization, and poor follow-up have undermined the effectiveness of most media-assisted informal education projects. The emergence of new projects and their evolution beyond the pilot stage has been hampered for the same reasons. To successfully build upon the satisfactory performance of a pilot project inevitably requires additional financial and human resources as well as careful planning and a clear set of development priorities. As the euphoria of the pilot experience declines over time, often there is little interest to build upon it, much less to vigorously redirect it into new areas. Many of the most promising informal education projects have died on the vine for lack of imagination and commitment to carry them beyond the pilot stage.

The Organization of the Media for Rural Education

It is possible to imagine an ideal instructional media system for rural education with a combination of optimum elements; a dynamic TV or radio teacher, skillful and imaginative programme producers, a carefully developed and pretested curriculum, and highly motivated rural audiences ready to participate actively at the local level. But given the circumstances in most developing countries, we have learned that a new media system must usually cope with almost the exact opposite conditions. This suggests that to increase the probability of success, structural weaknesses must be anticipated and, whenever possible, overlapping and reinforcing channels carrying the same message must be built into the system. What are the elements of a media system that planners need to take into consideration to insure the achievement of their objectives?

The message   One of the problems discussed above was the tendency of educational media projects in the past to emphasize technological aspects of their systems at the expense of programme content and quality. Saving operating costs by cutting corners on programme development and experimentation has proven to be a false economy. Production and transmission equipment are, of course, a necessary condition to the broadcast of a message via the mass media, but a high quality of programming is a prime necessity if a system hopes to hold the interest of its audience.

In a large formal ETV system, like that of El Salvador, the cost of operating a production facility is only a small proportion of the total education budget. Within such a framework, a relatively small increase in investment may be all that is required to improve the quality of programming by: paying higher salaries to attract the best production talent, increasing the amount of training given to all personnel, reducing programme production loads, and encouraging an extensive pretesting of all programme series.

Even before the quality of their programmes becomes a concern, however, educational planners have a number of basic policy questions to resolve. The most important question is what to teach. Should a special curriculum be developed for rural people or is it acceptable to have a single content for both urban and rural audiences? The answer to this question depends naturally on the development strategy being pursued by each country. Two quite different assumptions might be made with regard to rural audiences, particularly school audiences: (1) they are being prepared to leave the countryside for work in an industrialized, urban environment or (2) they are being trained to remain in the rural sector and to help modernize its economy. To our knowledge, no countries have consciously opted for the first alternative, although formal school in general certainly seems to have abetted the large rural exodus. In trying to counteract this phenomenon, Niger and the Ivory Coast have decided to retain the same curriculum for urban and rural students, but in their television lessons they have emphasized predominantly rural settings and values.

There are certain restrictions that the mass media impose on the content of any given message. To be cost-effective, radio and television must centralize teaching activities and reach large audiences. This means that individual differences within the audience cannot be directly served by the media. The problem of where to set the level of the message is also difficult for media systems attempting to serve different population groups. Cultural and educational characteristics may vary greatly within a country, and even within rural areas. Furthermore, educational programmes for rural audiences have experienced high attrition or dropout rates. For these reasons, programmes aimed at rural communities or schools should be as simple and as straightforward as possible. Instead of teaching many subjects in primary school, for example, it has been suggested that a basic curriculum be developed to stress only language and number skills. Niger originally aimed its ETV programmes at rural children and in so doing radically changed the classical French curriculum and reduced primary schooling from five to four years. Recently, however, the Niger ETV programme yielded to pressure from the formal school system and added a fifth year to its series and thereby moved somewhat closer to the traditional system.

In sum, even when a media system is aimed at a predominantly rural audience, the issue of what level to set programme content is likely to remain troublesome. Experience suggests that unless the media planners are willing to promote elitist tendencies and to accept a high dropout rate among its audience, they would be wise to concentrate solely on the communication of needed information and the instruction of basic skills keyed to mastery learning by the majority of its audience.

The channels Once the problems of the message are resolved, the channels over which they will be transmitted must be defined. We have suggested above that a single channel is rarely sufficient. Wherever possible, educators should use a multi-channel approach to accomplish their objectives. Such an approach is recommended not only out of fear that there is likely to be physical interference with any single channel. In rural areas, it is true, there may be periodic failures of electricity or delays in the arrival of supplementary learning materials. However, the obstacles to effective use of the media are more often a result of poor utilization and disorganization at the local level. Multiple channels provide more than a simple repetition of the same message. Ideally, each channel should also present the message with a different teaching or communication strategy in mind. For example, one channel may provide information, another may stimulate discussion, while still another may guide individual or group activities among members of the audience. Acting in different ways, each channel elicits some audience involvement and works toward some common objective.

Media system planners have divided channels into two basic types: direct and mediating. Direct channels include the broadcast programmes as well as ancillary learning aids. In addition to the pre-planned sequence of programmes, planners have sometimes added reinforcing review classes to their broadcast schedules. Sometimes printed materials containing the text of the lessons as well as review exercises have been distributed to the audience. Costs of such materials may become prohibitively expensive as the audience increases in size. This was the case in El Salvador where the size of student workbooks was reduced after the first year of ETV broadcasting. Under similar circumstances, Mexico and the Ivory Coast have had to re-evaluate how much they can afford to spend on such materials. All printed matter must be distributed on time if its cost is to be justified and many projects, particularly those engaged in informal rural education, have found this a major problem. Nevertheless, there is general agreement that simply broadcasting programmes without any supplementary material is of dubious value.

The most important mediating channel is the teacher in the classroom or the coordinator of the rural community group. These roles have been filled by older students, respected members of the local community, or even trained professionals in some instances. However, for most rural areas, we assume that the preparation and competence of local personnel is not too high. For this reason, experience with mass media projects has shown the wisdom of providing special orientation and training to such people. If planners expect the teacher or coordinator in a rural community not only to accept but also make effective use of the media, they need to consider him as a major focus of their change efforts. Without proper guidance and support, local personnel are unlikely to understand or accept the media as a help.

Strategies for preparing local personnel to use the media have varied widely. El Salvador, for example, was able to provide a full year of retraining to all her junior secondary teachers; Salvadoran teachers received courses in their subject specialities as well as in television utilization techniques. This is a rare luxury and one few countries would be able to afford. Many projects provide in-service orientation and training to local personnel through the media themselves, and some, such as Colombia's Radio Sutatenza, have combined such programming with highly effective strategies for bringing community development workers together for intensive short courses or seminars.

As yet, we have no clear prescription for how best to train people to use the media effectively in rural education. The stereotype impression that radio or television require only a passive monitor to be used effectively has been brought into question by classroom observation studies in El Salvador, Mexico, and the Ivory Coast.[15] Although it is too early to say definitely, preliminary results suggest that the media in a traditional setting can encourage a rural teacher or development worker to actively engage the audience in learning activities. It is possible that as retraining and orientation activities become more effective, more responsibility will shift to people working on a day-to-day basis in the rural schools and community centres. Thus, the burden of instruction may gradually evolve away from the media and into the hands of local people themselves.

The audience   We have already stated that if rural people are to be the target audience of a media system, planners must be aware of the great disparities in levels of ability, achievement, and interest that are likely to be found within any rural population. This makes the adjustment of a single, centralized message from the media a matter for constant concern and review. A second problem involves keeping rural people interested in the message, and indeed in the educational process itself. High desertion rates within most rural education projects are such that only in the first or second grades of primary school are educators guaranteed a large and relatively homogeneous rural audience. Although there is an hypothesis that with radio or especially television, dropout rates will decline sharply, there has been little evidence of this so far. Third, it is a commonly heard criticism that media instruction implies audience passivity. Yet the experience of numerous projects indicates that the media can stimulate active learning, provided local coordinators and teachers are given proper orientation and traditional authoritarian methods are not allowed to dominate. The Niger ETV project has often been singled out for its success in getting rural students to participate actively in the learning process. On the informal side, experimental community radio projects using dialogue pedagogy developed by Paulo Freire have encouraged rural audiences in Brazil and Bolivia to respond in an active way to the media stimulus.[16]

There are a wide range of additional audience problems that any rural education project must face, whether or not it uses the mass media. Learning is related to motivation, self-esteem, fatalism, and a number of other personal factors. Furthermore, if radio or television have success in extending educational opportunities and rural people seem to profit from their exposure to the media, the success may be due more to a high level of interest or aspiration among the people than to the particular ability of the media to teach. Correspondingly, if the educational experience itself does not lead to any betterment of rural life or a fuller integration of rural people into society, their motivation will certainly wane as it has historically in most rural education projects.

Feedback   The mass media are unidirectional communication mechanisms. For this reason, educators, who are accustomed to the interaction of teachers and students in the classroom, are often sceptical of media instructional systems, especially ones that purport to teach vast audiences with a single message. To allay this scepticism and to enhance communication between programme producers and their audiences, feedback loops have been built into most media projects.

Many kinds of feedback have been developed for the mass media. Schramm outlines a number of them in his monograph, *Feedback for Instructional Television*.[17] There are methods for *pretesting* to determine how well programmes will work and methods for *post-testing* to see how programmes actually did work in the field. Pretesting can help insure programme quality provided that the results of such investigations are interpreted and applied correctly and that the pretest itself is based on representative audiences and learning situations. Pretesting is often not done well because the above conditions are not fulfilled. Moreover, thorough pretesting is expensive and can rarely be done for all programmes. Niger was able to pretest all of its ETV programmes in pilot classes, although it is not clear what criteria the French evaluators used to determine programme effectiveness.

The post-test method is more common but its applications have been relatively weak in most projects. The common notion of feedback, reflected in the post-test strategy, is to solicit opinions from local personnel – classroom teachers, community organizers, etc. – about how the programmes seem to be working. Such information is customarily vague and virtually worthless as a means for determining how programmes might be improved. Response rates to this type of questionnaire have generally been low, questions have often been poorly phrased so that very little could be concluded from even a large number of responses, and, finally, the questionnaires have not provided a measure of what the programmes are teaching, but only a general impression of whether or not local utilization personnel are satisfied with the broadcasts. While such information is useful for some purposes, it cannot help programme planners pinpoint the specific content areas that most need to be changed.

As media systems have grown in complexity and expense, it has become necessary to evaluate in a more rigorous way whether or not they are accomplishing their basic objectives. This suggests that the most useful feedback should be some assessment of the programmes' impact. For formal school projects, impact is usually defined in terms of student learning, while in informal education, impact certainly includes learning, but also takes into account the attitude or behavioural changes advocated by particular programme series. In El Salvador's ETV system, for example, a feedback system has been based on student learning.[18] Toward the end of a particular content unit, a short multiple choice test is administered via television. An evaluation team then collects a representative sample of test results to determine if the key concepts of the unit were mastered by the students. This information is then fed back to the programme producers so that they can take appropriate remedial action such as the preparation of special review classes on themes that have proved to be particularly difficult for students.

The El Salvador example illustrates the elements that a good feedback system should include: the specification of minimum learning objectives, the determination through achievement testing of whether or not those objectives are being met, and the suggestion of appropriate remedial actions to assure that a satisfactory level of learning has been obtained throughout the system.

Yet, even if feedback is obtained on a continuing basis, additional research may be warranted to determine why certain results occurred. Often local problems such as teacher absenteeism, lack of materials, etc., may account for learning difficulties. This suggests that feedback information may imply corrective actions by a large number of people through the system. People at the local level may or may not be willing to cooperate and a production group cannot realistically be expected to remedy all learning problems in the course of a heavy taping schedule.

Feedback, then, is not only the gathering of information from the field, but also the use of that information to adjust an ongoing system. The adjustment process is often painful and may be complicated by the fact that feedback from the field is often open to different interpretations. If the system's minimum objectives always seem to be met, it may be that less time could be spent on particular content units. On the other hand, if minimum objectives are not met, different actions may be called for depending on the degree of failure. At the lowest level, a failure of rural audiences to comprehend or act upon some presentation may call for a review and reteaching of certain material. However, if poor results are consistent over a period of months, some more drastic measures may be called for, such as the replacement of a production team, the development of additional, reinforcing channels, or a reduction in the amount of material being taught. Finally, if failure to meet minimum objectives persists and continual readjustment of the system's elements does not help, planners may have to consider redirecting the whole system or changing its objectives.

Conclusions

The mass media do have a role in rural education; they are not magic wands that will miraculously eliminate the awesome problems of the rural sector, but for the solution of specific problems they can be most helpful. In the preceding sections we have summarized the state of the art as we see it. In this section we offer some general recommendations that have grown out of that evaluation as well as our own field experiences in education-media projects.

1. Educational objectives should stem primarily from a thorough and realistic determination of rural needs and only secondarily from the assessment of the media's potential role.
2. The principles of self-help and local control demand that educational problems as well as solutions emanate as much as possible from rural people themselves. These principles are particularly important in the relationships between rural people and urban decision-makers and between underdeveloped and developed countries.
3. At the operational level, planners should adopt a more experimental attitude toward the media so that different strategies for rural education can be tried and evaluated before final system designs are decided upon.
4. Planners should resist the more expensive and complex media

technologies offered by the developed countries unless it is clear that their educational objectives cannot be met by means of less sophisticated and lower cost alternatives.

5. When instituting a media-based instruction, reforms of non-media components of the educational system – curricula, complementary written materials, and classroom utilization – must not be neglected. Careful design of these components greatly increases the probability of a system's success.

6. Countries planning new media systems for rural education cannot afford to ignore the needs of local personnel such as teachers and community development workers. Local organizers and users of the media must be given proper orientation and training and they must be kept well informed once the new system is underway.

7. The media's effectiveness is enhanced when they are integrated within organizations that are strong and flexible enough to carry out complementary educational reforms. Also, without political and administrative leadership capable of sustaining interest in a particular rural education programme, the media's effectiveness is likely to decline over time.

8. Jurisdictional disputes over control of the media may be minimized by assigning them very specific functions (such as school broadcasting) at the earliest stage. Once established successfully in one area, the media's roles can be expanded.

9. More research is needed to summarize the experience of media projects in the past and to develop principles for the better use of the media in the future. Such research should include descriptive case studies as well as more extensive field testing and experimentation.

REFERENCES

1. Unesco conference for Latin American ministers of education, Caracas, Venezuela, 6–15 December 1971.
2. Paulo Freire, *Pedagogy of the Oppressed* (New York: Herder and Herder, 1970).
3. Unesco: International Institute for Educational Planning, *The New Media: Memo to Educational Planners* and *The New Educational Media in Action: Case Studies for Planners* (Paris: Unesco, 1967), Vols. I, II, III.
4. Herbert Shiller, *Mass Communications and American Empire* (New York: Augustus M. Kelly, 1970).
5. G. Comstock and N. Maccoby, *The Peace Corps Educational Television (ETV) Project in Colombia – Two Years of Research* (Stanford: Institute for Communication Research, 1966).

6. A detailed case study of the Samoa ETV project which includes new learning measures, attitude surveys, and an historical account of the first eight years is being prepared by Dr. Wilbur Schramm of Stanford's Institute for Communication Research.

7. A series of seventeen research and administrative reports on the El Salvador project has been published by Stanford's Institute for Communication Research, 1968–72.

8. Mexico's *Radioprimaria* and *Telesecundaria* projects are currently being evaluated by the Secretariat of Public Education in conjunction with Stanford's Institute for Communication Research.

9. Sylvia Schmelkes, 'Investigación Sobre las Escuelas Radiofónicas de la Tarahumara (Mexico),' *Revista del Centro de Estudios Educativos*, No. 3 (1971), 125–32.

10. Philip H. Coombs, *The World Educational Crisis* (New York: Oxford University Press, 1968) p. 138.

11. Wilbur Schramm, *Communication in Family Planning* (New York: Population Council, 1971).

12. Daniel Lerner, *The Passing of Traditional Society* (Glencoe, Ill.: Free Press, 1958).

13. Research by Everett Rogers and others has revealed that information about innovations can be delivered as well by the mass media as by human agents, but that the decision to adopt innovations often rests more on interpersonal communication such as that between a farmer and an extension agent. For this reason, the mass media are used most effectively in conjunction with interpersonal communication. In Dahomey, for example, although farm programmes are heard throughout the country, the target population for the broadcasts are the 600 villages where agents are currently at work.

14. Unesco, *An African Experiment in Radio Forums for Rural Development* (Ghana, 1964/65) (Paris: Unesco, 1968).

15. Judith A. Mayo, 'Teacher Observation in El Salvador' (Stanford: Institute for Communication Research, 1971). A more complete study of this kind is presently being completed in Mexico and similar work is being undertaken in the Ivory Coast by a group from the University of Liège.

16. Froilan Sanchez, 'Nuevas Formas de Educación Popular' in *Educación Popular para el Desarrollo* (Oruro, Bolivia: Instituto de Investigación Cultural para Educación Popular, 1971) Vol. 5.

17. Wilbur Schramm, 'Feedback for Instructional Television' (Stanford: Institute for Communication Research, 1969).

18. A. M. de Manzana, R. Hornik and J. Mayo, 'Feedback on Student Learning for Instructional Television in El Salvador' (Stanford: Institute for Communication Research, 1971).

5

Non-Formal Education for Agricultural Development: A System Perspective

Donald G. Green

Synoptic Overview

Nations currently involved in modernizing their agricultural sectors are experiencing difficulty in generating a shaping process which will stimulate and sustain a more rapid rate of development. The dimensions of the challenge indicate that a crucial central factor is the behavioural response of individuals and groups of individuals to that change process called agricultural development. More farmers must respond favourably. In addition, it is suggested that new behaviours, new productive capacities through new skills and understandings, must also be generated among the many individuals engaged in agricultural support activities. A dual but coordinate set of non-formal education activities directed at farmers and persons in agri-support activities is seen as an immediately available tool for enhancing the productive capacities of these many individuals.

Since non-formal education is not a new idea its potential viability resides in how it is used as an instrument of change. Therefore, a system perspective is developed which synthesizes some of the interrelationships between non-formal education and four other sets of basic nation-building activities: national socio-economic development activities, agricultural support activities, farmer participation activities, and formal education activities. The analytical framework presented by the system perspective should aid in strengthening the linkages among these five activities. Finally, the implications drawn are suggestive of the action needed to strengthen non-formal education for agricultural development.

The Shaping of Change

Individually and collectively, men are universally involved in a continuous process of shaping their social, political, economic and physical environments. Direction-giving goals are stated and restated as the process proceeds. Technological tools and skills are evolved, adapted, discarded, or new ones invented as knowledge and experience accumulate. Institutions for performing various functions are strengthened, modified, or replaced with new ones when stresses arise or when improved understanding dictates change. Individuals and groups of individuals struggle with the shaping and reshaping of their behavioural responses to the changing panorama affecting their lives.

In a period of such writings as Toffler's *Future Shock*, Myrdal's *Asian Drama*, the Pearson Report, and Brown's *Seeds of Change*, the drama of this shaping process is taking place on the world stage. Perhaps nowhere, however, is it brought into sharper detail than in the so-called third world. A developing nation and its people are faced on the one hand with more complete knowledge than ever before about the fruits of modernization. On the other hand are the realities of not one or two, but several simultaneous inadequacies which must be overcome – not the least of which is a citizenry which can increasingly capture, direct and enhance its creative and productive capacities, the foundations for the ultimate 'worth of a state'.[1] Beset with the rising expectations of their citizens, with frequently too little food for exploding populations, and with relatively few years of experience in managing their own affairs, the newly developing nations are struggling to find the ways and means to overcome the internal and external disparities which exist.

At centre stage in the drama is agricultural development, somewhat obscured under a contemporary veil called 'the green revolution'. Third world nations are increasingly cognizant that 50 to 70 per cent of their citizens will continue to gain their livelihood from the agricultural sector for many years to come. Thus, nations have taken a more balanced approach, upgrading the priorities given to rural and agricultural development. Stronger agricultural sectors will supply the increasing needs for food and fibre. Rural people with higher incomes can stimulate domestic industries through more purchases. Increased earnings from agriculture can pay part of the costs of industrialization. At least, such is the new hope of those charged with the task of nation-building who have 'tasted of the green revolution'.

Dimensions of the Agricultural Development Challenge

For the purposes of this chapter agricultural development means the sum of all those processes by which agricultural production per year is increased on land in farms. This definition is not as narrow as it may seem when one considers that the life of most rural people is very closely entwined with the production process. A sustained 'better life' for rural people must have its roots and its vitality in this process. Other facets of the 'good life' can then be logically and more easily superimposed.

The green revolution notwithstanding, there remains a pervasive, glacial quality about agricultural development. It has been slow to spread and to become sustaining except under what seem to be the most favourable of conditions in small pockets here and there involving relatively few farmers. Yet each nation intending to modernize its agricultural sector seeks the means to elicit favourable behavioural responses from thousands or millions of farmers. Favourable farmer response is that which involves increased productivity; those voluntary and largely independent decisions and activities of many farmers which generate a sustained flow of products and resources contributing to their own development as well as national development.

What are the constraints and processes which influence positive farmer response? Whence arise the flows of information, instruction, and inspiration which will help prepare the human resources to invent, assemble, organize and deploy the components of rural development?

Mosher, in a seminal writing, suggests the importance of a framework of essentials and accelerators for agricultural development. Farmers will respond and agriculture will develop if five complementary essentials are present in a country or portion thereof: (1) markets for farm products, (2) constantly changing technology, (3) local availability of supplies and equipment, (4) production incentives for farmers, and (5) a transportation system linking farms with services. There can and will be some growth in agricultural productivity wherever all of the essentials are present but without *all* of them there will be none. By adding the accelerators, each important but not indispensable, development can proceed more rapidly: (1) education for development, (2) production credit, (3) group action by farmers, (4) improving and expanding agricultural land, and (5) national planning for agricultural development.[2]

In the mid-sixties a new promise for agricultural development emerged in the form of 'miracle seeds' and the production package for their use. The technological breakthrough represented by the new seeds is stimulating changes which hopefully will sustain the process started. New irrigation strategies to quench the thirst of the new seeds, improved systems of research and growing research capacity, and the potential for multiple cropping, embryonic developments though they be, undergird the promise offered by the 'miracle seeds'.[3]

The myth that farmers do not respond to new technology has clearly been dispelled. They do respond when it is profitable to them. There is the danger, however, that a new myth may develop – one need only do the proper research and the innovations will sell themselves to the economically inclined farmers of the world. Mellor states:

What is not understood is that the profitability of innovation depends in large measure upon the care with which it is applied and that much of innovation involves a complex set of changes. A careful educational program run by competent technicians is needed to impart the necessary knowledge. Further, although innovators may make careful economic decisions regarding profitability of innovation, many farmers are followers who do not calculate carefully. The processes by which innovation spreads to such farmers and the means which could speed the spread of such innovations are not understood in most parts of the world, and hence the diffusion of complex innovation will occur less rapidly than is now expected. We have, in fact, little experience with improving extension programs because in the past we have had very little complex, profitable innovation to spread. As research programs improve, as they now are doing, the present failings of the systems for diffusing knowledge will begin to show clearly.[4]

Other countervailing forces exist. Wharton and others have called attention to a whole range of 'second generation' issues which will slow the spread of change or make it difficult to sustain initial momentum. Expansion of an entire complex of services and industries will be required. Improved input distribution systems must be developed to provide the insecticides and fertilizers needed by the new seeds. A seed industry, agricultural chemical plants, processing and storage firms, more viable credit institutions, improved marketing systems, and factories producing hand sprayers, dusters, water pumps and engines are just a few of the services and industries 'which must develop if the Revolution is to take hold'.[5]

Initial assessments of the spread of change suggest that the existing framework of institutional patterns presently distributes the socio-economic benefits unevenly. Those in favoured positions with ready access to the knowledge and resources required for the adoption of improved technology tend to gain first and most. Schutjer and Coward conclude that:

> The spread of the Green Revolution beyond the privileged few will require that traditional institutional patterns adjust, or that new institutional patterns emerge, to assure the access of cultivators with limited resources to the knowledge and physical inputs required for the adoption of the high yielding variety production package.[6]

For reasons that are not always clear, the activities of institutions designed to support agricultural development tend to accrue to the privileged few rather than to the many. Hunter reasoned that in India there is a correlation between size of farm, education, and likelihood of adoption of new practices. It is easier for the extension personnel to deal with the larger and better educated farmers since they can risk more money in inputs more safely and secure fertilizers and credit, if needed, more easily.[7] Unfortunately, this tendency appears to be widespread:

> . . . . the existing extension work, farm advisory services, 'encadrement', etc., operate mainly in very narrow production promotion schemes among a very limited number of selected farmers or farm groups. . . . In too many countries, however, little attempt is being made either to make increasing farm income the

main consideration of these production schemes or to extend the benefits of farm advisory services to include the general subsistence farm producers.[8]

Changes in technology and institutions present periods of transition when individuals at many levels of jurisdiction and function face unfamiliar tasks and problems. These periods are obviously learning situations. Far too frequently, however, the learning is haphazard at best and dysfunctional at the worst. A more ordered and deliberate approach is needed. Luykx suggests that there are four main elements in the process of providing individuals and institutions with the capacities to perceive the sequential nature of development and to do things which they have not done before:

.... (1) *organization* as a means of structuring the division of labor, and as a means of providing political and economic strength in approaching specific development objectives, (2) *training* in technical and problem-solving skills which permits dealing with emergent situations, (3) *supporting services*, appropriate to the objectives, which compensate for needs which participants cannot provide for themselves, and (4) *discipline* which channels and conserves the variety of scarce resources applied to the development process.[9]

A frequent disclaimer employed to explain the slowness with which new technology spreads is the notion of institutional lag. Institutions, like technology, are man-created instruments. If they lag, then man has lagged in shaping them to direct the dynamics which the new technology brings to the evolving system. Institutions are not organized simply to get more material goods or to utilize technology haphazardly, but rather to achieve a large number of goals. One infers, thus, that 'institutional innovations will have to be developed as joint products with the technology' if public policy and implementation are to be effective.[10]

Implicit in the foregoing is that sustained progress in rural and agricultural development will depend in large measure upon a variety of changed human behaviours. At issue here are those productive, functional behaviours of individuals and institutions – groups of individuals – which will influence the shaping of agricultural development. As Mosher has so aptly indicated, agricultural development is valuable not only because of added farm products but because of an additional, and perhaps most important product: it changes the people who engage in it. For agricultural development to occur, the knowledge, skill, attitudes and self-confidence of farmers must keep increasing and changing. A similar transformation must occur among research workers, extension agents, government officials, merchants, bankers, teachers and many others who make supportive contributions.[11]

The basic social instrument for helping individuals gain the requisite understandings and skills for altering personal and group behaviour is education. Education, formal and non-formal, also contributes to man's will and spirit – his determination to activate his energy and behaviour to meet the challenges of new situations. Unfortunately, the content and processes of education frequently become static. Then when the situation changes, educational content becomes obsolete, educational processes become inefficient and low productivity in education results. The will and spirit of people tend to deteriorate because learned behavioural responses no longer completely fit the demands of the new and changed situation.

An added dimension affecting agricultural development in the third world is the limited extent to which the educational system touches the lives of most rural people. Where it does touch, it orients rural youth away from the rural, toward the urban sectors. If, as seems likely, rural sector activities will have to absorb four-fifths or more of the labour force in many developing nations the 'educational systems and their basic orientation seem grossly out of line with the future needs of their students and with the development needs of their society.'[12]

The dimensions of the challenge ahead are clearly multi-faceted and complex. The crucial central thread which ties all of the dimensions together is the behavioural response of individuals and groups of individuals to that change called agricultural development. The following quote is apt:

> The really tough part of economic development is not fabricating improved technologies, but rather the organizational task of recombining human behaviors under new rules that enable more people to help each other in creating and putting to widespread use the more effective technologies. Here is why. Unlike physical materials and forces, the rules that combine behaviors into mutually helpful ways of living and making a living are not lifeless affairs. They are very much alive because, at least, the most important ones are interlocked with deep-seated convictions (beliefs) which people hold concerning the kind of rules which deserve their respect and allegiance, and the kind that merit their distrust and opposition. . . .
>
> Economic development is thus far more than a mere technological or physical transformation of inputs into increasing outputs; it is more fundamentally an organizational transformation of old ways of life and work into new rules of interpersonal behaviors. And this in turn is possible only to the extent that people are able to make revisions in their heritage of basic convictions concerning the kinds of interpersonal rules which do and do not deserve their respect and support.[13]

A System Perspective

Generating swifter agricultural development is a complex process. This is so because it involves an interrelated system of human enterprise activities, each of which is governed by the 'behaviours' of many individuals and groups of individuals.[14] The main sets of activities involved in this interlocking system are identified as national socio-economic development activities, agricultural support activities, farmer participation activities, formal education activities, and non-formal education activities. *Improved linkages among these sets of human enterprise activities will help determine the quality and rate of agricultural development within the confines of physical and climatic resources.*

This systems view of agricultural development can help increase individual understanding about what the nature of each set of human enterprise activities should be. Improved understanding can lead to improved actions. To illustrate the system, each set of activities is briefly characterized, linkages are examined and implications are drawn. Of particular note, for the purposes of this chapter, are the characteristics and the linkages of non-formal education activities with the rest of the system.

National Socio-economic Development Activities

Each nation has an economic and political system which creates an institutional and policy framework for expressing and attaining development goals through the utilization of resources available or which can be developed. This governmental process influences and frequently delimits what can and cannot happen in agriculture and other sectors. It does this through a complex of policy, legislative, investment and appropriation actions. These actions relate to policies on land tenure, prices, taxes and agricultural development. These actions affect what happens with regard to transportation, foreign trade, and domestic industries and services. They affect the extent to which farmers participate in the political process. They reflect and affect traditions and social values.

These national socio-economic development actions formulate what has been called an *agri-climate* or *agri-milieu* within which agricultural modernization and development proceeds. All of these activities form a general environment of opportunity, inducement, inhibition and attitudes which establish the 'rules of the game' for individual and group and public and private activities, or behaviours. *Changes or the lack of changes in this component affect behaviours in other components of the system.*[15]

Agricultural Support Activities

Closely related to the national socio-economic development process are public and private activities generated within a nation to stimulate agricultural development. Normally these two processes might be considered together. They are separated here for emphasis and because the process of deliberately modernizing agriculture is a relatively recent human enterprise. Nations intent on developing agriculture are still probing, experimenting and learning what constitutes the 'best mix' of activities to speed the rate of agricultural modernization. Whatever the particular mix of this set of activities, they are best characterized by their functional nature; *they are supportive of what farmers do.*

In traditional agriculture a farmer produces mainly for his family needs, marketing or bartering any surplus he might have. In nations attempting to modernize agriculture so that food needs and other goals can be met, the farmer is being asked to respond to his environment in a different way. He is being asked to produce substantially more for the market. Thus his old ways of producing will no longer suffice – new technology, new seeds, new inputs are needed. The larger society, therefore, must generate *agri-support* activities. These activities blended with farmers' responses to the alternatives presented constitute the agricultural development process.

An appropriate characterization of the kinds of agri-support activities required for agricultural development has been suggested by Mosher. An adaptation of his list for consideration here includes:

1. Research to find and develop new and improved farm (and related) technology on a constantly changing basis;
2. Provision, through importation and/or domestic production, of the farm supplies and equipment needed to put the new technology to use;
3. Creation of a new rural infrastructure which provides:
   (a) market outlets near to all farms where farmers can purchase production supplies and equipment and sell their products;
   (b) rural roads to expedite and reduce the cost of the flow of commodities, information and all sorts of rural services;
   (c) local verification trials that determine the best farm practices in the light of local conditions;
   (d) a non-formal education or extension service system through which farmers can learn about and learn how to use new technology; and
   (e) credit facilities to finance the use of production inputs.
4. Creation and maintaining adequate incentives for farmers to increase production;
5. Improving agricultural land through irrigation, drainage, or other appropriate means;
6. Improving capacities for the local planning and implementation of action programmes which blend local needs and goals with national goals; and
7. Educating and training the people involved (public and private) to accomplish all of these tasks competently.[16]

In the context of our system perspective, the interrelationships and complementarities among these agri-support functions should be noted. Also, while each nation may already have individuals involved in these kinds of activities, two important questions should be asked. In the light of efforts to modernize agriculture within a given nation is the quality of the functions performed adequate and is the amount of attention (and public resources) given to each activity sufficient in terms of the varying needs and circumstances within the country? Finally, it is important to recognize that, just as for farmers who must respond in new ways, *the individuals who perform these agri-support activities must respond in new ways.* Implicit are new understandings, skills and attitudes if behavioural response is to change.

Farmer Participation Activities

Rapid agricultural development requires participative response by large numbers of farmers. The response must be qualitatively different than past response and the rate of response must increase if agriculture is to modernize in a relatively short time span – two or three decades rather than the five to ten decades of the past. Crucial to the process is a better understanding of the kind of behavioural responses required and the implications for ways and means of improving and increasing farmer participation activities.

An important consideration in characterizing farmer participation activities is first to recognize that most farmers and farm labourers must have a wider variety of skills and understandings than factory workers. In factory production different persons perform specialized services as buyer, salesman, bookkeeper, manager, or mechanic. Most farm operators must perform all these functions; each farmer is simultaneously a manager, a cultivator, a buyer, a seller, and a bookkeeper. He is a *businessman*, making increasingly difficult and complex decisions among alternatives in the light of opportunities and constraints presented by his land and the agricultural environment around him. If agriculture is to modernize more farmers must participate through using new production techniques and more purchased inputs, requiring larger amounts of capital or production credit. Farmers will be confronted with the need to plan in different ways and to consider changes in land use, cropping patterns and enterprise combinations. Participation in group action may be necessary through active membership in cooperatives, farmer associations, and irrigation and drainage associations.

Clearly farmers must participate through learning and using new skills and understandings. Old ways of thinking and doing must change even though models for speeding the change must yet evolve. Many farmers have developed a 'subsistence-mindedness'[17] which makes them reluctant to shift from production primarily for the family to production for the market. Tully notes a range of value orientations among cultures which influence thinking and doing activities. Some cultures emphasize subjugation to nature while others emphasize mastery over nature. Some societies order their lives by the past, others live for today, while still others deny themselves present pleasures and plan for future gain. Some peoples are more concerned about 'being' while others value a 'doing' orientation. Some cultures value the immediate referent group of family, clan or other hierarchical relationships while others value a more individualistic orientation.[18] These ideas suggest some of the attitudinal differences that farmers and others may have to bridge if they are to participate in and contribute to a modern agriculture.

Farmer participation activities and their facilitation frequently loom large in the minds of many as being the most crucial and difficult part of development. However, in the context of a system perspective, the linkages between component parts of the system become the more crucial elements. One surmises that if farmers are not participating it is not because of a perverse nature, but rather because, from their reading of the system, a negative response is in their best interests. *Thus, if farmers are to respond positively, changes in other parts of the system must precede or coincide with farmer response.*

Formal Education Activities

Each nation has a pattern of formal education activities designed to prepare its youth and young adults for active citizenship – for active participation in and contribution to the fibre, life and growth of the nation. A basic intent in all nations is to equip its citizens with the skills and understandings they will need during their productive work years. Existing patterns of education in developed and developing nations alike, however, are undergoing substantial scrutiny. The current crucial problem being voiced and increasingly examined relates not to goals of formal education, but rather to the means being used which no longer appear to be as relevant and as productive in meeting the recognizable needs as was once thought. While this problem appears to have world crisis proportions, its burden is believed to be most detrimental to the newly developing nations.[19]

For the newly developing nations the formal education component may itself have to undergo substantial development before it can contribute more effectively to the agricultural modernization process. From the standpoint of the practical needs of farmers and agricultural development, the formal educational institutions have tended to have an isolation-like evolution which created an orientation toward knowledge for knowledge's sake. Thus, the focus of learning has been more on theory than on the integrative, applicative use of knowledge. Even as shifts have been made to formal educational institutions emphasizing the agricultural sciences, various cultural, pedagogical, and traditional factors have made a better balance between theory and practice an elusive goal in the preparation of youth.

Regardless of these rather formidable problems of formal educational development, from the point of view of our system perspective other points need to be considered. There is a weak linkage between formal education and farmers as a group. Relatively few of the present farmers have attained much education. Those who have tend to be the first to obtain benefits from new agricultural technology. The problem is to reach the majority.

On the other hand, most individuals providing support services to farmers have passed through the formal education system or at least parts of it. However, with agricultural development as a fairly recent national goal, graduates of the formal education system are not always equipped attitudinally and behaviourally with the competencies needed to assist farmers directly or indirectly. Additionally, problems of communication and information dissemination tend to maintain an isolation between the formal education institution, its graduates, and more crucial, the changing work-day world of its graduates. This seems especially true in those areas where the new technologies of the green revolution have spread rapidly from farmer to farmer. A situation has been created where many farmers are more experienced with the new practices than is the extension agent who graduated before the advent of the new technology.

In terms of a system perspective, formal educational activities as they now exist in nations striving to modernize their agriculture face an enormous challenge to establish and maintain strong linkages with the countryside and with rural sector activities. It is only from such contact that the formal education system can be gradually reoriented to give appropriate emphasis to the role and place of agricultural development in the nation building process. It is only through such linkages that changes in pedagogical content and techniques can emerge which will produce graduates more competent to serve the rural sector. Formal education institutions must acquire a greater 'now' orientation more sensitive to agricultural modernization and its needs while building a stronger and more relevant 'future' orientation.

Non-formal Education Activities

The final component of our system perspective is non-formal education.[20] Non-formal education activities are not a new phenomenon; they stem from the tutorial, guild and apprentice systems of old. Non-formal education capitalizes on the principle that 'learning it just before using it is more productive than learning it, saving it, and using it when and if you need it'.[21] Nations modernizing their agriculture do have a wide assortment of non-formal education activities. The contention here is that these nations, have not yet begun to use it as the potentially powerful tool it can be, given vitalizing policy direction and resource allocation which will allow it to grow and mature through the creativeness of those conducting it.

In the mounting effort to modernize agriculture, new policies, new plans, new projects and new resource allocations flow out of a nation's capital in a frequently bewildering flood of directives and documents. As they wash up on the desk of a local administrator or extension agent or on the doorstep of a farmer they are viewed all too frequently as the flotsam and jetsam of yet another government programme – a well-intentioned effort perhaps, but not providing much meaning or understanding or skill in recognizing how it will or can benefit the local situation and importantly, how it can lead to personal reward or satisfaction.

Farmers, for whom the programmes are designed to influence and presumably benefit, may view a new programme directive as an added risk in an already highly uncertain situation. While it is true that most nations are investing large sums in farmer education and training, some of the prior considerations of our system perspective interrelate. Have the essential agri-support services preceded or coincided with the introduction of the programme? Are those involved in 'farmer training' knowledgeable about what skills and understandings are needed and are they competent and confident to design and conduct appropriate learning activities for farmers? Are those who conduct the support services, whether administration, road building, fertilizer distribution, or production credit, capable of providing a quality of service that will build the confidence of farmers and all others involved?

When a new programme directive arrives the government functionary may not be able to integrate the directive with his present functions. He may only see it as an additional function among an already bewildering array of functions. The network through which the tasks and activities of a new programme or project are carried out are rarely 'the people' *en masse*.

> The first critical group is often the civil service, field extension agents and other 'agents of change'. A project may require almost as thorough and sudden transformation in their outlook, motivation and methods as it eventually will for larger groups of people in the sectors and communities they serve. In many cases, these leaders will also require orientation and training in techniques of communication that can help them to perform their tasks adequately and sensitively.[22]

The Dynamics of System Linkages

The system perspective is presented in its entirety in schematic form in Figure 1. The five components and their interacting linkages discussed in the foregoing section appear in substantially abbreviated form.

Central to the purpose of the perspective is the output goal: more farmers participating in and contributing to agricultural development as a sum of all processes by which agricultural production per year is

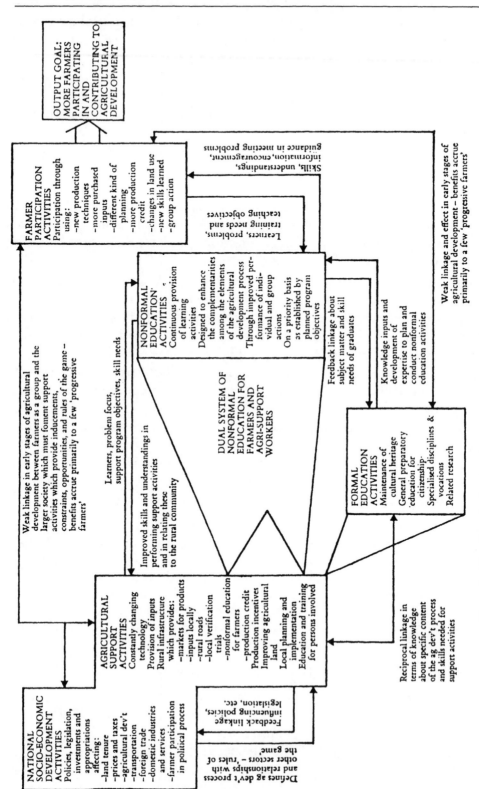

Figure 1. Non-formal education for agricultural development – a system perspective

increased on land in farms. Ultimately, of course, farmer response determines the amount of agricultural production achieved. The system perspective helps one ascertain the nature of the linkages between that response and other contributing processes. Then one can analyse how those linkages might be strengthened through the conduct of various activities which will influence the output goal positively.

In most developing nations political leaders, policy makers, and planners have started the process of modernizing the traditional agricultural sector. The quest is for a more productive agriculture that generates products for use, develops improved rural purchasing power, and creates more productive physical and human resources on a sustained basis. The quest has created a process of change – an interacting triangle of human activities including:

1. Governmental policies and plans;
2. Public and private supporting activities and services (e.g., provision of seeds, fertilizers, production credit, improved technologies, market incentives, and information and education services) which agriculture needs to modernize, but which a traditional agriculture did not provide and which farmers cannot provide themselves; and
3. Farmer response to the opportunities and alternatives created by the changed *agri-milieu* and *agri-support* conditions.

In the centre of this dynamic process, influencing and being influenced, are public and private employees charged with planning and implementing activities which will enhance the interactions in a positive manner. A graphic representation is suggested in Figure 2.

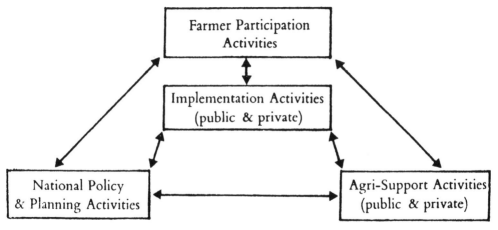

Figure 2. Activities interaction triangle

A first and general observation that can be made is that an activity at any corner of the triangle will influence and be influenced by activities at the other two corners. Thus a national policy decision to allocate more resources for agricultural development (triggered by reaction to the system) will be 'felt' and expressed by the nature of the activity change, *or lack thereof*, within the other two components. With additional resources it is now possible to do new and different things, like research for new technology or provision for new programmes promoting new methods. However, in the early stages of agricultural development the strength of linkages between components tends to be weak. For example, farmers as a group do not have a strong relationship with the national socio–economic development process. In a negative extreme, some officials may view farmers as poor, illiterate, ignorant 'peasants' who are hopeless learners requiring the paternalistic protection and guidance of their 'superiors'. When planning and taking actions these officials tend not to examine and consider the interests of farmers because farmers are not regarded as a strong reference or pressure group. Where such attitudes prevail through-out the official hierarchy they affect not only what is done by various functionaries but how it is done.[23]

On the other hand farmers who have survived under subsistence-like agriculture have had little need to articulate group interests. They regard officials as outside their primary referent group of family, friends and neighbours – outsiders who are impractical and not to be trusted. Farmers tend to resent being told what to do. They are guided by a 'conservative shrewdness' which dictates against taking chances with new methods, particularly if they have small farms, little capital and live near the margin of subsistence. Thus, in the early stages of development benefits tend to accrue only to a few 'progressive farmers' who can identify more closely with the official hierarchy or who have the resources and other capacities to respond independently of other farmers.[24]

Yet farmers can respond positively only by changing what they do on their farms in substantial measure. Learning to become a modern farm businessman is not a task that farmers can do alone. Most farmers will need the strength and the discipline of their own referent group on the one hand and the encouragement and help of the larger society through appropriate support and services on the other. Farmers as a group, need through more active participation and strengthened linkages with nonfarm individuals, to know and understand how the changing rules of the game and the agri-support activities generated provide viable opportunities and alternatives for them.

Weak linkages exist in early stages of agricultural development between those who plan, make policy, and legislate at the national level and those hundreds or frequently thousands of individuals who must plan and implement activities which are intended to execute the 'new rules' at various *other points within the system*.[25] This element is believed to be of such vital importance that it is given the prominent central place in the 'activities interaction triangle'. It is through these individuals that the 'ripples' of change-direction and farmer response must flow just as water in a pond carries ripples from a thrown stone to the bank and back.

Those who are most instrumental in setting the rules of the game and establishing agri-support activities need to recognize the imperative nature of adequate and quality support services and policies. Just as a modern manufacturing effort requires a physical plant, water, transportation, workers' housing and other amenities, and policies enabling the flow of raw materials and finished products, so does a modern agricultural industry require a comparable infrastructure and the aid of enabling rules of the game.

The provision of quality agri-support activities requires positive changes in behaviour of the many private and public individuals employed to perform the myriad of functions involved. The productive capacities of these individuals must be deliberately and systematically increased, just as those of farmers need to be increased. This involves first of all shifts in attitudinal perceptions about the nature and importance of functional roles as these relate to farmers and the agricultural development process. Secondly, it involves new competencies to perform new tasks, and old tasks in new ways. Thirdly, it involves some reorganization of the patterns in which these new behaviours are to operate – patterns which will unleash the creative capacities throughout the system. The diversity of the space locations in which agriculture operates demands that those close to the cutting edge of farmer participation have an increasing role in guiding and structuring the organization of the human activities needed. Positive and constructive feedback linkages to the policy and planning processes need to be developed so that support services can be quickly and adequately attuned to the variable needs of the farmer groups being served.

Knowledge about the specific ingredients, activities and strategies needed to influence positively and rapidly the bundle of interactions and responses implicit in the 'triangle' is relatively imprecise for a given country at any point in time. Ideas, theories and experiences from within and outside a country can be and are used. However, these are seldom useful without adaptation and integrative activities so that they fit the country situation or various situations within a country. Contributing to the agricultural development process, therefore, are the capabilities of all the persons involved to interrelate situational analyses and idea adaptation and integration. Strengthening the linkages between these individual implementation activities and the activities at each corner of the activities interaction triangle becomes extremely important.

The tools most readily available to forge productive changes in individual implementation activities are formal and non-formal education activities. Unfortunately, the system perspective analysis suggests that formal education has already failed the current actors in the agricultural development drama. This is not to imply that formal education has no role. Formal education needs to reflect quickly, strongly and positively to all classes and ages of individuals currently reached, the strategic and growing importance of a strong agricultural sector. A nation seeking to modernize its agriculture should imbue its citizenry with 'a spirit of agricultural development'. Educational institutions, especially those dealing with the administration, economic, political, business and agricultural sciences, need to reinforce the tone and the pace set by national socio-economic development activities. Such institutions must strengthen their linkages with farmers as a group and with the individuals and organizations that provide agri-support activities. This is possible through substantially increased individual contact of teachers, professors, lecturers, and researchers with the work-day world of agricultural development and its problems. The focus must be on increasing understandings about the kinds of change that will improve productive capacities of individuals and organizations. Curricula and methods of teaching need to be altered so that future graduates have skills which are more relevant to the nation's growing agricultural development needs. These adjustments, however, will take a substantial amount of time. Also needed is an improved means to learn quickly what content and what teaching methods will be more relevant and to learn the nature and the trends of the changes taking place and likely to take place in the future.

Implications for Non-formal Education: An Agenda for Action

Agricultural modernization is pursued through the implementation of planned programmes. Each programme or the projects comprising the programme have a set of stated objectives to be attained which introduce elements of change – something new or improved is involved. The attainment of objectives is pursued through the performance of a wide variety of functions by public and private employees and farmers. The quality of those performances will determine in large measure the extent to which the programme objectives are attained. The skills and understandings that each individual has or acquires will substantially determine the quality of his performance.

It is from this simple set of interrelated statements emanating from our system perspective that the first conceptual improvements in the guidance of non-formal education must flow. Increased agricultural production is only a partial goal; more productive farmers and agri-support workers is the real goal. Increased agricultural production becomes the measure of that productivity.

A first step in strengthening non-formal education is to define its intent and establish a rationale for its need. The following is offered for consideration. Non-formal education may be defined as: the continuous provision of learning activities designed to generate skills and understandings useful and relevant to the performance of mental and physical actions expected of various individuals in the attainment of planned agricultural development objectives and activities. The need for such continuing learning activities arises because:

1. Increases in relevant knowledge and understanding about the ingredients of agricultural development provide a changing perspective of the operational situation within which individuals must perform expected mental and physical actions.
2. Planned programme objectives introduce changes in the operational situation giving rise to the need for *improving* action performance or performing *new* mental or physical actions not previously deemed necessary.
3. Much of both the agricultural development process and the learning process is sequential and cumulative – one change gives rise to other changes in building-block fashion.
4. Formal education has not supplied all of the requisite skills and understandings needed by those now performing the various productive functions.

Most countries will spend much time and money to establish the rationale and feasibility for a major irrigation project, a multiple cropping programme, or a production credit programme. For an irrigation project, engineers will take test borings to determine a dam's location and will survey alternate routes to determine the optimum location of canals. Who is spending time testing and measuring the abilities of farmers and the many public and private agri-support persons to use effectively the resource represented by the dam, the canals, and the water which will be delivered to farms? In practice, comparatively little time and money appears to be devoted to planning a systematic strategy that will enable those involved to grow and develop; to begin shifting their attitudes in the light of the impending change and to gain some of the understandings and skills that will be required as the new resource or new programme comes into being.

A second item for action, therefore, is to create an enabling climate throughout the system which will permit, encourage and guide the formulation of continuing learning activities on a priority basis as established by programme objectives and an assessment of learning needs. The need for and establishment of this enabling climate does not arise from the assumption that no skills and understandings exist and thus must be provided. Rather it should be based on the notion of the multiplier effect; that the skills and understandings that do exist now need to be shared extensively among those to be involved in and influenced by a specific programme.[26] Similarly, there is little room for the notion that skills and understandings need not or cannot be improved. An enabling climate must flow from the nation's leaders and from the top levels of nation building departments. It need not be a wide open, permissive climate, but rather a cautious, guided and experimental climate which allows growth and development.

An appropriate climate for non-formal education must be accompanied by personnel, financial resources and intra-agency and interagency policies which will constitute the concern, the thrust, the guidance and the expertise for non-formal education activities. Since the attainments of a nation building department are accomplished through the performance of staff at all levels, a non-formal education strategy should be devised which will permit the conduct of a variety of learning activities appropriate for the needs at each level. Thus, individuals to guide non-formal education should be judiciously chosen with appropriate rank, abilities and interests in learning activities commensurate with the level involved. These individuals should be so located physically that they are in constant touch with the planning and implementation of programme activities at the level or levels for which they have responsibility. Their central task is to contribute to the attainment of programme objectives just like others in the agency, but their tool is non-formal education. Their principal resources are knowledge of programme objectives, ability to assess skills and understandings needed to improve the performance of activities and tasks crucial to the programme, and ability to identify and involve individuals who can contribute to the development or improvement of skills and understandings among participants of the learning activity. Enabling policies for intra-agency and interagency (public and private) interaction and financial resources to meet costs that cannot be borne within existing financial expenditure rules would be extra beneficial resources. The point here is that much more in the way of non-formal education is possible even within existing policies and financial arrangements, given an appropriate climate and leadership attuned to the interrelationships of the system perspective.

Another item on an agenda for action is consideration of whose functions will be changed or altered and in what fashion when a new programme is launched. Certainly the planners of a programme should give more weight to the importance of this aspect of implementing planned programmes. Systematic attention to a gross assessment of key behaviours implicit in the objectives of a programme would serve to call attention to the notion of the development of a 'people delivery system' and provide rough estimates of the magnitude of behavioural change that has to be accomplished. Secondly, it would establish a favourable climate for carrying out the necessary refinements in assessing the learning needs of the various subgroups involved throughout the system. Thirdly, it would provide useful feedback about the extent of need for early orientation learning activities for farmers and those within the official hierarchy of the departments or private agencies involved in the programme. Such learning activities would emphasize the positive implications of the programme before speculation and hearsay could build resistance. The system perspective with its characterization of component activities and linkages should serve to guide this type of assessment throughout the system.

A further implication for action is the identification of resource persons to be involved in non-formal education activities conducted throughout the system. Other resources can and should be used to supplement those within the agency. Training centres, institutes or agricultural colleges or universities may be used for specialized, resident instruction of selected staff for short or long terms. However, such instruction does not substitute for non-formal education within the agency. Lecturers, instructors or professors from these institutions can and should be involved in the within-agency non-formal education. On the one hand these individuals can contribute specialized technical knowledge as well as knowledge they may have about guiding the non-formal learning process. On the other hand their participation provides them with the opportunity to maintain a closer contact with the changing work-day world of agricultural development. This provides an important feedback linkage into the formal education process which can stimulate changes to produce graduates with the relevant skills and understandings requisite to rapid agricultural modernization.

The final implication for action to be discussed here centres around the nature of the non-formal learning activities to be conducted. In a very real sense, all that one experiences is 'educational' in nature, whether organized or unorganized. To be sure, self-study, self-learning and individual experiences can and do constitute frequently relevant and important personal learning activities. In fact, the daily experience of a farmer or a government functionary can be more convincing than an 'instructor', particularly if there is any variance between experience and the educational content. Thus, non-formal education should not be viewed in the same sense as a cookbook recipe where one takes measured amounts of specified ingredients, treats them in a certain fashion, and obtains a specified product. Non-formal education should build upon the collective experience of those participating. In some instances those participating may have to do some 'unlearning' – see things in a new light when change has established a new reality. Just as frequently, however, those who have the nominal role of 'instructor' or resource person may not have a clear picture of reality, particularly as it is perceived by the participants.

These aspects of learning suggest that non-formal education, whether it deals with mental activities (understanding, decision-making, planning) or physical activities (application of insecticides, conducting a method demonstration) should have a problem-solving approach. That is, a framework should be established between participants and resource persons that focuses on the function or task to be performed as a problem to be solved. The learning content then becomes the skills and under-standings needed. Additionally, much of non-formal education should be closely related to the work environment of the participants, using or stimulating that environment and its real life components as the 'class-room', the content, and the tools for learning.

There are, of course, additional implications for action in the planning and conduct of non-formal education. Additional questions of methods, the preparation of resource people or 'instructors', improved means of assessing needs, the phasing of learning activities over time in a cumulative fashion, and issues of learning priorities will all need consideration. How-ever, much of these aspects must be nation specific and must flow from systematic experience with non-formal education. The main purpose here has been to suggest a system perspective from which such experience might emerge.

Conclusions

The dimensions of the shaping process which has come to be known as agricultural development are complex. Much of this process, however, is rooted in change and individual behavioural response to that change. Farmers, extension agents, financial credit personnel, irrigation project staff, administrators and the many others involved in agricultural develop-ment must learn new behaviours. A system perspective helps analyse the interrelationships among the components and strengthen the linkages which will influence the farmer participation process.

It is concluded that a nation modernizing its agriculture should generate appropriate policies and support for non-formal learning activities as an integral part of its agricultural development effort. It is believed that more resources allocated to this process (even if at the initial expense of formal education) will provide more rapid gains in *productive capacities* both among farmers *and* those individuals engaged in agri-support activities. It is believed that the complementary effects of this dual system cannot and should not be ignored for the immediate present nor the more distant future. National goals tend to reflect the constantly growing store of knowledge about social and economic activities. Lastly, it is believed that action taken pursuant to the thesis of this paper will generate a strategy which can provide those citizens involved in agricultural development with the continuous opportunity to learn the skills and understandings of their changing functions implicit in national goals.

> It will have to be a development strategy which clearly and consistently aims at increasing self-reliance, increasing capacity for self-help each step of the way, especially in the rural areas, and at welding of the social structure which would make this possible. Such a strategy would also require reorientation of the educational system in a way that would provide the skills to handle the intermediate technology for rural activity, local pride, self-employment and innovation. It will also require a much more deliberate effort to provide access to educational and relevant skills for those who fail to gain entrance into the school system through new out of school education policies in a way and on a scale that is commensurate with the magnitude of the problem.[27]

REFERENCES

1. John Stuart Mill wrote, 'The worth of a State, in the long run, is the worth of the individuals composing it; and a State which postpones the interests of their mental expansion and elevation, to a little more of administrative skill, or of that semblance of it which practice gives, in the details of business; a State which dwarfs its men, in order that they may be more docile instruments in its hands even for beneficial purposes will find that with small men no great thing can really be accomplished; and that the perfection of machinery to which it has sacrificed everything, will in the end avail it nothing, for want of the vital power which, in order that the machine might work more smoothly, it had preferred to banish.'
2. A. T. Mosher, *Getting Agriculture Moving* (New York: Frederick A. Praeger, 1966).
3. Lester R. Brown, *Seeds of Change* (New York: Frederick A. Praeger, 1970).
4. John W. Mellor, 'Production Problems and Issues in Agricultural Development,' *Journal of Farm Economics*, 48 (December 1966) 1202.
5. Clifton R. Wharton, Jr., 'The Green Revolution: Cornucopia or Pandora's Box?', *Foreign Affairs*, 47 (April 1969) 464–7.
6. Wayne A. Schutjer and E. Walter Coward, Jr., 'Planning Agricultural Development – The Matter of Priorities,' *Journal of Developing Areas*, 6 (October, 1971) 35.
7. Guy Hunter, *The Administration of Agricultural Development* (London: Oxford University Press, 1970), p. 97.
8. FAO, Provisional Indicative World Plan for Agricultural Development, Vol. 2, Chapter 10, Part 4, p. 382.

9. Nicolaas Luykx, 'Rural Governing Institutions,' *Institutions in Agricultural Development*, (ed.). Melvin G. Blase (Ames, Iowa: Iowa State University Press, 1971), p. 208.

10. James Duncan Shaffer, 'On Institutional Obsolescence and Innovation,' *American Journal of Agricultural Economics*, 51 (May 1969) 245–67.

11. A. T. Mosher, *Getting AgricultureMoving*, pp. 11–12.

12. Philip H. Coombs, *The World Educational Crisis: A Systems Analysis* (New York, N.Y.: Oxford University Press, 1968), p. 81.

13. Joint Commission on Rural Reconstruction, 'Agricultural Development and its Contribution to Economic Growth on Taiwan,' *Economic Digest Series*, No. 17, Taipei (April 1966).

14. 'The term "systems" is generally used by social scientists to refer to an assemblage of components (characteristics of individuals or of groups of individuals) that have an ordered pattern of interrelationships. They have a recurrent pattern of interaction that is interdependent or complementary with respect to some common purpose or function and which is thus separated or "bounded" from the rest of the environment. To sum up, a system involves a set of identifiable elements or components; these system-components have interrelationships; the relationships have consequences; these consequences have further consequence (including the future set of interrelationships), and both sets of consequence have effects on the performance of the system.' From United Nations, *Appraising Administrative Capability for Development*. (ST/TAO/M/46), New York, 1969, p. 101.

15. This section is based on concepts discussed in substantial detail in two sources: 'What is Agriculture,' *The World Food Problem: A Report of the U.S. President's Advisory Committee* (Washington, D.C.: The White House, May 1967), Vol. 1, pp. 59–81; and A. T. Mosher, *To Create a Modern Agriculture* (New York, N.Y.: The Agricultural Development Council, Inc., 1971), pp. 3–15.

16. See especially A. T. Mosher, *Creating a Progressive Rural Structure* (New York, N.Y.: The Agricultural Development Council, Inc., 1969). Also Mosher, *Getting AgricultureMoving*.

17. D. H. Penny, 'The Transition from Subsistence to Commercial Family Farming in North Sumatra,' (unpublished PhD dissertation, Cornell University, 1964).

18. Joan Tully, 'Education for Change' (paper prepared for Symposium on Development and Social Change, Australia and New Zealand Association for The Advancement of Science, 43rd Congress, May 25–6, 1971).

19. See Coombs, *The World Educational Crisis: A Systems Analysis*. Also Burton C. Newbry and Kenneth L. Martin, 'The Educational Crisis in the Lesser Developed Countries,' *The Journal of Developing Areas*, 6 (January 1972) 155–62.

20. Non-formal education refers to organized learning activities designed to provide knowledge, skills and understandings outside of the formal system of education. While formal education operates within a structure of schools, colleges, universities and higher institutions which receive major public support, non-formal education operates under widely scattered sponsorship, control and financing among public and private agencies. See Coombs, *The World Educational Crisis: A Systems Analysis*, pp. 138–44; and International

Council for Educational Development, 'Outline of Research Project on Non-formal Education for Rural and Agricultural Development,' mimeograph (New York: January 1971), p. 2.

21. Paraphrased from Huseyin Yegin, 'The Role of Irrigation Foremen in Irrigation Projects,' in a report on the Seyhan Irrigation Project in Turkey (title unknown), p. 114.

22. Clinton A. Rehling, 'A Critical Link in Development,' Explosion Hunger-1975, Second Development Decade Number (October-December 1971) 463.

23. This problem of attitudes and behavioural response is not restricted to third world nations developing their agriculture. For example, similar stereotyped attitudes regarding the poor, blacks and youth characterize current weak linkages among groups in the US.

24. See Hurbert F. Lionberger and H. C. Chang, *Farm Information for Modernizing Agriculture: The Taiwan System* (New York, N.Y.: Frederick A. Praeger, 1972) pp. 11, 14–15, 349; and Mosher, *Getting Agriculture Moving*, pp. 25–38.

25. The phrase 'other points within the system' is used deliberately in lieu of the subordinating concept of 'lower levels in the system.' While elements of subordination will probably always prevail in human relationships, the point being stressed here is that in a system perspective the output or achievement of the system is tied to the weakest component or linkage in the system. A fine Mercedes car will not operate as intended if the carburettor is missing or poorly adjusted or the gas line is clogged or cut.

26. A Director of Agriculture in an Indian state explained that he could not afford to use a particular district officer as a trainer for inservice training programmes because he was too valuable as a field officer. Yet, in the writer's view, what was sorely needed was to use the capabilities of this officer to multiply the number of field officers who had his skills and understandings. This latter use of the officer would be a more productive use of his particular talents even in the short run.

27. Soedjatmoko, 'Technology, Development and Culture: A Memorandum for Discussion,' unpublished note, 1972.

BIBLIOGRAPHY

Lester R. Brown, *Seeds of Change* (New York: Frederick A. Praeger, 1970).

Philip H. Coombs, *The World Educational Crisis: A Systems Analysis* (New York, N.Y.: Oxford University Press, 1968), p. 81.

FAO, Provisional Indicative World Plan for Agricultural Development, Vol. 2, Chapter 10, Part 4, p. 382.

Guy Hunter, *The Administration of Agricultural Development* (London: Oxford University Press, 1970), p. 97.

International Council for Educational Development. 'Outline of Research Project on Non-formal Education for Rural and Agricultural Development,' mimeograph (New York: January 1971), p. 2.

Joint Commission on Rural Reconstruction. 'Agricultural Development and its Contribution to Economic Growth on Taiwan,' *Economic Digest Series*, No. 17, Taipei (April 1966).

Herbert F. Lionberger, and H. C. Chang, *Farm Information for Modernizing Agriculture: The Taiwan System* (New York, N.Y.: Frederick A. Praeger, 1970), pp. 11, 14–15, 349.

Nicolaas Luykx, 'Rural Governing Institutions' *Institutions in Agriculture Development*, (ed.) Melvin G. Blase (Ames, Iowa: Iowa State University Press, 1971), p. 208.

John W. Mellor, 'Production Problems and Issues in Agricultural Development,' *Journal of Farm Economics*, 48 (December 1966) 1202.

A. T. Mosher, *To Create a Modern Agriculture* (New York, N.Y.: The Agricultural Development Council, Inc., 1971), pp. 3–15.

— . Creating a Progressive Rural Structure (New York, N.Y.: The Agricultural Development Council, Inc., 1969)

—. *Getting Agriculture Moving* (New York: Frederick A. Praeger, 1966).

Burton C. Newbry, and Kenneth L. Martin, 'The Educational Crisis in the Lesser Developed Countries,' *The Journal of Developing Areas*, 6 (January 1972) 155–62.

D. H. Penny, 'The Transition from Subsistence to Commercial Family Farming in North Sumatra' (unpublished PhD dissertation, Cornell University, 1964).

Clinton A. Rehling, 'A Critical Link in Development,' Explosion Hunger–1975, Second Development Decade Number (October–December 1971) 463.

Wayne A. Schutjer, and E. Walter Coward, Jnr., 'Planning Agricultural Development – The Matter of Priorities,' *Journal of Developing Areas*, 6 (October 1971) 35.

James Duncan Shaffer, 'On Institutional Obsolescence and Innovation,' *American Journal of Agricultural Economics*, 51 (May 1969) 245–67.

Soedjatmoko, 'Technology, Development and Culture: A Memorandum for Discussion,' unpublished note, 1972.

Joan Tully, 'Education for Change' (paper prepared for Symposium on Development and Social Change, Australia and New Zealand Association for The Advancement of Science, 43rd Congress, May 25–6, 1971).

U.S. President's Science Advisory Committee. 'What is Agriculture,' The World Food Problem: A Report of the U.S. President's Science Advisory Committee (Washington, D.C. The White House, May 1967), Vol. 1, pp. 59–81.

United Nations, *Appraising Administrative Capability for Development* (ST/TAO/M 46), New York, 1969, p. 101.

Clifton R. Wharton Jr. 'The Green Revolution: Cornucopia or Pandora's Box?', *Foreign Affairs*, 47 (April 1969) 464–7.

6

Schools and Rural Development: An Anthropological Approach

John Singleton

Introduction

Public, political, and professional[1] expectations of school proceed from the assumption that what goes on in schools is education and that schools are effective instruments for achieving an unlimited range of cognitive and affective educational purposes. This has been nowhere more evident than in the wide and inconsistent variety of prescriptions for schooling made in the name of development. Though public, political, and professional leaders have had a common institution in mind, the local public school, their perceptions of that school, its activities, and what it might accomplish have varied widely. Moreover, consistent definitions of development or agreement on developmental goals have not been achieved, even though universal and extended popular schooling has often been seen as both a basic element, and instrument of, the different definitions of development.

We have had, therefore, world and regional conferences that promoted plans for universal schooling and minimum percentages of gross national product which governments should invest in the maintenance and development of existing school systems. Educational planning at the national level has been primarily based upon the assumption that schooling is education, especially as economists have elaborated manpower plans, estimates of social demand, and calculations of cost effectiveness. Standards of efficiency have come from industrial models in which it was assumed that the educational product of schools was measurable in available statistical records, usually in degrees awarded or time served by inmates of the system. From the same models has come the assumption that some forms of 'profit' accruing to the larger system – the economic returns on capital investment in education – are measures of school efficiency.

In this atmosphere of post–World War II concern for 'development' and models of educational planning derived from economics, schools have competed for development investment on the basis of popular political support, on their image as social instruments for democratization (equalizing opportunities for individual and communal social mobility), their contribution to national economic or political development, and, occasionally,

on their involvement in something labelled 'community development'. While different arguments for the support of schools have been
used with different audiences, intra-government dealings between bureaucracies controlling schools, finance, and development planning, have often
stressed economic and political criteria – as have negotiations with external
aid-granting agencies.

Educational planners and professional educators have also been interested in the technology of education. When it was perceived that
schools were not meeting their own professed expectations of educational
achievement, professional interests turned to technological innovations –
at first in hardware for teaching machines, educational television, and
computer-assisted instruction. Curriculum development and pedagogical
technology, too, have had attention: programmed instruction, the 'open
classroom', and the new math, have been widely diffused.

These activities have not, however, stimulated the political or professional actors in most of the systems involved to re-examine their assumptions about the schools' processes and products. Such questions have
recently begun to arise from social critics, disenchanted educational
planners, anthropologists, and scholars concerned with the political
economy. They have suggested that the schools serve other social functions than education and that these other functions are often antithetical to
the commonly held myths or images of the schools.

Because these recent observations make sense in an anthropological view
of social institutions and education, it is my purpose here to suggest an
anthropological framework for new professional conceptualizations of
schooling and education which can help us to redefine the larger problems
of relating education to social and developmental purposes. The focus is
upon rural communities because some of our best current research comes
from rural settings and is relevant to those problems usually associated
with rural development – but the analysis is not limited in applicability to
rural settings. The anthropological models have, of course, come from
traditional disciplinary concerns with isolated small communities and are,
perhaps, better adapted to the understanding of social institutions at the
local level than at the national and international levels.[2] The local emphasis is justified here because it is the local schools which are commonly
expected to act as the educational instruments of development, rural,
community, or otherwise, by national planners and administrators. It is
the political and social context of the local community within which
larger development goals will be achieved, subverted, or ignored –
whether by schools or other social institutions, agencies and movements.

Schools, Schooling, Education and Culture

The emphasis in the model proposed here is that schools are social institutions within which there are a number of activities and by which a number of purposes are served. To assume that their activity and purpose is, by definition, education is to immediately ignore the rich variety of social life and tradition which is encompassed in schools (cf. Wax and Wax, 1971a). The proliferation of schools in our modern world is a social movement of unprecedented proportions. In this context I am speaking of schools as those institutions which require or selectively allow the attendance of specific age groups of children in classrooms supervized by professional teachers for the study of graded curricula (adapted from Reimer, 1971:51). There is, in many ways, an international culture of schools which prescribes the norms, forms, content and goals of the activities which proceed in their name.

In larger context, schooling refers to 'those processes of teaching and learning carried on at specific times, in particular places outside the home, for definite periods, by persons especially prepared or trained for the task'. (Herskovits 1948, p. 310.) While 'schooling' has arisen in some form in most societies, 'schools' are primarily a feature of modern Western society transferred to every nation and politically-organized territory in the world by colonial authorities, missionaries, and other 'educationaries' (as Freeman Butts has called them). Even societies with indigenous school models, like Japan, have been heavily influenced by the Western models. These schools are, by public definition, the location for formal schooling and the most visible locations of professional teaching, but they are not the only social institutions of schooling.

Though some children still escape the ministrations of schools, there is an almost universal myth that they are thereby deprived and inadequate to assume the social and material perquisites of an 'educated' (meaning schooled) member of their society. While those who escape the schools may never fully realize what they have missed in potential social rewards, there are large numbers of children who participate only long enough to be convinced of their unworthiness because they have not graduated from the system (cf. Paulston's chapter on Cuban education in this volume).

As social institutions in the sense defined by Malinowski, we mean that schools have 'a set of traditional values for which human beings come together' (1944:39). An institution is 'a group of people united for the pursuit of a simple or complex activity; always in possession of a material endowment and a technical outfit; organized on a definite legal or customary charter; linguistically formulated in myth, legend, rule, and maxim; and trained or prepared for the carrying out of its task' (1945:50). The customary charter under which schools operate, i.e. their public reason for being and their traditional mandate, is, of course, schooling, though it is usually called education. Under this charter there are a variety of activities, but it is an empirical question to determine which of these activities are educational and what functions they serve. Activities performed in any social institution are by no means limited to, nor even necessarily inclusive of, the purposes and values stipulated by their charters.

Within this anthropological model, the process of education is viewed as cultural transmission, encompassing but by no means limited to schooling. Culture, itself, can be defined in essentially educational terms as 'the shared products of human learning'. More precisely, and from a psychological orientation, culture can be seen as 'standards for deciding what is, standards for deciding what can be, standards for deciding how one feels about it, standards for deciding what to do about it, and standards for deciding how to go about doing it' (Goodenough, 1963, pp. 258–9). Thus culture encompasses patterns of meaning, reality, values, actions and decision-making that are shared by and within social collectivities. A culture is not, in this view, a group of people nor even necessarily a complete system of human behaviour since most people participate in several significant cultural systems. It is a conceptual abstraction that helps us to analyse individual human behaviour as that behaviour is shared among groups.

Because anthropologists are so often connected with the study of social tradition, I must add that cultural transmission includes both the transmission of tradition from one generation to the next *and* the transmission of new knowledge or cultural patterns from anybody who knows to anyone who does not. It should also be obvious that there is a dynamic process of cultural systems in transmission which led Redfield to speak of education as 'the process of cultural transmission and renewal' (1963:13). People are both products of, and creators of, culture; they are not passive receptacles of culture.

Education viewed as cultural transmission contrasts with the more usual professional definition of education taken from psychology – a process of individual behavioural change – which implies an individualistic process, isolable from social context, in which one behaviour is substituted for another and in which the patterns of learning are separable from the content. The results of sophisticated psychological testing have, for instance, been accepted as a measure of education, and universal achievement tests are currently under construction. Professional educators recognize, however, even though their linguistic terms tend to hide the fact, that cognitive and affective learnings are inextricably intertwined, and that there are important group as well as individual differences.

The anthropological definition of education is suggested here to emphasize that the learning processes which go on in school, and that which is traditionally measured as educational achievement, are only a small part of an individual's total education and only one of the results of his contact with the schools. We have too often implied that education is something which goes on in schools – and that all that goes on in schools (or that which is really important there) is education. We have assumed that the internationally recognized content of schooling is the prime educational result rather than observing it as a distinguishing feature of the social movement of Western school education. We have not conceived of education as a pluralistic process as diverse as the various cultural traditions within which the process occurs and from which its content is derived.

It is from these limited assumptions, for instance, that professional educators have been able to talk about some of their clients as 'culturally deprived' – without recognizing the cultural systems hidden by differences between themselves and their clients in their perceptions of the world, their values, their patterns of decision-making, and their strategies for action.

A peculiar and truly international myth of educators, colonial officials, and many politically powerful people has been what the Waxes aptly labelled a 'vacuum ideology'. It is the idea that their clients, who are poor and come from different social origins than those associated with the dominant society and schools, have no culture. 'Children who come from lower-class and impoverished ethnic groups are regarded as empty and cultureless rather than as having a culture and social life of their own which educators must learn about in order to be competent in their jobs' (Wax and Wax, 1971b:132).

While education is a necessarily universal cultural process, it is not an easily isolated activity in any context. Whenever communication is occurring, there is always the possibility that the participants are engaged in an educational transaction, sharing elements of a cultural tradition within which their communicating behaviour is relevant. Whether or not the educational transaction is significant to one or more actors will depend on a variety of contextual and personal factors.

Our usual policy-oriented research on education deals with those institutions which publicly specify an educational charter as the legitimating base for their support. Schools are only one such public institution with educational functions – but they are the first that come to mind when we specify an educational purpose. It is with reference to their public charters, however, that they are defined as educational institutions. The mass media, churches, extension services in health and agriculture, apprenticeship systems, prisons, and other institutions, too, are supported under public charters proclaiming their educational purposes. Many other institutions operate as educational agencies, even without such legitimating public charters for education – such as the legal system for the administration of justice, hospitals, social welfare agencies, advertising, and many voluntary associations. The family, the community, and the peer group are also important channels of cultural transmission and reinforcement – often resistant to the educational intentions of other agencies.

Activities and Functions of Schools

That schools are the sacred institution of modern and modernizing societies has been noted by several recent observers. Most dramatic, perhaps, have been the pronouncements of Ivan Illich, a Catholic priest who became disenchanted by both the institutionalized church and the institutionalized school. 'School has become the world religion of a modernized proletariat, and makes futile promises of salvation to the poor of the technological age' (1971:10). He, and others, point out that compulsory school attendance is demanded because it is 'good' for children, holding out the promise of 'salvation' in this world for those who are worthy and will complete the more or less rigorous obstacle course of requirements and examinations. School attendance is seen as an initiation rite through which children gain adult status, recognition and social privilege.

An anthropologist, Barnett, and his Ibaloi peasant informant in the mountains of northern Luzon, in the Philippines, made similar observations. In more traditional times, the Ibaloi people had celebrated an elaborate series of rituals, called *peshit*, designed to enhance a man's prestige in the community. Butchering three to ten pigs for a feast and dance in the home of the celebrant, at given intervals, provided prestige through the redistribution of accumulated wealth, in pigs.

An older Ibaloi peasant remarked to some students, 'You practise the *peshit* by going to school, having learned to read and write'. Formal schooling was seen as providing the same kind of local prestige as the *peshit* ritual. As Barnett noted, the tangible rewards of successful schooling were also important – the few students who made it through certain levels of advanced schooling were the ones given civil service or teaching jobs (Barnett, 1969:292).

While looking at schools in this sense, however, it is not necessary to become a militant disbeliever or school-atheist. Rituals have always served educational and other purposes. It is only necessary to look at what goes on in them more broadly – to describe the activities that take place within them and to describe their functional relationships to the society and its other social institutions.

One of the most provocative contrasts of certain patterns of 'primitive' schooling with the activities of modern schools was noted by the anthropologist Hart when he looked at the many forms of schooling developed for new initiates in rites marking the transition to adult status. Almost universally, the emphasis of the 'curriculum' was upon the teaching of religious knowledge – 'such things as the learning of the myths, the tribal accounts of the tribe's own origin and history, and the performance, the meaning, and the sacred connections and connotations of the ceremonials'

(1955:138). Surprisingly little attention, even in the most elaborate and protracted patterns of schooling which could last for more than a year, was given to economically practical skills of subsistence or even to specialized crafts. Schooling seems to have been reserved for what was considered most importantly taught by specialists in formal settings – the cultural heritage of the tribe. As Pettit noted in looking at the initiation rites of American Indian groups, these forms of schooling provided 'a constant challenge to the elders to review, analyse, dramatize, and defend their cultural heritage' (quoted by Hart). We should not be surprised that schools continue to perform this sacred cultural service, even while their chartered purpose has been increasingly dominated by a concern for the transmission of practical and economic skills and knowledge.

Formal teaching (schooling) is, of course, the chartered activity of the school. Education, cultural transmission, the teaching and learning of knowledge, skills, and attitudes, is the activity that we most often notice. Two other activities, however, are equally important in the Western-model schools of our world – social certification and custodial care.

Social role selection and certification is certainly one of the most deeply embedded activities of the school. Selection procedures for admission, categorizing, or tracking pupils within the system; examinations; and other evaluation procedures all serve to channel and certify, or decertify, children not only inside the school but also for social opportunities in the wider society. The ideology of schools specifies that this is a democratizing process, if all children have equal access to the schools, giving each the opportunity to compete on his own merits. In practice, it is most often the socio-economic status of a child's parents which is associated with his chances of success in formal schooling. The schools have consistently reinforced, and certified, class status; they have rarely subverted its influence. Parents and the public know this important role of the schools and come into natural conflict with school authorities as they attempt to protect their children's chances in the social class selection process while school authorities seek to uphold universalistic criteria.

Many of the supposedly universalistic criteria of the schools are, however, particularistic and discriminatory in their application – witness the current controversy over the correlation between intelligence-testing and race in the United States. Some professional educators have had a particularly difficult time choosing between their professional faith in intelligence-testing, their egalitarian political faith, or in their faith that educational research will ultimately reconcile the 'facts' with their different ideologies. Even though intelligence tests are based upon correlations with academic success, few researchers have perceived them as an evaluational or diagnostic device for schools. School success is assumed to be an adequate test of individual intelligence. One does not read the tests to see what kinds of knowledge, skill, and cognitive style the schools or society reward. (See R. Cohen 1969 for an exception.)

The second important non-educational activity of schools is the custodial care of children. The models for organizing schools have come from those societies in which it is expected that children will be cared for by teachers for six or more hours a day, five or six days per week, nine to eleven months of the year. Families are relieved, thereby, of supervisory responsibility for their young children, and usually resist any organizational changes which would once again put the children back in the home for longer periods of time. Secondary and higher school education, too, has had this function – keeping older children off the streets and out of overcrowded job markets. Even when schools have been transferred to rural agricultural environments, there have been few adaptations to reduced social expectations of custodial care except in the scheduling of vacations to coincide with times of needed child labour. Schools and parents in rural areas have, at first, engaged in a competition for the time of the children when they were an economic resource to their parents. In most cases the schools have won without a major compromise on the time demanded from children.

Little attention has been given to time-saving organization of school activities. The basic measure of educational achievement remains that of time spent in school. I know of no suggestions that teaching proceed in units of content which would provide for the early dismissal from school of children when they had accomplished their daily, weekly, or yearly objective. Though some garbage collectors and college professors are assigned professional tasks which they can complete at their own rate of speed, without punching a time clock, students and most school teachers have their work defined in strict requirements of time spent within the physical plant of the school. The custodial purpose of the schools thus overrides the educational purpose which might be served, as in prisons, by promise of time off for good behaviour.

Besides social certification and custodial care, there are other activities associated with schools that could and should be described. Many of these activities are not universally associated with schools but are features of particular school systems. School-related sports, musical, and dramatic activities often become a major recreational event of the larger community as well as for the students. As centres for fun, play, creative, and expressive activities, some schools mitigate their compulsory custodial function. The schools can also serve to create integrating social networks in divided or extended communities, even as they symbolically serve the integration of racial, ethnic, national, and international social systems.

It is, of course, primarily in their educational activities that schools are expected to serve developmental purposes. But the educational activities are inevitably limited and often controverted in school contexts where all the activities of education, custodial care, and social certification are taking place simultaneously and indivisibly.

In one brief example, I still remember the linguistically sophisticated Japanese middle school teacher of English who told me she knew what was necessary to develop English language competence in her students – but she could not teach in this way because of the structure of the examinations for entrance to high school which demanded objective answers to questions about English grammar. Preparation for those examinations, the first crucial selection for differentiated tracks of social mobility, had to be her students' most important concern.

The activities of the school, educational and otherwise, are obviously related to many other social institutions – though we often rationalize these relations by reference to the educational charter of schools. The students of our own political economy like to point out that the behaviours taught to pupils, what we might call the pupil-making process in schools, separated from the explicit formal curriculum, is most important for preparing children to work in depersonalized and alienating industrial factories and bureaucracies. Unquestioning acceptance of the hierarchical authority of teachers and school administrators, adherence to highly organized time schedules, docility, and other behaviours form a hidden curriculum of more importance to the social institutions of production in modern societies than the explicit technical skills recognized in the public curriculum descriptions. It is important to ask about the relationship of these behaviours to proposals for rural development educational programmes. (Are these, indeed, the cultural attributes of successful farmers?)

Schools in rural and ethnically differentiated communities have often served as social boundary-maintaining systems through which contact with and information about the larger society was filtered, and by which children were generally discouraged from thoughts of active participation in the larger society. The Hunts (1970) describe this process in rural Mexico much as the Waxes do for an American Indian reservation (1964). The 'vacuum ideology' of the teachers effectively communicates that they and their social system are disvalued by the larger society and they have little chance of attaining its economic rewards. Even though the official purposes of the schools in this situation are to promote the mobility of Indians into the larger Mexican or US societies, they are effectively, though unintentionally, subverted by the social processes of the local classroom.

It is also true that schools have served more democratic purposes in accord with their social charter. With relation to ethnically discriminated groups in US society, for instance, the schools have been disproportionately the instruments for social mobility of children of Jewish and Japanese ancestry. These groups have found within the schools a system within which they can win on the system's terms. One can continue to turn to the hypothesis of genetic correlation between race and intelligence, this time at a disadvantage to American WASPs, or one can take the anthropologist's assumption that different cultural systems in interaction will produce different effects.

Thus, the central activities of the school – education, social role selection, and custodial care – serve a variety of social functions. As part of the 'sacred' institution of modern societies, they serve as both ritual and transmitter of myth and ideology. The hidden curriculum of modern institutionalized behaviours can be seen as a direct preparation for participation in bureaucratic and industrial organization. The differential organization of schools for discriminated ethnic and social classes may serve to maintain and certify the privileged status of socially dominant groups. And, of course, the school may serve those educational functions claimed for it in its customary charter. Whether it does or not is, however, a question for investigation – not a definitional assumption.

Case Studies of Rural Schools in Thailand and the Philippines

Two case studies of rural schools viewed as social institutions in the anthropological model presented here have recently been completed. Dealing with schools in the Philippines (Manalang, 1971) and Thailand (Gurevich, 1972), both were initiated to better understand the role of schools and teachers in rural communities and the developmental roles which they might be expected to play.[3]

In these studies, completed as doctoral dissertations in the International and Development Education Program of the University of Pittsburgh, educational researchers with broad professional experience in the country concerned and with linguistic competency in the national languages chose public elementary schools in rural villages that were neither very remote, nor particularly close to large metropolitan centres. Their intention was to find schools and communities which could be considered typical of large sections of their national systems. Proceeding with an ethnographic research methodology, they each spent more than a year living as participant-observers within the communities of their study, looking at the social institution of the school and its relations with other social institutions, especially the local community and the administrative institutions of education. While there is a fairly extensive educational research literature for both countries, no detailed ethnographic accounts focused on the schools as social institutions could be found. In both Thailand and the Philippines, school authorities have characteristically included rural community development as an area of school and teacher responsibility. Often competing with other governmental agencies for the community development action, and the bureaucratic resources which go with this assigned function, a variety of programmes have been officially sponsored in schools, teacher-training programmes, and in experimental community projects.

In the Philippines there had been a sharp conflict between governmental strategies of community development organized by the schools versus those organized by a separate corps of village-level extension agents. While the 'community school' concept lost out in intra-governmental competition for funding and control of community development programmes, the slogan continued to play an important symbolic role in the pronouncements and programmes of the Bureau of Public Schools. Community development was a politically profitable platform for educational administrators as they sought to justify larger school expenditures on the basis of school contributions to national development. Faced with problems of surplus and unemployed graduates of high schools and colleges, contributions to local development efforts could counter charges of an over-expanded school system.

The Philippine elementary school, which Manalang studied, was located in a small village on the shore of a large inland lake. A Tagalog-speaking population of about 2,000 people participated in an economic system of mixed farming, fishing, and wage employment, but only 28 residents, including one male and 15 female teachers, held white-collar jobs. While many employed people held part-time jobs outside the village, they were not close enough to any large city to work there without moving away from the community. The most distinctive development-related feature of the village was the designated site for a large electric-generating plant, not yet built, which would eventually furnish power for the Manila metropolitan region, about 70 kilometers away.

The most obvious feature of the local school which comes out of Manalang's report was the extent to which it was organized as an extension of the national bureaucratic school system. This was not the result of looking at an organizational chart, but rather a summation of the behaviours and attitudes evinced by teachers, students, and community as they related to the school. Ultimate and real authority for explicit activities of the school rested with the chain of command that went from teacher to school head to district office to division office to the Bureau of Public Schools. Numerous reports requiring statistical precision were demanded of the school, some with only short notice. Teachers would be regularly summoned from classes, especially those who could type, to help the head teacher in the preparation of the reports. Impending visits of school officials, likewise, required a good deal of teacher attention, as detailed plans were laid for activities during the visit. Even the details of a luncheon menu for the officials could be the subject of faculty deliberation.

Tremendous teacher time and organizational effort went into school money-raising schemes, one purpose of which was to provide for the expenses of these visits.

The Service Manual for the Bureau of Public Schools contained extensive and detailed instructions for school personnel, even prescribing the size and margins for official correspondence. It indicated that 'programmes and courses of study are intended not as prescriptions or blueprints but rather as suggestive patterns and models for the guidance of local school officials and teachers'. While encouraging adaptations to the needs and conditions of local communities, the Manual says that 'any radical departure from prescribed subjects and the curriculum requirements should be made only with the prior approval of the Director of Public Schools'. In the climate of a school dependent upon bureaucratic support and approval, the distinction between 'local adaptations' and 'radical departures' must necessarily be drawn rather conservatively. Exceptions require going all the way to the top.

The formal organization and prescription of the educational administration nowithstanding, there were highly organized patterns contravening the explicit intentions of the Manual – but these were adaptations aimed at protection and survival of those most intimately caught up in the system, the teachers and the administrators. Local funds had to be raised for school improvements which would be noticed by official visitors and reflect creditably upon the local teachers and administrators. One of the points of contention between the local community and the school was over who should bear the burden of these contributions. Parents thought that the salaried teachers, considered very well-off in the socio-economic hierarchy of the village, should contribute from their own salaries. The teachers, with the support of a community school slogan, thought that the parents should contribute and devised numerous ways, primarily through the children, to accomplish this. One teacher was especially successful with candy sales to the children.

Local expectations of the school, shared by both parents and teachers, were that it was responsible for transmitting certain traditional values and basic literacy skills. The values of obedience and submission to authority, respect for age, a proper sense of indebtedness for favours received, and good inter-personal relations were most often stressed explicitly by both teachers and parents. The basic literacy skills were perceived as important in a credentialing process that would allow those who graduated to go on to the higher levels of schooling. While subjects and activities relevant to local community improvement were prescribed by school officials from Boy and Girl Scout organizing to gardening, there was criticism, resistance, and only superficial compliance from teachers. The school was not a force for social change but an instrument by which some children might begin to move into the urban economy and away from the difficult subsistence of village living. As Manalang says, 'the school taught survival behaviours rather than innovative ideas' (248).

Important for understanding the meaning of basic literacy skills in the village was the fact that school instruction was conducted in three languages. Though beginning with the vernacular, English was the language of instruction from the third year on. The national language, Pilipino, was expected to replace English in this capacity, but Pilipino curriculum materials had not yet been adequately developed. The spirit behind this change is, of course, national integration and identity, major political issues in Manila and particularly important to the bureaucracy. Local teacher and community attitudes, however, did not parallel the nationalistic directives. Since Pilipino is primarily based upon Tagalog, the community was not much affected by the change, but there was a continuing demand for English instruction since it was perceived as the language for higher schooling and advancement to urban employment.

Reflecting some development prescriptions from social science, the Bureau of Public Schools officially proscribed the traditional values of *utang no loob* (a deep and proper sense of indebtedness) and *pakikisama* (good interpersonal relations, getting along well with others). They were perceived at the national level as deterrents to national development objectives, but they continued to be regarded locally as descriptions of appropriate behaviour. Teachers, caught in the bind of conflicting expectations, endorsed the community values but reserved their explicit teaching for other bureaucratically endorsed values.

The ideology of community development, like that of the teachers' 'vacuum ideology' described by the Waxes,[4] assumed that external agents were necessary to organize a community for its own developmental goals. Much like the social scientists who have prescribed the 'necessary' values which will lead to developmental social change, usually incorporating those values attributed to the Western 'Protestant ethic', the agents and agencies of community change have often sought development through more or less specific attitudinal changes of people as well as in the extension of new technologies and other forms of community-level investment.[5]

The greatest changes in the community of Manalang's study were obviously going to come from the new electric generating plant, but there was nothing in the school programme related to this change. The school functioned in very real ways as an agent of bureaucratic socialization, more apparent in the effect upon teachers than students. As the only village occupation which required higher education, teachers were the major community models of successful schooling. Others who successfully negotiated the school system were drawn into civil service or other jobs elsewhere. That the teachers themselves would not have chosen school careers of their own accord was probably a sign of their occupational status, even though they were well-off by local standards. It is not surprising that many students dropped out before graduation; that economic activities at home often took precedence over school attendance. As Manalang concluded,

> That the schools continued to be perceived by some sectors as institutional agencies for social change and community improvement, and more recently, as organizations for manpower development was as much due to the glib repetition of this aphorism over a long period of time as to a blindness in school people deriving from close identification with a system. The important thing was that the school was successful in teaching survival behaviours rather than innovative ideas. Consequently the bureaucracy of which it was a part appeared less intent on social change than on self-maintenance. (268–9)

In Thailand, too, there has been a history of school-centred community development programmes for rural areas. One of the best known was the Thailand–Unesco Rural Teacher Education Program (TURTEP) in which the Department of Teacher Training and Unesco jointly sponsored programmes for future rural teachers. The training included rural student teaching during which the students were expected to engage in village development projects as well as conduct classroom teaching. As part of Unesco's programme in fundamental education, it was expected that rural school teachers would play important development leadership roles in the communities to which they would be assigned. The educational bureaucracy, as in the Philippines, found the rural development emphasis effective for its purposes and promoted both the training programme and the slogan.

For the ethnographic study of a Thai school, Gurevich chose a rural community in Northeast Thailand not far from the administrative and university centre of that region, Khon Kaen. With just under 1,000 inhabitants, the prime economic activity of the village was farming, both commercially and for subsistence. There was also a variety of supplementary occupations in the village, primarily involved with small commercial enterprises.

Having previously worked in the TURTEP project, as well as conducting research on its history, Gurevich was familiar with the intentions of its planners. He was, however, concerned about the assumptions relating to the role of the rural teacher on which it was based. TURTEP planners assumed that rural Thai teachers were village leaders and that special training would make them more effective in leading rural development projects.

In choosing a village for study, he deliberately selected one which appeared to have the optimum conditions for teacher influence in village affairs. The local primary school was fully staffed with separate teachers assigned to each of the four grades. The headmaster and the teachers were native or long time residents of the village. They had strong kinship ties there and had been assigned to the school long enough to have established their community roles. One teacher served on the Village Development Committee.

Community support for the local school was strong. Villagers took pride in the school and liked to refer to their village as a place where people 'love education'. They had participated in the construction of the existing primary school facilities and were raising money for the construction of an upper primary school in the village.

Many local children had been successful through schooling in securing highly valued civil service employment and other rewards. During the period of the research, one graduate of the school was in New Zealand for post-graduate university study. Though only four residents were teachers in the local schools, seven other teachers lived in the village and commuted to jobs in nearby communities.

Even with such enthusiastic community support for the school, however, the teachers were accorded more prestige than leadership by community residents. Their professional province was the school, and they were expected to be fully involved with their work there. While one teacher was customarily appointed to serve on the Village Development Committee, this membership did not appear to be a special recognition of local leadership. The incumbent teacher member was also the owner-operator of a central village coffee shop, whose daughter was also one of the school teachers and was included as a member of his household. His appointment to the Committee reflected governmental views that one member should be a teacher.

The headmaster of the school is the son-in-law of the most influential man in the village and is looked to for matters of educational leadership. He is leading the effort to raise local funds for the new upper primary school to be organized in the village. Because he lives with his father-in-law, he does not play a dominant role in his own household or in his household's relations with the larger community.

The local status of teachers is quite high, even though they are not perceived as the initiators of community action outside of the schools. This status is usually attached, in the villagers' thinking, with the designation of teachers as government officials. The status of teachers was referred to by a term literally translated as 'lord and master' and used for all civil service officials. It was not only as civil service officials that they were given status in the village, but it was also through their participation in the civil service system that they could anticipate future social mobility and advancement. Rigidly structured, all civil service positions and promotions depended upon examinations, completion of formal educational requirements, and the goodwill of one's superiors.

Two of the younger teachers were enrolled in night courses at the nearby university in order to qualify for higher positions and the younger male teachers were definitely caught up in the system. The headmaster and the older teacher-coffee shop owner had outside economic interests in their local households, but the younger teachers had only the civil service system to depend upon for their future.

While bureaucratic values were, therefore, important to the teachers as they sought to maintain a good record, none of them had originally chosen for himself to enter teaching. In all cases, rural parents had chosen their children's occupation since it provided the one opportunity for a salaried income without removing their child from the village. All other salaried occupations took children permanently away from the countryside. On the economic side, teacher training required the least investment and risk by the parents.

Just as the teachers were personally caught up in the civil service system, so was the school a direct extension of the bureaucracy. The headmaster had numerous required reports to file with the District Education Office. Over the period of a year, the headmaster filed 42 regular handwritten reports apart from special requests for statistical or other data, all of which were personally delivered to the District Office. The administrative workload was in addition to his regular full-time teaching responsibility in the school.

Since school success was identified with opportunities for further schooling that would lead to civil service positions, the organization of the school was definitely relevant to those who would succeed within it.

Much like the Philippine school, teachers were expected to contribute financially for school improvements and the costs of hospitality for visiting officials. Villagers thought this only fair since the teachers stood to benefit from the goodwill of their superiors. While the community accepted responsibility for building and repairing the school itself, they did expect disproportionate teacher contributions of cash and labour. Teachers must also participate in other communal projects in order to maintain community rapport and in order to be able to count on continuing community support of the school's needs. When conflicts arise between the desires of the community and a teacher's superiors in the civil service, however, it is the civil service that will prevail.

In the school curriculum literacy is complicated by the fact that the vernacular language of the Northeast is not Central Thai, the national language. All formal teaching is done in Central Thai and children must learn the language as well as reading and writing within it at the school. In the village, the national language is used outside the school primarily on ceremonial occasions. Further complicating the problem of language teaching is the official position that Central Thai and the Northeast dialect are so close as to pose no substantial learning problem. Thus teachers are directed to use Central Thai in all of their teaching and the teachers' main concern is to teach the children enough of the language to pass their required examinations. They do seem to be quite flexible in their use of the local dialect in the classroom, in spite of the formal proscription.

There appears to be no overt conflict in formal values between the schools and the community. Most of the learning is structured in rote fashion and teachers generally follow the detailed procedures in their official lesson manuals. Little attention is paid to the products of student effort – even in art. The American observer was shocked to see a teacher systematically destroying clay animals the children had made in an art lesson after he had entered a grade in his book for each child's production. Neither the children nor the teacher saw any intrinsic value in the objects.

Along with the subject matter prescriptions in the teachers' guides, teachers were instructed to conduct Boy and Girl Scout activities on a regular weekly basis.

In each of the four elementary grades there is a highly formalized system of evaluation including a yearly final examination that increases in importance as a child moves through the grades. Final exams for the first three grades are prepared at the District level and administered within the school. While the headmaster is held responsible for certifying the results of these exams, the District Education Officer must do so for the fourth grade. That exam is developed and administered on a province-wide basis with pupils from several schools assembled at a common testing site. During the fourth grade, teachers hold special evening and weekend classes to supplement their preparation for both the final examination and the entrance examinations to upper primary schools. No child is allowed to take the examination without an 80 per cent or better attendance record.

Thus both teachers and pupils are part of a highly formalized system in which they are judged by the results of examinations and admitted to the examinations, in the first place, by certified school attendance. From the very beginning of their school experience, children are subjected to the formal examination experience.

That schools are bureaucratically organized in both the Philippines and Thailand is an empirical fact – not a value judgment. Within this context the school obviously serves particular purposes for which it is recognized and supported by both local communities and educational authorities. It is in this context that suggestions for development-oriented school activities must be made.

Some Suggestions for Development Education

It has been the purpose of this presentation to suggest the need for an empirical view of the school as a social institution and of education as a cultural process occurring in many contexts, by no means limited to the school. The brief descriptions of two case studies of schools in Thailand and the Philippines were intended to show what such a view would reveal about schools in specific social contexts – their limitations and their strengths in developmental effectiveness.

Because much has been expected of the schools, the preceding descriptions appear quite caustic, regardless of their validity or generalizability. But certainly our professional disappointment must be directed beyond the schools to those who have expected the schools to be malleable multipurpose tools of unlimited development objectives. One unrealistic development objective, for instance, has been the goal of changing rural attitudes to conform to thinly disguised replicas of an idealized Protestant ethic. Such a goal has neither relevance to the needs of local development nor appropriateness within the schools described. More developmentally appropriate, but antithetical in the school contexts described, is an attempt to reinforce an attachment to rural patterns of livelihood. To the extent that schools are an extension of an attractive metropolitan-centred national bureaucracy, the models they present through teachers and the behaviours they value will be much more likely to prepare for and encourage rural defection. The underlying social message will be much clearer than the formal statements of texts and teachers.

There are two educational objectives which are easily defensible from the standpoint of rural development and from the realities of school institutions: (1) basic literacy, broadly conceived as the ability to use the skills of reading, writing, and arithmetic for real and local purposes, and (2) those skills and technologies relevant to survival in particular community context, which would seem to be the natural curriculum of schools in any setting. Local relevance of particular curricular content will be a matter of local perception and negotiation. Those skills and knowledge which already exist in the local community with established patterns for their transmission are not the stuff of effective curricular concern in the schools. It is those skills and knowledge which come from outside the community for which schools or alternative patterns of schooling are required. Where schools and development programmes exist, local communities are increasingly engaged in wide-ranging social, political, and economic transactions with larger and alien systems.

For both individual and community survival, people will need linguistic skills in the non-vernacular languages of their region; technological understanding and skills relevant to local resources; understandings of the economic and political systems and transactions which will inevitably impinge upon them and the ability to achieve their own purposes within this framework; understandings of their own relative locations in space (geography) and time (history) with reference to the rest of the world; and the abilities to deal with, and maintain some sense of individual and collective integrity within cultural systems foreign to the local community. These skills and understandings are not very different from the conventional elements of school curricula – it is just that their purpose as substantial skills and understandings for survival in the modern world has been submerged by the institutional forms used for their transmission and evaluation.

Ultimately, it will be necessary for the schools and their educational agents to negotiate regional and local adaptations of their curricular proposals with the communities in which they wish to establish them. Much like the models of agricultural extension agents, it is possible to bring national influence and purpose to bear upon local institutions and communities. In the end, legitimate national and international educational interests will be better represented and implemented in the local community when they are related to and made complementary with locally perceived needs.

REFERENCES

1. 'Professional' refers here to the administrators, teachers, supervisors, teachers of teachers, and others professionally involved with schools – those whom we usually label professional educators.
2. See Y. Cohen, 1971, for the beginnings of larger scale anthropological analysis of education and schooling.
3. Data and quotations in this section, unless otherwise noted, are taken from the two dissertations. Manalang and Gurevich are not, however, responsible for my interpretations.
4. One of the specific examples of the 'vacuum ideology' cited by the Waxes was a Filipino educator who contributed to the Philippine community school ideology by a pre-World War II experiment in community school organization on the US Pine Ridge Indian Reservation – the field location of the Waxes' research which led to their concern for the attitudes of teachers (1971: pp. 133–4).
5. A summary and discussion of research dealing with values attributed to peasants (Rogers 1969) and an excellent critical review of the implications of these statements (Castillo 1969) should be consulted by those who believe that the greatest development problem is the attitudes of people who 'should' change. As Castillo noted, 'We need to know and understand the motivations, attitudes, and values of planners, policy-makers, researchers – foreign "experts" included. The values of such people exert more influence in evolving so-called grassroots development programmes than we realize or care to admit.' (1969: p. 141).

BIBLIOGRAPHY

Milton L. Barnett, 'Subsistence and Transition Among the Ibaloi in the Philippines' in Clifton R. Wharton (ed.), *Subsistence Agriculture and Development* (Chicago: Aldine, 1969) pp. 284–95.

Gelia Castillo, 'A Critical View of a Subculture of Peasantry', in Clifton R. Wharton (ed.), *Subsistence Agriculture and Economic Development* (Chicago: Aldine, 1969) pp. 136–42.

Rosalie A. Cohen, 'Conceptual Styles, Culture Conflict, and Nonverbal Tests of Intelligence' *American Anthropologist*, 1969, 71: 828–56.

Yehudi Cohen, 'Schools and Civilizational States', in Joseph Fischer (ed.), *The Social Sciences and the Comparative Study of Education* (Scranton, Pa.: International Textbook Co, 1970) pp. 55–147.

H. Ward Goodenough, *Cooperation in Change: An Anthropological Approach to Community Development* (New York: Russell Sage Foundation, 1963).

Robert Gurevich, *Khru: A Study of Teachers in a Thai Village*, unpublished PhD Dissertation, University of Pittsburgh, 1972.

C. W. M. Hart, 'Contrasts Between Prepubertal and Postpubertal Education', in George D. Spindler (ed.), *Education and Anthropology* (Stanford: Stanford University Press, 1955) pp. 127–44.

Melville J. Herskovits, *Man and His Works: The Science of Cultural Anthropology* (New York: Alfred A. Knopf, 1948).

Robert and Eva Hunt, 'Education as an Interface Institution in Rural Mexico and the American Inner City', in John Middleton (ed.), *From Child to Adult: Studies in the Anthropology of Education* (New York: Natural History Press, 1970).

Ivan Illich, *Deschooling Society* (New York: Harper and Row, 1971).

Bronislaw Malinowski, *A Scientific Theory of Culture and Other Essays* (Chapel Hill: University of North Carolina Press, 1944).
The Dynamics of Cultural Change: An Inquiry into Race Relations in Africa (New Haven: Yale University Press, 1945).

Priscila S. Manalang, *A Philippine Rural School: Its Cultural Dimension*, unpublished PhD Dissertation, University of Pittsburgh, 1971.

Robert Redfield, *The Social Uses of Social Science* (Chicago: University of Chicago Press, 1963).

Everett Reimer, *School is Dead: Alternatives in Education* (Garden City, N.Y.: Doubleday, 1971).

Everett M. Rogers, 'Motivation, Values, and Attitudes of Subsistence Farmers: Towards a Subculture of Peasantry', in Clifton R. Wharton (ed.), *Subsistence Agriculture and Economic Development* (Chicago: Aldine, 1969) pp. 111–35.

Murray L. and Rosalie H. Wax, 'Great Tradition, Little Tradition, and Formal Education' in Murray L. Wax, Stanley Diamond, and Fred O. Gearing (eds.), *Anthropological Perspectives on Education* (New York: Basic Books, 1971a).
'Cultural Deprivation as an Educational Ideology' in Elanor Leacock (ed.), *The Culture of Poverty: A Critique* (New York: Simon and Schuster, 1971b) pp. 127–39.

Murray L. Wax, Rosalie H. Wax, and Robert V. Dumont. *Formal Education in an American Indian Community*, Monograph No. 1, Society for the Study of Social Problems, 1964.

7

Developing Educational Alternatives: Some New Ways for Education in Rural Areas

A. W. Wood

Despite the Illich furore, the principles of 'deschooling' have been applied for years in the rural parts of the low-income world. Where the formal elementary school has not been able to provide either a vehicle for basic education on a wide scale (e.g. in many parts of Africa), or where the returns from mass elementary schooling in terms of skills and attitudes conducive to development are increasingly questioned (e.g. in several Caribbean countries and Malaysia), the emergence of parallel systems of informal education is an accepted fact.

In many instances alternatives to formal education have developed as salvage operations moving behind the formal school system and seeking to pick up some of these young people who have dropped out of it, or perhaps more correctly were pushed out of it. They have a distinct 'second best' image, a factor which helps to account for many of the difficulties encountered by out-of-school education schemes in the early days in, first, retaining the loyalties of the young people who participated in them, and secondly, in involving these young people in the kind of vocational ends to which the schemes were directed (cf. the early difficulties of such differing experiments as the Swaneng Farmers Brigade in Botswana and the Western Nigeria Farm Settlement Scheme). Into this category fall many of the national youth service schemes which were a product of the late 1950s and early 1960s, sponsored by governments, aiming primarily to absorb, secondarily to train vocationally and otherwise, primary school leavers.

Arising from this, however, has been a more fundamental approach, starting from the basic premise that in many societies the hard-pressed primary school is not of much *direct* relevance in the stimulation of the development process in 'backward' communities. Secondly it is argued that there should be a more comprehensive cataloguing of the overall educational requirements of rural communities, with a consequent elaboration of education and training programmes designed to meet these requirements in whatever form is appropriate to the local situation. The product of this approach is already visible in a wide range of countries, covering the communication of vocational skills, social development needs or a combination of these. Clear examples are the educational aspects of the unofficial *ujamaa* village development programme in the Ruvuma District of Tanzania, the settlement and training programme of the Guyana Cooperative Union, the experimental multi-purpose training centres set up in Kenya as an aspect of the follow-up to the 1966 Kericho Conference on 'Education, Employment and Rural Development'. All of these examples make do with limited material structures and work to satisfy limited training goals in contexts in which these goals once achieved can have immediate application.

It is sought here to trace the evolution and diversification of alternative educational programmes for rural communities from what might be called the shock-absorber approach, aimed at a particular sector of society which presented a very visible need, towards community education in the broad sense and to indicate some of the working principles behind this latter approach.

On examination of the first category, an evolutionary process can again be observed. A convenient starting point is what might be defined as traditional (in a Western sense) youth work. Youth clubs spread throughout the developing world, often but not exclusively located in the towns, in roughly the same fashion as the primary school. As a consequence of the extreme selectivity of the conventional education system, the dropout adolescent – and potentially therefore the delinquent or extreme political activist – became the preoccupation of the missionary, of the voluntary worker, of the private philanthropic organizations in the commercial community such as Rotary or the Jaycees and ultimately of governments. In many countries there is a long history of such structures, frequently scantily equipped and staffed, aiming at offering young people in some cases recreational opportunity, in others shelter.

Urban and Rural Youth Centres

In Jamaica the original youth centres, located in both urban and rural areas are perhaps the classic examples of this method, what might be seen as the sporting approach to youth work. The formula offered was a fairly low-cost, permanently supervized building in and from which various recreational activities were organized. Similar centres were prompted in Kenya in the late 1950s as part of the Kenya Colonial Government's hasty reaction to the social factors which stimulated young adolescents to involve themselves in the Mau Mau rising. Malaysia, facing a not dissimilar situation in the 1950s, reveals a similar pattern – a widespread network of primarily recreational centres with initially at least no educational purpose.

The progressive transformation of these centres into informal education and training structures serving an assortment of development needs has gone ahead steadily in recent years. In Jamaica most centres now offer to the young people who become associated with them the opportunity, should they wish it, of beginning to acquire a usable skill; this might subsequently be developed further either at a residential youth training camp offering longer and more professionalized training courses or at a formal Labour Department vocational training institution. The centres in West Malaysia have evolved still further, both through the supplementation of their traditional social and cultural content by various vocational activities and, perhaps more hopefully, by the attribution of responsibility for village development among the Malay community to village youth groups. A group in Pahang District working outwards from a youth centre built from local materials by the members themselves includes in its overall programme such diverse activities as large-scale cooperative rice cultivation, running the village taxi, a poultry project, a nursery school for village children of pre-school age, training in typewriting and elementary bookkeeping, adult literacy and child care – in addition to the recreational and cultural programme which in a fairly traditional Muslim community is understandably prominent. In Botswana, where recent years have seen much innovative work in various aspects of informal education, the Mochudi Centre illustrates an even more complex evolution. In this case a village community centre, serving general recreational and cultural needs, first developed a series of small commercial and industrial activities, with the aim of setting up development models for the village as a whole; thereafter the Centre focused its activities heavily on a series of interrelated training and employment-creation schemes for young people out of school, covering activities such as cooperative ranching, dry land agriculture, building, leatherwork, as well as continuing and developing further the previous community work. Thus a conventional community programme was able to move in various directions to meet with more precision particular education and training needs in the immediate society.

Government and National Schemes

A similar development process can be seen in the large-scale governmental youth training programmes, the national youth services. These originate from a later era – in most cases dating from the period of attainment of national independence. They can be seen in certain respects as the critical reaction of new governments, anxious for development gains and anxious also to provide outlets for young people who could not be fitted into the selective formal educational systems, to a loose system of mainly voluntary youth activities which did not at the time appear to have much development-orientation or which was identified with alien norms. In Malawi one rapid consequence of the establishment in 1963 of the Malawi Young Pioneers[1] (whose programme is available in some respects to all Malawi youth in school, and a selected number of young people who are not so fortunate) was the abolition of conventional youth movements such as Boy Scouts and Girl Guides. The various services have many similarities – a somewhat military flavour, an emphasis on physical development and on various forms of morale boosting, in some cases frankly described as political education. The main common emphasis is on providing young people outside the conventional education streams with vocational skills.[2]

Initially, the training and absorption element was most prominent and there was little systematic thinking in the early stages of what the consequences of training might be. In the case of the Ghana Young Pioneers, the model in Africa at least for very many of the national youth services, although at the outset an employment-related training was considered, service with the Pioneers became in fact a full-time job. By the time of its abolition on the fall of President Nkrumah,[3] the Ghana Young Pioneers had all the trappings of a permanent career structure. In Malawi, which had certain direct affinities with the Ghana organization at the outset, an end to training was foreseen, it being assumed that after the ten month training period the former Pioneers would return to their villages and spread progressive ideas among the traditional community, while at the same time organizing local-level MYP clubs. The predictable reaction of the established community to the pressure from 'trained and motivated youth', coupled with the frustration of many of the young people concerned at the prospect of terminating their training with no prospect other than reversion to what they knew before, led MYP to attack systematically the central problem of the national youth services and their function in rural development, that is to consider how, through a structured settlement programme, MYP trainees could as a group, and with continued outside support both from the training organization and from other relevant agencies such as the Department of Agriculture, build what would amount to new villages and in so doing change the image of small-scale agriculture in Malawi.

This movement away from training *qua* training towards a consideration of how training can mesh with the employment situation at the end of it can be seen in the records of similar organizations elsewhere. The Zambia Young Pioneers have assumed the role of leading the way towards President Kaunda's vision of rural Zambia organized in diversified cooperatives. Cooperative groups are formed among trainees while still in the service. The service lends direct support to new cooperatives in the testing early phase after they have been established. Tanzanian National Service, at least those aspects of it not concerned with reconditioning the educated elite, feeds trained young people into the *ujamaa* village programme.

In Guyana the Tumatumari youth camp has set up its own settlement scheme and is closely involved in the priority programme for the development of the Guyanese hinterland. In a different respect the Jamaican youth camps, established since the mid 1950s, have also in recent years placed heightened emphasis on the development of effective job-placement services, linking the camps among other things to existing land settlement schemes so that trained ex-campers should receive special consideration in the selection of settlers for these. In Malaysia the principle has been projected one stage further in the youth settlements – in effect agricultural training schemes run along familiar national youth service lines but with the training being combined with the development of extensive tree-crop plantations to which the trainee ultimately as part of a cooperative group will have a title.

In the national youth services there has been a move towards solving the question 'training for what?'. There has perhaps not as yet been much consideration of how selective and intensive youth training can fit into the overall rural development picture. In many instances, the youth services have retained a image of the bulldozer in view of their association, particularly in Ghana and in Kenya, with large-scale public works. It could perhaps be argued that in their attitude towards the more subtle problems of bringing about change in rural communities, this image is inappropriate. With the obvious exception of Tanzania, the national youth services in their rural development aspects have turned their backs on existing rural society and gone ahead with the establishment of alternative systems; in some cases, especially in Malawi, this has been remarkably successful. Presumably the accusation that this is in fact an alternative form of plantation agriculture holds some force and that consequently the services with their considerable advantages of staff, material and specialist skills should broaden their focus in a more wide-reaching way to involve the established rural community more directly in their activities. There are no models as yet which could be related to this general need, the Tanzanian situation being unique to that country.

Smaller Schemes

On a smaller scale, however, outside the heavily structured national youth service schemes, there are several examples of the transformation of what began as a special youth training scheme into an overall community education programme. The Nyakashaka tea scheme in Western Uganda,[4] beginning with a carefully selected one hundred and twenty primary school leavers, has multiplied in its impact from being concerned with a small, as it turned out very privileged, group of young men into an agency which has caused an almost abandoned county to be repeopled, transformed its economy by the introduction of an unknown crop and acted as a progressive influence on the entire new community which returned to the Buhweju Hills following the project's success. On a wider scale, the present plans in Jamaica for integrating the Jamaican youth camps with the youth and community centres throughout the island are well advanced. Each camp becomes a major development centre for its area. The centres in turn, as well as providing various training courses at local level, feed into the camps and are serviced from them, thus pointing the way to a less narrowly focused national youth service.

The justification for the exercise by the national youth services of a broader community responsibility is, of course, their cost. All the services might be seen as creating a new form of privilege. With the exception of Malawi, where cost cutting has been given close consideration from the start, numbers of trainees have been low and training costs high. Given the investment required to keep them in being, it would seem important that such a valuable resource that the services represent be turned to the broadest possible use and that the benefit that could derive from them be shared more widely.

Whilst the national youth services can be seen as the governmental reaction to perceptibly growing needs outside the formal school system, the voluntary bodies which had themselves originally developed a concern for young people out of school also began to move towards more innovative methods of communicating skills and combating the social and economic problems of under-development. Arguably, it is in the experimental work of the non-governmental organizations from the mid-1960s onwards, working within realistic limitations of capital and manpower, that the real guidelines for widespread systems of informal education appropriate to the wider needs of developing rural areas can be seen.

The starting point is the fact that the voluntary bodies very frequently have the advantage of a close rapport with the people with which they are concerned. They tend to be less trammelled than governments by bureaucratic procedure. They do not have the disadvantage with which governments very frequently start out in all societies of being regarded as a creditor body to all. Simple examples of the latter phenomenon can be seen in the attitudes of those involved in the Ghana Workers' Brigade farms who successfully demanded a status for themselves as paid servants of government rather than participants in a settlement and training scheme. The position was similar in the Western Nigerian Farm Settlement Scheme where the eventual termination of government monthly subsidies to settlers produced wholesale desertions. Against this, the record of private settlement ventures such as Nyakashaka and Wambabya in Uganda stand out as remarkable examples of endurance in the initial stages by the settlers, inspiring leadership by the technical staff involved and comparatively low capitalization, all related in turn with what turned out to be two remarkably successful settlement and training schemes.

Private Experiments

The point is perhaps best illustrated by examining three different private experiments in three very different but not unrelated fields which illustrate a willingness to tackle a variety of needs in deprived rural communities; the 'Faith and Farm' rural training scheme in the Benue-Plateau State of Nigeria,[5] the craft training work of the Social Centre in Dominica in the Eastern Caribbean and the Project for Early Childhood Education in Jamaica.[6] Each of these projects is focused on different aspects of educational and social need in rural communities (although the Jamaican project has operated in both rural and urban areas). Their working method is in essence the same. It is to locate and understand what the milieu and the immediate community have to offer, develop a training programme around this local situation and by a slow and careful process build up on and improve that situation until the development process becomes self-generating.

The 'Faith and Farm' scheme was a consequence of much previous experimentation and frustration. The sponsoring organization, the Christian Rural Advisory Council, had sought for some years to develop appropriate training forms for improved young farmers. Institutional training away from the traditional agricultural situation was tried at length, with the consequence familiar in so many situations. Recruits could be found but after what understandably to the trainees appeared to be a lengthy course of post-primary education, the latter did not regard themselves as being farmer material. Their aspirations had risen above the aim of the training course. In consequence the course was radically restructured and indeed grafted on to another aspect of the agricultural work of the sponsoring organization – the promotion among selected farmers in the Benue area of ploughing with bulls. This exercise also had had a slow start. However, by 1960 a nucleus of progressive farmers had been established, using ploughing bulls otherwise unknown in the area and substantially improving on the normal returns of the small Benue-Plateau farmer. These farmers became in turn trainers, small groups of trainees being attached for a full cropping cycle to the farmer's own household, sharing his everyday tasks with him, learning the techniques of handling ploughing bulls, periodically being visited in the workplace by the training team. At the end of the training period transfer was organized from the trainer/farmer to the former trainee's own holding, initially very close to his former master. The trainee himself would be loaned the capital to equip himself with bulls and a steel plough after which, apart from occasional follow-up visits by the training team, and the proximity of his former 'master', the trainee was on his own. Over the period 1960 to 1968, the wastage rate from the scheme was approximately 20 per cent. By 1968, all trainers, now named master farmers, were themselves former trainees.

The Dominican example contrasts sharply in its nature. Dominica has little employment to offer outside small-scale agriculture, and the problem is particularly difficult for girls. The Social Centre's craft training and production scheme started therefore from the premise that adolescent girls out of school presented a particular training need. The answer initially lay in the development of the Dominican mat-making industry which has won for itself something of an international reputation in a region where the standard of craft work is not particularly high. As in the Nigerian case, the first task was the availability of a suitable raw material, a particular long grass suitable for craft purposes, building up the design ideas, setting up the training structures and organizing the production and marketing. Once again the training element was one component in an overall scheme. The unusual aspect of the Dominican project is that in its overall operation it combined the promotion of village industry involving the adult community – collecting and preparing the grasses and the execution of the first part of the actual production process in the villages – with the youth training and production facet, in this case the final work of producing the finished mat, located in the central workshop.

Thirdly, the Project for Early Childhood Education, Jamaica (PECE) and again the same principle in operation is revealed – locating what is on the ground and centring the development effort on this. In PECE's case what was available was an unusual Caribbean educational institution, the basic school, in many respects the product of the West Indian islands' peculiar social history.

In effect the basic school remains a privately run (and often privately owned) establishment where children from the Jamaican poorer classes receive from the age of three upwards (normally until enrolment in primary school at six years of age) whatever the proprietor perceives as an appropriate educational foundation. The proprietors typically are middle-aged ladies primarily concerned to supplement their income. The customers are the children of working mothers from the poorer sectors of society, a particularly important feature of Jamaican society where fathers are often not present in the home and mothers are of necessity the bread-winners. The schools are located in various unusual situations, from verandahs, to garages, to shady trees, but most usually in community centres or church halls. Prior to the launching of the Project, no systematic attempt had been made to reach the basic school teachers or to improve their teaching performance; indeed a former Minister of Education had written off the basic school teachers as 'unteachable'.

From 1966 to 1972 an experimental training team operated from the University of the West Indies Institute of Education trying to disprove this contention. The training approach was based on three operating premises; firstly, close day-by-day contact with the teachers in their schools, by peripatetic project supervisors, building up confidence on both sides; secondly, the preparation and distribution of tightly structured lesson guides indicating in exact terms a teaching programme over a two-week period, this programme being in turn rehearsed with the teachers at fortnightly one-day training sessions in local community centres; thirdly, twice yearly one-week training sessions at the University, something of a traumatic experience for teachers who rarely move very far from their own community. That the formula works can be indicated by some of the research findings on the Project so far[7] which show PECE children behind but not still falling behind children in middle-class nursery schools and in turn gaining progressively on children in basic schools outside the Project. By other indicators the Project has also succeeded. The Jamaican Ministry of Education has set up its own training team on PECE lines and using PECE materials. The Jamaican Basic School Teachers Association flourishes. Politicians associate themselves happily with new building projects. Parents readily attend work sessions to make learning materials, repair furniture, and maintain buildings. The unteachable have been taught.

Conclusions

It is evident that the rural areas of the developing world constitute a clear case of what current jargon would rate as multiple deprivation. Faced with such a situation, there is probably little that education in itself, whether of the conventional in-school variety or of the less usual out-of-school sort can achieve. As far as the out-of-school sector goes, over the last two decades there has been a mounting volume of experimentation by governments and voluntary bodies which have produced in limited areas their own solid achievements. The Kenya National Youth Service has demonstrated that road construction in remote areas and pre-vocational training can be effectively, and indeed economically, combined.[8] In Malawi it has been shown that low-cost agricultural settlements, emphasizing a large measure of self-help, can succeed even when high-aspiring primary school leavers are involved.[9] In the voluntary sector, youth settlements and youth training in Western Uganda and Northern Nigeria have shown in the one case dramatic economic returns, and in both cases that effective training does not require heavy inputs in terms of training structures. In Jamaica rural-based training camps feed the burgeoning Jamaican hotel industry with chefs and waiters. In Jamaica also the rural child in his early years can now receive through informal and improvised structures, and through teachers with the most marginal of academic backgrounds, an early stimulus hitherto confined only to the privileged urban-dwelling child.

Despite these achievements (and not overlooking the many failures) all these approaches have one shared characteristic which perhaps detracts from their value in regard to the broader, more diffused problem of overall rural backwardness. This is clearly that their focus is normally on one of the manifestations of what is a multi-faceted phenomenon, with perhaps in certain examples a secondary incidental impact on other areas. In the most successful cases in terms of the promotion of economic transformation, for example the Nyakashaka Scheme in Uganda, it would appear that the repercussions of the youth settlement on the area as a whole have been felt in matters such as roads, housing, formal educational and other social facilities, the general raising of wealth of the local population apart from the settlers themselves. However, the particular conditions which produced the Nyakashaka Scheme, although perhaps they can be found in other situations, are highly localized and of limited replicability. Indeed it might well be argued that such 'successes' can have a distorting effect on the formulation of a practical training strategy for rural development as a whole since they tend to lend support to the 'backing winners' philosophy with its stress on the 'selective/intensive' approach to rural communities, an approach which might cynically be seen as locating the rural privileged and assisting them to become more so.[10] Viewed another way, achievements in one sector can be vitiated by continued stagnation in another – agriculturally trained youth in a traditional farming community; 'stimulated' Jamaican pre-schoolers in unregenerate primary schools.

The question remains whether training and development models can be set up which accept the 'deprived' rural community in its totality and through the communication of information, skills, back-up facilities, assist that community to move forward organically. In such a situation the demarcation between in-school and out-of-school education would be blurred as would the distinction between what constitutes education in the broad sense and specific development activities. There are few achievements so far which give any practical guidelines. The Tanzanian *ujamaa* village idea subscribes outwardly to many of these precepts and is built upon an educational plan which is refreshingly frank about the limitations (and potentialities) of the formal primary school. It is perhaps to the non-governmental origins of the *ujamaa* village idea – the former Ruvuma Development Association – that one should look for a starting point. By the time of their dissolution in 1969, fourteen villages had emerged, built on the work of the founding village at Litowa, farming cooperatively, cooperatively developing small industries, setting up their own formal school facilities with a highly diversified curriculum emphasizing the potential contribution even of children in school to village development,[11] providing on-the-spot various forms of appropriate vocational training (with specialized assistance where necessary) in areas such as dispensary work, tractor driving and maintenance, bookkeeping, and finally providing different forms of adult education ranging from literacy to political education. The official move against the Association culminating in its dissolution in 1969 is perhaps an outstanding instance of the inability of the administrative elite, even when working within a political system which recognizes the need for self-reliance at village level, to accept that the direction of their own development efforts should lie in the hands of village people and not in the hands of an omniscient, paternalistic bureaucracy.

The second example of the community education approach is contained in the later development of the Swaneng experiment in Botswana. This experiment, which itself provides an excellent instance of the tortuous evolution of educational forms appropriate to a highly deprived rural community,[12] has moved from a low-cost, self-reliant secondary school, to an increasingly diversified youth training scheme covering perhaps a wider range of activities than any comparable project at least in Africa (cattle-farming, dry-land agriculture, leatherwork, lime-burning, soap-making, textiles, weaving, engineering, building and carpentry among others) to the ultimate evolution of the *boiteko* idea, itself a product of the youth training activities. In a widely diversified training programme such as the Swaneng brigades offer, the problem of employment after training presents special difficulties except in training areas such as building which are in demand in the modern sector of the economy. Swaneng is prepared to meet this demand but only up to a point. The main emphasis in the informal education activities based on the Swaneng complex has swung round to focus on the village community and how the reserves of skill and know-how which the Swaneng brigades constitute can be brought to bear on the traditional village and on the deprived sections of the village communities who are untouched by even the relatively low-level brigade activities. *Boiteko* is designed with two purposes. Firstly, it is an opportunity for village people, without any strictures on age, but inevitably to a large degree young people, to come together for a practical training and production activity. The association offers various practical activities, as well as cultural and social activities, with which the education and training as well as managerial resources of Swaneng are associated. Theoretically goods produced within *boiteko* are exchanged among the members, thus satisfying needs (for bricks, boots or milk, for example) or sold and the returns diverted back to the members. Secondly, since the assumption is that the *boiteko* idea will spread out from Serowe to other villages (one additional village has been so far located) and these villages will in turn require leadership and training in the skills which the Swaneng brigaders have to offer, it is expected that *boiteko* will provide a long-term solution to the post-training problems of the Swaneng brigades. More important it is designed to provide a formula for organic as opposed to selective development and for the diffusion of modernizing ideas through whole communities.

The other side of education is nothing new in the low-income countries of the world. Indeed despite the fulminations of international gatherings on educational plans and the imposition of regional and national targets for school enrolment, which perhaps give an impression of a preoccupation with the idea of education as a matter of desks and square feet per pupil, there has been in these countries a hard-headed awareness that school systems are an inadequate base upon which to base expectations for a change in attitudes at a popular level towards development and for the production of the practical skills necessary to foster this. This perhaps tacit recognition has given rise to a very wide diversity of experimentation designed to devise alternative educational vehicles. What remains is the task of pulling together conclusions on this body of experience, recognizing that in practice the product of 'deschooling' also has numerous limitations, and the shifting from this of those lines of development which appear most appropriate to the real needs of deprived rural communties.

REFERENCES

1. The first training course of the newly constituted Malawi Young Pioneers was launched in August 1963 although in the previous year nine instructors went to Ghana for training with the Ghana Young Pioneers. MYP was radically reorganized in 1964; the organization in its present form dates from then.
2. For a brief overview, see 'Special Youth Employment and Training Schemes for Development Purposes', paper for ILO Conference, 53rd Session, Geneva 1969.
3. The Young Pioneers were abolished. The consequences in terms of employment of abolishing the equally Nkrumahist Young Farmers League and Workers Brigade deterred even the Ankrah Government. These latter bodies have survived two further changes of government.
4. See C. R. Hutton, 'Making Modern Farmers: Case Study of the Nyakashaka Resettlement Scheme for Unemployed School-Leavers', paper delivered to African Studies Association (UK) September 1967 and also in *African Affairs*, vol. 67, no. 267, April 1968. Also A. W. Wood 'The Experiment at Nyakashaka' in *Youth and Development in Africa*, Commonwealth Secretariat, 1970, pp. 177–85.

5. See P. Batchelor 'Faith and Farm' – a Community Orientated Rural Training Project in *Youth and Development in Africa*, pp. 186–94.

6. See *The Project for Early Childhood Education*, Bernard van Leer Foundation, The Hague, 1972.

7. Various mimeographed papers on research findings by N. Wein on the Project for Early Childhood Education are available from PECE Centre, University of the West Indies Institute of Education, Kingston, Jamaica.

8. See G. Griffin in *Youth and Development in Africa*, pp. 195–206.

9. See A. W. Wood 'Training Malawi's Youth, the Work of the Malawi Young Pioneers' in *Community Development Journal*, July 1970.

10. Guy Hunter in *Modernising Peasant Societies* (London: Oxford University Press, 1969, p. 94), ably sets out the case against this approach, citing in support the record of the early agricultural stages of the Japanese Entwicklungswunder whereby '. . . . the increase in farm output and productivity . . . resulted from the widespread introduction of improved techniques by the great majority of the nations farmers' . . .

11. Described at length by S. M. Toroka in 'Education for Self-Reliance', a paper for CREDO/EDC Conference on Social Studies in Africa, Mombasa, August 1968.

12. Various papers by Patrick van Rensburg, the initiator of the Swaneng experiments, have been gathered together for publication by the Dag Hammarskjöld Foundation, Uppsala, Sweden. See also van Rensburg's contributions to *Youth and Development in Africa* and *Education in Rural Areas*, Commonwealth Secretariat, 1970.

8

The Educational Needs of Farmers in Developing Countries

E. Ronald Watts

Introduction

Education is only one of a range of factors influencing agricultural development. Much of the controversy over its role has resulted from exaggerated claims for what education can achieve. As Harbison[1] has pointed out, 'education becomes a relevant factor in economic growth only when it is properly integrated with all other factors in development'. By itself education can achieve relatively little. Mosher[2] only lists education under his five 'accelerators' for agricultural development rather than under what he terms the 'essentials'. This is a clear indication of its role as a catalyst of development rather than a basic ingredient.

In order to determine the educational needs of farmers, we need to relate them to Mosher's 'essentials' and 'accelerators'. His five essentials are incentives, markets, transport, input supplies and research. The five accelerators are education, credit, group action, an improving land base and planning. In many countries education has failed to produce results because it has been superimposed on a situation where one or more of the essentials were absent. Virtually all of the essentials have little direct connexion with education. Incentives, largely through the prices obtained for farm products, are in many areas uncertain because of the absence or ineffectiveness of controlled prices. Markets are strongly influenced by government in most countries, although well-run cooperatives may give farmers some control. Transport and inputs are, in many nations, provided by private enterprise although there is scope for farmers to organize these themselves. Research is invariably a function of government.

It is usually accepted that educated farmers are more innovative, have higher incomes and are more knowledgeable than illiterate farmers. However, there are also indications that education can have an adverse effect on a peasant farming situation. Odeke,[3] commenting on his home area in Uganda, considered that 'illiterate people tend to be more effective agriculturally'. Most farmers in the area were found to be old people. While education may help understanding, it can also depress people's motivation for the hard work which is inevitable in a small-scale peasant farming situation. Too rapid a development of literacy in Ghana may well account for the rapid inflation in food prices despite a high level of unemployment that has been seen in recent years.

Education has had a negative influence where it has been applied in isolation. In fact, any of the 'accelerators' if stressed in a situation where one or more of the 'essentials' are missing can lead to frustration. The world abounds with agricultural programmes started without a secure market for the product being promoted. Farmers are taught the techniques but are frustrated when they cannot sell what they produce. As a result, they may well be less responsive to future efforts to assist them. Schultz[4] concludes that education is of most importance where improved factors of production must precede a rise in output.

If economic development were to become the main preoccupation of developing countries, it is likely that the proportion of government finance spent on education, health and defence would be reduced. At present many developing nations pay lip-service to their concern for economic development but, in practice, do not give it high enough priority when they allocate resources. Country after country is going through a financial crisis brought about by a too rapid expansion in government expenditure and bureaucracies have swelled until they have outstripped the ability of the economy to pay for them. The main sufferers are the rural population, most of whom are farmers. In many developing countries, they are faced with constant or falling prices for their products, accompanied by rampant inflation on the things they want to buy.

The Needs of Farmers

For several thousand years farmers have farmed without having received any formal education. They have, of course, acquired skills and knowledge but this has been largely handed down from father to son rather than acquired from outside the family and even today for millions of farmers this is the main source of information. However, a survey by the author in Kenya, in an area with one extension worker to only 200 farmers,[5] found that the extension worker was a major source of information even on a fairly specialized subject (Table 1).

Traditional skills and knowledge have in the past been adequate in areas where agriculture has changed very little but there are few areas of the world where this situation still exists. Many developing countries are dependent on agricultural export expansion for any considerable improvement in their standard of living. Where there has been substantial non-agricultural development, such as in Zambia, this has often been accompanied by food shortages. To meet these challenges farmers

TABLE 1

INFORMATION SOURCES FOR MAIZE GROWING PRACTICES IN EMBU DISTRICT
KENYA, 1966

Information Source mentioned	Number of mentions	Per cent
Non-Agricultural Department Sources		
Neighbour	79	21
Traditional knowledge or parent	21	6
Formal education	2	0
Experience	22	6
Agricultural Department Sources		
Farmer Training Centre	108	29
Research Station	18	5
AO and AAO	0	0
TA	59	16
JAA	37	16
Combination (Demonstrations, Field Days, etc.)	28	7
	374	100

need new knowledge and new skills. Well-planned education should also help to equip farmers for the increasingly commercial approach that they will need to adopt.

Wharton[6] has suggested that a farmer requires three major kinds of new knowledge if he wishes to change. First he needs knowledge about new inputs, secondly knowledge about new techniques of production and thirdly economic knowledge. He stresses rightly the need for farmers to be good businessmen as well as farmers. Wharton also points out (op. cit., page 214) that extension education programmes have too often stressed technical knowledge and neglected the equally important economic knowledge.

Farmers need to go beyond the production orientated kind of knowledge stressed above. In many countries greater knowledge of nutrition and in the wider field of health education could have a major impact. Research in East Africa[7] indicates that much time is lost in visiting dispensaries both by farmers and their wives. Malnutrition amongst children must limit their contribution to farm labour. A broad science-orientated education should help to create farmers who can respond to the challenges they will undoubtedly meet in the future. The lack of a scientific approach to farming is a stumbling block even to many of today's educated farmers; too often such farmers reject profitable innovations because they misinterpret their initial trials.

Teso District in Uganda provides an interesting example of a technical innovation being introduced with too little stress on basic education. Teso is remarkable for the speed with which the area adopted ox cultivation in place of the traditional hand hoe. Today virtually all primary cultivation is done by oxen whereas in many other areas of the country the hand hoe is still the most important cultivation tool. It is remarkable that between 1923 and 1935 ploughs increased from under 300 to around 12,000[8] and the cotton acreage increased by 100 per cent. But a report in 1937 stated that the Iteso are 'still essentially a very primitive tribe'. Yields fell over the 1921–35 period by some 20 per cent. Today Teso is still a problem area as regards agriculture and there seems little chance of an early solution to the problems of falling yields and overgrazing.

A major need for the farmers of the future is in the area of practical skills. These are difficult to teach through formal school education. Often they are highly specialized and if they are taught too early they may be forgotten by the time they can be used. Ideally they need to be taught to those who are already committed to farming for they can then make fairly immediate use of the skills. Ideal for this purpose are the Farmers Training Centres now being developed by many African countries. Table 1 shows that such centres can be major sources of information as well as centres of skill training.

Wharton points out that skill training and practical knowledge of agriculture are a major deficiency in most developing countries. It is, of course, true that many of those being trained to teach farmers come themselves from farming backgrounds. However they have often been divorced from practical farming by several years in boarding schools and if they have any farming skills at all they are usually the traditional skills which farmers already possess. There is a great need for special programmes designed to improve agricultural skills amongst extension staff, teachers and leaders of the farming community: these could include apprenticeship schemes, pre-entry practical training for all agricultural courses and short courses. To supplement such programmes there is a need for a series of proficiency tests so that staff have some level to aim at. Amongst government employees these would need to be supplemented by financial incentives such as promotion bars or special allowances.

The Role of Primary Education

We have seen in the previous section that technical innovation can take place in a situation where few if any farmers are literate. However the experience of Teso District gives but one example of the frustrations that may follow. One technical innovation such as ox ploughing is not enough. For if it is not followed by other innovations the results may be disappointing. In Teso District there are now serious labour shortages at weeding time and a critical need exists for crop sequences that will minimize these labour bottlenecks. Increased acreages under cultivation mean more attention must be devoted to insect pest control. While illiterate farmers may have readily adopted the original ox ploughing innovation they seem to have been reluctant to adopt the *complementary* innovations, which would have provided a real breakthrough. Agricultural development involves a sequence of innovations and adjustments which increasingly demand a more sophisticated and hence better educated farming community.

While education is an important factor in the whole picture of agricultural development it may not be so critical in individual cases. A study by the author of 'progressive'* farmers in Embu District, Kenya, in 1966 showed a very wide range of educational background. A more recent survey in Uganda[9] has produced the interesting results summarized in Table 2. This shows a general correlation between years of education and

TABLE 2

RELATIONSHIP BETWEEN YEARS OF EDUCATION OF FARMERS
AND VARIOUS OTHER FACTORS. UGANDA. 1970
(Percentages unless otherwise stated)

	Years at school					
	None	1 or 2	3 or 4	5 or 6	7 or 8	9 and over
Use of mass media score (9 and over)	2	11	21	36	69	75
Extension participation score (over 20)	19	15	24	31	36	42
Adoption of farming practices score (over 150)	3	3	12	19	30	36
Mean Annual Income (Shillings)	478	644	822	980	1,448	1,912
No ploughing implement	74	65	69	63	54	57
Traditional type house with thatched roof	60	50	48	49	42	34

various factors which are related to progressiveness in the broad sense. Perhaps of most interest is the mean income figure. It seems likely that a substantial part of the income of the over nine years schooling group may come from non-farm sources and further studies in this direction would be of great interest. It would seem from the writer's experience that other factors such as army service, travel and particularly experience in business outside of farming may be equally as important as education in affecting

* 'Progressive' here is used in the official sense of being a farmer who is cooperating with the Government's Agricultural Department.

the performance of a farmer although in the broadest sense these could all count as part of 'education'. The crucial point that should be made is that farming in all countries is increasingly becoming a business. Even primary education needs to be orientated more towards simple skills of business and this is particularly important in the developing countries where so many children receive no further formal education once they leave primary school. This business orientation is of greater importance than the teaching of detailed agricultural skills.

Agriculture as a primary school subject has been a dismal failure in most countries. The fault has not been primarily that of the subject itself for the main problems have been the teachers and the way in which the subject has been taught. For years it was thought that agriculture should be taught very practically to show the dignity of labour, but the practical side lacked interest and children who slaved for their parents at home were not interested in great physical effort at school. Nigeria in the 1950s made a brave attempt to get away from this image; specialist teachers were trained in Rural Education Centres; school gardens were regularly inspected and an effort made to devise a broad syllabus. There was however still too much routine practical work due to the plot sizes selected. Moreover, the preoccupation that British-trained agriculturalists have with *rotations* has also contributed to the designing of school gardens with large areas requiring annual cultivation. This is quite unnecessary in those tropical countries whose main crops are perennial.

There is no doubt that agriculture can stand on its own as a primary school subject but the syllabus should not be designed to produce skilled farmers. Topics would be selected on a basis of their potential interest to primary school children and the subject could of course be termed 'Rural Science' although the agricultural content should remain considerable.

The emphasis on agriculture at the primary level should be retained so long as secondary education is for the favoured few. Such an emphasis will be made easier by the changes in age of entry for primary education. Castle[10] in a recent study favours what he considers to be almost identical proposals in Tanzania and India (the Wardha Scheme). These both involve a schooling period of only seven years and a delay of age of entry to seven years. Nyerere's proposals in Tanzania include a strong case for the inclusion of agriculture in primary schools.

Post-primary Education

In several developed countries agriculture has been taught at the secondary school level. In Britain this emphasis has usually been confined to a small number of rural or private schools but in the United States the vocational agriculture programme was a much larger affair. It was natural, however, that as the percentage of the population employed in agriculture dropped

(1·7 per cent of all employees in the UK by 1970) this emphasis would be continuously reduced.

It will be many years before a substantial number of secondary school leavers become farmers in most developing countries. In Kenya a pioneer programme based on the American Vo-Ag schools has now been expanded to cover the whole country. But a follow-up study by Maxwell,[11] the first teacher of the pioneer programme, reveals that very few have become farmers although a number have gone for further training and are performing a useful role in the farming industry.

Uganda pioneered a special type of secondary school which did not feed into the higher education system. These 'Farm Schools' were all closed down during 1969–70 but at least one of them was successful enough for the experience to be useful to other countries such as Tanzania, which seems to be moving in that direction. The Busoga Farm School at Wairaka near Jinja is described by Castle as a 'model of its kind'. The history of farm schools[12] dates from 1934 when two grants were given to Catholic and Anglican missionaries to start schools of this type. Their subsequent failure was due to intermittent finance, poor staffing and the obstructiveness of both colonial and indigenous bureaucracies. Agricultural education too often falls between the stools of Agriculture and Education. The final closedown of all schools of this type in 1970 was due to their being handed over from the Ministry of Education to the Ministry of Agriculture without any allocation of funds to run them.

However, enough is now known about the Uganda experience to mount a thorough farm school programme. Table 3 demonstrates that to train people to be farmers does not necessarily make them into farmers, for without land, capital and few profitable enterprises the opportunities for making a reasonable living are limited in most countries.

TABLE 3

OCCUPATIONS OF BUSOGA FARM SCHOOL LEAVERS. 1959–70

	No.	%
Farmers on own land	42 ⎫	
Tenant farmers	8 ⎬	15
Teachers (mainly Agriculture)	44	13
Employed on Estates, etc	80	24
Government (mainly Agriculture)	126	38
Working in Business (not Agriculture)	18 ⎫	
Police and Army	6 ⎬	10
Miscellaneous	9 ⎭	
Total	—	—
	333	100

(Not a random survey but covered all who could be contacted out of 639 ex-students).

Although only 15 per cent of ex-students were actually farming on their own, some 90 per cent were usefully employed in agricultural occupations. From this viewpoint the Farm School cannot be said to have been a failure.

If a major objective is to produce farmers then programmes must go beyond training. They must be provided with land and capital, and have access to relatively guaranteed outlets for produce. Further, intensive follow-up is needed. Without these elements farmers will not be produced. Indeed some of the most successful schemes for producing farmers have included a minimal amount of formal education. Thus Stephen Carr's settlement schemes[14] in Sudan and Uganda have been based on commitment to the land first and training second. Training consists of on-the-job instruction when a task is due to be performed and each primary school leaver settler is visited approximately once a week. The schemes in Uganda are fortunate in having been based on high value cash crops such as tea and it would be virtually impossible to mount similar schemes for food crops to be sold on the free market: price fluctuations when one is competing with subsistence producers are too great for a commercial farmer to stay in business for long unless he has great technical advantages.

Adult Education

The idea of commitment to farming as a prerequisite for training fits well into the arguments put forward by Darling[15] for concentrating on short courses at residential centres. These centres are not, however, an alternative to non-vocational agriculture in primary and secondary schools. In fact there is a strong movement throughout East and Central Africa for the expansion of Farmer Training Centres and both Kenya and Uganda now have such institutions serving all the major agricultural areas of the country. Uganda experimented with long-term training on small-holdings as early as the 1930s but the trend now is toward shorter courses of a week or less. Such training is more effective when farmers already have some basic education and a Uganda report in 1934 commented that better results would be obtained 'if pupils were better educated'[16]. A more recent study by the present author showed that Farm Institutes in Uganda tend to take a high proportion of farmers who have had some education already (Table 4).

As Farmer Training Centre courses become more sophisticated and oriented to commercial farming, it may be necessary to have some basic entry qualification for certain courses, for the mixing together of illiterate and literate farmers in the same course may, in the end, suit neither group. Increasingly a knowledge of English or some other international language is important for understanding the more technical aspects of agriculture.

TABLE 4

EDUCATIONAL LEVEL OF FARMERS ATTENDING DISTRICT FARM INSTITUTES COMPARED
WITH THE EDUCATIONAL LEVEL OF FARMERS IN THE AREAS SERVED, 1968
(Percentages)

	Farmers attending		100 Per cent Survey of Villages		
	Tororo DFI	Mukono DFI	Bumboli	Kimwanyi	Nalyama-gonja
No formal education	12	3	54	30	46
Over 8 years education	7	32	8	10	10
Can speak some English	47	47	31	22	23
Can read Luganda	95	100	45	74	60

At Kenya's Large-scale Farmers Training Centres the courses are directed at owners and managers farming areas of hundreds or even thousands of acres. Much of the content of these courses is directed to instruction on the operation and maintenance of farm machinery and to take full advantage of them (they last over six months) farmers need to understand both Swahili and English as well as their tribal language. Ability to read instructions on manuals and on the labels of agricultural chemicals is also important and, as with small-scale farmers, financial success increasingly depends on the ability to keep and use records and accounts.

Table 1 has shown that the Farmer Training Centre in one typical Kenya district was a major source of knowledge. As a distinct source of information it had more mentions than the extension staff despite a very dense staffing rate. At the time of this author's study in 1966 there was approximately one member of the Agricultural Department to every 200 holdings (5, page 71). The fact that these staff did not score more highly is probably a reflection of the fact that a high proportion of them had received very inadequate training for the job; many of the older, semi-literate staff could not speak English and so could not benefit fully from short course training. This apparent failure of the extension staff in this particular case does not mean that agricultural extension itself must always fail in a developing country. In general I would agree with Ruthenburg[17] when he states: 'A well managed agricultural extension service, supported by training, research, small loans and social work at village level, represents the most effective instrument for promoting agricultural development.' To this I would only add that there must be viable innovations for the extension service to feed to farmers and these will invoke the supply of profitable inputs and particularly provision for marketing and price control of the end product.[18]

Although viable programmes for increased agricultural production are the way to rural development their success depends on whether farmers can readily apply their new knowledge and skills. If there are bottlenecks in marketing or if over-production leads to serious falls in price, extension instruction can lead to frustration among them. In Uganda a national campaign to promote onion growing in the late 1960s ended in frustration. Farmers succeeded in growing the new crop and technically it was a success. Where the campaign failed was at the national and regional level for there were inadequate channels for marketing and storage, and a flood of the crop on to small local markets led to catastrophic falls in price.

Functional literacy plus major investments in agricultural extension are probably best concentrated in areas where new profitable enterprises are being introduced. Fogg[19] shows, using Nigerian statistics, that small-holder investment schemes can give an output : government input ratio of from 26:1 (oil palm) to 37:1 (rubber). This compared very favourably with plantations which give a ratio of only 2·3:1 (oil palm) to 2·8:1 (rubber). Research in East Africa by Ruthenburg has also shown that there is often a direct return to government from expenditure on agricultural extension through increased taxation. In view of the acute financial problems of most developing countries government expenditure will increasingly have to be justified in this way.

Education for Women

No distinction has been made in this paper between the educational needs of men and women farmers. Women are a major part of the farming community in many developing countries. A survey by the author in Uganda showed that in one part of Buganda Region only about 60 per cent of farms were solely controlled by a man (Table 5).

A study of 1968 Department of Agriculture Annual Reports revealed that between 16 and 47 per cent of those attending Farm Institutes were

TABLE 5
STATUS OF PERSON IN CHARGE OF FARMS IN THREE SAMPLES OF FARMERS.
BUGANDA REGION, UGANDA, 1967. (Percentage)

	Kimwanyi Village (all farms)	Nalyamagonja Village (all farms)	Farmers attending Mukono DFI*
Husband	59	58	41
Wife	18	7	22
Widow	11	8	3
Joint control by husband and wife	5	18	22
Others	7	8	12

* DFI – District Farm Institute (Ugandan name for a Farmers Training Centre)

women. The lowest figure was for Karamoja District where women have yet to be emancipated. The higher figure is for Buganda where women wield considerable power in the rural areas. Of the 47 per cent, however, very few were attending specialized farming courses.

There is now much greater emphasis on the training of women farmers in East Africa. All Farm Institutes in Uganda now have women Vice Principals and between 1961 and 1965 attendance by women at the Kenyatta Farmers Training Centre in Kenya rose from nil to 609. Indeed, in the last three years women have outnumbered men. However the training of women alone is less useful than joint trading for in many situations the husband is still the arbiter, particularly where a new technique costs money.

Special courses for women have been mounted in some Farmers Training Centres and these tend to concentrate on the area of Home Economics. But even within agriculture there is room for specialization, for in many countries there is a pattern where women concentrate on food crops while the men deal with the cash crops for export. Increasingly however, as towns grow, 'food' crops become 'cash' crops, and thus even courses for women should emphasize the commercial aspects of production. As Ruthenburg states, 'The promotion of cash crop production is in the long run . . . a better starting point for improving the nutrition of farm families. The idea that the development cycle begins with better nutrition should be regarded sceptically' (page 62).

This is not to say that nutrition education should cease or be underplayed: it is extremely important for healthy, well fed farmers are obviously more productive than malnourished ones. However, the core of the development cycle is economic: only when farmers increase their incomes can there be a major long term improvement in their standard of living and this fact must be central to *any* educational programme which is directed towards promoting agricultural development.

The Future for Agricultural Education

Agricultural education, while of declining interest in the developed countries, seems to be on the rise in other parts of the world. Stimulated by problems of school-leaver unemployment and the need for more exports, many third world countries are anxious to stimulate greater agricultural production. There is also a desire to cut down the enormous annual budgets for education by making schools more self-sufficient, for they could then develop self-reliant children who would not be so dependent on obtaining employment.

There is, at the same time, a move towards more integrated efforts at rural development: piecemeal schemes have too often failed. Intensified agricultural extension in a situation of over-production of food crops has led to frustration followed by stagnation. Production campaigns with no guaranteed markets have led to complete disenchantment with government extension services. Functional literacy programmes have too often yielded disappointing results in a static agricultural situation. Yet a number of countries, ranging from India to Kenya and Uganda, have made serious attempts to develop comprehensive rural programmes. The most adventurous, like the Kenya Special Rural Development Programmes, aim to cover aspects as diverse as roads, schools, crop production and marketing. Obviously the education of farmers will play a critical role in such programmes. But the emphasis is increasingly on educating those who are *already* farmers rather than those who might become farmers in the future.

There is increasing recognition that the problems of rural development are primarily economic. Even the poorest farmers save against a 'rainy day' but where they are deficient is in the ability to invest their savings to obtain the largest return. Education for rural development must increasingly stress the keeping of accounts and their use. Ways of developing entrepreneurial ability through student-run cooperative societies, farms and shops should be found. There may also be a case for relaxing restrictions on trading in order to encourage more business activity amongst young people, for it must be remembered that a successful farmer is invariably first a successful businessman.

One of the challenges facing both developed and developing countries is the increasing complexity of modern life. An agriculturalist trained in his teens is out of date before he is 30 unless he has constant re-training. Farmers are increasingly faced with complex mechanical devices or techniques requiring high degrees of skill and all these challenges must be faced by those involved in educating farmers. In fact, the constant re-training of teachers and extension workers is too often neglected, usually for lack of finance.

Shortages of finance are a constant headache for developing countries and agricultural education is sometimes neglected, often because it is not strongly demanded by the electorate. It is important that ways be found for reducing costs. Agricultural extension in countries like Denmark and Taiwan is, to a substantial extent, paid for by farmers themselves and the Harambee School Movement in Kenya has shown how rural communities can shoulder a high proportion of costs when they are sufficiently strongly motivated. At the same time as central government costs are reduced, ways need to be found to improve the effectiveness of rural extension work. In too many countries farmers are not getting the assistance they desperately need and in too many countries the bureaucracy works on balance against their interests. A new deal for farmers is overdue in a large number of countries in Asia, Africa and Latin America.

BIBLIOGRAPHY

1. F. Harbison, chapter in *Education and Development of Nations*, J. W. Hanson and C. S. Brembeck (eds.) (New York: Holt, Rinehart and Winston, 1966).
2. A. T. Mosher, *Getting Agriculture Moving* (New York: Agricultural Development Council).
3. B. Odeke, *Crop Production in Orungo, Teso District, Uganda*, Special Project (unpublished manuscript) (Makerere: Faculty of Agriculture, 1971).
4. T. W. Schultz, *Transforming Traditional Agriculture* (New Haven: Yale University Press, 1964).
5. E. R. Watts, 'Agricultural Extension in Embu District of Kenya', *East Africa Journal of Rural Development*, Vol. 2, No. 1. 1969.
6. C. R. Wharton, 'Education and Agricultural Growth: The Role of Education in Early-stage Agriculture', chapter in C. A. Anderson and M. J. Bowman (eds.), *Education and Economic Development* (Chicago: Aldine Publishing Co., 1965).
7. E. R. Watts, *Family Health under a Peasant Farming System*. Paper at Conference of the Association of Medical Schools of Africa, Kampala, December 1971.
8. Dept. of Agriculture, Report of the Teso Informal Committee. Entebbe Government Printer, 1937.
9. R. E. Nelson, *A Baseline Survey of Uganda Agriculture*. USAID, Box 1528, Kampala.
10. E. B. Castle, *Education for Self-Help* (London: Oxford University Press, 1972).
11. Robert H. Maxwell, *The Chavakali Case Office of International Programs* (W. Virginia University, 1970).
12. A. D. R. Ker, *The Development of Uganda Farm Schools*, unpublished manuscript (Faculty of Education, Makerere, 1971).
13. J. Bakaluba, 1971. Personal communication quoted in Ker above.
14. Stephen Carr, 'The School Leaver Problem', chapter in E. R. Watts (ed.), *New Hope for Rural Africa* (Nairobi: East Africa Publishing House, 1969).
15. H. S. Darling, 'The Training and Education of Farmers with Special Reference to Developing Countries', *Legon Agricultural News*, Ghana, February 1971, Vol. 4, No. 2.
16. Department of Agriculture. Annual Report 1934 (Entebbe Government Printer, 1935).
17. Hans Ruthenberg, *Agricultural Development in Tanzania* (Berlin: Springer Verlag, 1964).
18. Fergus Wilson, 'Education and Training for Agricultural Development', in *Education in Rural Areas* (London: Commonwealth Secretariat, 1970).
19. C. Davis Fogg, 'Economic and Social Factors affecting the Development of Small Holder Agriculture in Eastern Nigeria', *Economic Development and Cultural Change*, Vol. 13, No. 3, 1965, pp. 280–6. University of Chicago Press.

9

Research, Extension and Schooling in Agricultural Development*

Robert Evenson

The improvements in the conceptualization of relationships between schooling and economic factors achieved in economics and related disciplines in recent years have been impressive. Studies of the schooling-income relationship have clearly contributed to the quality of public discourse and decision-making with respect to public investment. It is perhaps unfortunate, but not surprising, that the great bulk of theoretical and empirical work on the role of schooling has been concentrated on developed, growing economies. The studies which have investigated schooling in less developed countries have by and large identified schooling-income relationships that exhibit patterns similar to those revealed by data from the United States.[1] For example, measured rates of return to schooling are highest for primary schooling.

It would not be accurate, however, to state that development economists agree that investment in schooling in a given country will have a clear and measurable effect on productivity, especially in the agricultural sector.[2] The available evidence lacks consistency. Not all studies have shown size able schooling-income effects. A substantial number of economies have invested heavily in schooling over the past 20 years, without achieving rapid growth.

The thesis of this chapter is that, in interpreting existing evidence in evaluating schooling programmes in less developed countries, a richer theoretical base is required. In particular, it will be argued that activities which generate new production technologies and facilitate the transfer of existing technologies should be incorporated directly into the analysis.

The Theoretical Basis for the Schooling-Research-Extension Interaction

Much of the early quantitative investigation of schooling-income relationships interpreted the evidence in a skill creation framework. That is, schooling created, or rather an individual participating in the schooling experience acquired, skills of economic value. Welch [15], among others, has raised important new questions about the nature of these 'skills'. Becker [1], in his pioneering work, had shown that schooling-associated

---

* Support for portions of this research was provided by NSF-GS-2803.

skills did not exhibit the property of diminishing returns. Returns to schooling did not fall over time as the ratio of schooling-associated skills increased relative to other factors of production.

Welch developed a distinction between worker skills and allocative skills which proved useful in interpreting the schooling-income data over time.[3] This new emphasis on allocative skills has served as a point of departure for further investigations which incorporate both information supply and the supply of 'new' potentially economically viable inputs and production techniques into the analysis.

The basis for the analysis is relatively simple. Allocative skills reflect a capability to economize under conditions of uncertain and imperfect knowledge of both technical and economic parameters of production processes. These 'conditions' are largely the result of 'new' and potentially improved inputs and techniques of production, the end products of research activity. It is important to note that new inputs and techniques of production are only potentially better in an economic sense than existing inputs and techniques. In practice, a great many products of the research system turn out not to be economic improvements at all. Most improvements in agriculture are real improvements under a very limited set of economic and technical conditions, a point central to understanding technology transfer from one region to another.

To develop an international and interregional perspective on the generation and transfer of technology, it will be useful to define major geo-climate regions. Geo-climate factors are of major importance to technology uses in agriculture. The major geo-climate regions that we will utilize here are those of Trewartha [14]. The 11 major crop-producing regions of the world are:

Humid Continental Climates (coldest month below 32°F)
1. Humid Continents – cool summer
2. Humid Continents – warm summer
Humid Mesothermal Climates (coldest month above 32°F, below 64·4°F)
3. Humid Subtropical
4. Humid Subtropical (dry winter)
5. Marine Coastal
6. Mediterranean
Dry Climates
7. Middle latitude Steppe
8. Subtropical Steppe
Tropical Climates (coolest month above 64·4°F)
9. Savanna
10. Tropical Rainforest
11. Monsoon Rainforest

Within each of these major *regions*, we can define a number of *sub-regions*. For example, Region 8, the Subtropical Steppe climate zone, encompasses the areas where the 'green revolution' in wheat has taken place. It includes portions of Mexico, North Africa, Turkey, Iran, Pakistan and North India. It also encompasses portions of Australia, South and Central Africa and Brazil. Sub-regions could be defined on the basis of differences in soil types and more detailed gradations of temperature and rainfall than used in regional definitions. In North India, for example, some four or five sub-regions (in Region 8) have been prepared by soil scientists [11]. We have not attempted a full definition of sub-regions for all regions, but a rough idea of their magnitude can be given. Within Region 8, for example, roughly 20 sub-regions would be defined. The continental United States actually includes portions of five Regions (1–4 and 7) and recent work by the author delineates some 29 sub-regions.[4]

The chief criterion for sub-regional definitions is derived from the interactions of geo-climate factors and technology itself. Hybrid corn companies, for example, define sub-regions on the basis of growing seasons. In the US corn-belt, typically six to eight distinct sub-regions based on different growing seasons are utilized. Most developers of crop varieties implicitly produce varieties suited to a sub-region. Thus, the appropriate definition of a sub-region (as used here) is determined by economic and technical factors. For a given level of research investment, there will be some optimal allocation of research effort toward the production of sub-region specific crop varieties and other forms of technology and some optimal degree of detail in the definition of the sub-region.

The degree of detail in the definition of sub-regions will not be complete enough to adequately encompass all of the differences in production conditions, however. We introduce the *micro-region* as a sub-unit of the sub-region to distinguish between fine detail in soil type, topography, and other climate factors that affect production. Within a micro-region we can then describe production of a single crop (or aggregate production under appropriate aggregation procedures) by the following relationship:

$$1.\ Q_m(t) = F\left[\gamma_m(t),\ X_m(t)\right]$$

This is a standard production function relating output Q_m in time period t, to a vector of inputs, X_m (land, labour, fertilizer). The term $\gamma_m(t)$ is an index of technique use which will differ among farms in the micro-region. Thus, within each micro-region, m, there will be a distribution of levels of technique use with a mean, γ_m, and a maximum, $\gamma_m^\star$, which will be defined to be the level of 'technology'.

Since all producers are not actually utilizing $\gamma_m^\star$ (the maximally efficient techniques, given factor and product prices), production in the micro-region will be less than what it could be. The difference between what could be produced and what is actually produced in the sub-region is:

$$2.\ Q_m^\star(t) - Q_m(t)$$
$$= \gamma_m^\star(t) - \gamma_m(t) + \alpha(\sum_x [P_x - F_x])$$

This expression distinguishes between technique choice errors, $\gamma_m^\star \gamma(t) - \gamma_m(t)$, and economic efficiency errors, given technique choice.[5] The size of this term, which measures a kind of economic 'slack', plays an important role in policy discussions. The 'labour surplus' model of economic development presumes that large errors in economic efficiency exist in that the marginal product of labour is well below the wage rate. It is also often presumed that large technique choice errors are being made as well, and that a relatively simple reorganization of production will lead to substantial productivity gains in the agricultural sector.

It was partially on this basis that extension has received great emphasis in development programmes over the past two decades. In addition to the presumed existence of micro-region slack, it was also supposed that huge opportunities for relatively low-cost productivity gains were to be had by reducing sub-regional and regional disparities in technology levels. Extension activities were prescribed as the appropriate form of investment to achieve this technology spread.

As evidence has accumulated over time, it is now becoming relatively clear that (a) micro-regional slack was more apparent than real and (b) that the scope for direct transfer of technology via extension activities has been and continues to be extremely limited. Furthermore, the hoped-for transfer is unlikely to be realized by investment in the 'adaptive research', now much in vogue in development circles.[6]

The process of technology transfer is complicated. Within a micro-region, for example, the process of evaluation begins with the emergence of the new technique. Each new potentially valuable technique has a life cycle with a component of 'information capital' attached to it. Upon first emergence, little information may be available. It may be a crop variety new to the area, but with some production evidence from other areas. Perhaps some yield trials have been completed in other micro-regions. At this point, a number of producers have a demand for information. They seek out experimental data and begin to develop information capital. The more capable the producer is to process and understand information from various sources, the more capital he will build (obviously the value of information capital will depend on the size of the production unit). Typically, experimentation and evaluation in the sub-region then occurs. As more information is obtained it becomes clear whether adoption in the micro-region is justified. In a great many cases it will not be.

Typically the cost of acquiring information falls with the passage of time as more evidence becomes available. Not all cases are clear-cut, however. Some techniques, such as a change in row-width or in cultivating procedures, are such that several years of evidence may be required before the technique can really be shown to be superior. Even experimental stations cannot always identify superior techniques without several years' data.

It should be rather obvious that a new technique may prove to be superior to existing techniques in only a limited number of micro-regions. In general, the great bulk of changes in $\gamma_m^\star$, $\Delta\gamma_m^\star$, are confined to micro-regions within only one sub-region. Superiority is, of course, relative to the existing technology and hence to the economic activities devoted to generating or facilitating indirect transfer of technology. Cases of new technologies which are widely transferred in direct form over a number of sub-regions are usually the result of a misallocation of research resources.[7]

The fact that direct transfer is limited does not mean that transfer in an indirect form does not take place. The generation or creation of new techniques can be characterized as a combination of search and learning which utilizes antecedent knowledge. The division of labour in most agricultural research systems, especially regarding crop technology, is such that experiment stations and departments are organized to produce (and test to some extent) new production techniques suited to a number of micro-regions, usually to a sub-region. The personnel with this objective are usually considered 'applied' researchers. These include agronomists, plant breeders, entomologists, pathologists, irrigation engineers and even economists.

In the search-learning research process, the indirect role of the outcome of non-applied research and 'feed-back' information from micro-region experience with technologies is important. Researchers have at their command a certain body of knowledge, intellectual capital, if you will. In addition, in the process of discovery and search, they must search out and process new information. The amount of intellectual capital possessed, as well as the rate of production of new elements of such capital, determines the productivity of the applied researchers. In those research situations where applied researchers have acquired little intellectual capital and lack ability for further acquisition, and where little relevant fundamental research is being done, a pure search situation holds. That is, researchers simply search for superior techniques in a fixed distribution of possible techniques. It is well known that there are diminishing returns to search and that the limited potential for finding new techniques is rapidly exhausted.[8]

To formalize the transfer process, several 'plausible' specifications relating certain kinds of technology change are presented here. The specifications are oversimplified, but are designed to emphasize factors about which we are accumulating evidence. In the following expressions, a constant time unit is assumed. That is, the relation between one change and another holds for some time unit (for example, two years).

Consider first the transfer of an improvement in micro-region technology to producers in the micro-region:

$$3.\ \Delta\bar{\gamma}_m = A\ \Delta\gamma_m^{\star}/(1+\alpha_1/SC_m)EXP^{-\alpha_2\ EX\ m}$$

This particular specification is a logistic expression with the following properties: (a) When investment in both extension (EX_m) and schooling (SC_m) is relatively high, the value of the function approaches the ceiling parameter, A, which in this case should be close to one for most kinds of improvement in $\gamma_m^{\star}$; (b) When extension is equal to zero, the fraction $1/(1 + \alpha_1/SC_m)$ of the ceiling is realized. This fraction increases with schooling (which we arbitrarily will not allow to be zero). The relationship is easily seen with the aid of Figure 1. As extension is increased, a logistic transfer pattern is given.

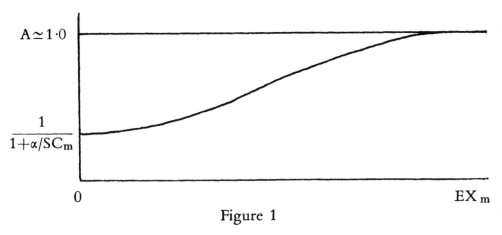

Figure 1

In expression 3, 'slack' from previous change was ignored, but the fundamentals are not greatly changed by introducing a sequence of changes.

Now consider the factors related to $\Delta\gamma_m^{\star}$.

$$4.\ \Delta\gamma_m^{\star} = \Delta\gamma_m^{!} + BC_m\Delta\gamma_{m(b)}^{!}/(1+\beta_1/C_mSC_m)EXP^{-\beta_2EX\ m}$$
$$+ CC_m\Delta\gamma_s^{!}/(1+\gamma_1/C_mSC_m)EXP^{-\gamma_2\ EX\ m}$$

In this expression we have somewhat arbitrarily allocated a given change in micro-region technology to three sources. The first source $\Delta\gamma_m^{!}$, is the micro-region sub-invention and technology modification that is related to the evaluation process. The second term, $\Delta\gamma_{m(b)}^{!}$ is the sum total of counterpart inventions in other micro-regions in the sub-region.

The most significant term is the third, relating a change in technology generated at the sub-region level to a change at the micro-region level. The first two terms depend on the third. That is, without real sub-region technology change, the micro-region technology is not produced.

The transfer process in the third term differs in one major respect from the relationship in equation 3. A term C_m, a scalar which reflects differences in climate factors, is associated with each micro-region. It reflects the fact that it is economically inefficient to produce a bundle of sub-region technologies that will be equally well suited to all micro-regions. Some micro-regions may systematically be able to utilize only a fraction of the increases in the sub-region stock of new crop varieties and other production techniques. C_m will generally be less than one for most micro-regions, at least for certain periods of time.[9] The lower C_m, the lower both the ceiling, $(C)(C_m)$, and the intercept of the logistic relationship.

Extension and schooling play a similar role in equations 3 and 4. By substituting 4 into 3, we have an expression which captures the basic relationship between technology change, extension and schooling. As specified here, if $\Delta\gamma_s' = 0$, the value of extension will go to zero as slack is taken up over time and the value of schooling derived from technique choice and economic efficiency will also go to zero.

We next turn to the sources of $\Delta\gamma_s'$:

$$5.\ \Delta\gamma_s' = DC_S\Delta\gamma_s'(b)/(1+\delta_2 EX_S))EXP^{-C_3 R_s}$$
$$+GC_S(\Delta K_r + g_1 K_r)(1-EXP^{-g_2 R_s})$$

Here we distinguish between the 'borrowing' of technology from other sub-regions (the D term) and the production of sub-region specific technology (term G). The borrowing term is logistic in form with sub-region research effort (R_S) being the key variable in its transfer. The intercept term is $DC_S/(1 + \delta_2 EX_S)$. It represents transfer when $R_S = 0$. It is lower, the lower is C_S, the sub-region climate factor, and the lower is the level of extension in the sub-region. The ceiling parameter is $D C_S$ and is likely to vary considerably between sub-regions.

This term is of great policy importance. It captures the extent to which one country can benefit from research done in another country with sub-regions in a common region. The intercept term is the fraction of the potentially borrowable technology that will be borrowed if the recipient country does no research. In a recent paper by the author and a colleague, Yoav Kislev [9], this intercept term was estimated to be approximately 0·05 for transfer of technology in wheat production and approximately zero for maize and related technology. This estimate was derived for moderate levels of extension activity. To the degree that they are borne out by further studies, these estimates indicate that a policy of emphasis on extension with little attention to research is a serious misallocation of resources.

The second term in equation 5 is a crudely specified 'production function of research'. It should be interpreted as 'expected' technological change. The principle feature of the specification presented here is that when $R_S = 0$, production of technology will be equal to zero. The K_r variable is a measure of the non-applied or fundamental research that is relevant to the region. The units in which it is measured are somewhat arbitrary. In the study referred to above (Evenson and Kislev [9]) the number of scientific publications adjudged to be of sufficient scientific value to justify inclusion in international abstracting journals was utilized as a measure.

In the form presented, research activity will be productive even if $\Delta K_r = 0$ in the time period in question. Research activity will be subject to diminishing returns however. The ratio of research in the sub-region, R_S, to the stock, K_r, (subject to measurement comparability) will determine the productivity of research if the usual production function properties hold.

We present a final relationship determining ΔKr.

$$6.\ \Delta K_r = HC_r(1-h_1EXP^{-h_2R}r)(\Delta K_r(b) + h_3K_r(b))$$
$$+\ I\ [1-i_1EXP^{-i_2R}r)\Delta\gamma_r^!(-1)$$

In this expression, $\Delta K_r = 0$, if R_r, regional research (including mission oriented sub-regional research) is 0. There is an important interaction between technology production in the past, $\Delta\gamma_r^!(-1)$, in the region and fundamental knowledge expressed in the last term.

Combining equations 3–6 we get (in shorthand form) a general accounting relationship showing the 'sources' of real technical change in a micro region

$$\Delta\bar{\gamma}_m = A_m\Delta\gamma_m^! + A_mB_m\Delta\gamma_{m(b)} + A_mC_mD_S\Delta\gamma_{S(b)}$$
$$+\ A_mC_mD_SG_S(\Delta K_r + H_r\Delta K_{r(b)} + I_r\Delta\gamma_r(-1))$$

This is an accounting relationship, not a growth equation.[10] It does serve as a kind of basis for judging the effects of certain policies:

1. The contribution of producer generated technology (terms 1 and 2) is directly proportional to the contribution of borrowed sub-region technology (term 3) and produced sub-region technology (term 4). Both A_m and B_m are functions of schooling and extension. A_m is likely to be approximately 1 when normal investment in extension is undertaken. B_m will be substantially less than one because of climate factors.

2. The contribution of the third term, technology borrowed from other sub-regions, will, in normal circumstances, depend almost entirely upon whether a contribution is forthcoming from the fourth term as well. In other words, if a sub-region is not doing any sub-regional research, it will

not borrow from other sub-regions. The intercept term for D_S (equation 5) is close to zero, even with substantial extension investment. This is due to the climate factors involved. The foregoing statement is supported by evidence in the case of wheat and maize production in the 1948 to 1968 period. Some modification is required in the light of the 'green revolution' experience in wheat production in the past few years. If the sub-regional gains in Mexico, for example, are of 'large' magnitude, as in the case of the new wheats, they will be borrowed to some degree, even in sub-regions in Northern Africa which do little research. Nonetheless, the existence of sub-regional research in India facilitated the borrowing greatly.

3. Sub-region technology generation is the key element in the process. As we have noted, without it, only unusual 'green revolution' type gains are likely to result in real micro-region gains. The process of producing such gains is a complex search-learning process that depends not only on directed 'applied' research effort, but on the availability of a stock of regionally relevant knowledge of fundamental physical and biological properties of plants and animals. It further depends on the capability of the applied researcher to understand the relevance of the fundamental knowledge. The lower the regionally relevant stock of knowledge and the lower the capability of applied or 'adaptive' researchers to utilize such knowledge, the less productive will such researchers be.

4. This schema has not admitted direct transfer of technology from one region to another. We know of no appreciable evidence of such transfer in the form of plant varieties. Even the Mexican wheats are confined basically to one region. This is perhaps less true of animals, though when one carefully examines the matter it appears to hold here as well. Beef cattle in the tropical climates are bred for heat resistance, for example. Animal breeding has reduced to some extent the diversity among native animals (which is very climate specific), but gradations still exist. Cultivating techniques and machines and implements are transferred across regions to a much larger degree. Cultivation techniques, however, are quite specific to the particular crop and to climate conditions. Monsoon climates require practices that differ to some degree from Rainforest climates. Improvements in practices in one region are not usually direct improvements in the other. The introduction and utilization of machines depends heavily on the relative prices of machines, labour and animal power. Because of this, the climate based scheme developed here is not fully appropriate for this technology. Until recently, however, mechanical power and implements have contributed negligibly to technology change in less developed countries.

The International System of Agricultural Research and Extension
This section presents data on research and extension investment in the

year 1965. It is presented in both a political regional basis and a geo-climate regional basis. The basic data were compiled by the author and a colleague and are reported in detail in Evenson and Kislev [4].

Table 1 is a summary table of expenditures in US dollars on both research and extension in the public sector for the year, 1965. In addition, data on the number of scientist man years (SMYs) and extension staff in agriculture are given. The figures in parentheses are estimates. All others are based on reliable data. (The notes to Table 1 list the major qualifications to the data.)

It is of interest to note that public sector spending on agricultural research is relatively low. The spending by less developed countries is especially so and a substantial number of countries have very rudimentary systems. In many cases, research stations are isolated from extension services and from graduate teaching and research in the discipline-oriented sciences. The less developed countries spend 11 per cent of the world's public sector research budget and 20 per cent of the extension budget, though they produce 28 per cent of the agricultural products and provide employment to two-thirds of the world's farmers. Since they can purchase the services of agricultural scientists for about 60 per cent of the developed country costs and extension workers for 22 per cent of developed country costs, the proportions of agricultural scientists and extension workers in the less developed countries are 17 and 47 per cent respectively.

The pattern of investment in the less developed countries has been heavily influenced by technical aid programmes of the developed countries after World War II. The relative emphasis on extension is apparent. We do not have data on the extension programmes for these countries in an earlier year. We do know that the share of less developed country research publications in the world total increased from 10·6 per cent in the 1948–54 period to 13·2 per cent in the 1962–68 period [4]. It is quite likely that the less developed countries' share of extension work rose to a much greater extent over the period.

Table 2 presents comparisons based on these data, organized by major geo-climate regions. The 11 major climate regions are those defined earlier. The notes to the table describe the coverage of the regions.

These comparisons are designed to reveal major differences in investment activity. Ideally, we would like to have research investment per sub-region and extension investment per micro-region. Since we have not defined sub-regions completely, we utilize, as a proxy, the dollar value of agricultural product. It is a good proxy if sub-regions are of roughly equal economic size. Extension investment should be related not only to micro-region size, but to the number of farmers to be contacted.

Research is measured in terms of research *input*, i.e. dollar expenditures and SMYs, and in terms of a particular kind of research *output*, scientific

TABLE 1
AGRICULTURAL RESEARCH AND EXTENSION – 1965 INTERREGIONAL COMPARISONS

Region	Exp. on Research (Million $)	SMY	Exp. on Extension (Million $)	No. of Ext. Workers
1. North America	390·2	15,283	204·4	9,137
2. Northern Europe	190·0	8,232	106·4	17,480
3. Southern Europe	23·1	2.236	25·1	5,335
4. Oceania, S. Africa, Rhodesia	86·7	3,671	(43·0)	(7,950)
5. Eastern Europe and USSR	(233·2)	15,340	(144·0)	(33,400)
6. Latin America	20·6	2,431	22·9	3,883
7. Middle East and North Africa	33·3	1,608	(33·0)	(15,500)
8. South and South East Asia	36·0	4,220	(45·9)	38,892
9. East Asia	65·7	5,195	47·4	18,443
10. Sub-Sahara Africa	33·5	1,344	28·0	23,820
Developed Countries*	985·7	49,262	559·2	87,428
Less Developed Countries	126·6	10,298	140·9	76,412
World Total	1,112·3	59,560	700·1	163,840

* Developed Countries=categories 1, 2, 3, 4, 5 plus Japan, (LDC=6 through 10 minus Japan).

1. The data were compiled from a number of sources, including FAO and OECD regional surveys, as well as published experiment station budgets and responses to a survey questionnaire. It is inevitable that certain problems of consistency exist in the definitions used by different agencies. Fortunately, the regional surveys by OECD did produce a set of definitions of research and of researchers which serve as a standard. We have attempted to make these data as consistent as possible with that standard.

2. Conversion of local currencies to US dollars is a source of error in the expenditure data. We have simply used official exchange rates.

3. In general, we have attempted to include only that research and extension activity directed to increasing agricultural production. We do not include research on food technology and home economies, for example.

4. Definitions of scientists in the SMY data are reasonably consistent for most developed countries. A scientist is generally defined to have 'graduate training at the PhD level' in the OECD countries. This definition was not very applicable to many less developed countries, particularly in Latin America, where the basic academic degree (Ingenero Agronomo) is more of a professional degree than a research degree. In a number of countries, civil service categories (such as Senior Research Officer) were used. We cannot claim that the SMY data are standardized for quality. The graduate research training of most LDC scientists is of lower scientific standard than in the OECD countries.

5. All data are by location of the scientist, not by nationality. Thus, French and British scientists in Africa are treated as African scientists.

6. In general, all data for public sector activities. Where private associations, such as sugar cane growers' associations, support research stations, they are included. R & D activities by private chemical and machinery companies are not included.

publications. The use of the publications measure is justified if it can be standardized in a meaningful way and if it has economic meaning. In the measure reported in Table 2, the scientific publications include those accepted for abstraction by three international abstracting journals, *Plant Breeding Abstracts*, *Dairy Science Abstracts* and *Biological Abstracts*. These journals have as their objective the abstracting of all scientific publications of scientific merit throughout the world. Their editorial staffs screen publications from more than 2,000 journals in all languages.

The publications data probably reflect more uniformity, as a result, than the SMY data or the expenditures data. The ratio of publications to output is the most meaningful indicator of real regional research activity. As the table shows, on this basis, regional crop oriented applied research in the less developed countries as a whole is only a little over one-third of the research activity in the developed countries. The ratio of plant physiology publications (not included in crop-oriented work) gives an indication of the region relevant fundamental research. It indicates that the less developed countries are producing by their own research activity roughly one-sixth as much per unit of agricultural product as the developed countries.

When this comparison is made on a regional basis, only the Rainforest region (10) is below the norm for all less developed countries by this measure. The other regions with substantial coverage of less developed countries (6, 8, 9 and 11) fare somewhat better as they include some developed country sub-regions. Region 8, the wheat revolution region, appears to have substantial research activity, but much of it is concentrated in Australia.

When the comparison is based on SMYs per unit of agricultural product, some variations from the pattern are observed. There are two sources of this. One is the quite different pattern in publications per dollar's worth of livestock product. The other is variation in publications (crops plus livestock) per SMY. The less developed countries have a relatively high research investment in livestock, although livestock products account for a very small share of total agricultural output in most. Variation in publications per SMY is partly due to measurement errors, but a substantial component is due to variation in the region relevant fundamental knowledge. (Evidence is presented on this point in the next section.)

Extension investment is actually highest on a workers per unit output basis in regions with substantial less developed country sub-regions. If the comparison were made on the basis of extension workers per farm, the developed countries would have roughly a 2 to 1 advantage [4]. The 'right' basis for judgment is not easily defined. If costs of information transfer were independent of the number of farmers, extension per micro-region would be appropriate. Obviously this is not the case and some weighted average of the measures is probably appropriate.

TABLE 2

GEO–CLIMATE REGION, RESEARCH AND EXTENSION COMPARISON, 1965

Geo–Climate Region (% of World Product)	% Agr. Prod. spent on Research	SMYs per $10m. agr. Product	Ext. workers Per $10m. Agr. Product	Scientific Publications Per $10m. Agr. Product		Ratio Plant Phys. to Crop Sc. Publications
				Crops	Animals	
Humid Continental						
1. Warm Summer (0·16)	0·50	5·3	9·2	5·9	4·2	0·58
2. Cool Summer (0·8)	1·19	5·3	5·9	7·6	5·6	0·81
Humid Mesothermal						
3. Humid Subtropical— (Even Rainfall) (0·14)	1·01	5·4	8·8	5·5	5·7	0·85
4. Humid Subtropical— (Dry Winter) (0·02)	0·60	5·3	18·3	7·1	12·1	0·40
5. Marine Coastal (0·13)	1·27	5·7	10·0	8·6	7·7	1·22
6. Mediterranean (0·09)	0·58	4·0	20·9	2·9	4·1	0·83
Dry Climates						
7. Middle latitude Steppe (0·12)	0·76	4·9	7·2	6·2	5·0	0·63
8. Subtropical Steppe (0·07)	0·63	3·8	26·6	4·1	7·9	0·32
Tropical Climates						
9. Savanna (0·11)	0·57	2·8	14·9	3·2	7·4	0·38
10. Rainforest (0·04)	0·41	5·8	20·1	2·1	2·9	0·11
11. Monsoon (0·04)	0·21	·24	14·0	3·3	10·7	0·36
All Developed Countries	0·87	4·4	7·7	6·5	6·6	0·84
Less Developed Countries	0·26	2·1	15·7	2·8	4·5	0·39

1. *Humid Continental: Warm Summer*
   US (Corn Belt), Japan (North)

2. *Humid Continental: Cool Summer*
   US (NE and Dairy States), Canada (Eastern half), USSR (Northern 70%) N. Korea

3. *Humid Subtropical: Even Rainfall*
   India (North Central), Taiwan, China (South, no data), Australia (NE)

4. *Humid Subtropical: Dry Winter*
   Brazil (South), China (North), Japan (South), Italy (North), Yugoslavia (North), S. Africa (NE), Austria (East), US (South and South Atlantic), Uruguay, Argentina (North)

5. *Marine Coastal*
   Brazil (SE), Argentina (NE), Chile US (West Coast), Australia (SE), New Zealand, Northern Europe, Canada (West)

6. *Mediterranean*
   Southern Europe, North Africa, Middle East (Coastal regions)

7. *Mid-latitude Steppe*
   Turkey (Central), USSR (Southern and Eastern), Spain (Central), US (Great Plains) Argentina (Central), Canada (Central)

8. *Subtropical Steppe*
   India (North), W. Pakistan, Mexico (North), Venezuela (Interior), Brazil (NE), S. Africa (Northern), E. Africa (Plains), N. Africa (Interior), Middle East (Interior), Australia (Northern Interior)

9. *Savanna*
   Australia, (North Coastal), Indonesia (Outer Islands), India (Central Interior), E. Africa (except Plains), W. Africa (except Coastal), Brazil (Interior), Mexico (South), El Salvador, Venezuela (Coastal)

10. *Tropical Rainforest*
    Indonesia, Philippines, Malaysia, Nigeria (South), Brazil (East Coast), Colombia, Ceylon (East), Central America and Caribbean

11. *Tropical Monsoon*
    Burma, India (NE and SW), Sri Lanka (West), Liberia, Sierra Leone, Brazil, (East Coast), Bangladesh

Evidence from Recent Studies

Studies of technical change in agriculture have only recently dealt with the testing of hypotheses implicit in Part I of this paper. This section reviews studies which provide evidence on four aspects raised in Part I. They are:

1. A study of the extension-schooling interactions in nitrogen application to corn by US farmers by W. Huffman [8].
2. A study of aggregate agricultural productivity by Hayami and Ruttan [6].
3. A study of technology borrowing in wheat and maize by Kislev and Evenson [9].
4. A study of agricultural scientist productivity also by Evenson and Kislev [4].

The study by Huffman utilized a formulation similar to the one proposed in equation 3, page 168. His procedure is first to derive an estimate of 'optimal' nitrogen usage on a country basis. This gives a measure of 'slack' (equation 2, page 166). He then postulates an adjustment equation similar to equation 3. His estimates of the parameters imply:

(a) That extension activity and schooling of farmers both contribute significantly to reducing the slack.

(b) That extension and schooling are substitutes in improving adjustment. That is, the marginal contribution of extension decreases, the higher is the level of schooling.

(c) That the value of the contribution of extension to reducing the slack implied a handsome return to extension investment (approximately $50 per extension hour spent working with farmers).

This study is one of the first to directly estimate the contribution of information supplied to productivity. Others [3, 5] have estimated the contribution of combined research and extension to production, but did not develop specifications suited for separating the effects of information supply from the contributions of research.[11]

Hayami and Ruttan [6], in an extensive work, utilize international data to estimate parameters of a 'meta production function' which they claim to be free of some of the restrictive assumptions underlying an 'international production function'. It is true that the conventional production function specification is simply not rich enough to be capable of explaining inter-country productivity differences. However, it may be doubted that the Hayami-Ruttan specification is rich enough. They incorporate a measure of schooling of farmers and a composite variable, technical education in the agricultural sciences, which is interpreted as a proxy for extension and research in both public and private sectors. They do not specify an international borrowing relationship.

Their results are of some interest. They claim significant schooling and technical education effects. In the Cobb-Douglas specification, these variables are complements. That is, an increase in schooling levels increases the marginal product of extension and research. The Huffman work [8] indicates that schooling and extension are substitutes, and a result by Evenson [3] suggests that this is the case for schooling and research plus extension as well.

Perhaps the work of most significance and relevance to the transfer question is contained in a study of productivity gains in wheat and maize by Kislev and Evenson [9]. In that study, cross-section-time-series data for a number of countries were utilized in a regression analysis of inter-country differences in land productivity. The regression results were:

Wheat: $R^2 = 0.93$: 't' ratios in parentheses; 64 countries: 1948–68

$$Y_{it} = 23.65 + 4.65\ R_i(t) + 6.4 \times 10^{-4}B_i(t) - 1.3 \times 10^{-4}A_it$$
$$(9.35) \qquad (9.01) \qquad\qquad\qquad (2.35)$$
$$+ 0.23t + \Sigma D_i$$
$$(1.47)$$

Maize: $R^1 = 0.85$: 't' ratios in parentheses: 49 countries: 1948–68

$$Y_{it} = 36.35 + 3.01\ R_i(t) + 1.8 \times 10^{-3}B_i(t) - 1.1 \times 10^{-3}A_it$$
$$(6.66) \qquad (5.63) \qquad\qquad\qquad (5.68)$$
$$+ 0.34t + \Sigma D_i$$
$$(13.6)$$

Y_{it} = Yield per hectare, country i, year t. $R_i(t)$ = Indigenous or sub-regional research: scientific publications oriented to wheat (or maize) cumulated to time t from 1948. $B_i(t) = [1/1 + \alpha e^{-\beta R_i(t)}]R_i(b)(t)$: where $Ri(b)(t)$ is the research done in other sub-regions in the same region as country i. Regions were defined approximately as in Table 2. Sub-regions were arbitrarily defined on a country basis; that is, one sub-region per country. α and β were estimated by iterative methods (wheat $\alpha = 500$; $\beta = 6$; maize $\alpha = 100$; $\beta = 2$).

A_it = Area harvested

t = time

ΣD_i = country dummy variables for all countries except one.

These results offer rather strong support to the specification put forth in this chapter (eq. 5, p. 169). The intercept term in this case is approximately zero. That is, if a country does no research, it borrows nothing. In an alternative form (the exponential) the intercept term for wheat was 0.05, indicating a small amount of borrowing not induced by research.

The estimated economic contribution of sub-regional research can be calculated for these two crops. The contribution of an incremental unit of research activity (in this case measured by a scientific publication) can be divided into three parts: (1) the direct indigenous contribution (measured by the coefficient on R(t), (2) the contribution to the country from accelerating the borrowing of research results from sub-regions in other countries (measured by the coefficient on B(t)) and (3) the contribution to other countries with common sub-regions who benefit from the research.

For the results reported above these marginal contributions (at the mean of the sample) were:

	Direct Contribution	Transfer Acceleration	Contributions to Other
Wheat	$29,737	$135,000	$17,997
Maize	$15,040	$15,100	$9,302

These can be viewed as earnings streams which can be purchased with additional research. There will be a time lag of roughly 6 to 8 years[12] before the full stream is realized and it may depreciate after a number of years. The research unit which generates these streams ranges in cost from about $40,000 in Asia and Latin America to roughly $100,000 to $125,000 in the North American and Northern European countries.[13] Even at higher prices for research, these estimates indicate that very high rates of return are being realized. Recall that the intercept term indicates that if a sub-region does not conduct any research, virtually no technology from other sub-regions is transferred to it. These estimates indicate that, when research is undertaken in the sub-region, transfer is facilitated and that the marginal contribution of research through transfer acceleration is probably as great or greater than the direct contribution. The contribution to other countries, of course, depends on the research that they undertake.

A final bit of indirect evidence on the relationship between applied and fundamental research (the second term in eq. 5, page 169) is of some interest. In the discussion of this relationship, it was postulated that the productivity of applied research activity will decrease as the ratio of applied research to the stock of fundamental research findings relevant to the region declined. Equation 6 (page 170) postulated that the 'borrowed region relevant fundamental research findings are closely related to the indigenously produced findings. If they are related by a factor of proportionality, and if all fundamental research findings are proportional to plant physiology research findings, the following regression specification will test the effect of fundamental research on the productivity of applied research. This is a result from a paper by Evenson and Kislev (4).

$$\log(SP_i) = A + 0.38 \log(SMY_i) \times 0.43 \log(PP_i) \quad :R^2 = 0.84$$
$$(3.1) \qquad\qquad (5.7)$$

't' ratios in parentheses

SP_i: Publications in Agricultural Sciences

SMY_i: Agricultural Scientist Man Years

PP_i: Publications in Plant Physiology

The interpretation of this result is that, holding constant plant physiology and related work, an increase in agricultural scientist man years of 10 per cent will result in a 3·8 per cent increase in agricultural science publications. On the other hand, an increase of 10 per cent in plant physiology work, holding constant agricultural scientist man years, is associated with a 4·3 per cent increase in agricultural science publications. This result is, of course, subject to other interpretations. For example, the plant physiology variable may be serving as a quality index of agricultural research. Even this interpretation suggests that the fundamental research is valuable, perhaps through improved graduate programmes, where of course much of this knowledge is acquired by applied scientists. Errors in measurement of SMYs also exist and tend to bias the SMY coefficient downward. And finally, it may be claimed that scientific publications are a poor measure of the output of agricultural scientists. We can only say that the wheat and maize study has shown this particular measure to be economically meaningful.

Implications for Schooling Policy

It would be overstating the case to say that a well specified model integrating research, extension and schooling has been achieved and that its parameters have been estimated with reasonable confidence. It will take much further work to realize that objective. In this chapter, certain aspects of such a model have been suggested and a small amount of evidence has been cited in support of several propositions. In this section, some policy implications of these propositions are discussed.

Efficiency growth in a micro-region has been crudely postulated to be determined by: (1) micro-region extension, (2) micro-region schooling, (3) extension and schooling in other micro-regions, (4) sub-region research activity, (5) technology gains in other sub-regions or indirect research in other sub-regions, (6) fundamental research in the region and institutions which enable sub-region research activity to express a 'derived demand' to guide it, and which foster the acquisition of knowledge of applied research and (7) fundamental research done in other regions.

Micro-regions may have some control over 1 and 2, but little over 3. Depending on institutional arrangements they may be able to express a voice in policy with respect to 4. If a small region or commodity group is unable to affect sub-regional research policy, it has little real control over its productivity growth. Investment in extension and schooling will only marginally alter its economic performance.

Sub-regions, on the other hand, have a much larger range of policy options and we will focus on these. They can, through political institutions, invest in schooling, extension and research. They will have little or no control over sub-regional research in other countries, and may have little control of regionally oriented fundamental research. Within the range of options regarding schooling, extension and research, one of the fundamental postulates of this paper is important. It is that *little borrowing from other sub-regions can be accomplished by extension and schooling investment alone.*

It is understandable that less developed countries will wish to use their scarce resources to maximum advantage. It is also true that, by and large, extension services are low priced relative to research services in most low income countries. But extension, bargain or not, does not have a high productivity unless the sub-region invests in research.

Schooling is much like extension as far as productivity growth is concerned. In terms of reducing 'slack' it is a substitute for extension, though not a perfect one by any means. Without research activity, it does not produce growth. It may produce other things, however, including future growth. It may induce migration and occupational change. It also is likely to alter the institutions extant in the sub-regions and depending on the distribution of schooling among the population this could produce future growth.

The potential for high pay-off among alternative investments in almost all less developed sub-regions is greatest in the establishment of research systems. This is true even where the services of scientists are expensive because of limited supply. The productivity of sub-region applied scientists is importantly determined by the quality of its scientists. By quality, we mean the holding of intellectual capital, acquired by exposure to first-rate graduate training, including the understanding of available region relevant fundamental knowledge.

There is a widespread view that, since low quality researchers are lower cost (not always of course), most less developed country researchers can get by with less graduate training. Missionary zeal is considered to be a good substitute for sound adequate training. Unfortunately, the current emphasis on 'adaptive' research is translatable into emphasis on low quality research. The wheat-maize study referred to earlier implied that it is not just research, but 'publication-producing' research that is productive. Of course, one can cite numerous examples of non-publishing researchers who have developed new crop varieties, but they are largely exceptions.

If sub-regions have no effective control over research done in other sub-regions, they will have some optimal mix of low quality research, high quality research and fundamental research. It is not obvious that the ratio of low quality research to fundamental research should be lower, the lower are the 'borrowable' stocks being generated in other sub-regions. In fact, it is the existence in other countries of institutions producing substantial region relevant fundamental knowledge which allows a country the prospect of economizing, by having less investment in fundamental research. Even in that case, it will invest in high quality applied research effort.

Most sub-regions have an incentive to influence regional policy and have an interest in the research policies of other countries. In some cases, with small countries, regional research organizations can be supported through cooperation, as in East Africa. It is probably true that there is currently serious underinvestment in fundamental research in all of the Tropical climate regions and in the Subtropical Steppe regions. Many sub-regions have simply failed to establish research programmes of significance. Some less developed sub-regions may have research programmes which are currently not very productive because there is little to borrow.

International agencies can and should be guiding the international systems towards a more efficient mix, as well as encouraging resource transfers from rich to poor sub-regions. It is not possible to review the success of aid agencies in doing so to date, but two points might be mentioned. First, aid agencies have sometimes encouraged and fostered a mix of research and extension resources in less developed regions that appears in retrospect to have been quite inefficient. Extension programmes have been emphasized. Resources have gone into research, but it is probably true that not a single really first rate research centre (on a par, say, with the best US State Experiment Stations) has been established as a result of aid programmes.

Second, the current emphasis is on International Centres, to the detriment of building indigenous research institutions. The spectacular success of the centres which produced the new wheat (CYMMT) and rice (IRRI) varieties is used as a basis for this policy. The contribution of these two centres has indeed been enormous. They were successful partially because of the misallocation of research resources in the regions where these crops were important and their comparative advantage over indigenous research institutions may not be as great as it appears to be. They do not appear to be giving emphasis to fundamental research and graduate training where their greatest comparative advantage may lie.

REFERENCES

1. For a review of Human Capital studies and a rich discussion of the importance of research to human capital theory see Shultz [12].
2. The labour surplus models of development usually imply that incomes in the agricultural sector are determined by institutional factors. Thus by this view, largely discredited by the evidence, a schooling income association would not imply that schooling made farmers more productive.
3. Chaudhri [2] and Nelson and Phelps [10] have developed formulations with similar interpretations.
4. These sub-regions are based on classifications provided in the 1958 *Yearbook of Agriculture* [16].
5. This expression is a refinement of the Welch [15] and Nelson–Phelps [10] definitions. The term

$$\sum \alpha(x\left|P_x - F_x\right|)$$

measures departures in cost minimization, since $P_x - F_x = 0$ under cost minimization. A term to encompass errors in product choice could be added as well.
6. Technique choice and economic efficiency errors are the net result of (1) changes in $\gamma[\overset{*}{m}]$, and (2) producer activity directed toward reducing the errors. The size of observed errors or slack will tend to be largest in those economies which have experienced a sustained and rapid flow of new technique. The US probably has higher observed slack than most less developed economies. A recent study of Huber [7] of 'underemployment' bears this out. Because of this, most attempts to interpret this slack as a measure of under-employment are meaningless.
7. This point is addressed in the first section of the chapter.
8. See Stigler [13] for a discussion of the search phenomenon.
9. C_m cannot be greater than one by definition. That is, $\Delta\gamma'_s$ is defined to be the maximum $\Delta\gamma_m$ after complete transfer.
10. A growth model would have to specify the relationship between micro-region generated technology and sub-region generated technology.
11. Evenson in an earlier study [3], provided evidence that extension and research are substitutes for schooling.
12. See Evenson [3] for the time lag estimates.
13. Some African countries pay in excess of $200,000. See Evenson and Kislev [4].

BIBLIOGRAPHY

1. G. Becker, *Human Capital*, National Bureau of Economic Research (New York: Columbia University Press, 1964).
2. D. P. Chaudhri, 'Education and Agricultural Production in India,' University of Delhi, doctoral dissertation, 1968.

3. R. E. Evenson, 'Economic Aspects of the Organization of Agricultural Research,' in *Resource Allocation in Agricultural Research*, W. Fishel (ed.) (Minneapolis: University of Minnesota Press, 1971).

4. R. E. Evenson, and Y. Kislev, 'Investment in Agricultural Research and Extension: A Survey of International Data,' Yale University, *Economic Growth Center Discussion Paper* No. 154, 1971.

5. Zvi Griliches, 'Research Expenditures, Education and the Aggregate Agricultural Production Function,' *American Economic Review*, 54: 967–968, 1964.

6. Y. Hayami, and V. W. Ruttan, *Agricultural Development: An International Perspective* (Baltimore: Johns Hopkins Press, 1971).

7. Paul Huber, 'Disguised Unemployment in U.S. Agriculture – 1959,' PhD dissertation, Yale University, 1970.

8. Wallace Huffman, 'The Contribution of Education and Extension to Differential Rates of Change,' PhD dissertation, University of Chicago, 1972.

9. Y. Kislev, and R. E. Evenson, 'Research and Productivity in Wheat and Maize Production,' *Journal of Political Economy*, forthcoming.

10. R. Nelson, and E. S. Phelps, 'Investment in Humans, Technological Diffusion and Economic Growth,' *American Economic Review*, 56: 69–75, May 1966.

11. S. P. Rayehaudhury, and S. V. Govindarajan, Soils of India, IEAR Technical Bulletin 25, Indian Council of Agricultural Research, New Delhi, 3rd ed., 1971.

12. T. W. Schultz, *Investment in Human Capital: The Role of Education and of Research* (New York: Free Press, 1971).

13. G. T. Stigler, 'The Economics of Information,' *Journal of Political Economy*, 69 (1961), 213–15.

14. Glenn T. Trewartha, 'Climates of the Earth,' in E. B. Epsenshode, *Goodes World Atlas*, 12 ed. (Chicago: Rand McNally, 1968).

15. Finis Welch, 'Education in Production,' *Journal of Political Economy*, 78 (1970).

16. USDA, 'Soils,' *1958 Yearbook of Agriculture*, Government Printing Office.

10

Recent Developments in Rural Education and Training

Nadia Forni

Introduction

In recent years the notion that lack of formal education is the one stumbling block that obstructs social and economic development has lost ground. It appears more and more uncertain, for instance, whether education follows or precedes economic growth. As Malassis[1] rightly puts it, the problem is to know if rural education is the cause or the consequence of growth. Thus while the role of informal training is gaining in momentum, formal education in its traditional forms shows its limitations as a development catalyst.

The prevailing opinion is that education promotes rural development only when it is included in a package effort touching all economic and social aspects. Education is only one of the ingredients of development; it may, however, be particularly relevant when increases in production affecting wide masses of rural people can be fostered by extending new techniques and better management without an increase in existing farm resources. The economic value of education is, however, difficult to measure. Schultz[2] states that 'only if schooling increases future productivity and earnings, do the contributions of schooling become a source of measured economic growth'. Moreover, if the effects of schooling (returns to investment) are difficult to measure, this is even more true for education in more general terms.

Clearly, what is meant by education is a wider learning process than actual schooling which may be too long and indirect a process to generate needed improvements. The mere creation of a group of formally trained people is not sufficient to overcome the inertia of organizational structures which have inherent survival ability. On the contrary, in these cases, while traditional societies are not able to utilize the new skills, the aspirations of those who have enjoyed formal training increase in a disproportionate way, and education is seen as a way to enter other types of occupation and raise one's social status. In the rural areas, in particular, education is not usually seen as a way of improving the performance of the rural economy but uniquely as a route to urban wage employment.

Without going into detail over the many issues related to rural education, it may be said that the most relevant developments in recent years
involve a few main themes.

FIRST THEME: THE INTERLOCKING OF RURAL AND URBAN FORMAL AND NON-FORMAL EDUCATION

We may risk saying that the first reason for this educational flux is
financial. New countries undertaking revolutionary innovations want to
raise the educational level of the masses with minimal discrimination
against any group or class; at the same time, they are making tremendous
efforts to increase production and raise the standard of living. The moment
comes when the financial burden of providing adequate educational
facilities appears too great. Moreover, the time-lag between training and
its effective results in the productive sector is considerable and therefore no
immediate contribution is apparent. The need to link training effectively
to production, together with an ideological movement stressing the
dignity of manual work, has given rise to a number of experiments where
trainees are also producers and vice-versa in a continuous process of
education.

The Chinese and Cuban Experiments

China, with its continuous interchange between urban and rural occupations, theoretical and practical training, is probably the most outstanding
example of the tendency towards the abolition of discrimination between
categories, particularly the rural and urban sectors. Especially since the
'cultural revolution', training has been reorientated: engineers and other
types of professional personnel will from now on be recruited from the
ranks of farmers and workers who will undergo a permanent technical
education coupled with political education. University teaching has been
completely reformed and pre-university schooling, formerly lasting
twelve years, has been reduced to nine. On its completion, all boys and
girls are to work for three years either in farms or factories and only then
may they apply for entrance to a higher institution where, in any case,
they will continue to perform manual work which will support the
training institution itself.[3]

If China is the most popular example, it is surely not the best known for
Cuba provides us with more information regarding similar experiments.
The situation is still highly fluid: the general tendency is toward the non-
separation of technical and vocational training from the general stream of
secondary education, and there is a proposal to abolish all general schools
preparatory to university, and have everybody attend technical schools.
Even while maintaining the present system of general schools, Cuban
students are urged not to isolate themselves in an academic sense. In fact,

from 45 to 120 days per year (depending on the year), are to be spent by each student in practical productive work, mostly on farms. (One should be careful here not to confuse practical work with technical teaching.) Also at the university level, teaching is strictly linked to productive work. One of the first reasons for the practical slant in education was economic need. In the first years of the revolution all technicians were considered necessary for production activities and the recruitment of adequate teachers for vocational and technical schools was very difficult. A system was therefore devised in which teaching was done directly in the production units – factories and farms became training centres.

One of the first steps in the Cuban educational revolution was the eradication of illiteracy through special courses for workers and farmers. These involved approximately one half million adults every year between 1962 and 1969. Cuba, where 24 per cent of the population was reported to be illiterate before the socialist revolution, was probably at the right stage of informational structure and economic development to make this campaign an asset for development and for maintaining the literacy and numeracy skills thus acquired.

Within the campaign to offer educational opportunities to those who had missed them in their early youth, were special directed-study programmes organized at every level for those engaged in work, and the 'workers and farmers education' system, including 'farmers and workers faculties' at the university level. For those attending normal schools, the link with the surrounding world is maintained mostly through the 'interest clubs' in each school where students conduct supervized research and discussion on technical and political topics they themselves have selected.

A special feature of Cuban education has been the existence of a very wide age bracket in all types of education. This is a symptom of the massive drive for the education of the whole population at the same time. The phenomenon is, however, likely to disappear in the future when no backlog of uneducated people exists at the basic education level.

Tanzania

Let us now rapidly examine the Tanzanian experience. The Republic of Tanzania has had to solve the problem of the need for technically trained personnel which it could not, in fact, afford to pay while, at the same time, social pressure was being exerted for increased educational facilities. Hunter[4] estimated that, in the five years following 1966, Tanzania would produce increasing numbers of standard IV and VII[5] graduates and that formal education would run ahead of the opportunities open to ex-pupils. On the basis of his experience in the sixties, he suggested (given the impossibility of altering cultivators' attitudes through primary school teaching) stressing education efforts through extension agents who, on average, were supposed to cater for over 1,700 families each: 'a major redirection of educational effort should now take place towards those educative services, particularly extension, which are directly aimed at rural development'.[6]

In fact, while over 50 per cent of the educational budget was spent on formal training, for the majority of school leavers there was no productive activity to be engaged in outside traditional agriculture. 'Each year the threshold of the "modern", educated salaried world seems to be rising higher, beyond the reach of the standard VII/VIII leaver'.[7] Accordingly, the government decided to give priority to agricultural and rural development, restricting further expansion of formal education until it could be matched by economic advance.

The most forthright spokesman for this new policy was without doubt President Nyerere: 'Individually and collectively we have in practice thought of education as a training for the skills required to earn high salaries in the modern sector of our economy. It is now time that we looked again at the justification for a poor society like ours spending almost 20 per cent of its government revenues on providing education for its children and young people, and began to consider what that education should be doing.'[8] This may show a tendency to rationalize economic stringencies, but it may also have been the occasion to rethink an educational philosophy introduced by the former colonial power and to seek for deeper 'decolonization' by inculcating commitment to the community and to an egalitarian spirit. Education must '. . . prepare young people for the work they will be called upon to do in the society which exists in Tanzania – a rural society where improvement will depend largely upon the efforts of the people in agriculture and in village development'.[9] In such a society – and here lies the limitation on entrance to secondary education for the selected few – secondary education can only be provided for a few to service the many, and the role of the educated elite in aiding the masses should not result in undemocratic developments. In addition, schools, where they exist, should not forget manual labour and should try to support themselves through a farm or workshop activity carried out by students.

A consequence of this policy was the Declaration of 1970 as 'Adult Education Year' and the stress put on cooperative action to mobilize public attention.

Moshi Cooperative College, established in 1964, and with the associated Cooperative Education Centre, was given wide responsibilities for formal training for cooperative personnel and supervisors, for short educational courses and for mass programmes through radio and other channels. The cooperative system, in a sense, has served as a test for the whole effort in adult education.[10] Mobilization of the masses with a basic message in a short time was tried in one-day induction courses. At the same time, co-operative officers were trained in specific topics related to their work and inspectors received two years training based on a system of practical field training alternating with more academic sessions.

It may be pointed out that one of the features of the experiments mentioned in Tanzania, as well as in other countries, is the return to the land for at least part of the year during the working life of each individual. This may, at the same time, represent a cathartic function for people who feel the need for complete decolonization and see in the land the original national tradition, and the recognition of the role of agriculture and rural crafts, in general, in speeding up general development.

Urban and Rural Education at the Primary Level

Undifferentiated education has its advocates and detractors. The provision of uniform education in both urban and rural areas is often criticized because it allegedly induces alienation of the children from their environment. It may be pointed out, however, that the scholastic approaches adopted are often borrowed from other societies or continents and are thus implicitly alienating. In fact, they are invariably urban oriented and thus little concerned with the values useful to a child who will stay in the rural areas. Systems as they now exist surely push the rural child toward an environment where he hopes to find the type of life he has learnt to admire and wishes to emulate.

On the other hand, the opposition to differentiation may be justified if rural education turns out to be simply a poor and cheap copy of urban education, closing any possibility to enter further training for the rural people. Clearly, the right way stands somewhere between differentiation and undifferentiation, although the wisdom necessary to strike the right balance is rare.

SECOND THEME: EDUCATION IN THE COMMUNITY MORE THAN IN THE SCHOOL

The tendency to education in the community is a result of the drive to less formally and traditionally oriented education. It has induced an increased interest in extension and 'animation' techniques and their linkages with local traditions, and a decreased emphasis on the traditional concept of farmer training – a group of selected farmers undergoing training, often at high cost, in a boarding institution removed from their home and local conditions.

In most newly independent countries, attention has been concentrated recently on the training of higher executives, while the training of farmers and village instructors has been given little attention often leading to the failure of ambitious development efforts. One could, however, argue about the extent to which these failures are due to faulty training at the grass-roots level, or to a lack of basic philosophy in applying a specific development policy. In fact, it is much easier to plan theoretically for change from a higher level than to find the way to motivate farmers to make change in spite of persisting structural difficulties. One could agree with Dumont that '. . . rural awakening which is to instil the readiness for development, the acceptance of change and the desire for innovation, is essentially a moral and political matter . . .'[11] and that a higher status should be conferred on agriculture from the top.

In human manpower mobilization an important role is assigned to extension services, beyond the limited interpretation of dissemination of agricultural information, and to 'animation' techniques. The latter were first elaborated and applied by the IRAM (*Institut de Recherche et d'Application des Méthodes de Développement*) in Morocco and later spread to other French-speaking countries of Africa. The method stresses the selection of village leaders and is usually considered a pre-extension activity and includes action on all aspects of rural life including farm production.

Extension ideology is too well known to need description. An interesting debate is going on at present concerning its financing, which may eventually have an effect on policy. In some countries, particularly those of Latin America, extension services are financed by a fixed percentage charged on agricultural export earnings. The problem is whether this results in a concentration of effort by the extension agents on export crops, which already enjoy better market facilities and technical support, thus neglecting efforts where they are most needed, i.e. in the food producing sector. Moreover, since the extension budget is linked to export-oriented markets, this would be larger in the richer regions and smaller in poorer ones where, for lack of economic information and favourable physical conditions, the extension service is most needed to stimulate the best use of available resources.

A Programme of Education in Upper Volta

Let us now note briefly a specific case where a trial was made to link formal education and extension work. In Upper Volta, the impossibility of financing universal primary education in the short run led, in 1961, to the creation of a special programme of rural education for community improvement, including a strong literacy component. The first innovation over the traditional primary education is the admission age of pupils, which is supposed to be at least 14 years in order to obtain a more motivated group. (Incidentally, raising the entrance age to primary schools seems to be a common device now in developing countries for decreasing the dropout rate.) This tendency is completely opposite to what happens in most developed countries where children are supposed to reach the necessary maturity for school at an earlier age. This clearly depends on the time that is required for teaching a minimum level of educational attainment. Another reason is that these schools are supposed to be at the same time vocational centres and literacy centres, with a limited amount of land for practical farm instruction and production for sale. Teenagers, it was believed, would be more eager to learn, better prepared to absorb simple vocational teaching and, finally, more willing to work on a farm, thus increasing school income and lowering school costs. This system, however, underestimates the social aspirations associated with education and this is often responsible for a lack of enthusiasm on the part of parents and communities.[12]

There is also the need to link strongly the educational effort with local background and tradition. In Upper Volta, for instance, there has been one major stumbling block: all teaching is in French, a language which practically none of the students knows, so that two of the three years of teaching are spent on language training, thus creating lack of interest in the whole programme which is very far away from the rural reality in which the pupils are expected to live (as compared with, for example, their colleagues in normal primary school who are preparing for occupations in the modern sector). In places where many unwritten dialects are spoken, oral transmission through person-to-person contact or via the mass media may well be the only real way of promoting modernization.

An Experience in Rural Teacher Training: Turkey

Linked to the preceding point is the problem of teacher training for the rural areas.

A system which tried to combine primary teacher training with agricultural training existed for a few years in the forties and fifties in Turkey. Boys and girls with a rural background and middle-level education were selected for one year of training in 'village teachers schools' where they were prepared for work which went far beyond teaching literacy and numeracy to rural children. Emphasis was laid on agricultural and rural crafts and on the obligation of teachers to participate in the manual work and efforts of the community to which they were sent. It may be noted that this represented a revolutionary philosophy in terms of the social status of teachers in that national society. In fact, the results of the experiment could be considered revolutionary, not so much in terms of actual technical improvements in the villages but for the amount of information, often forcefully presented, that came from those teachers who felt themselves to be the interpreters of rural people's aspirations in relation to urban society and political powers.[13] This was the first wave of articulate expression of the peasants' claims for rights and was probably one of the main causes of the abandonment of the experiment. The lesson that may be learnt from this experience is that a desire to introduce change and promote economic improvement in the countryside must be coupled with a readiness by the authorities to question the existing power structure.

The Comilla Project, Bangladesh

In the field of community improvement, through a coordinated set of efforts most of which can be classified as educational in the wide sense, one should include the famous Comilla Project in Bangladesh.[14] The area has characteristics common to many other developing countries: a high illiteracy rate, the concentration of educational facilities in urban areas, high dropout rates increasing with enrolment and a rapidly increasing educational budget. Agricultural transformation in a zone of very small farms and high population density is only possible through mobilization of human resources. It appeared, however, very early that the formal education available in schools was of little help in this transformation.

The Comilla integrated approach to rural education and development is basically centred around an agricultural cooperative supported by the Academy of Rural Development of Comilla, which started in 1959 as an experiment in rural development. This cooperative had a mushrooming effect in the whole area, where smaller cooperative units were formed. The Central Cooperative, through a Training and Development Centre, provides a series of educational services ranging from accountancy to tractor driving.

The Academy of Rural Development carried out an evaluation of the work in the sixties by comparing a series of socio-economic indices in Comilla and in another district before and after the integrated approach, which showed considerable relative improvement in Comilla. Basically, the experiment suggests the advantages of integrating educational efforts into the total development effort and stresses the use of non-formal education for those who are in the productive age group. It also suggests coupling extension information with the provision of inputs and administrative help, and insists on a democratic approach to farmers who have to define their own problems and look for solutions.

Although this is only a very rapid sketch of what Comilla does and is, some scepticism may be expressed. It has often been stated that, where all efforts are pooled, results are certain to come. In fact, the existence of the Academy of Rural Development, the availability of several sources of external financing, the existence of a group of relatively rich farmers – who are reportedly those who really participate in the cooperative work and enjoy the training facilities – have established the pre-conditions for success. Unfortunately, the problem of under-development is one involving millions and millions of people and it would be much too costly to diffuse the Comilla approach on a wide basis.

THIRD THEME: HOW TO WIN THE RACE AGAINST TIME

The realization of the need for trained personnel for planned and rapid economic development has led to a number of stop-gap measures. Accelerated training is one of the temporary measures adopted pending provision of the necessary annual outputs by the formal education system. The number of different situations which the developing countries have to face has led to the creation of just as many mixed systems (e.g. accelerated training coupled with traditional formal education) which may eventually evolve into solutions including formal and non-formal components or may revert to traditional solutions, once the emergency is over.

Accelerated Training in Algeria

Algeria has chosen to promote the accelerated training of technicians as an alternative to the intensive use of expatriate personnel and FAO is assisting the government through a UNDP-financed project. This project aims at training technicians, the so-called 'trainers' and particularly agricultural personnel to work at the farm level. About six months' intensive training in a special centre gives basic technical knowledge and, especially, a problem-solving approach to a group of technicians who are already assigned to one of the 30 Rural Training Centres spread over the country, each of which has a specialization in line with national and regional needs. The advantage is that the whole learning process is focused on the practical job the individual technician is going to do. Shorter periods of training and follow-up courses are organized regularly for all the 'trainers' already on the job, to assist them in their performance. The training of this level of technician by more formal means, which anyway could not give the specific preparation based on job analysis, would last at least two or three years.

Lower level technicians receive short training sessions in the 30 centres where there is also provision for training workshop foremen, accountants and skilled farm workers. Particular attention is given to the preparation of the teaching materials and visual aids that the 'trainers' will use in their work with technicians and workers who have enjoyed only limited formal education. In total, about 18,000 persons are expected to pass through the training facilities of the project in the 1970/73 period, aiming at the greatest possible multiplier effect. The project is an attempt to shorten a development phase in the educational sector with a temporary nucleus of international assistance. It can be successful only if motivated by the needs of the country involved. It is still early to evaluate if such accelerated training over short periods is as effective as longer training in more formal systems. This is, nonetheless, an alternative to consider for those countries that do not wish to rely on substantial foreign technical assistance until their basic personnel are trained as a result of the long process of formal schooling.

FOURTH THEME: EDUCATION FOR, AND THROUGH, LAND REFORM

There is a tendency for rural education to be seen as a part and function of a total programme of reform in the rural areas that involves changes in the relations between the cultivator and the land, between urban and rural populations and in other general areas of social and economic interaction.

The new Chilean situation seems to provide the best example of this approach. In Chile, there is a large urban market for agricultural products; less than 25 per cent of the population is dependent on agriculture. In spite of this, per capita income in agriculture before 1970 was less than half the national average and over 300,000 families were landless or living on minifundia (below-subsistence holdings, usually with unstable tenure rights).[15] However, extensive farming techniques with mechanization were used on the latifundia. This indicates that structural change was necessary to break the vicious circle.

The extensive reforms introduced by the current regime in the rural areas have met with difficulties arising from the complete lack of training, particularly in respect of management and marketing skills, among farmers. Under the preceding government, the farmer cooperatives, usually composed of better educated farmers, with a reasonable amount of land, had difficulties because of a lack of farm management and accounting skills. At present, the beneficiaries are no longer a few selected farmers, but whole villages including previously landless labourers. This makes training an even more important factor. It is believed in Chile that extensive trade union participation can facilitate mass training. The socio-economic conditions and the development stage which would permit trade unions to have a position of influence in mass organizations and training would be worth studying in relation to other countries. In Chile, in 1971, about 60 per cent of the farmers were unionized.

The INDAP (*Instituto de Desarrollo Agropecuario*) in charge of credit and technical assistance has identified some of the basic faults of agricultural training under previous regimes.[16]

First, training was divorced from the economic realities under which farmers worked; therefore the graduates of the training schools were usually giving inappropriate advice in view of the farmers' limited resources. Second, training at all levels was done without the participation of the farmers or farmers' organizations. Third, farmer training was not available for agricultural workers and both groups developed separate organizations and aspirations thus segregating the agricultural working class.

This is why the first efforts were aimed at strengthening unionism and the cohesion of the working class through cooperative organizations. In 1971–72, a total of over 140,000 small farmers and agricultural workers, 28 per cent of the total number of persons in this category, were selected to attend short courses aiming at improving the quality of the *campesino* movement. Courses were oriented to strengthen the internal organization of the unions, offer accounting and administrative assistance and basic ideological and political information. There was no distinction between political and technical assistance, the difficulty being to give a balanced share of each.

The importance of technical training is stressed in the two year plan (1972–73) for agricultural production.[17] This is the first plan for the 'reformed' areas of Chile (the total expropriated area up to September 1971 was approximately one million hectares). The aim for these areas is to use labour-intensive techniques and increase productivity at the same time. It has been pointed out in this context that, due to lack of knowledge among farmers, campaigns for improved fertilizer use and other techniques had not led to the expected results and actually a decrease in productivity has been observed in many places. Therefore, the need to train technicians intensively and continuously to make technical advice available to farmers has been underlined.

A fall in production following land reform seems to be a constant phenomenon in many countries. Simple fragmentation of big holdings leaves the farmer alone to fight against management and marketing problems with which he cannot cope. Only the injection of assistance both for purely technical matters and for marketing purposes (together, of course, with the credit and other inputs that the *big landowner alone* had previously had access to) can reverse this trend in the first phase.

Responsibility for organizing technical agricultural training in Chile is given to the so-called 'integrated cultivation teams' that try to break the traditional duplication of effort by several public bodies. The teams are composed of representatives of the Agrarian Reform Corporation (CORA), the Agriculture and Livestock Service (SAG), the State Development Corporation (CORFO) with the assistance of the regional units of the National Agricultural Research Institute (INIA) plus other specialized agencies dealing with pest control, fertilizers, etc. Several types of course are organized by these teams, usually lasting only a few days on very specific subjects. They try to cover the needs of specialists and other technicians as well as of farmers by giving refresher courses through the organization of practical demonstrations.

It is early to analyse the results of this training drive. Too many other factors are involved to measure the real impact of training. What is felt strongly is a need to link the technician with the life and needs of the farmer. It has been proposed, for instance, in line with traditional US practice, that the technician be dependent for salary and be responsible as regards performance to the community he serves and that the future technician should be selected from that community for training. Traditionally, however, in Latin America as well as elsewhere, the agricultural technician is socially closer to the land-owner, i.e. the educated class, than to the farmer. The adjustment therefore requires political propaganda and a change in the scale of values, propagated also through formal training institutions. It should be noted also that the adjustment may be attainable in a relatively short time in Chile which has a potentially advanced rural society with the lowest rate of illiteracy in Latin America. It may be more difficult to achieve in other parts of the world.

REGIONAL ASPECTS OF RURAL EDUCATION

Some of the main features of new forms of rural education have been outlined above. Although this is far from being a comprehensive list, we can see a number of developments that fall under one or other of these major headings in most regions of the world. There are however a few developments that are peculiar to certain geographic areas.

ASIA

The Higher Level

The creation of fully-fledged agricultural universities is typical of some countries in Asia. In the late sixties there were thirteen agricultural universities in Asia which attempted to achieve integration of research and extension and also to make formal higher level teaching relevant and directly useful for the needs of the farming masses. These institutions could be responsible for improving the image of agriculture as an effective path to economic advancement and also possibly for the increased number of students choosing agriculture as a course of study: 4·1 per cent of total university enrolments in 1968 compared with 2·9 per cent in 1957 and an actual increase in numbers of 347 per cent over the period.

The Intermediate Level

In most countries, this level of education represents only a small part of the responsibilities of ministries and the lack of sufficient policy direction and support is often felt. Moreover, it is common practice to staff these institutions through transfer from other branches of the agricultural services, disregarding teaching attitudes and appropriate training, and without providing good career prospects.

TABLE 1
ASIA – AGRICULTURAL EDUCATION AT THE UNIVERSITY LEVEL
IN SELECTED COUNTRIES*

	1957	1968	Increase 1968 over 1957 (1957 = 100)
Number of institutions	81	143	176
Number of students	23,316	81,033	347
Agricultural students as per cent of total number of students	2·9	4·1	
Number of graduates	5,538	13,172	238
Agricultural graduates as per cent of total number of graduates	2·9	3·5	

* 1957 and 1968 were considered as basic reference years for a decade. National data included in the totals refer to the basic years or to surrounding periods. The sample includes seven Asian countries: Sri Lanka (Ceylon), India, the Republic of Korea, Malaysia, the Philippines, Taiwan and Thailand. Scattered data were also available for other countries but were not included because their bases were largely non-comparable. Although errors may exist in the national figures the basic trends and the order of magnitude ought to be correct.

SOURCES: Unesco, *Statistical Yearbook* 1970, Paris, 1971; C. W. Chang, *Rural Asia Marches Forward*, Los Baños: University of the Philippines, 1969; Unesco, *Agricultural Education in Asia*, Paris, 1971.

In spite of these shortcomings, enrolments are generally rising. Some exceptions were pointed out in one Unesco study[18] but the lack of comparable statistics over the years may be responsible for the apparent decline. This publication gives a total enrolment of over 200 thousand students in the late sixties in agricultural education institutions below university level in 19 countries. It should, however, be mentioned that relatively little quantitative information is available on this level. It is therefore difficult to indicate the main patterns of growth since national statistics often include different categories of school and are hardly comparable.

LATIN AMERICA

The Higher Level

One problem that seriously hampers university level agricultural education concerns high wastage rates during training. Part-time commitment to the university is characteristic of both students, whose attendance is intermittent, and teaching staff, who often occupy other more remunerative positions outside the university. This phenomenon is possibly one of the most immediate causes of high wastage rates. In one Latin American country, out of an enrolment of 2,500 at the National Agricultural University, the annual output is reported to be only 150 graduates which would mean a wastage rate of approximately 70 per cent. Moreover, those who graduate from Latin American universities seem to remain in the student body for substantially longer periods than the minimum required. A statistical survey of the University of Buenos Aires[19] reports, for instance, that the average time necessary for the students to graduate from the five year course of the agricultural faculty is 7·4 years.

The Intermediate Level

The World Conference on Agricultural Education and Training[20] exposed another area of weakness in Latin America. Middle level education and training is far from adequate. It does not supply the numbers needed for the agricultural and related sectors of the economy, and fails also to train the individuals in a practical sense. It seems evident that if progress is to be made in the next decade, the area of middle-level education and training should be given high priority.

At this level there is now a tendency to try to introduce economies of scale by developing multi-purpose technical schools in which agriculture constitutes only one stream. But, unless the schools are rural in outlook and training, integration is difficult and the danger exists of creating substantially academic types of training.

As far as the programmes of teaching are concerned, while curricula are generally highly technical in content, farm management and other economic aspects are neglected and there is a lack of basic information in these subjects. These deficiencies exist at all levels but are more evident at the intermediate level. Another area which is neglected in almost all countries of the region is the preparation of agricultural teachers. This often leads to the appointment to teaching positions of technically competent people who have not mastered the art of communication and have an imperfect understanding of the social significance of their job.

In the past, FAO has produced manpower estimates for the region.[21] However these have often been based on ideal ratios which often imply an absorptive capacity in the agricultural services far above reality. It has been necessary to revise the estimates in view of the extensive changes that are occurring in many countries of the region in terms of agrarian reform and the latter may require different types of input. In Peru, for instance, extensive changes in the whole educational structure are being considered and a law is under discussion to promulgate the new organization. Thus, there will be a new type of secondary school (*Escuelas Superiores de Educacion Profesional, ESEP*), attendance at which will be compulsory for all those going to the university. A proportion of these schools will specialize in agriculture. However, what is mostly needed in Peru, as elsewhere where agrarian reform is either in progress or contemplated, is a shift from preparing technicians who largely relate to large landowners to training more broadly based rural development agents who personally participate in the peasants' life and aspirations, thus abolishing the present 'class' distinction which makes dialogue difficult. It is also most desirable for these people themselves to come from a rural background.

AFRICA

Typical of this continent is the large number of expatriates in the professional category. To take an extreme example, it was estimated that in Zambia in 1971 87 per cent of university trained agriculturists in all fields were expatriates. This necessarily affects the whole structure of basic rural education since the planners and supervisors are often not local people and the danger of introducing and reinforcing in the educational system foreign elements which are difficult to assimilate at the grass-roots level, is very high. This fact only emphasises the need for rapidly developing a corps of indigenous technicians relying as much as possible on local institutions.

The Higher Level

There are now relatively few countries in the region which do not have a higher level agricultural institution. A number of regional institutions, built in the fifties and early sixties, have been dissolved and replaced by national ones. Some of the new institutions are still in the developmental stage and, therefore, the quality of output over the region as a whole is variable. As a result of the proliferation of institutions, the number of students at the degree level is now fairly impressive. The creation of many of these institutions has only been possible through the use of large numbers of expatriate staff and there are still indications that there is a shortage of adequately trained Africans to fill specific positions. This point is perhaps underlined by the fact that the majority of postgraduate training still has to be done abroad and postgraduate schools of adequate standard are only just beginning to emerge. African staff are still often relatively young and inexperienced and facilities are limited. As a result, the output of adequate applied research in the agricultural and social sciences is small. So far, there are rather limited signs of regional and sub-regional co-operation, except in specific subject-matter areas and at Makerere University, which is increasingly taking over the role of a postgraduate training centre for East Africa.

The Intermediate Level

As at the higher level, the influence of the ex-colonial powers has been strongly marked in the creation of intermediate training institutions. There has been a substantial increase in numbers with an almost bewildering variety of levels and types. Throughout these intermediate institutions, there is a notable tendency to upgrade them toward higher levels,

thus often defeating the original objective of providing field level technicians. In fact, many of these intermediate level institutions have failed
to produce people with a sufficiently practical orientation toward field
work.

The contribution of women to agriculture and rural life in most
countries of the region is of great significance and it should be noted that
a number of countries have made good progress in providing intermediate
training in a range of subjects for girls.

In general, however, the provision of adequate training for staff for
intermediate institutions has been unsatisfactory. It is useless to assume that
young graduates from higher level institutions are properly equipped for
the very practical teaching required at this level unless they receive careful

TABLE 2

AFRICA[1] – AGRICULTURAL TRAINING INSTITUTIONS BY LEVEL AND MAIN
GEOGRAPHICAL REGION

Geographical Regions	University level	Higher intermediate level[2]	Lower intermediate level[2]	Vocational level[3]
North West Africa	6	30	66	10
Central Africa	4	22	38	11
Eastern and Southern Africa	7	16	19	6
Western Africa	11	15	35	48
Total	28	83	158	75

[1] Includes only independent countries. The Arab Republic of Egypt, the Libyan Arab
Republic, the Somali Democratic Republic and the Democratic Republic of the Sudan are part
of the Near East Region of FAO and are therefore not included.

North Africa: Algeria, Morocco, Tunisia (3)

Central Africa: Burundi, Cameroon, Central African Republic, Chad, Congo, Gabon
Rwanda, Zaire (8)

Eastern and Southern Africa: Botswana, Ethiopia, Kenya, Lesotho, Malagasy Republic,
Malawi, Mauritius, Swaziland, Tanzania, Uganda, Zambia (11)

Western Africa: Dahomey, Gambia, Ghana, Guinea, Ivory Coast, Liberia, Mali, Mauritania,
Niger, Nigeria, Senegal, Sierra Leone, Togo, Upper Volta (14)

[2] Some difficulty exists concerning the classification of schools given the difference between
the English and French systems. In principle, schools of the deuxième cycle have been classified
together with the Diploma level schools in the Higher intermediate category; while premier
cycle schools have been classified in the Lower intermediate category together with 'certificate'
schools of the English system.

[3] Only schools offering a formal curriculum of at least one year's duration are included. The
borderline between this type of training and informal farmer training is, however, hard to
define.

NOTE The institutions listed are of variable size. It would have been more meaningful to
give the number of students in addition to institutions. However, the situation is changing
so rapidly that data of this kind become obsolete, and also enrolment figures are not available
for all the institutions covered.

SOURCE: FAO Directory of Institutions in Forty African Countries, Rome 1969.

preparation and unless they are selected on the basis of their aptitude for teaching. Some countries have adopted a common career structure for the products of the intermediate institutes and the extension services, but there is a need in all cases for a closer link between intermediate teaching, the extension services and other forms of non-formal training. In too few intermediate institutions are farm facilities of adequate standard available for proper instruction; it is also true to say that far too little use is made of the surrounding district as a living agricultural and social teaching area.

Farm Families

Quite clearly, the major endeavour in the last decade has been aimed at the creation of institutions to train people to serve the farming community (farmer training centres). Comparatively little effort has been applied to the development of non-formal types of education aimed at the farm families which numerically constitute an enormous challenge. Indeed, even assuming that the majority of those graduating from formal institutions are actually employed in extension or similar work, they can only ever reach a small proportion of those actually farming, and the prospects for extension in its present forms having a really significant impact are very limited. Equally critical is the serious problem of rural youth for whom little has been done so far. A number of countries have developed club programmes and formal training of varying length for small numbers, but these have had little impact on the very limited and sometimes hopeless prospects for rural youth.

Some indication of the relative importance of the different levels of agricultural education in the different regions of Africa is provided in Table 2.

THE NEAR EAST

In this region, it is possible to observe two extreme situations: in some countries the lack of trained personnel in agriculture slows down the development process because of the technical isolation of the agricultural producers from modern sources of information; in others, such as the Arab Republic of Egypt, an excess of trained personnel in comparison with the absorptive capacity of the public sector structures is apparent at all levels (Table 3).

In the case of Egypt with 14 agricultural faculties and colleges and 49 intermediate agricultural schools, the employment of technicians implies the spending of practically all scarce resources on salaries so that the effectiveness of these persons for development purposes is minimized because of lack of equipment and supporting inputs. Some redirection of technical teaching toward more practical skills for work in direct contact with the farmer is under way. A sign of this is the possible establishment

TABLE 3
THE NEAR EAST: AGRICULTURAL EDUCATION AND TRAINING
NUMBER OF STUDENTS AND INSTITUTIONS OF UNIVERSITY AND INTERMEDIATE LEVEL[1]

Country	Agric. Pop. 1970[2] (000's)	Agric. pop. as percent of total Agric. Pop. in Region	University Level — No. of institutions	University Level — No. of students	University Level — No. of students as percent of total in region	Intermediate Level — No. of institutions	Intermediate Level — No. of students	Intermediate Level — No. of students as percent of total in region
Afghanistan	13,691	10.9	1	800	1.9	5	907	2.0
Cyprus	244	0.2	—	—	—	1	200	0.4
Egypt (Arab. Rep. of)	16,655	13.3	14	30,496	71.7	49	31,500	69.5
Iran	15,440	12.3	6	2,300[5]	5.4	29	4,983[5]	11.0
Iraq	5,062	4.0	3	2,012	4.7	14	3,771	8.3
Jordan	672	0.5	—	—	—	4	535	1.2
Kuwait	74[3]	0.1	1	253	0.6	1	50	0.1
Lebanon	1,291	1.0	1	313	0.7	2	90	0.2
Libyan Arab Rep.	1,106	0.9	4	3,808	8.9	8	256	0.6
Pakistan	44,000[3]	35.2	1	500[5]	1.2	—	851	1.9
Saudi Arabia	3,189	2.6	—	—	—	1	60[5]	0.1
Somali Dem. Rep.	2,543	2.0	1	377	0.9	2	395[5]	0.9
Sudan	11,574	9.3	2	1,668	3.9	12	1,619[6]	3.6
Syrian Arab Rep.	3,083	2.5	—	—	—	—	—	—
Yemen Arab Rep.	5,498	4.4	—	—	—	—	—	—
Yemen People's Dem. Rep.	924	0.7	—	—	—	2	76	0.1
TOTAL REGION	125,046	100.0[4]	34	42,527	100.0[5]	131	45,293	100.0[5]

[1] The information refers mostly to the early seventies. It includes formal training in agriculture and animal husbandry (veterinary assistants' schools at intermediate level are also included). It does not include forestry, fisheries, veterinary medicine.

[2] (Forecast) FAO 1970. Note that these data tend to be lower than the 1970 rural population figures given for a limited number of countries in the *UN Demographic Year Book*, 1970.

[3] Country estimate 1971.

[4] Errors due to rounding.

[5] In most cases only capacity figures were available. The total enrolment is thus likely to be overestimated.

[6] Some underestimation is possible.

Source: FAO *Directory of Agricultural Education and Training Institutions in the Near East Region*, Rome, 1971.

of a training centre for agricultural and related skills, with attention to intermediate technologies, that would draw its enrolment from rural youth. The Centre which is to be located in an intensive cultivation area of the Nile Delta will receive international support.

The Higher Level

Very few institutions at this level existed before the late fifties outside Egypt and Pakistan; but in the last decade, university faculties of agriculture have multiplied and many now offer postgraduate training. As Table 3 shows however, almost 72 per cent of the total student body is in Egypt, which accounts for only 13 per cent of agricultural population in the region although many students in the Arab Republic of Egypt come from other countries.

The tendency in many universities of the region is toward extreme specialization, which is often criticized as being costly and not suited to the existing pattern of labour market mobility. Uncoordinated expansion of the student body is another challenge that most educational planners will have to face in future years.

The Intermediate Level

At this level, beside a few excellent institutions, we find a large number of schools that are not equipped to produce practically-oriented generalists for extension and other farm services. It may be noted also that enrolment in the intermediate schools is slightly lower than at universities. Of course, university courses are of longer duration, so that the two figures are not strictly comparable. However, this indicates a serious imbalance if the internationally accepted ratio of one professional to five technicians is considered valid. It may also be pointed out that about 70 per cent of the total enrolment is in Egypt and that some countries (see columns 2 and 8 of Table 3) have a very inadequate coverage at this level of education. Assistance and training for farmers necessarily reflects this lack of field personnel, with the remarkable exceptions of some irrigation and development areas (notably in the Sudan).

Iran has tried to cope with the lack of trained personnel in the rural areas by mobilizing educated people through the army. Young men and women engaged on military service are allowed to apply for three types of public service: the Literacy corps, the Health corps, and the Extension and Development corps. The first of these programmes started operating in 1962 and they are under continuous expansion. Candidates are selected from among university and secondary school graduates whose training is pertinent to the corps' speciality. Those selected are given an initial four months of training, a quarter of the time being devoted to military training and the rest to technical subjects. For the remaining 18 months, they are under the supervision of the appropriate technical ministries (Agriculture, Health, Education) and are assigned to work in villages. While the Extension and Development corps is more directly related to agriculture, the Literacy and Health corpsmen are given training in rural subjects so that they may advise on the different problems arising in rural communities.

CONCLUSION

Before concluding, one issue should be mentioned which is highly relevant to the future of all developing regions. This concerns the participation of one half of the rural population – the women – in the development effort. This calls for special programmes of appropriate training. As Dumont writes:

> An essential fact for Africa is that numerous fields, especially for food crops, are cultivated almost entirely by women. In certain regions these latter even carry the major part of the work of cultivation. Now advice for improvement is given to the men, by men. The rare women advisers speak to the women of the housekeeping problems, of gardens and of the rearing of smaller animals. It seems necessary to talk to them also about large-scale cultivation, about food crops, and for this reason, an increase in the number of women advisers, and of the quality of their training, has seemed indispensable to us.[22]

The sentiments expressed are applicable to many other regions of the world. In the Eastern European countries, there has been an increase in the number of women undertaking agricultural training but in most other countries, and particularly in the developing world, the whole social pressure has been to keep women as unskilled agricultural workers, be it in big holdings or on the small family farm, while advancement in social status is only possible by leaving agriculture.

How much is being done to correct this distortion is hard to ascertain, but it is surely insufficient. While female participation in formal education generally increases steadily, in agriculture it is often still very low (Table 4). It seems, however, imperative both for economic and socio-political motives to start action in order to mobilize this half of the population who could have a far-reaching impact on the development of rural areas.

This has been a rapid review of some of the main topics relevant to rural education in developing countries. Educational change is a slow process and no dramatic results are to be expected in the short run. However, new ways are being tried all over the world to make rural education an effective vehicle for development. Which of these initiatives will survive cannot be easily forecast; it is clear that, apart from their inherent merits, their success will depend on the complex of socio-economic circumstances in which the educational system operates and on how well

TABLE 4
Number of Farm Families and Agricultural Enrolment at Degree and Diploma Level in Selected Countries in Asia and the Near East

Countries	Number of farm families (000's)	Enrolment in agriculture at degree level[4]		Enrolment in agriculture at diploma level[1],[4]	
		Total	Percent female	Total	Percent female
Afghanistan	2,372[2]	468	0·2	—	—
Burma	3,067[3]	822	17·0	422	1·1
Ceylon	1,170[2]	110	17·3	246	16·3
Iran	2,972[2]	1,732	10·3	257	21·8
Japan	4,658[3]	13,413	5·7	4,260	5·7
Philippines	3,027[2]	14,434	30·5	567	—
Thailand	3,998[2]	1,668	29·7	536	3·1

[1] Junior Colleges and other post-secondary institutions below degree level.

[2] FAO *Provisional Indicative World Plan for Agriculture Development*, Vol. 2 p. 486 (data refer to 1962).

[3] 1965 FAO agricultural population estimate assuming an average size of family of five persons.

[4] Enrolments refer to the academic years 1968–69 and 1969–70

Source: FAO *The State of Food and Agriculture 1972*, Rome, 1972, Chapter 3.

this system serves and interprets the development objectives of the country.

REFERENCES

1. L. Malassis, *Développement économique et programmation de l'éducation rurale* (Paris: Unesco, 1966).

2. T. W. Schultz, *The Economic Value of Education* (New York: Columbia University Press, 1963).

3. Two interesting sets of articles touching these problems were published by the French journal *Le Monde* in September 1971 and February 1972. Unfortunately, professional documentation on these developments is presently available only to limited groups of Sinologists.

4. G. Hunter, *Manpower and Educational Needs in the Traditional Sector* (Paris: IIEP, 1966) p. 13.

5. Lower and upper primary.

6. G. Hunter, ibid; p. 74.

7. G. Hunter, *Manpower, Employment and Education in the Rural Economy Tanzania* (Paris: IIEP), p. 33.

8. J. K. Nyerere, 'Education for Self-Reliance' in *Ujamaa, Essays on Socialism* (Dar es Salaam: OUP, 1968) p. 44.

9. ibid. p. 52.

10. S. Grabe, *The Cooperative Education System of Tanzania* (Paris: IIEP, 1966).

11. R. Dumont, *African Agriculture and its Educational Requirements* (Paris: IIEP, 1966).

12. See also V. L. Griffith, *The Problems of Rural Education* (Paris: IIEP, Unesco, 1968) p. 16.

13. See, for instance, M. Makal, *A Village in Anatolia* (London: Valentine, Mitchell & Co, 1954).

14. A. F. Raper, *Rural Development in Action – The Comprehensive Experiment at Comilla, East Pakistan* (Ithaca: Cornell University Press, 1970). FAO/Action for Development, *Comilla: An Experiment in Non-Formal Education* (Panel of Experts on the Involvement of People in their Own Development) Rome, 1971.

15. S. Barraclough, *Agrarian Reform in Chile* (Santiago: ICIRA, 1970) (Draft).

16. INDAP, *La Nueva Politica de Desarollo Social* (Santiago: INDAP, DESOC, 1971).

17. Equipos Agropecuarios CORA-SAG-ICIRA, *Marco de Programación 1972* (Santiago, 1972).

18. Unesco, *Agricultural Education in Asia* (Paris, 1971) p. 27.

19. Universidad de Buenos Aires, *Anuario Estadistico 1971.*

20. FAO/ILO/Unesco, *World Conference on Agricultural Education and Training,* Report, Vol. II, Rome 1971.

21. FAO, *Provisional Indicative World Plan for Agricultural Development,* Rome 1970, Vol. 2, Chapter 12.

22. R. Dumont, *Tanzanian Agriculture after the Arusha Declaration,* (Dar es Salaam: Ministry of Economic Affairs and Development Planning, 1969) p. 33.

Case Studies

Philip Foster and James R. Sheffield

There can be no doubt that contemporary transformationist or radical models for rural development as exemplified in the policies pursued by Mainland China, Cuba and Tanzania have aroused considerable interest. It is, of course, virtually impossible to obtain the kinds of data that would enable us to meaningfully evaluate the outcomes of these vast social experiments, but some descriptive materials are available and it is clear from these that a 'total mobilization' of society is at least being attempted. H. P. Lee thus places rural education in China within a broad framework including ideological education and rural public health programmes as well as more conventional forms of technical and agricultural training. As in China it is apparent from Rolland Paulston's description of how Castro has tried to 'make Cuba one big Revolutionary School' that in the latter country ideological commitment is viewed as the primary factor in stimulating rural development. Tanzania by contrast, hardly possesses the logistical resources necessary to undertake programmes on the scale that has been attempted in China or Cuba, but Solomon Odia's essay demonstrates that Tanzania does, in fact, share a number of premises concerning development in common with the other two countries. Whether her rural masses are willing to be mobilized in terms of the objectives adumbrated in Nyere's 'Education and Self-Reliance' or 'Socialism and Rural Development' remains to be seen.

Although the more radically oriented nations have accorded education – both formal and informal – a central role in transforming their societies the remaining case studies in this section reveal a more cautious and pragmatic orientation. The writers attach far less importance to ideological questions and are more inclined to see issues in terms of economic incentives and market opportunities. Thus Guy Hunter suggests that, at least in Africa, educational reform – however important it may be in other contexts – cannot solve the continuing problem of rural underemployment: the creation of new job opportunities is largely a function of trends in local economies. John Anderson also addresses himself directly to the question of the underutilization of rural, human resources when he describes the village polytechnic movement in Kenya – a series of small, mainly self-help, training schemes for primary school leavers.

Whatever the merits of informal education may be, it is obvious that at some point or the other formal training institutions must exist to prepare the cadres of agricultural scientists, technologists and fieldworkers without efforts the farmer cannot be expected to effect substantial transformations in agricultural practice. Therefore, André Voisin describes the various formal training programmes in agriculture that have developed in Francophone Africa as a result of colonial and post-colonial experience. But Gelia Castillo's following reflections on the contribution of an extensive system of formal agricultural training to rural development in the Philippines obliges us to realize that this kind of input is of extremely limited utility when other conditions are not met.

Finally, we return to a series of contributions more explicitly oriented to the social sciences. Manning Nash examines the developmental role of rural education in Burma and Malaysia from the viewpoint of the cultural anthropologist but his essay is followed by two others in a markedly different methodological tradition. Using path analysis as his principal tool Bruce Harker examines the relation of education to innovatory behaviour among Japanese farmers, and his rigorous, quantitatively oriented study is followed by D. P. Chaudhri's equally careful empirical piece that lends support to the view that agricultural productivity in India is significantly related to the level of education. Hard data of this kind are all too seldom available in the literature but more investigations in this tradition are vital if we are to develop any real understanding of the relation between education and developmental processes.

Education and Rural Development in China Today

H. P. Lee

Although the revolution in China today, as claimed by its leaders, must be continued and has yet a long way to go, the success so far in transforming and modernizing the rural areas, as one of the achievements of the revolution, has won world-wide recognition. This chapter is a study, based on instances rather than theories, of the role of education in the transformation and modernization of rural areas in China today. Education here, in pragmatic terms, means an instrument which is used to rectify people's ideology and to train socialist workers for national reconstruction. This study begins with a brief review of the reforms and innovations that have led to a reorientation of pre-1949 education in China and then investigates some of the major educational programmes which have successfully embodied the plans for rural development. The most notable achievements of China's rural development programme have been the elevation of the cultural level of the rural masses; the increase in farm production and the relative disappearance of destitution and ill-health which had dogged China's rural areas before. In the context of these three achievements, a variety of programmes will be discussed under three headings: literacy and mass ideological education; agricultural and technical education and rural public health education. Finally we examine some of the potentialities and problems of China's education for rural development schemes.

Reforms, Innovations and Revolution

Since coming to power in 1949, China's leaders like those of many other nations of the so-called 'Third World', have been eager to stimulate their nation's development and have been preoccupied with the notion of achieving a general standard of living comparable to that prevailing in the well-developed nations. Therefore most of the programmes in the 4th Five-year Plan (1971–75) have concentrated on 'striving to change China's economic and scientific and cultural backwardness within several decades and enabling it rapidly to reach advanced world level.'[1] As the great majority of China's population live in rural areas, China's development strategy has been to give priority to rural areas and thus programmes for rural development are specially emphasized.

In order to provide the necessary technology and manpower for the improvement of rural conditions, and to ensure that supply will meet demand, education in China has been drastically reformed and reoriented over the past two decades. In establishing the new educational order China has adopted a double-track system, known as a policy of 'walking on two legs' – formal schools and non-formal schools. In the former, both primary and secondary, and particularly those in the large cities, many traditional features remain, despite some fundamental changes in curriculum and teaching. The non-formal schools, particularly those in the countryside, set up on an *ad hoc* basis and for immediate use, are *sui generis*. Curriculum and teaching in these schools are determined by practical needs, and the education offered by them stops when student needs have been met. Nevertheless, it is these non-formal schools that have contributed most markedly to what has been accomplished in China's rural areas today.

In the early fifties, schools, particularly the institutions of higher learning inherited from the Kuomintang regime, were completely reformed. The reform included the nationalization of foreign and missionary schools and others sponsored and run by private citizens. As a result, through consolidation and relocation at the college level, from the 227 institutions of higher learning in 1953, 18 new comprehensive universities, 50 new institutions of technology or polytechnology, and 167 new specialized institutes were organized.[2]

At the secondary school level, the general vocational schools were all converted into schools specializing in subjects such as agriculture, mining, chemical engineering, trade, pharmacy, etc. Altogether 22 different kinds of specialized school emerged throughout the country.[3] In addition, technical courses were added on to the curriculum of the general middle schools, so that the graduates of these could acquire some kind of technical skill for productive work if they chose not to go on to higher education. This reform brought an end to the traditionally literacy-oriented and urban-centred schooling, and spelled the beginning of a new era and new meaning for Chinese education.

Under the pressure of demands to produce more, better, faster and more economically in order to speed up the socialist reconstruction of the nation, workers in factories and on farms felt an increased need to learn new knowledge and skills in order to improve their productivity. Consequently, a great variety of schools for short-term and on-the-job training have been instituted. Most of these schools are operated on the principle of *min-pan, kung-chu* (local people manage and government subsidizes). The innovations culminated with the launching of the 'Great

Leap Forward' movement in production, and also with the advent of the people's communes in 1958. As a result, there are schools almost everywhere in the country, and almost everyone, regardless of age or sex, has become a student.

In the wake of the recent Cultural Revolution came the revolution in education. As the Cultural Revolution was seen by the Chinese proletariat as an attempt to right what was wrong in the society at large, so too was regarded the revolution in education. According to a decision made by the Central Committee of the Chinese Communist Party the former educational system and the extant principles and methods of teaching were to be remodelled, and new policies and forms of operation were to be adopted.[4] Under the new policy, for instance, a student who wants to continue his education does not have to pass the competitive entrance examinations, which formerly deprived many of the opportunity to receive a higher education. Instead, students are now selected and recommended by the commune to which they belong. The pattern of school administration has also been changed: the former office of the president or principal has been replaced by a revolutionary committee composed of workers, soldiers, and representatives of students and teachers. It is believed that schools operated under such committees are more able to meet the needs of the people, for the members of the committee know more about the real social, economic, and political problems of the country than do professors and academic authorities. In the new curriculum, courses are 'few but essential', and theoretical learning is followed by practice and application. In many cases, teaching materials are prepared and compiled by workers and soldiers together with students and teachers. Obviously, this revolution in China's educational system results in more people having access to an education that is more practical for rural development.

Literacy and Mass Ideological Education

It is believed by Chinese revolutionary leaders that to ensure success in a revolution, programmes for revolutionizing people's thinking should be carried out first. Therefore, education for remolding the attitudes of the rural masses is regarded as a strategic necessity, and a new attitude among the masses is believed to be the driving force through which a new society can be created.

To suit the cultural level of the rural population, the content of rural mass ideological education is simple but essential. The channels through which such education is disseminated are not formal schools, but rather the activities of the non-formal schools and literacy classes.

The most successful example of applying literacy and mass ideological education to rural development has been the transformation of Tachai

Village, despite the fact that the Tachai episode reflects only the rudimentary programmes of the Chinese Communists undertaken in their
early days. The transformation has been considered so successful that
Tachai has become a model village and a centre of 'pilgrimage'. Each year
it receives millions of visitors from all parts of China, and thousands of
foreign visitors. In 1964, the Chinese leaders used the slogan: 'in agriculture, learn from Tachai'. This was repeated in 1968. Today, millions
of Chinese peasants, motivated by the aspiration to 'let the flower of
Tachai bloom all over the country', are labouring to create their own
Tachais.

Prior to its transformation, Tachai was a small northern Chinese
mountain village with a population of 288 from 73 different households,
scattered over the slopes of the Taihan Mountains in Shansi Province.
Nearly 70 per cent of its population were landless peasants, and the total
acreage of farmland owned by the Tachai people was about 800 mu (one
mu is approximately equal to one-sixth of an acre). This acreage was
divided into 4,700 tiny plots spread out over gullies, ridges and slopes.
(Some of the plots were literally not even big enough for a tractor to
stand on). Stony soil and unruly waters reduced the yield of grain to a
minimum so the villagers continually lived under the shadow of poverty
and the constant threat of starvation.[5]

Since 1945 when Tachai Village was first liberated from the Japanese by
Communist guerrillas, the Tachai people began to try to transform their
land. By 1964, the old poverty-stricken village had taken on a new look,
and had turned into a place of hope, security and pride. New brick
buildings had replaced the old caves, and electric light had driven away
the old shadow of poverty.

In the process of the transformation and modernization of Tachai, mass
ideological education, which had been specially designed for changing
people's attitudes and motivations, played a vital role. Chen Yung-kuei,
the protagonist of the Tachai effort, said, 'People can change the land,
technique, output and village because they have changed their thinking.
This change is the result of arming them with Marxism-Leninism and
Mao Tse-tung's thought.'[6]

Literacy and the Raising of Mass Cultural Standards

A rise in cultural standards in China today necessitates an increase in
literacy, for the high rate of illiteracy has been a persistent obstacle to
modernization. In 1945, after the Communists had driven the Japanese
out and moved into Tachai, they launched a literacy programme in which
was embodied a scheme for starting a programme of land reform as a
precondition for the development of the village. The initial phase of the
literacy programme was to introduce the name of the Communist Party,

which in Chinese is *Kung-ch'an-tang* (the commonly sharing property party). While the people were learning these characters and their meaning, they were encouraged to start a redistribution of land in the village and finally, after several fierce struggles against the landowners, the peasants shared equally the land and property in the village.

When the peasants obtained their share of land, they found that they were not able to tend it for lack of the necessary animals and tools. Consequently, these landowning peasants still had no means of improving their condition. Under these circumstances, the literacy programme began to introduce a new phase *tsu-chih ch'i-lai* (get organized)[7] through which the peasants were taught the significance and advantage of being organized. Therefore, a mutual-aid team of nine peasants gradually took shape under the leadership of a 32-year-old man, Chen Yung-kuei, who later became a leading figure in the development of Tachai. The team members worked together assiduously, and their farm production was consequently higher than those who worked individually. Soon others saw the advantage of organized labour and came to join the mutual-aid team. This team developed into a primary-stage agricultural cooperative in 1952, and a higher, or socialist, agricultural cooperative in 1956. Finally in 1958, Tachai Village became a production brigade following the formation of the People's Commune which was named after the village.

These literacy programmes that incorporate ideological education usually follow no fixed schedule. Those peasants who can read teach those who cannot. Twigs, stalks and even fingers are often used to write characters on the ground and the characters introduced and practiced are always related to farming and crops, such as *tu* (soil), *shui* (water), *fei* (fertilizer), *chung* (seeds), *mai* (wheat), *ku* (millet), *yumi* (corn), etc.

Group Study

For those peasants who are at a relatively advanced level of literacy there is a group study organization, which takes three different forms: group meetings in the village, small study groups in the field, and family meetings. The subject matter for these study groups is mainly Mao's 'three constantly read articles'.[8]

The village group study meetings are held mostly in the evenings and on rainy days when the people cannot work on the farms, and also during daytime or evenings in the winter season. At the meeting, everyone is required to have a copy of the 'three constantly read articles'. A group leader is elected from among the participants to conduct the meeting. At first, the study group in Tachai was divided into youth groups and adult groups. Later it was found that there was a generation gap: the young people encountered little difficulty in reading the articles, but they had

more difficulty than the adult members in understanding the real meaning
of the articles due to their lack of experience. An alternative schedule for
meeting was then made: a separate meeting was followed by a mixed
meeting of the old and the young. At the mixed meeting, in addition to the
reading of the three articles, the old members are always asked to recount
their experience in the old days, and their experience in studying Mao's
works and applying them to their daily lives.

After the meeting, young members are required to use their own free
time to make family visits, to interview the old peasants, and to write
their own family history. These activities are intended to enable the
young members to thoroughly understand the bitterness and suffering of
the peasants in the old society. Thus their enthusiasm for revolution and
confidence in the new society is firmly reinforced.

The small field study group often takes place during the break from
work on the farm and its main aim is to improve the reading ability of the
adult peasant. When the study begins, a leader is elected from among the
members to lead the other members to read the three articles aloud in
unison or individually. Sometimes the study leader gives his own explanation of the reading. Because of the limitation of time, no discussion
is undertaken during the small group study meetings. When the study
session is over, the members immediately go back to their farm work.

For the female members of the village, particularly the older ones who
are unable to work on the farm, literacy and cultural education are provided at home. Usually the younger members of the family become
teachers of their mother and grandmother after the evening meal. The
teaching materials are quotations instead of full texts of Mao Tse-tung's
works. In many cases, although the Chinese characters proved too difficult for the older people to master, nevertheless, the old seem to be
equally influenced as the young by Mao's words.

Public Discussion and Mass Criticism

In the centre of Tachai Village there is a huge old willow tree. Almost
every day, if weather permits, the villagers, after returning home from
work, get together under the willow tree to have supper and to hold
open-air-talks. So the ground under the willow tree is known as the 'dining square'. While they are having their supper, the villagers more often
than not enter into discussion about matters concerning public interest
and welfare, and individuals who have done outstanding work as well as
those who have erred. Many of their problems and construction projects
are also discussed in this symposium-under-the-willow-tree. It was said
that once a young commune member expressed his desire to have a
certain degree of relaxation in working conditions and less thriftiness in
people's daily life. He and other 'delinquents' were therefore summoned

to the willow tree to receive public criticism and were told of the bitter former days of the village and its people. Sometimes awards and recognition of model farmers are also made at this place while people are eating.

As an outcome of the literacy and mass ideological campaign, the people in Tachai, emulating the heroism of 'The Foolish Old Man Who Removed the Mountains', decided to reshape their land, and to collectively transform their village. They vowed that if they could not finish the work in a short time, they would complete it in a longer period of time; if they could not finish it in their lifetime, their sons and grandsons would complete it. As a result of determined and constant labour over a period of ten years, the craggy slopes have been turned into level terraced fields, and the deep gullies into well cultivated land with high yields. Because of the Tachai people's determination and courage, and their remarkable achievements, the 'spirit of Tachai', symbolizing self-reliance and hard work, has become a powerful driving force leading people elsewhere to make massive efforts to develop China's rural areas.

Agricultural Technical Education

In the past, a vicious circle prevailed in China's rural areas. The destitution of the rural masses denied them the possibility of improving their primitive agricultural methods and tools and this in turn led to low productivity which contributed to continuing destitution. In order to break the vicious circle, a double-pronged programme designed to disseminate new agricultural knowledge and skills by way of rural mass education has been the most significant realistic measure taken by the Chinese government.

The decentralization of control over education was a bold and significant step for this enabled the people in rural areas to set up their own schools according to their practical needs without interference from the government. Thus in China today the number of rural schools is very impressive, and their achievements in helping agricultural and rural development have been remarkable. These rural schools are diverse in form. In conventional terms, they are non-formal schools with no fixed schedule and no definite pattern of curriculum. The school offers whatever education is needed by the people, and the activities in the school are solely determined by local circumstances. However, the content of the education offered by these schools is similar if not uniform for they are all, in one way or another, related to the measures for increasing farm production, which were suggested in the *Draft Programme for Agricultural Development*. These included water and soil conservation projects; the use of improved farming tools and gradual introduction of mechanical farming; efforts to discover every possible source of manure and improved methods of fertilization; extension of the use of the best and most suitable strains of crop; soil improvement; extension of multiple cropping areas;

planting more high-yield crops; improving farming methods; eliminating insect pests and plant diseases; opening up virgin lands, reclaiming waste-lands, and extending cultivated areas.[9] These measures were subsequently summarized by Mao Tse-tung into eight single-syllable words; *tu* (soil), *shui* (water), *fei* (fertilizer), *chung* (seeds), *mi* (closeness), *pao* (protection), *kung* (implements), and *kuan* (management). Nowadays these words, well-known as the 'eight-word chatter' in agriculture, are widely quoted in China.

Among the mushrooming rural schools, there are two established types, the agricultural middle school and the communist labour univer-sity. In addition a new type of multi-purpose rural school, known as the 'May 7' school,[10] has recently been widely established in the countryside of China.

The Agricultural Middle School

The establishment of agricultural middle schools is an unprecedented event in the history of Chinese education. It was originally conceived of as a transitional measure to cope with the problems of an insufficient number of middle schools to accommodate all the primary school graduates in the rural areas. As available statistics show, in 1958 there were more than thirty-seven million youngsters from ages 13 to 16 in China, and the existing middle schools could accommodate only seven million of them.[11] In order to provide education for rural youth while not neglecting their obligations on the farm, the agricultural middle schools, established on the 'half-farm, half-study' basis, have become very popular.

The agricultural middle school first appeared in Hai-an Hsien of Kiangsu Province, as an experiment, in early March 1958. It took only four days from the planning to the opening of the school. At first there were 156 students divided into three classes with one full-time teacher in each class, these teachers being graduates of senior middle schools. The school was housed in a public building of the county, and the desks and chairs were borrowed by the students from local people. The daily working schedule for both teachers and students consisted of classes in the morning and farm work in the afternoon. The courses offered by the school were politics, Chinese language and literature, arithmetic, fun-damentals of agriculture, and public health.

Due to the simple requirements, in little more than one month, from 15 March to 27 April 1958, 6,568 similar schools were established through-out Kiangsu Province with a total enrolment of 342,605 students.[12] In the same year, the 4th National Convention of Educational Administrators was held in Peking from 24 March through 8 April when the establish-ment of agricultural middle schools in Kiangsu Province was hailed as a very important measure in China's rural and agricultural development.

Thereafter, in the short period of a month, the movement for establishing agricultural middle schools spread all over the country. As a consequence, there is today no province without an impressive number of agricultural middle schools within its boundaries.

So far as agricultural development is concerned, the agricultural middle school has proved to be a useful innovation. In Anhui Province for instance, two years after its establishment the Haung-k'ou agricultural middle school was reported to have succeeded in manufacturing more than two hundred kinds of insecticides and chemical fertilizers through the collective research and experiments of teachers and students. It was reported that in late April of 1958, within a month of its establishment, the rice sprouts in the area of Huang-k'ou were seriously affected by insects. The peasants did not know what to do, so sought the help of the agricultural middle school. The principal of the school then called a public meeting of experienced farmers, teachers and students of the school, to discuss the problem and to try to find a solution. After discussion, the participants decided to make an insecticide by mixing powdered croton-oil bean with caustic lime to spray over the damaged areas. The result of the first trial was not satisfactory and after further discussion and study, powdered croton-oil bean was replaced by powdered arsenic. The application of this new mixture inactivated the insects, but did not kill them, and it was finally discovered that the insects could not be killed unless they ate a certain amount of the insecticide. A new formula was worked out which tempted the insects to eat the right amount, and this new formula proved to be very successful when it was applied to the fields.[13]

In the course of more than ten years, variations in agricultural middle schools have gradually developed, but their basic function, to help the development of agriculture, remains the same. In one agricultural middle school in Hsiu-chang, Honan Province, for instance, students are grouped according to their practical needs into long-term classes for a period of about two years, and short-term classes for a period of only several days or a few months. The commune can send students to the school at any time it wants; and whenever the students have to return to their commune, they can leave the school. The courses offered by the short-term classes vary in length and in terms of local needs. For instance, in 1969 there was a movement to electrify the villages in this area. The agricultural middle school undertook the responsibility to train through short-term classes 38 electricians for fourteen production brigades. On another occasion the commune needed people who would be able to teach the masses to sing revolutionary songs. The school organized short-term music classes to train more than 400 singing leaders for twenty-eight production brigades in the commune.

According to statistics collected by the school, in the past seven years there have been 158 graduates from the long-term classes, and 1,018 graduates from the short-term classes who have all become agricultural technicians. Some have been very successful in improving farm products, and others have become electricians and mechanics.[14]

The Communist Labour University

The Communist Labour University is also an institution operated on a half-work and half-study basis. The guiding philosophy upon which the university has been established is that education must be combined with production and that theory must be related to practice. Students are expected to be new socialist men with a communist ideology, a high level of personal morality and professional competence. This kind of institution does not fit the traditional pattern of a university since it offers a multiplicity of courses designed to aid the development of agriculture and rural areas. The first communist labour university was established in August, 1958 in Kiangsi province where the Chinese communists made their base from 1930 to the beginning of the 'Long March' in 1934. Besides its main campus, the university has eighty-eight branches throughout the province. These branches include university classes, technological classes, secondary technology classes all lasting four years, and three-year technological classes, two-year technical training classes and short-term technical training classes. In 1960, the university had a total enrolment of about 50,000, of whom 10·3 per cent had not completed their primary education; 58·9 per cent had completed primary school; 30·4 per cent were junior middle school graduates; and 0·5 per cent were senior middle school graduates.[15] The courses offered on each campus vary according to their feasibility and the practical needs of the immediate locality; thus classroom learning and field practice are related. In many cases students are required to undertake field work in the daytime and theoretical work in the evening.

Since a half-study and half-work university must be self-supporting, the education it offers has to be combined with production, and sometimes production is given more emphasis in order to meet the expenses of the university. Students in the four-year university class are therefore required to do manual work for six months and study for five months in their first year; work five months and study six months in their second year and work four months and study seven months in their third and fourth years.[16]

The students are grouped into different classes; these function as research groups when projects are carried out; and they are also organized as production teams when the students go to work in the fields. In addition to their regular teaching responsibilities, teachers are also required to take part in manual work and experimental research. So a teacher is at the same time a worker and a researcher. The technicians in the production teams are all experienced workers. In addition to their regular jobs, they are sometimes asked to teach students and to take part in research. Hence a technician is at the same time a teacher and a researcher. Thus workers, teachers, students and technicians join together and mutually help each other in their efforts to improve productivity and learning.

The selection of teaching materials closely follows the 'few but essential' principle. All unnecessary and redundant courses are eliminated, and the requirements in general education are minimized to the extent that students are expected to have background sufficient only for their professional and technological learning. In the field of professional and technological education, precision and conciseness are stressed, and broad background work is considered wasteful. Each professional and technological department offers only the courses which are essential for that field, and each course is supplemented by application and practice. For instance, students of the forestry department are required to work in the forest in the daytime and have their classroom education in the evening.

As a result of the students' half-work and half-study and the teachers' half-work and half-teaching, the university has succeeded in opening 35 farms in a period of six years; cultivating more than fifty-four thousand mu; developing four hundred thousand mu of forests; operating 46 small factories and refineries; and building houses needed on the eighty-eight campuses. By the end of 1963, the total value of production of the university reached about thirty-seven million Chinese dollars. Among the eighty-eight branches, ten had been able to support themselves; seven had sufficient food but received partial subsidies for operational expenses. Eighteen branches had sufficient operating funds, but imported part of the food from other sources; and the rest could be said to be largely self-supporting. By 1964, the university sold three hundred thousand jin (1 jin is equal to 1·1 lb.) of surplus grain. In addition to these achievements in production, over six years the university also prepared 1,300 university graduates; 8,800 secondary technology graduates; and 6,200 graduates from short-term technical training classes. All these graduates returned to their villages to become agricultural technicians, rural school teachers and commune administrators.[17] The faculty of the university is composed of party cadres who have been sent to the country for re-education; discharged army officers; graduates of regular schools and universities; and experienced workers and peasants.

The Kiangsi experience has shown that the communist labour university, a multi-form institution, comprising in conventional terms, a university, secondary schools, primary schools and vocational and technical schools, is economic to operate. Unlike bourgeois intellectual elites the graduates of this communist labour university are farm workers close to the rural masses. As a result other major provinces, such as Hopei, Kiangsu, Fuchien, Yunnan, Kwangsi and Sinkiang, have established their own communist labour universities.

The 'May 7' Labour School

In China today there are two different kinds of school which are prefixed 'May 7': the 'May 7' cadre school and the 'May 7' labour school. The former is an institution where party cadres and government office workers receive re-education; the latter is a multi-purpose rural school designed to train versatile, skilled farm workers for rural and agricultural development. Such multi-purpose schools are the product of the recent proletarian revolution in education. The schools have extended themselves into rural communities, farms, and villages, which are in turn used as school laboratories. Education is combined with agricultural production. Teachers and students are also farm workers.

The 'May 7' labour school in Kuei-ping County of Kwangsi Province has been regarded as a model of its kind. Established in December 1968, this school is at the same time a production unit, and an experimental station – a 'three-in-one' combination of school, farm and factory.

The students are all selected from peasants who have had farming experience and primary, junior or senior middle school education. Upon graduation from the 'May 7' labour school, students are required to go back to the farm or factory to engage in productive work. City youths are also admitted to the school on the condition that they stay in the countryside after graduation.

Of the thirty-one teachers in this school, fourteen are experienced workers, and poor and lower-middle peasants; ten are party cadres; and seven have been selected from among former teachers and college graduates. According to local conditions and practical needs, the school is organized into classes in agriculture, animal husbandry, rural medicine, agricultural machine-repairing, and rural electrical engineering. The duration of schooling in most classes is one year.

Teaching-learning activities take place mostly in the fields and sometimes in classrooms. In many cases, experienced farmers, rather than teachers, teach the class and give demonstrations on how to tend certain kinds of crops. After the demonstrations, teachers draw conclusions by summarizing the processes of the teaching-learning activities. The teaching material used is compiled mostly from the practical experience of the workers, poor and lower-middle peasants, and technicians, and sometimes teachers. But the materials compiled by the teachers are subject to criticism, group discussion, and revision by students, experienced workers, and poor and lower-middle peasants.

Learning followed by application is the guiding principle upon which courses are offered. Students in each class are required to practice what they have learned in the field or in the laboratory. For instance, students from the agricultural machine-repairing class are reported to have repaired 800 rice planting machines and 20 tractors for the local people while students from the rural medicine class have established health stations in nearby villages.

According to statistics published in March 1970, of the 491 graduates from this school's first graduating class, 30 became cadres of production brigades; 108 leaders of production teams; 14 members of propaganda teams; 8 agricultural technicians; 5 tractor operators, 29 'bare-foot doctors'; 43 teachers; and 21 factory workers. The rest went to other communes to advance the socialist reconstruction of the country. Moreover, as a result of the joint labour of teachers and students, the school farm produced 560,000 jin of rice, 30,000 jin of corn, 50,000 jin of peanuts, and 800 tons of sugar cane in 1969.[18]

Currently there seems to be some tendency, on the part of many of the regular primary and middle schools throughout the country, to attempt to transform themselves into a kind of 'May 7' labour school.[19]

Public Health Education

The condition of public health in China prior to 1949, particularly in the rural areas, was the same, if not worse, as in any other developing country. Especially during the first half of this century, because of war and successive famines, the level of public health was very low and an immense number of people became victims of epidemics. According to the 1934 statistics, the number of deaths in China's population was about 30 out of every thousand, compared with 10 in the United States, 15·8 in France, 16·2 in Russia, 17·7 in Japan, and 24·8 in India.[20] The diseases from which China's population suffered most seriously were schistosomiasis, Kala-azar, bubonic plague, malaria, dysentery, leprosy, diphtheria and cholera. It was reported that in the areas south of the Yangtze River, about ten million people suffered from schistosomiasis, and in the southwestern areas, a great number of people suffered from malaria, encephalitis and filariasis.

But China today is no longer a country of 'sick people'. Through the collective efforts made by the government and the people in public health campaigns most major diseases have been controlled or virtually eliminated. It is reported that in China it is now difficult to find a case of venereal disease to show medical students. Obviously, the achievements in public health in China reflect the success of the programmes in rural mass education, of which public health is an integral part. The development of China's rural public health campaign will be examined in terms of three dimensions.

Investigation and Prevention of Disease .

In 1949 the new government of the People's Republic found that hundreds of millions of its people were subject to epidemics, and tens of millions of lives had been lost. Such a massive loss of life naturally meant a substantial loss to the productive labour force in rural areas and this was certainly a major cause perpetuating the 'culture of poverty' in the country. In coping with such a long-neglected problem the First National Health Congress, held in Peking in 1950 announced three guiding principles for medical work.

1. Medical services should be available to workers, peasants and soldiers.
2. The main concern of health work should be preventive medicine.
3. Chinese traditional medicine and western medicine should be combined in practice.[21]

At the same time in order to fulfil its commitments to the health of the people of China during the early years of the new regime, efforts were made by the government to investigate health conditions in different regions; to conduct professional discussions through successive conventions and meetings of medical workers; and to awaken the people to the dangers of disease while suggesting feasible ways of preventing it. In the fifties when the people were encouraged to establish their own community schools, public health together with communist ideology and agricultural development, constituted a major theme in the curriculum. For instance, the Chi-li Agricultural Cooperative in Kwangtung Province consisted of 26 villages which had been long plagued by dysentery and malaria. In 1952, with the help of local schools, the cooperative started a public health campaign and urged its members to observe the 12 public health rules:

1. Everyone must have his own toothbrush and face towel.
2. In spring, summer and autumn, everyone must take a bath and change his clothes once every three days; once a week during the winter.
3. Drinking water must be sterilized.
4. No grass should grow within a limit of 15 feet around the living quarters.
5. No impure water must remain in ditches.
6. Backyards must be kept clean.
7. People and animals must stay in separate rooms.
8. The toilet must have a wooden lid; hands washed after using the toilet.
9. Tableware must be washed in boiling water before use.
10. Utensils must be washed in boiling water once every day.

11. No spitting.

12. Eliminate flies.[22]

As a result, in a period of ten years, this area has been reported to have become a very clean and disease-free place.

The draft programme for agricultural development from 1956 to 1967, formulated by the Planning Committee of the Central Government of the People's Republic of China, planned to eliminate within seven to twelve years, major diseases such as schistosomiasis, filariasis, hookworm, Kala-azar, encephalitis, bubonic plague, malaria, smallpox, venereal disease, dysentery, typhoid fever, diphtheria, leprosy, goitre, Kaschin Beck's disease and tuberculosis.[23] The programme for eliminating the major diseases began with a campaign to wipe out the 'four evils' – rats, sparrows, flies and mosquitoes to be completed in 5, 7, or 12 years. It was reported that rats and mosquitoes were killed by chemical spraying but most of the sparrows and flies were eliminated by school children who were too young to take part in any kind of productive work. The children were taught to carry out their assignments not by physical killing, but by exhausting the birds through not allowing them to alight. Only a year after the campaign started many areas were reported to have become areas of 'four nos' – no rats, no sparrows, no flies and no mosquitoes. Later the sparrow was replaced by the bedbug as one of the 'four evils'. The success in disease control may be attributed in large part to the campaign to wipe out the 'four evils', the carriers of disease.

Reform and Reorientation of Medical Education

To meet the urgent needs of a population of about seven hundred million, the quantitative increase in China's public health programme is emphasized although its quality is still far from adequate. According to available statistics in 1947, there were 65,760 hospital beds throughout China; the number was increased to 261,930 by 1956. There were 9,499 medical college graduates produced between 1928 and 1947, but between 1949 and 1956, a period of only eight years, 27,426 new medical college graduates were added. At middle school level, there were 1,700 medical middle school graduates in 1947, and 10,386 in 1956. The total enrolment in medical schools in 1947 was 10,400, and 86,000 in 1956.[24] On the other hand, the revival of traditional Chinese medicine was believed to be a valuable resource worth exploring, and led to a tremendous increase in medical facilities and personnel. For instance, there are four Chinese medicine colleges among the 38 newly established medical colleges, and six Chinese medicine middle schools among the 176 medical middle schools. In addition, there are 144 Chinese medicine hospitals with half a million Chinese medicine doctors and 40,000 apprentices.

A national convention on rural medical education was held in Peking in

August 1956 where, in addition to a discussion of rural medical problems, it was decided that a rural health network throughout the country ought to be established. Henceforth, many provinces and counties began to organize their own health network by establishing health centres and clinics in key spots in the provinces and counties and to train medical workers with the help of local hospitals and medical colleges. In Kweichow Province for instance, 3,640 anti-malaria districts were established, in which four million four hundred thousand malaria patients received treatment, and four million nine hundred thousand people received preventive treatment.

As the public health network continued to grow the demand for health workers increased particularly in remote areas. Relying on the support of the local people's hospitals, many counties throughout the country undertook the task of training these workers. For example in Shansi Province in northern China, the people's hospital of K'o-lan Hsien, at the end of 1954, established a village 'medical school' on a half-study and half-farming basis. The 31 students of the school were selected from among the junior middle graduates in the communes. Upon graduation from this medical school, each student is expected to be half-farmer and half-doctor, and to care for public health work in the village without interrupting his farm work. The classrooms and laboratories of this school are all in the people's hospital, and two doctors from the hospital are assigned as full-time teachers in charge of the whole programme of training public health workers. The courses offered by the school include politics, pathology, microbiology, entomology, medical and surgical practice, obstetrics and gynaecology, pediatrics, sanitation, examination of regulators of bodily functions, traditional Chinese medicine, and acupuncture. The duration of the training programme is two years and each year every student is required to work for four months and study for eight months. Work during the final six months is concentrated on clinical practice. The 31 students, together with the two full-time teachers, organized themselves into a travelling medical team and visited twelve communes and more than twenty production teams, and treated 213 patients in the area. These students are all under the supervision of the local hospitals, and are committed to take part in public health work when they return to their communes after graduation.[25]

In addition to the reduction of study requirements in all medical colleges from five to four years (two years for basic medical courses, half a year for basic theory of medical and surgical practice and eighteen months for clinical practice), the medical services of hospitals and medical colleges were reoriented to place more emphasis on rural needs. In 1965 Shanghai Hospital No. 2, for instance, established two-year medical training classes in which the students were mainly poor and lower-middle peasants. Training in the first year includes basic medical courses and disease-prevention. In the second year the students must join in travelling medical teams to visit communes and villages. Also in 1965, Peking Medical College started a three-year rural medical school for rural youth selected and recommended by the communes around the national capital. The Wuhan Medical College established a half-study and half-work medical school to train senior middle school graduates in the Wuhan area, and also a short-term class to train primary school graduates to become rural medical workers.[26] Moreover, some hospitals in large cities have organized their personnel into travelling medical teams to visit the countryside. Peking Hospital, for instance, organized three travelling medical teams in 1965 which visited the outskirts of Peking. They treated about 5,000 patients and helped to establish 32 health stations. In other large cities such as Shanghai, Tientsin, Canton and Chungking, hospitals all organized travelling medical teams to supply medical services to the homes of the peasants.[27]

Furthermore, since 1966 many hospitals in large cities have begun to send their medical staffs (most of whom are graduates of the regular medical colleges) to settle in the countryside. For instance, about 2,000 medical personnel from Tientsin were sent to service the countryside; 4,460 from Heilungkiang Province; 1,400 from Kirin Province; and 15,000 from Hangchou City. In Kiangsu Province, the hospitals jointly selected more than 100 specialists and sent them to settle in the rural areas to train about 20,000 'bare-foot doctors' for the rural population. Hunan Province sent 2,000 medical personnel to the countryside to train 22,600 'bare-foot doctors' and health workers for rural people. In addition, the military hospital from the People's Liberation Army sent 30,000 medical personnel to the rural areas near their stations, and helped to train another 141,000 'bare-foot doctors'.[28]

The Shenyang Medical College is considered to be the outstanding example of a college aiding medical rural services and public health. This college was established in Kiangsi Province as a medical school for the Red Army in 1931 when the Chinese communists first established their Chinese soviet in the area. Following the 'Long March', the college was moved to Yenan and changed its name to the Medical University of China. During the war of liberation the University was moved to the northeast to supply medical personnel for the army. Finally, it was moved to Shenyang and was given a new name, the Shenyang Medical College.

In 1965 the college established over 30 short-term medical training classes and specialized medical classes on the campus and in neighbouring communes which produced about 1,700 health workers for the area. Based on this experience, a plan for developing rural medical education was devised. Since April 1969, a revolutionary committee, composed of workers, soldiers and students, led 1,200 students and professors of the college to settle in 33 cities and counties, 84 communes and 113 production brigades in Liaoning Province, of which Shenyang is the capital. For the 113 production brigades, they trained about ten thousand medical workers, and established 80 'red medical villages', able to meet the medical needs of both peace and war.

By the end of 1969, the college had set up four rural medical bases in the province for medical education and medical service. In each base there were 100 hospital beds and 130 professors, administrators, students and workers who had settled there with their families, so that each base could independently carry out programmes of teaching–learning, medical treatment and research. Each base is responsible for a three-part programme: first, they send professors to nearby production brigades to help them establish medical centres and train medical workers; second, they organize travelling medical teams to make medical services available to peasants in remote areas; third, they cooperate with local hospitals in establishing health stations and 'red medical villages'. Thus the medical college has moved out of the urban centre and taken permanent roots in the countryside.

For the first time in June 1970, the college in its Shenyang headquarters enrolled 470 worker-peasant students. For this new group of medical students, the first part of the training programme requires each student to do all the kinds of work usually done by nurses and nursing aides in order to oblige students to develop humane attitudes and to understand the feelings of patients. Then, students are sent to the rural areas for clinical experience, and they are responsible for treating patients with common local diseases. The teaching work at the bases is usually carried out by a team composed of professors, students, workers, peasants and 'bare-foot doctors'. Sometimes, the teaching takes place in a production team in order that there will be no social gap between the peasants and the medical college students. The students must also try to cure or prevent diseases by using a combination of traditional Chinese medicine and Western medicine. Each is encouraged to do research on common local diseases in order to advance medical knowledge and to discover new methods of treatment.[29]

'Bare-foot Doctors',[30] Cooperative Medical Care and the Patriotic Sanitation Movement

The training of 'bare-foot doctors' and the introduction of cooperative medical care are two remarkable medical innovations, both indispensable to the success in popularizing medical services in the country. The 'bare-foot doctors' go to the people in remote areas where regular medical services are usually unobtainable. On the other hand, cooperative medical care provides equal medical care for all regardless of financial status.

It is said that the term 'bare-foot doctor', was first heard in a suburb of Shanghai where the people called the health workers in the area by this name. However, although never said so officially, it may have derived from the former 'straw-sandal doctors' who were the products of the army medical school during the war of liberation. In contrast to conventionally dressed doctors, the 'straw-sandal doctors' were trained to practice their profession in an 'unconventional' way. Now 'bare-foot doctors' are even more 'unconventionally' trained, and practice their profession in a more 'unconventional' manner. The professional status of the 'bare-foot doctors' is between that of professional doctors in hospitals and local health workers whose primary responsibility is to supervise environmental sanitation and reinforce disease-prevention measures in rural areas. Most 'bare-foot doctors' are originally local health workers who have continued their training and acquired some basic techniques in treating common diseases from members of the travelling medical teams sent to the countryside from city hospitals. In many cases, they have the opportunity of being selected and recommended by the commune in which they are working as candidates for admission to regular medical colleges. Because of their experience, they are always given preference when the medical colleges select students from numerous applicants.

The training of 'bare-foot doctors' takes place mostly in commune hospitals, with the help of city hospital travelling medical teams. The duration of training ranges from two to six months. Practice is stressed in the training, and more often than not the prospective 'bare-foot doctors' acquire their medical knowledge and skills as apprentices to doctors in the travelling medical teams. Usually the professional courses include methods of preventing common local diseases, physiological anatomy, medicine and acupuncture. In most cases, training is conducted as a combination of basic medical theory and clinical practice, prevention and treatment, common and rare diseases, traditional Chinese and modern Western medicine.

In addition to the diagnosis and treatment of disease, this new kind of doctor is also responsible for preventive measures in the areas where they are stationed. They vaccinate the villagers, teach farmers the correct use of pesticides, and help them improve community sanitation. They are well received because they are integrated with the masses. They are farmers and shopworkers with medical duties, and receive no special financial reward for their medical work. Their income, like everyone else's in the community, is calculated on the work-point basis.

The proliferation of 'bare-foot doctors' since 1966 has provided a good base for the extension of the cooperative medical care system and by

1970, throughout China, this system had been established in every production brigade. Cooperative medical care is a system of mutual help in dealing with medical problems of the rural population and is operated by the production brigade. Each member of the brigade pays an annual fee of about one American dollar to the medical fund and treatment and medicine are then free. If a member is not able to pay this fee, the production team makes the payment and deducts the amount from his monthly wages. This system was initiated in 1958 with the advent of the people's communes but due to the inadequacy of both medical facilities and personnel, it did not go beyond the experimental phase. Since 1965, the number of 'bare-foot doctors' has increased significantly, and the medical facilities in communes have also improved; the system has consequently become a nationwide medical programme.

There are some basic principles on which the cooperative medical care system is operated throughout the country. First, participation is voluntary and the system is managed by the poor and lower-middle peasants. Second, for all members who have paid their dues, treatment (except for chronic diseases) and medicine is free. Third, those who want to obtain medicine without a doctor's prescription must pay. Fourth, if the disease cannot be treated in the local hospital, and the patient must be transferred to another hospital, the transportation fee must be paid by the patient. If the fee is beyond his financial ability, it will be paid from public funds upon approval of the revolutionary committee. Anyone who wants to transfer to another hospital without the doctor's permission must pay the expenses. Fifth, for anyone injured on duty the treatment and medicines are free.

Because the use of traditional Chinese herbal medicines has been revived, and also because the cooperative medical care system is operated on principles of self-reliance and frugality, the collection and cultivation of herbal medicines in China now has become very important. Thus one commune in Hupeh Province suggested that since herb cultivation was an item of farm production, herb farmers should receive payment like crop farmers and herb collectors should be paid on a work-point basis.[31]

The Chin-chiao Production Brigade in Kiangsu Province may serve as an example of cooperative medical care. The system was started in November 1968 and in the first year of its operation, the members of the brigade collected 10,014 jin of herbal medicines and received an income of $1,702 from selling the surplus. Since November 1969, every member of the brigade has received free diagnosis and treatment from the brigade medical centre where emphasis is placed on the use of Chinese remedies. (In 1969, 72 per cent of all treatments used were Chinese remedies.) The brigade has established its own medicine store and constructed a factory to refine the herbs collected by its members.

To reinforce the public health system there is a programme of public health education at the mass level, known as the patriotic sanitation movement. Its purpose is to convince the rural population of the importance of environmental cleanliness as an effective means of preventing disease. At each level of government, there is a committee of the patriotic sanitation movement responsible for carrying out its programme which includes wiping out the 'four evils', sanitation in restaurants, hotels, airports and train and bus stations, and the maintenance of healthy conditions in factories and farms. The programmes vary from season to season, and region to region. During the peak farming season, the emphasis of the mass health movement is directed to the farms. For instance, farmers are advised to carry enough water with them when they work in the fields, and to work and rest according to a proper schedule. They are also taught ways of treating minor injuries on the farm; methods of checking food contamination; means of controlling livestock and preventing them from affecting the sanitation of the community. Assisted by radio and low-cost aids, such as pictures, filmstrips and exhibitions, the 'bare-foot doctors' and health workers of each commune visit the villages each season and the results of these regular campaigns have been extraordinarily successful.

Potentials and Problems

There are both potentials and problems in the efforts to develop China's rural areas through education. On the one hand commune organization has provided greater opportunities of education for all; but the Chinese language, because of its complicated writing system, poses a formidable problem in the efforts to wipe out illiteracy among China's population.

The people's commune created in 1958, is a new type of organization which has had a considerable impact on traditional Chinese social structure. Within the commune, decisions concerning agriculture, industry, trade, education, military affairs, and even the individual's social life and activities are made by administrators at the commune headquarters. Commune organization is roughly the same throughout the country; a commune is divided into several production brigades, each of which is in turn composed of several production teams. Therefore, each production team constitutes the basic unit of a commune.

The highest authority in a commune is the congress of the representatives of the commune members; the revolutionary committee (formerly the administrative committee) of a commune, whose members are democratically elected by the commune every two years, is in practice the governing body. Under the committee there are different departments such as agriculture, water conservation, forestry, animal husbandry, industry, commerce, finance and food, culture and education, military affairs, planning and research, transportation, etc.

Each production brigade has its own revolutionary committee headed by a brigade commander, who is elected at the general meeting of the brigade members. The brigade revolutionary committee derives its authority from the commune revolutionary committee and reports directly to the committee. The leadership of each production team bears some resemblance to that of a production brigade. Each team holds its own general meetings at which a commander and several deputy-commanders are elected.

Regarding education, a commune is charged with the full responsibility of educating all its members regardless of age or sex. This decentralization of control over education has brought a proliferation of schools as the commune is free from centralized bureaucratic regulations and controls and it can establish whatever kind of school the local people need and can afford.

In the same way that commune organization is divided into three different levels, so is its responsibility for education. Generally, a commune is responsible for middle schools; a production brigade for primary schools and the production teams for lower primary schools and various non-formal schools. As a result of such a division of responsibility primary education, at least, has become universally available to China's rural masses because there is today no production team without a school of one kind or another.

Nevertheless, the Chinese written language has remained an enormous obstacle to the efforts to make China's population literate due to its extreme complexity. Literacy has been a very serious concern of Chinese governments since 1912 when Sun Yat-sen founded the Republic. But even now, illiterates still constitute a large part of China's adult population and there can be little doubt that the effectiveness of literacy campaigns would be increased if the present writing system could be extensively reformed.

Several attempts have been made to solve the language problem, but none has proved successful. In 1954, a Chinese Written Language Reform Committee was formed under the sponsorship of the State Council, and a list of 500 simplified new characters was compiled which has since been enlarged. These characters are useful for those who are beginning to learn the Chinese language, but they are a problem for those who are already able to read Chinese in the unsimplified form.

An attempt was also made to Latinize, or Romanize, the Chinese written system, and to write Chinese phonetically. However, since there are so many dialects in China, a person from Shanghai could not communicate with his compatriot in Peking by using the Shanghai dialect written in alphabetic form. Thus the existing writing system, despite its complexity, has the advantage of serving all dialects in China and makes it possible for people of different dialects to communicate with each other through writing because a written symbol conveys the same meaning throughout the country, even though it is pronounced differently. If the language is written phonetically, however, more barriers will be created among the Chinese people. This does not suggest that the present system of writing needs no reform; on the contrary, the possibility of changing the writing system must be explored in order to make the language easier for illiterate Chinese to learn.

Summary and Conclusions

China's rural development programmes have three dimensions: mass education, agricultural development and public health, and each reflects Chinese Communist ideology. Thus development in one area reinforces development in another. Such a strategy has effected tremendous changes in China's rural areas and reflects the bold revolutionary ideals which have been cherished in the past half-century.

Chinese Communists take an inconoclastic attitude in coping with China's national problems and do not hesitate to break with many of China's traditions but neither do they readily adopt alien systems wholesale; they depend on their own pragmatic and creative abilities to do whatever they think is best for national development.

As progress is contingent upon the initiative of the people then what is good for the people is best managed by them. In the field of education, decentralization of control has not only strengthened local initiative but also enabled the population to express its creative abilities to the full in devising whatever kinds of education it needs. As a result of being isolated from the international scene for more than two decades, the idea of self-reliance has been firmly instilled in the minds of the Chinese people. Now there is a willingness among the Chinese to stand on their own feet and work for their own future – a process that has led to continued growth in their own self-confidence.

REFERENCES

1. *China Reconstructs*, Vol. XXI, No. 4 April 1972, p. 2.
2. Report by Chang Chien, head of the Department of Planning in the Ministry of Higher Education. *Jen-min Jih-pao* (People's Daily), 17 March 1956. For a complete list of the institutions, see Leo A. Orlean, *Professional Manpower and Education in Communist China* (Washington, D.C.: Government Printing Office, 1960), pp. 176–213.
3. Yuan Tsun-chao, *Kung-fei chung-teng chiao-yute p'i-p'an* (China's secondary

education under communism) (Taipei, Taiwan: China Cultural Service, 1959), pp. 73–6.

4. See Article 10 in the *Decision of the Central Committee of the Chinese Communist Party Concerning the Great Proletarian Cultural Revolution* (Peking: Foreign Languages Press, 1966), pp. 9–10.

5. Source: *Tachai – Standard Bearer in China's Agriculture* (Peking: Foreign Languages Press, 1972), p. 2.

6. ibid., p. 4.

7. This is a very common expression in Chinese. But today it has become an underlined phrase in all printed materials in China because Mao Tse-tung once used it as the title of his speech delivered at Yenan on 29 January 1943.

8. The 'three constantly read articles':

(1) *The Foolish Old Man Who Removed the Mountains* is a Chinese version of Aesop's fable – once upon a time there was an old man who was trying to remove the two mountains which blocked the roads leading to his house. One neighbour ridiculed him, but the old man told him that if he could not finish removing them, his son would continue, and so would his son's son and so on. Finally the gods sympathized with his determination and sent two spirits to move the mountains away. Mao used this theme, in 1945, to write the articles and metaphorically stated that there were two mountains, namely, imperialism and feudalism, which blocked China's development, and the Chinese Communists were determined to remove these two mountains. Nowadays, the mountains are used to imply difficulties of any kind.

(2) *In Memory of Norman Bethune* was written in 1939, in memory of a Canadian doctor who came to China in 1937 to render medical service in the liberated areas to the soldiers in the Sino-Japanese War. On 12 November 1939, he died of septicemia caused by an untreated wound on his finger – early that November he had slashed his finger during a hurried operation while the Japanese were moving in on his unit. Mao praised his profound compassion and love for mankind and regarded him as a symbol of the true spirit of communism and internationalism.

(3) *To Serve the People* was written, in 1944, in memory of a soldier named Chang Szu-teh, who was an old and loyal member of the Communist Party. On 5 September 1944, he was working by a kiln which suddenly collapsed and buried him. Mao used him as a model of giving one's own life for the people.

9. *The Draft Programme for Agricultural Development in the People's Republic o, China, 1956–1967* (Peking: Foreign Languages Press, 1956, p. 16).

10. On 7 May, 1966, Mao Tse-tung wrote a letter to Lin Piao urging Lin to try to make the People's Liberation Army into a big school. Besides military affairs, soldiers should also learn farming, factory work, and language and literature. So too should the peasants, workers and students. The passage concerning students reads: 'Same with students, while taking study as the primary duty, they should learn other things as well. In addition to literature, they must also learn about industry, agriculture and military science, and they must criticize the bourgeoisie. The years of schooling must be shortened and education must be revolutionized. The ruling of our schools by bourgeois intellectuals must be discontinued.' *Jen-min Jih-pao* (People's Daily), 25 October 1967.

11. *Hsin-hua pan yueh k'an* (New China Biweekly), No. 7, 1959, p. 102.
12. *Hsin-hua pan yueh k'an* (New China Biweekly), No. 12, 1958, p. 115.
13. Li Chien, 'Huang-k'ou nung-yeh chung-hsueh te liang-nien' (Two years of Hung-k'ou agricultural middle school). *Hung-ch'i* (Red-flag), No. 13, 1960, pp. 25–30.
14. *Hung-ch'i* (Red-flag), No. 8, 1970, pp. 50–54.
15. *Jen-min Jih-pao* (People's Daily), 12 June 1960.
16. Liu Chun-hsiu, 'Wo-men shih tsen-yang ch'uang-pan lao-tung ta-hsueh te' (How did we run the communist labour university), in *Pan-kung (nung) pan-tu yu hsin-jen – Kiangsi kung-chan chu-yi lao-tung ta-hsueh pan-huseh ching-yen ch'i* (To educate the new communist man through half-work and half-study – a collection of reports on the Kiangsi Communist Labour University) (Nan-chang: Kiangsi Education Publications, 1965,) p. 9.
17. ibid., p. 3.
18. 'Pei-yang you-she-hui-chu-yi chueh-wu-te you-wen-hua-te lao-tung-che – Kwangsi Kuei-ping-hsien 'wu-ch'i' lao-tung hsueh-hsiao-te tiao-ch'a pao-kao' (To train rural workers with socialist consciousness and culture – a report of Kwangsi Kuei-ping 'May 7' labour school), in *Hung-ch'i* (Red-flag), No. 6, 1971, pp. 26–51.
19. For detail, see *Hung-ch'i* (Red-flag), No. 6, 1971, pp. 26–51.
20. Hsueh Chien-wu, *Hsiang-ts'un wei-sheng* (Rural public health) (Shanghai: Cheng-chung Book Co., 1947), p. 12.
21. *Hsin-hua yueh-kan* (New China Monthly), No. 9, 1950, p. 152.
22. *Hsin-hua pan yueh kan* (New China Biweekly), No. 3, 1958, pp. 115–16.
23. For details see 'The Draft Programme for Agricultural Development in the People's Republic of China', 1956–1967 (Peking: Foreign Languages Press, 1956), or Yi-chiu-wu-liu nien tao yi-chiu liu-ch'i nien ch'uan kuo nung-yeh fa-chan kang-yao (ts'ao-an) chiang-hua (Lectures on the draft programme for agricultural development in the People's Republic of China, 1956–1967) (Peking: China Youth Publications, 1956).
24. *Hsin-hua yueh kan* (New China Monthly), No. 21, 1957, p. 150.
25. *Kwang-ming Jih-pao* (Kwang-ming Daily), 10 August 1965.
26. *Kwang-ming Jih-pao* (Kwang-ming Daily), 5 September 1965.
27. *Jen-min Jih-pao* (People's Daily), 15 August 1965.
28. Yung Hsin, 'Reform in Communist Medical Education and "Send Down" of Medical Personnel' in *Studies on Chinese Communism*, No. 11, Vol. III, pp. 53–62. Taipei, Taiwan. 10 November 1969.
29. Source: 'Yung-yuan fa-hui hung-chun wei-hsiao ch'uan-t'ung – Shenyang yi-hsueh-yuan tiao-ch'a pao-kao' (Forever to develop the revolutionary tradition of the health school of the Red Army – a report of the revolution in medical education in Shenyang Medical College), in *Hung-ch'i* (Red-flag), No. 6, 1971, pp. 98–104.
30. For some interesting stories of the 'bare-foot doctors', see Sah Ying (ed.), *Ch'ih-chueh i-sheng hao* (Bare foot-doctors are good). (Hong Kong: Ch'ao-yang Publications, 1969).
31. *Jen-min Jih-pao* (People's Daily), 14 June 1972.

12

Cuban Rural Education:
A Strategy for Revolutionary Development

Rolland G. Paulston

Cuban efforts since 1959 to break out of underdevelopment, to create the socialist 'new man,' and to achieve a more just, egalitarian society have all placed a high priority on rural education. With the triumph of the guerrillas, rural education programmes for youths and adults, both in the formal school system and in the non-formal, out-of-school educational sector, have experienced a radical transformation. Under the Batista dictatorship, the scant, impoverished, and generally neglected rural educational programmes clearly indicated the power and dominance of urban commercial and political elites over the rural masses. As in most of Latin America yet today, the peasantry or rural working class was integrated into national society in a way that denied them access to institutions and knowledge essential for economic advancement and social mobility.

In this chapter, the writer examines some of the major consequences for rural education of recent Cuban efforts to favour the rural population and to achieve a rural transformation. Organization of the paper will be in three parts. The first will examine something of the extent and nature of pre-revolutionary rural education-programmes and their functionality in an unevenly developed plantation economy powerfully influenced by the United States. The second section describes and evaluates major innovative efforts after 1959 to harness rural education to national goals for ideological, political, and economic development. Section three looks to the future; it examines current planning efforts to remedy past failures and draw up a new strategy for rural education that will place it at the very centre of efforts to create the new socialist society.

As a case study of rural education and the Cuban development model, the paper also speaks to the theoretical concerns of social scientists seeking to better understand problems and strategies for national development. In sum, is, as many Latin Americans claim, neo-capitalistic domination the major constraint on development in poor backward countries such as Cuba? (See, for example, Quijano, 1971). Or, on the other hand, as numerous North American social scientists profess, is Latin America kept underdeveloped by dysfunctional attitudes and behaviours, by essentially cultural constraints? (Hutchinson, 1968) Cuba offers an interesting test of these competing theoretical frames. The country has broken out of capitalistic domination but yet remains, at least in the short run, relatively underdeveloped. Powerful and persistent efforts continue, nevertheless, to replace still prevalent personalistic, authoritarian, and 'macho' behaviours with greater social consciousness, to create a new Latin American who will view the world in societal-centric rather than egocentric perspective.

Cuban documents define urban areas as 'any population centre with over 2,000 inhabitants', and the rural population is accordingly defined as those living in population centres of less than 2,000 population. As all Cuban data on the rural sector are gathered on this basis alone, the definition of rurality embodied in official statistics is unidimensional and unfortunately fuzzy. Rural education is defined here as structured learning activities in rural areas. These may be offered as part of the national, articulated formal school system, or they may take place in non-formal settings on the job, in the fields, or in the community. Participants may come from the rural area where instruction is offered, from other rural areas, or from urban centres. Cuban rural education is offered in two essentially different modes. The more visible is formal schooling offered in rural primary or secondary schools.[1] These schools, although they share a common national curriculum, are geographically distinct from their urban counterparts as is the case throughout most of Latin America. Less apparent and frequently only superficially understood, non-formal or non-school educational programmes for adults and out-of-school youth comprise the second major component of Cuba's educational complex in rural areas.

Sources used include Cuban primary and secondary materials and government publications, recent social-science research studies by students of the Cuban revolution, and personal observations of rural educational programmes made during a three-week visit to Cuba in December 1970.[2] These materials are listed in a bibliography at the end of the work.

Gunnar Myrdal has astutely suggested that objectivity in social research is enhanced by explicitly stating the value premises upon which a study is based. As this is rarely done, one might question the utility of a good bit of the literature on social problems and processes. Be that as it may, my biases favour efforts such as Cuba's to break dehumanizing bonds of dependence, to place the social welfare of the nation over the material welfare of individuals, to give all individuals access to knowledge and institutions, and to define development as improvement in which no one is left behind.

Part One: Rural Education and Underdevelopment before 1959

There has been a good deal of descriptive research on the so-called dysfunctional aspects of rural education in Latin America. The problem has been generally viewed as lack of such educational resources as schools, books, teachers on the one hand, and 'irrelevant' curriculum, ill-prepared teachers etc., on the other. The line of reasoning follows that shortcomings of rural education could be largely eliminated with greater material inputs from the Ministry of Education and greater motivational inputs by teachers, parents, and youth in the countryside. As the litany goes, if rural students would only stay in school and stay on the *finca*, or farm, then rural development would become more innovative, entreprenurial, and democratic.

Unfortunately, neither the scholarly study of rural development problems, nor the intervention programmes of national and international organizations seeking to ferment rural educational development during the past several decades have come to grips with structural obstacles to induce these so-called 'more functional behaviours.' As the conditions of rural education and rural life deteriorate in much of Latin America, explanations have focused on what are viewed by interventionists as 'dysfunctional aspects', on behavioural constraints that have kept the recipients of technical assistance from becoming more like the grantors.

It would seem to me, that if we really seek to understand the outcomes of attempts to induce change in a sub-system, in this case the rural sector, we must more diligently and honestly seek to understand not only 'how did it not work,' but 'how did it work'; how was, or is, rural education, for example, functional within the larger national context of, as Harold Lasswell has asked, 'who gets what, where, when, and why?'

An understanding of the *modus operandi* of pre-revolutionary rural education in Cuba is especially pertinent in this regard if we are to view it as an indicator of rural deprivation and underdevelopment. Before looking at how Cuban rural education worked under a plantation economy largely dominated by US capital, it may be instructive to first briefly examine several theoretical frameworks that attempt, in part, to explain how institutions function in the type of plantation society as found in Cuba before 1959, and still prevalent today in many of the Central American republics, in Northeast Brazil, and throughout much of the impoverished third world.

In a study of plantation economies, Beckford has argued persuasively that structural factors inherent in the plantation system retard the process of development and introduce what he calls a dynamic process of under-development.[3] (Beckford, 1969) He views the persistent poverty of plantation societies, despite their frequently long exposure to so-called modern' influences, as a direct consequence of their institutional environment, i.e. the nature of their economic, social, political, and not least, educational organization. This means that in attempts to understand how instituitons such as rural education work, we must examine them in terms of their historical legacy and from a political-economy point of view in studies which attempt to synthesize human activity in holistic analysis.

What might be called 'the underdevelopment biases' induced by plantation systems are easily identified. They are plural social orders divided by race, class, and caste and characterized by dissensus, societies which are to use M. G. Smith's term, 'pregnant with conflict'. In such settings of continuous social instability and tension, there is a tendency for the privileged to invest in land, while the underprivileged invest in education for their children: assets which can survive protracted conflict. (Beckford, 205) Plantation societies are socially integrated along the lines of economic production for export markets. All social groups seek to emulate the life style of the planter class, while interpersonal rivalry to win favour with plantation owners makes cooperative effort difficult to mobilize and keeps social cohesion weak. Absence of local government also tends to undercut efforts to mobilize local resources for community-development projects. Inter-personal relations clearly reflect the authority structure of the plantation. Those at the top of the social hierarchy with most of the power, as well as those at the bottom who are virtually powerless, all characteristically exercise what power they possess over others in an exploitative authoritarian manner.

The negative influence of plantation systems on attempts to motivate and mobilize people for change, to provide sufficient incentives and rewards, and, in sum, to establish the concrete social requirements of development have recently been emphasized by several social scientists. Following a rigorous study of the Caribbean situation, Beckford contends that:

> On the whole the plantation has a demoralizing influence on the community. It destroys or discourages the institution of the family and so undermines the entire social fabric. It engenders an ethos of dependence and patronage and so deprives people of dignity, security, and self-respect. And it impedes the material, social, and spiritual advance of the majority of people. In these circumstances we could hardly expect to find a highly motivated population displaying the kinds of characteristics that development demands. The energies of most people are spent in trying to beat the system in one way or another. (206)

Although all plantation societies do not in the same degree share the same values, there are pronounced similarities in their traditions, attitudes, and behaviours, and in the extent to which the values of much of the population coincide with those of the elite planter class. Hutchinson's study of the Brazilian Northeast suggests that:

The sum of these value orientations in the Northeast plantation context does not add up in a way which promises modernization . . . . Starting with a rejection of nature as a viable partner, the rejection of innovation, the rejection of cooperation, and a rejection of long-range planning, they add up to a continued tradition and to a continued cycling of crises. (88)

Evidence of the social economy of underdevelopment in the United States' South as well has been presented by Nicholls in his study, *Southern Tradition and Regional Progress*. He argues that:

Southern traditions that have seriously impeded economic progress are a rigid social structure dominated by the aristocratic ideal of the planter class; a spirit of extreme individualism, and a tradition of leisure which discouraged enterprise; a subordination of the rural middle class; dominant agrarian values that are a legacy of the slave plantations which have impeded balanced and broadly based regional progress; an undemocratic political structure dedicated to white supremacy at whatever cost; the weakness of social responsibility resulting in inadequate support for public education. This has kept the majority of the population in relative ignorance and encouraged a continued belief that low-income groups in society are poor because they are innately inferior, thus preventing action towards improvement of the social and economic organization; and, among others, that conformity of thought and behavior in the Southern tradition has created a general intolerance of intellectualism and encouraged an acceptance of violence as an ultimate weapon against non-conformity and dissent. (Nicholls, 157–63)

In rural areas of Latin America devoted not to plantations but to subsistence agriculture and tenant farming, the mechanism of dominance has been usually one of internal colonization, i.e., the internal colonization of rural areas by urban centres and elites. Although this pattern has not, to a significant degree, been present in Cuba, it is prevalent in much of Andean America and is equally detrimental to efforts at mobilization, participation, and the development of rural education. The theory of internal colonization has been elaborated in detail in the works of Rodolfo Stavenhagen, Julio Cotler, and, among others, Dale Johnson. (Stavenhagen, 1970; Cockcroft, 1972)

As pre-revolutionary Cuban rural education took place primarily in the plantation sector of the rural economy (i.e., children in the peasant sector went, for the most part, unschooled), we might examine in a general way how the plantation system tends to introduce underdevelopment biases in education before examining the specific Cuban case.

Traditionally plantation societies have been slave societies with education available only to children of the planter and managerial class. During the colonial period, these children would usually return to the colonial metropole for schooling; with independence, schooling in the metropolis or national capital replaced study abroad. Non-formal or on-the-job training was limited to the mechanic or artisan class and disseminated knowledge directly related to the requirements of plantation production. With independence and the increase in size and influence of the middle sectors, national agencies, usually ministries of education, began to provide public schooling that was patterned on urban institutions but located in rural areas. It has only been in this century, however, that the ex-slaves, the field hands, have gained some degree of access to free public schooling. In the past several decades, the growth of social demand for schooling among rural working-class adults and youth has been a key factor in what has come to be called 'the world education crisis.' Receiving at best several years of primary schooling, these children are systematically exposed to the elite value system embedded in the national curriculum. As has been described well by Illich and others, they are thus taught not only the legitimacy of the existing rigid social structure, but the correctness of carrying the blame for their failure to rise in the educational and social system. This experience demonstrates that for plantation workers, and similarly dominated groups, a little education is not necessarily a 'dangerous' thing. Quite the contrary, if it is offered in such a way that the majority of students will fail and assume the responsibility for their failure, then rural education can be a powerful device to legitimize privileged elites and gross inequalities in power, consumption, and life chances.

In 1958, the Cuban class structure was made up of a small upper class of landowners, owners of large ranches, and manufacturers; a middle group of some 18 per cent of the population comprised of small businessmen, tradesmen, manufacturing, and the agricultural middle sector; a group of non-farm wage and salaried workers in public and private employment made up of about one-half of the labour force; and agricultural wage workers who were, for the most part, unionized plantation workers comprised about 22 per cent of the total, while small farmers and tenants accounted for perhaps ten per cent or so. (O'Connor, 55)

The large agricultural population (see Table 1), although they had achieved certain minimal services, lived in another world and another century when compared to the rapidly modernizing urban sector. A study of rural living conditions by the Association of Catholic students at the Universities in Habana (ACU) in 1956 gave a picture of cultural domination and rural neglect that might be duplicated throughout much of Latin America today. A representative sample of 1,000 households distributed throughout Cuba's 126 municipalities was selected to represent the universe of some 400,000 rural families in Cuba at that time. The survey and the subsequent 1953 population census show that while an imported cultural life flourished among the upper classes of Habana, over 43 per cent of the adult rural population were illiterate. They were,

TABLE 1
CUBAN RURAL AND URBAN POPULATION, 1943–1970

	1943	1953	1966	1967	1970
Rural Population	2,574,500	2,832,620	3,640,200	3,700,300	3,381,290
% total population	53·9	48·6	46·7	46·6	40·0
Urban Population	2,204,090	2,996,410	4,159,400	4,236,900	5,172,100
	46·1	51·4	53·3	53·4	60·0
Total Population	4,778,590	5,829,030	7,799,600	7,937,200	8,553,390

SOURCE: Data for 1943–66 are from Roberts, 1970, p. 24; the 1970 figures from the national 1970 census are provisional. See 'Creating a Statistical Base for Development,' *Granma Weekly Review* (10 January 1971), pp. 8–9. (All figures are rounded to the nearest tenth.)

as later events were to bear out, starved for books and knowledge of all kinds. Housing conditions were little better. Over 60 per cent of all rural families lived in palm-thatched huts with earthen floors, two-thirds had no toilets, and only one house in 14 was electrified. As a North American social scientist has observed:

> Poor housing was matched by deficient diets; only four per cent of all rural families consumed meat regularly; rice furnished 24 per cent of the average diet; beans, 23 per cent; and root crops, 22 per cent. For the health of Cuba's country people, diets and living conditions had terrible implications: 13 per cent of the population had had a history of typhoid, 14 per cent of tuberculosis, and over one-third had intestinal parasites. Of Cuba's social resources, country people consumed a tiny share. (O'Connor pp. 57–58)

Although rural consumption of educational services at the same time also lagged far behind urban standards, the discrepancy, at least at the level of primary schooling (see Tables 2 and 3), was not as notable as in matters of housing, diet, and health.

Part Two: Major Innovations in Rural Education after 1959

As a mass movement seeking to implant a new egalitarian value system and create a new society, the Cuban revolution has placed a high priority on eradicating inequalities and giving all Cubans opportunities to participate in the institutions and processes of national life. The rural population, for example, has received special attention in this regard. Castro, on taking power, began a number of 'crash' assistance programmes to redistribute land, to organize, and to educate the formerly isolated and exploited rural agricultural population and to link them to national society and the ongoing process of revolutionary change.

A two-stage land reform in 1959 and 1963 turned 35 to 40 per cent of

TABLE 2

Expansion of Cuban Rural Primary Educational Programmes, 1958/59—1968/69

	1958/59	1959/60	1960/61	1961/62	1962/63	1963/64	1964/65	1965/66	1966/67	1967/68	1968/69
Number of Schools											
Urban	2,678	2,026	2,943	2,709	2,634	2,565	2,604	2,599	2,632	2,445	2,454
Rural	4,889	8,355	9,305	10,134	11,146	11,189	11,395	11,542	11,810	12,124	12,353
Total	7,567	10,381	12,248	12,843	13,780	13,754	13,999	14,141	14,442	14,569	14,807
Number of Teachers											
Urban	12,019	14,135	15,812	19,272	29,752	22,171	22,155	24,988	25,760	28,502	30,357
Rural	5,336	10,308	14,112	14,644	15,861	15,870	16,318	16,934	17,296	18,429	18,637
Total	17,355	24,443	29,924	33,916	45,613	38,041	38,473	41,922	43,056	46,931	48,994
Number of Students Enrolled											
Urban	500,567	631,881	653,320	646,497	651,841	712,973	756,370	748,423	775,024	809,292	858,430
Rural	218,850	460,383	482,957	519,770	555,445	567,691	567,555	573,345	578,875	582,875	602,341
Total	719,417	1,092,264	1,136,277	1,166,267	1,207,286	1,280,664	1,323,925	1,321,768	1,353,899	1,392,167	1,460,771
Number of Student Graduates											
Urban	—	—	—	—	31,161	34,618	43,903	54,264	49,823	48,454	
Rural	—	—	—	—	7,474	9,539	14,374	18,820	16,259	16,426	
Total	21,616	21,310	34,786	55,658	38,635	44,157	58,277	73,084	66,082	64,880	

SOURCE: *Juceplan*, and Roberts pp. 92–3. Data on private primary education which would affect the significance of the data prior to 1968 is excluded.

TABLE 3

CUBAN SECONDARY EDUCATION: RURAL AND URBAN SCHOOLS, TEACHERS AND
STUDENTS IN 1958/59 AND 1968/69

	1958/59	1968/69
Number of Schools		
General	21	434
Basic Secondary: Rural	0	8
Basic Secondary: Urban	. . .	391
Basic Secondary: Pre-University	21	35
Technical and Professional	40	114
Industrial	20	39
Agricultural	0	11
Fishing and Marine	0	2
Business Administration	20	26
Languages	. . .	29
Art	0	7
Teacher Training (normal)	19	26
Number of Teachers		
General	2,580	10,703
Basic Secondary: Rural	. . .	150
Basic Secondary: Urban	1,400	9,353
Pre-University	1,180	1,200
Technical and Professional	1,277	3,547
Industrial	818	2,016
Agricultural	0	421
Fishing and Marine	0	173
Business Administration	459	229
Languages	. . .	344
Art	0	364
Teacher Training (normal)	692	1,194
Number of Students Enrolled		
General	63,526	186,358
Basic Secondary: Rural	—	1,571
Basic Secondary: Urban	26,278	167,486
Pre-University	37,248	17,301
Technical and Professional	15,698	45,974
Industrial	6,259	20,052
Fishing and Marine	0	2,786
Agricultural	0	3,668
Business Administration	9,439	1,630
Languages	. . .	15,853
Art	—	1,985
Teacher Training (normal)	8,899	21,779

SOURCE: Estadísticas (p. 97) and Roberts, 1970, pp. 98–100.

all land over to small tenant farmers, and rent disappeared as a means of pumping out the surplus product of peasants for the benefit of urban elites. The second land reform in 1963 eliminated all private holdings over 165 acres and put vast numbers of unemployed labourers to work on idle land previously held as reserve by the large foreign corporations. (Aranda, 1969)

After 1930, Cuban farmers could receive bank credit and export licenses only if they were members of agricultural producer associations such as the Association of Tobacco, Rice, Cane, etc., Producers. These powerful organizations were, however, controlled by the large land-owners and foreign interests and served them well as instruments of domination over the small peasantry. (Gutelman, 1970) In 1961 the revolu-tionary government replaced these associations and the Asociacion de Colonos (small land owners) with a single mass organization, the As-sociation of Small Farmers, known in Cuba as ANAP. ANAP soon began to play a vital economic and political role in rural areas. It has coordinated private production with government plans, become the normal channel for credit, employment, spare parts, and the mechanism by which the landowning peasantry is incorporated into the political life of the Republic. ANAP has also been active in supporting the extension of formal school-ing in rural areas, and the provision of non-formal educational pro-grammes to upgrade the technical skills of small farmers and their children.

Thoroughgoing land reform has been a cornerstone of revolutionary ideology and practice. It has been the essential pre-condition which has enabled Cubans to acknowledge the fact that they live in a poor under-developed country and to reorder their priorities and investments for a rural-development approach to national development. Agricultural acti-vities have been expanded and diversified. Roads, dams, reforestation, housing, and other key elements in the rural infrastructure are given investment priority. With agriculture now the favoured sector, the chronic pre-revolutionary unemployment and underdevelopment prob-lem has been eliminated, and there is now a painful labour shortage. (Mesa-Lago, 1972 B)

In a number of ways, the agricultural population has been singled out for preferential treatment by the revolution. They are now assured employment throughout the year; schools, hospitals, and other human services are available, in many cases for the first time, and free to all. They receive the same ration of food and clothing as the urban population and are usually able to supplement it with their own production. They par-ticipate in mass organizations such as trade unions, the Communist Party, Committees for the Defense of the Revolution, Peoples' Courts, and the like. In sum, their lives have been radically altered for the better, and they are, for the most part, fervent supporters of the Revolution. (Jacoby, 1969)

Most favoured of groups in the rural sector, indeed of all Cubans, have been the ex-tenant peasant farmers. They comprise some 40 per cent of the agricultural population and work about 30 per cent of the agricultural area, largely as tobacco farmers in Pinar del Río. With average holdings of 50 acres, this peasant sector produces only for the government and in exchange receives fixed prices, credit, and labour supplies. Labourers supplied by nearby state farms work on an equal footing with peasant owners, and everyone is addressed as *compañero*, or comrade.

As rural youth are caught up in the Cuban revolution through their formal and non-formal educational activities and through participation in voluntary organizations, and as the income gap between agricultural workers and peasant farmers narrows, the landowning peasant class is rapidly contracting. For largely ideological reasons, increasing numbers of peasant children are declining to succeed their fathers: thus, as members of the old generation raised in the pre-revolutionary society die, their farms are now, for the most part, acquired by the government and added to state farms. This change presents significant evidence of how the new value system emphasizing collectivistic over individualistic behaviours has become woven into the very fabric of life, culture, and politics in the Cuban countryside. (Jacoby, 30)

Simultaneous with basic change in rural structures in the early 1960s, large numbers of youth were recruited in urban centres to teach in rural areas. Rural school construction dramatically increased, thousands of police and military buildings became improvized schools, and for the first time in Cuban history, primary schools became available to all. The Frank Pais Brigade, for example, has taught in the most remote mountainous areas as 'shock troops of the revolution' who, by their very presence, make their revolutionary message credible and vibrant to the peasants and farmers who, through their support, had done much to make the guerrillas' success possible (see Table 4).

TABLE 4
ENROLMENT IN ADULT EDUCATION PROGRAMMES IN RURAL AND MOUNTAIN
AREAS, 1965–67

	1965	1966	1967
Rural Zones	160,666	173,898	200,708
Mountain Zones	46,450	36,680	35,755
Total	207,116	210,578	236,463

SOURCE: Valdés, 1972, p. 430.

Although the movement of teaching volunteers to rural areas crested in the national literacy campaign of 1961, over 800 literacy-education centres, largely in rural areas, with over 16,000 students had already been in operation only a few months after the guerrillas took power in January 1959. During the Year of Education in 1961, Government efforts sought to raise the level of adult education, and to involve the entire population in the revolution's most urgent task, the eradication of illiteracy. Ubiquitous slogans stressed the need to and the possibility of accomplishing this objective as a consequence of Cuba's newly won independence. Thus the call to become 'the first Latin American country free of illiteracy' followed logically from the view of Cuba as the 'first liberated country in the Americas' (i.e. free of US 'capitalistic and imperialistic domination and intervention').

The details of the campaign are well-documented and need not be repeated here. (Fagen 1969) It is enough, perhaps, to note that volunteers located 929,207 illiterates and some 126,000 youthful 'peoples' teachers', plus 34,000 professional teachers learned about rural deprivation as well as the goals of the revolution while teaching 707,212 illiterates to read and write. (Cuba, NCTU, 1970) While the overall national illiteracy rate dropped appreciably as a result of this vast mobilization effort, as may be seen in Table 5, the impact on the largely rural provinces was especially profound. Gross differences in the literacy of urban and rural areas, as well as between Habana and the more remote provinces became minor differences (Table 6).

TABLE 5
LEVELS OF LITERACY AND ILLITERACY IN CUBA, 1899–1962

Year	Literate		Illiterate	
	Total	Per cent	Total	Per cent
1899	882,000	56·20	691,000	43·80
1953	3,344,000	76·40	1,033,000	23·60
1961	5,964,000	84·45	929,000	15·55
1962	6,777,000	96·10	222,000	3·90

SOURCE: Valdés, 1972, p. 42. Figures are rounded to the nearest thousand. The some 222,000 people still illiterate after the campaign include the senile and mentally deficient, those who refused to cooperate and, among others, some 25,000 non-Spanish-speaking Haitian immigrants brought to Camagüey and Oriente provinces before 1959 to cut cane. See *Verde Oliva*, August 16, 1968, pp. 40–3.

Programmes continue to be divided, as in pre-revolutionary times, into urban schooling oriented towards higher education, and rural schools oriented towards agricultural life and production. (Cuba, *Planeamiento*, 1969) That the obvious contradictions of a dual school system in a society professing equal opportunities have been painfully apparent to educational decision makers, there can be little doubt. The choices, given a continuing

TABLE 6

PERCENTAGE OF PROVINCIAL POPULATION (OVER TEN YEARS OLD) LITERATE
AND ILLITERATE IN 1953 AND 1962

Province (listed from west to east)	Literate		Illiterate	
	1953	1962	1953	1962
Piñar del Río	69·2	94·9	30·8	5·1
Habana	90·8	97·6	9·2	2·4
Matanzas	80·8	96·8	19·2	3·2
Las Villas	75·2	96·1	24·8	3·9
Camagüey	72·7	94·5	27·3	5·5
Oriente	64·7	94·8	35·3	5·2

SOURCE: Valdés, 1972, p. 43.

teacher shortage and heavy investment in education (18·8 per cent of the
national budget in 1967), have been to expand the existing formal school
system to modify its more inequitable aspects through the scholarship
programme, and to complement it with a wide range of non-formal
activities outside the school in what has come to be called 'the parallel
school system' (see Table 7). Many intellectually able and ideologically

TABLE 7

YOUTH AND ADULT ENROLMENT IN CUBAN NON-FORMAL EDUCATION,
OR THE 'PARALLEL SYSTEM OF EDUCATION'

	1968/69	1969/70	1972
1. Worker-Farmer education Primary and Secondary Level	457,888	404,149	—
University Preparatory Level	7,201	19,058	12,000 (est.)
2. Military Technical Education MINFAR	46,604	—	—
3. Public Health Technical Education MINSAP	7,516	—	—
4. Centennial Youth Columns Agricultural and Technical Education	—	24,000	60,000
5. Teacher In-Service Education	6,549	—	—
6. Others (School in Industry, on-the-job training, etc.)	60,000	—	—
Totals (informed estimates)	600,000	500,000	450,000

SOURCES: Cuba, Ministerio de Educación Estadísticas, 1969, pp. 81, 85, 86; Cuba. The Educational Movement, 1970, pp. 30–31; Granma, July 25, 1971; Granma, April 23, 1972; and
Educación, July–September, 1971, No. 2, p. 24.

dedicated rural youth are sent with full scholarships to board and study in urban schools both at the primary and secondary levels. In 1972 the total number of such scholarship students totalled over one-quarter million. (Castillo, 1971) At the same time, all urban secondary-school students have for a number of years been required to spend some 45 days a year in a programme of rural encampments called 'Schools to the Countryside.' This period is principally devoted to a minimum of class-work and a maximum of working with state farms, private farmers, and the military in the production of such agricultural products as sugar cane, coffee, tobacco, citrus fruits, vegetables, and others. (Aguilera, 1971) Benefits of the programme for students and teachers claimed by Aguilera include the development of a 'producer's mentality,' greater under-standing of agricultural problems, new organizational and self-leadership skills, new relations between students, as well as economic contributions. In 1969–70, 85·2 per cent of all secondary basic students participated; in 1970–71, the number of students dropped to 80 per cent.

Efforts to provide basic educational services for rural youth and to give all rural adults the equivalent of a sixth-grade education during the past decade have been less dramatic and exciting than the initial literacy campaigns but, nevertheless, impressive in their scope and evidence of commitment. The government's strategy of making Cuba, in Castro's words, 'one big Revolutionary School' has been to adapt and reorient existing school programmes so as to implement new develop-ment priorities and, when necessary, to create new structures, organiza-tions, and programmes largely in the non-formal educational sector.

Part Three: Plans to Revolutionize Rural Education

Cuban efforts to make six years of primary schooling available to all rural children have been impressive. Even the most isolated village accessible only by mule path has its school and teacher in residence. At the secondary level, the pre-revolutionary situation where secondary schools were, for the most part, located in urban centres continues, much to the chagrin of educational authorities. True, all deserving rural teen-agers now have access to these schools through full scholarships, or *becas*, from the government. Also technical training and volunteer youth education and service programmes give rural youth widespread and significant opportunities to learn new skills and use them in the ongoing struggle to mechanize agriculture.

If one compares Table 1 with Tables 2 and 3, it is clear that although the rural population as a percentage of the total population continues to decline, the relative percentage of schools, teachers, and students in rural primary education in relation to the national educational system has significantly increased since 1959. In 1959–1961 the total number of primary schools increased 61 per cent while the increase for rural schools was almost 100 per cent. During this same period urban schools actually decreased in number from 2,678 in 1959 to 2,026 in 1960 as many middle-class school teachers began to flee the revolution, mostly to Miami. At the same time, other primary teachers and a vast army of volunteers drew upon urban educational resources to open and staff new schools in backward rural areas that had previously never seen a school teacher. By the late 1960s this contemporary effort, fuelled by idealism and a revolutionary concern to draw the campesinos into the nation and the revolution, had been largely accomplished. After 1962, the rapid growth in rural school construction and conversion levelled off, while the decline in urban primary establishments has been reversed and their number has remained fairly constant despite considerable enrolment increases.

Data on numbers of teachers and enrolments in rural primary schools also indicate the enormous quantitative explosion that took place during the revolution's first years. Clearly rural education has been powerfully favoured, frequently at the expense of the urban educational sector, in the area of educational inputs. The results of this revolutionary shift of national education priorities to favour the rural sector might very roughly be evaluated in terms of quantitative increases in the number of graduates and qualitative behaviour changes sought. If we examine the first category (see Table 8), it becomes painfully apparent that the internal efficiency of rural primary schooling, and urban as well, is low and little different from other poor but non-revolutionary Latin American countries. In sum, Cuba is different primarily because the schools and teachers are available to all; the majority of students, nevertheless, continue to drop out at an early age to work, or simply to loaf. Over 300,000 youth in the 6-to-16 age bracket have left school, while within the educational system, between the first and sixth grades, over 620,000 school children have fallen behind one or more grades, and only some 40 per cent of those who begin primary grade one complete grade six. The corresponding number of 'over-age' students for the seventh to the tenth grades is some 77,000, while in the eleventh, twelfth, and thirteenth grades the number 4,600 is still relatively high. These students are viewed as a cause for grave concern in a society that is seeking to raise traditionally low rural educational achievement to national norms. The enormity of this goal is indicated in the continuation of an exceedingly steep-sided educational pyramid. Although the base has been expanded, i.e., some 85·8 per cent of all children at least enrol in primary education if only for a short period, the percentage of the age cohort enrolling in intermediate-level courses in 1972 was only 12·6 per cent, and in higher education 1·6 per cent. (Cuba, July 1971)

Perhaps the second most critical goal of education in rural settings

TABLE 8
GRADUATES OF MINISTRY OF EDUCATION PROGRAMME LEVELS
OF INSTRUCTION 1967/68

Educational Level	Number of Graduates	Total
1. Primary		
(a) Urban	48,454	
(b) Rural	16,426	64,880
2. Middle Schools		
(a) General		
(i) Basic Urban	—	
(ii) Basic Rural	40	
(iii) Pre-University	5,421	
		5,461
(b) Technical and Professional		
(i) Industrial	979	
(ii) Agricultural	893	
(iii) Fishing and Marine	992	
(iv) Administration	791	
(v) Languages	1,137	
(vi) Art	—	
(vii) Teacher Training	2,005	6,797
3. University		
(a) Preparatory	331	
(b) Normal	715	
(c) Higher	1,573	2,619
4. Adult Education	40,428	40,428
	GRAND TOTAL	120,185

after schooling of rural youth is the attempt to teach urban youth in rural educational programmes seeking ideological development and agricultural production. Although evaluation of results in this regard is even more difficult and informal, a number of recent comments on these programmes provide some qualitative insight into their aims, operation, and outcomes. At the recent First National Conference on Education and Culture, for example, efforts in the compulsory Schools to the Countryside Programme and in voluntary work in agricultural production were indirectly criticized as follows: (1) the goals of the activity are not clear, and the encampments consequently lack organization directed at specific outcomes; (2) the time lost from formal-school programmes in urban settings has serious effects on the academic programmes of students preparing for higher education; (3) urban students make few meaningful contacts with campesinos and largely maintain attitudes of urban superiority vis-à-vis their rural countrymen; (4) the productivity of students is generally low, leadership is lacking in the camps, while the activity has often been poorly integrated into the formal-school programme and viewed with suspicion by many secondary-school teachers. The programme has recently been cut back to five weeks, and it now appears that the entire effort to carry urban schools to the countryside for short encampments will be replaced during the next few years by a bold new strategy to locate all general secondary programmes, beginning at the junior-high school level, in rural areas and link them with agricultural production. (Aguilera, 1971)

Prime Minister Castro's speech of 4 April 1972 to the Second National Congress of the Young Communist League, discussed in detail current failings of the formal school system, presented a plan to build a massive new secondary system of boarding schools in rural areas, and gave the League a charge to implement the task in concert with 'the mass organizations, the labor movement, the Party, and all the people.'[4]

Because Castro's critique and the global solution he proposed will very likely shape the direction and content of Cuban rural education for at least the next decade, it is important to ascertain his view of rural education today, as well as its potential for revolutionary development. His blistering criticisms of the shortcomings of Cuba's educational system, and especially that part in the rural sector, confirm the data on low efficiency presented in Table 9. They also indicate that problems in creating the new socialist man through education have recently grown more critical and are now viewed as threatening to the very survival of the revolutionary state.[5] During the first years of the revolution, problems of illiteracy and lack of educational facilities were rightly viewed as part of Cuba's colonial heritage. They were attacked as intolerable social ills and largely eradicated. By mobilizing the masses and changing spending priorities, the revolution's first educational battles were conspicuously won. And if the outcomes were costly in terms of human-resource utilization, production losses, and other efficiency criteria, they were imperative at almost any cost if one used ideological criteria. But as vastly increased numbers of youths entered schools and educational costs skyrocketed, problems of efficiency in the educational system, and of its relevance to national production goals have greatly intensified. Now 13 years after Castro's victory, several basic educational problems are being critically assessed as indicators of educational-system failures.

The first major problem is that over half of the children in primary

TABLE 9
PERCENTAGE OF AGE COHORT ATTENDING
PRIMARY SCHOOL IN 1965/66

Age	Percentage attending	Number not in school
8	99·8	
9	—	
10	97·5	
11	—	
12	94·5	
13	86·9	20,804
14	76·7	35,428
15	55·7	68,042
16	39·8	91,239
(Incomplete total)		215,513

SOURCE: Castro, 1972.

schools, some one and three quarter million in 1972, are over-age grade repeaters. There are, for example, over 400,000 students in the first grade, over 'double the number that would be registered if the system were functioning as it should, if the graduation rate were what it should be, and if the students entered school at the required age.' (Castro, 1972) In all, some 720,000 primary students are two or more years behind their grade level. Of these about 130,000 are in the first grade, and 115,000 in the second grade. With barely 60 per cent passing, the fourth grade has the greatest number of repeaters.

The problem of school leavers is equally critical. Castro notes that the following percentages of age cohorts attend school: using the data from the 1965–66 school year, which would seem to indicate that the problem is little changed today, Castro explained that 387,000 students registered in the first grade, and some 124,000 in the sixth grade; but that only 82,3000, or 21·2 per cent, graduated. Moreover, in comparison to the national rate of 21·2 per cent, graduation rates for urban schools were 34·2 per cent. In rural elementary schools, they were only 11·7 per cent. (Castro, 1972)

The educational pyramid grows even steeper at the junior-high school level where, in the 1966–67 school year, 59,300 students enrolled in seventh grade, but only 17,213 reached tenth grade. Of these only 8,073 passed. This figure represents a 13·6 per cent graduation rate, a figure in large part understandable in light of Cuba's underdevelopment, rurality, and lack of trained teachers, but nevertheless totally unacceptable in a country desperately short of technicians. The consequences of low internal efficiency that are viewed as most serious are the nearly one-quarter million youth who neither work nor study, and the low enrolment in technical-education programmes. Of the 23,960 students in these crucial training programmes, 16,203 study industrial subjects, while only 7,757 study agriculture. At the university level as well, the number of students selecting agricultural science has been equally discouraging (see Table 10).

TABLE 10
University Enrolment in Agricultural Sciences,
1959 to 1969

Year	Agricultural Sciences	Agronomy	Veterinary	Animal Husbandry
1959	1,202	948	254	—
1960	1,359	1,150	209	—
1961	851	704	147	—
1962	886	689	197	—
1963	880	592	237	51
1964	1,194	908	262	24
1964/65	1,617	1,236	1,236	29
1965/66	1,300	923	923	21
1966/67	1,857	1,449	1,449	—
1967/68	2,908	2,083	2,083	—
1968/69	2,203	1,667	1,667	—

Source: Cuba. *Estadísticas*, 1969, pp. 80–81; and Roberts, pp. 104–5. In the 1967/68 academic year, approximately ten per cent of Cuban university enrolment was in the agricultural sciences. The figure appears to have fallen off in recent years. See Juceplan, Compendio Estadístico de Cuba, 1968. La Habana, 1968, pp. 34–5; and Paulston, 'Education,' 1971, p. 390.

For a poor agricultural country seeking to mechanize the agro-industrial sector, these figures indicate a serious lack of student interest in technical studies. Castro laments that, 'There are few young people who are thinking about getting agricultural or industrial training. . . . There are agricultural and industrial technological institutes that are empty.' In marked contrast,

> . . . there are 24,033 people studying languages. That's fine. We should be glad that so many people realize the importance of studying foreign languages. But who is going to produce the material goods in the future, and how? How will we be able to introduce technology in agriculture and industry? (Castro, 1972)

The Prime Minister also criticized Cuban education for its continued overemphasis on theory and intellectual preparation, for the poor study habits of students, and for their resistance to work and study programmes in rural areas. In this regard, he acknowledged the problem of motivation faced by all rural educators:

Who wants to go to work in the countryside? The countryside is rough, it's poor. Moreover that rough, poor countryside doesn't change from one year to the next, and we'll be having a rough, poor countryside for years to come. All these factors have a bearing on each other and give rise to certain attitudes of evasion.

Even more serious has been the ineffectiveness of those educational and rural service experiences such as the Schools to the Countryside and voluntary labour programmes that seek to internalize the new values. Castro frankly stated that, 'We still don't have the new man, and we no longer have the old one.' He sees Cuba living through a difficult transitional period between the old plantation system under capitalism and the new socialist society:

> The new man doesn't exist yet. . . . The irresponsible fellow that destroys equipment, who doesn't work or study is not yet a new man. The old man who lived under capitalism knew how hard it could be to find a job. He learned how to handle a bulldozer or a centrifugal in a sugar mill by working ten years as an apprentice. He learned about discipline because life, the factory, and hunger imposed it upon him. When you arrive at a sugar mill today, you do not see this discipline. The discipline of the old man is gone, and we don't have the new man with the corresponding discipline – self-discipline and awareness of his obligations and tasks. (Castro, 1972)

Interestingly, Castro views non-formal education programmes in the army during compulsory military service and in the 'Voluntary' Centennial Youth Column as the 'two key factors that have instilled discipline . . . in the mass of males who could not be won over and forged by the formal educational system . . . who didn't study or work and hadn't learned a skill or a trade.' (See Santié, 1970) He also observed that because girls have not participated in either of these activities, they have even fewer opportunities 'to learn a skill, to develop work habits, and elements of discipline. . . . This is a serious problem, and even more so in a country where there are old traditions that women shouldn't work.' (Castro, 1972)

Empty agricultural and industrial technological institutes and failure to produce the much vaunted 'new man' lead Castro to warn that the danger signals have been put out for education. He underscored that, 'There is not the slightest doubt that all things point to the need for effecting a true educational revolution.' His strategy for radical reformation of the educational system is based on a 'full-scale application of the principle of combining work and study. This is to be done at all levels of education: elementary school, junior- and senior-high school, and the university.' (Castro, 1972) This new revolutionary offensive began in 1972 first in Camagüey, Cuba's most rural and backward province, under the leadership of the Young Communist League and in collaboration with the closely allied Ministry of Education, and the ministries of the armed forces and interior.

Primary schools where fourth, fifth, and sixth grade students work two hours a day in agricultural production exist now only in one or two localities, but Castro is enthusiastic about developing this kind of school in the countryside. With reference to the primary school at Mencses, he claims that students now supply 'the fruits of their labour' not only to meet school food programmes, but also to the workers' dining rooms. 'And it wouldn't be a surprise if they could supply the town itself with some of the things they have grown. And all with working only two hours a day.' (Castro, 1972) Counterpart urban schools combining work and study are yet to be developed because of difficulties in finding truly useful forms of activity for fourth to sixth graders 'at the industrial level.' Rather, junior-high schools will be the first target institution.

Ten rural secondary schools have been constructed since 1970 using standardized pre-fabricated concrete construction. With 500 boys and girls boarded at each school, some 5,000 young people are presently enrolled in junior-high school programmes and working three to four hours a day in agricultural production. (Martinez, 1972) Ambitious plans call for the construction of 300 more junior-high schools a year of the Ceiba 1 type in 1973, 1974, and 1975. In September 1972, 40 of these junior-high schools with a combined capacity of 20,000 students were inaugurated on the same day at the same time. Construction is organized on a brigade model. Over 80 construction brigades were at work on this programme in early 1972 using labour inputs from the construction sector, the army, from volunteer workers' 'minibrigades', and others. After 1975, increased output of cement and steel rods will permit the implementation of a second stage of school construction to locate all senior-high schools, normal schools, and technological institutes as well either in rural areas, or close to a factory. Cuba's 150 sugar mills are, for example, each to have a polytechnic school, a plan that would involve 75,000 youth in the production of sugar while learning agro-industrial skills.

Special primary schools in the countryside are also viewed as the solution to the problem of 'backward students in our schools.' Thirteen- to fifteen year old grade repeaters will be isolated in these institutions and offered remedial studies and productive labour experiences 'just like the ones in junior-high schools.' Overaged 16- and 17-year-olds in the seventh- and eighth-grade programmes will be sent to the new polytechnic schools. Thus, notes Castro, 'our schools will be divided according to educational and age level.' (Castro, 1972) This proposal to create a dual system of remedial and regular schools would appear to be a surprisingly elitist solution for what is undoubtedly an egalitarian society. It indicates the surprising degree to which Cuban schooling continues to practice traditional concepts of grade promotion and individualistic competition.

The cost of creating a new system of boarding schools in largely rural settings has not been made public. One might observe, however, that Cuba's admittedly inefficient educational system in 1972 cost somewhere in the vicinity of 400 million pesos. Even if the costs of school expansion and relocation increased to the 1,000 million mark, to quote Castro, the value of youth labour 'should easily pass the 1,000 million mark.' The expectations are clear: students will pay for the new schools with their labour and in the process internalize revolutionary norms of sacrifice, solidarity, and service.

With 40 new Ceiba-type junior-high schools opened in 1972, and 'at least 120 in 1973,' where will teachers, already scarce, be found? With each school requiring a staff of at least 40 teachers, Cuba must launch a crash teacher-training programme to match the coming explosion of educational facilities in rural areas. The plan is to encourage junior-high school graduates (there were some 10,000 of these tenth graders in 1972) to volunteer for teaching positions in the rural junior-high schools. Student organizations such as 'the guerrillas of education' movement, the Young Communist League, and others, are to encourage tenth-grade graduates to stay on as teacher trainees and receive pedagogical training on the job. Castro concludes that 'at present there simply isn't any other formula except to go to out tenth graders and recruit at least 2,000 of them this year and at least 5,000 next year, and so on.' (Castro, 1972) Little has been said, however, about the fact that only 25,000 of Cuba's 80,000 teachers have been professionally prepared. The need to improve the quality of the teaching corps has at times been recognized, but the task is arduous and time-consuming. Rather than enter into a massive in-service training programme, it would seem that Castro is largely counting on enthusiasm and ideological commitment on the part of teachers, student teachers, and the League of Young Communists to prepare the new teachers required by the plan.

The fact that Cuban youth do not all equally share in the tasks of the revolution is viewed as a matter of great potential danger. Some youth study, for example, and are exempt from military service, in which only about one-third of all 16 and 17 year olds serve three years. Some volunteer for work in agriculture or construction, others don't. (*Cuba is 'Colonizing' Isle*, 1972) Current plans call for an extension of compulsory schooling from 16 to 18 years of age so that all Cuban youth will be required to work and study in the new schools in the countryside. In this way, Castro claims 'we'll get more mature, better trained, and more knowledgeable young people.' (Castro, 1972)

The need for 16 to 18 year old youth in rural high schools, especially in the sparsely populated cane-producing province of Camagüey, might also be interpreted as a necessary step to insure semi-skilled manpower for sugar production. As previously noted, pre-revolutionary Cuba had a dominant plantation sector that demanded large numbers of seasonal workers. During the long 'dead season' canecutters barely survived either through small-plot subsistence farming or through supplemental occupations outside the cane industry. Whatever the alternative, it had to be compatible with the need for workers to be available to the sugar producers for the next harvest season. (Hicks, 1972)

With the social revolution and a basic change in the ecology of sugar-cane production in Cuba, an alternative structural response has developed, i.e., non-sugar workers are made temporarily available for harvest-season labour. Volunteers from urban centres, farm labour, the military, foreign volunteers, as well as forced labour have all been used in varying degrees.[6] (*The Venceremos Brigade*, 1971) It will appear now, however, that future plans will increasingly call for rural secondary schools to provide year after year a significant labour contribution to the cane harvest season.

Conclusions

In sum, rural education in Cuba is increasingly viewed as the basic strategy for accomplishing key revolutionary objectives in the areas of production, ideological formation, and educational preparation. The need to involve all youth in work-study programmes, functionally linked with production, has been established as the number-one priority of the revolution in the years to come. Previous revolutionary offensives in Cuba have sought to mobilize the masses and involve them in efforts to achieve moral victories – often at great material cost. (Edel, 1970) The rural education offensive now getting under way is no exception to this pattern. It is an audacious, frontal attack on the still traditional formal school system and continuing attitudes of urban superiority and elitism. It is, moreover, indicative of belief that the new socialist man with his attributes of dedication to collective rather than individual interests will be best formed in rural settings where youth can supposedly be removed from family and urban influences. In a larger sense, Cuba's attempts to seek salvation in schooling and in rural development provide a revealing indication of cultural continuities and discontinuities in what must be Latin America's most ambitious effort to find a way out of poverty, under-development, and dependency.

REFERENCES

1. Although Cuba's three universities at Habana, Las Villas, and Oriente are urban in location, their growing efforts to prepare agricultural specialists and to involve students in agricultural extension and surface extraction activities will be treated as rural education here because of the degree to which instruction is located on the job in rural settings. (See Table 10.) At the University of Habana, for example, 12,000 students are directly involved in productive work, largely rural, for half of their time. This releases some 12,000 farmers and workers for half-time study in special workers' facilities.

2. See 'Cuba: Education,' *Latin America*, Vol. 6, No. 24 (16 June 1972), p. 189. See also: Santiago Cardosa Arias, 'Far From the Walls of the University,' *Granma Weekly Review* (14 November 1971), p. 6, which describes efforts by student volunteers of agronomical engineering at the University of Las Villas to create 'the first school of cattle-raising engineering in the Escambray Mountains . . . and to put into practice Fidel's idea to universalize universities and locate them in development projects, in factories, in research centers.'

3. Underdevelopment is viewed here not as a stage or a condition, but as a process.

4. Created in 1962 from the Association of Young Rebels, the League is a 'Marxist-Leninist organization based on the principle of selectivity whose main mission will be to provide the moral and ideological education of the new generation leading it to participate in all revolutionary activities and prepare it to live in a classless society.' The League also works with farmers and their organizations to promote 'their social and political development.' See 'Final Declaration of the Second Congress of the Young Communist League.' *Granma Weekly Review*, 23 April 1972, p. 7.

5. During his trip to Chile in 1972, Castro stated that illiteracy in Cuba still stood at 4 or 5 per cent, and despite great investment in education and continuous revolutionary talk and indoctrination, that the majority of students had not really changed. See *Granma Weekly Review*, 21 November 1971, p. 8.

6. See, for example, Fernando G. Dávalos, 'Youth in the Development of Agriculture and Construction Work in the Countryside', *Granma Weekly Review* (April 2 1972), p. 5. The author reports that in Oriente province alone 8,500 volunteers are cutting cane, 2,300 are building dairies, 500 are installing electric power lines, 1,000 are aiding the tobacco harvest in Piñar del Rió, while thousands more are working on other agricultural and construction projects.

BIBLIOGRAPHY

José A. Aguilera Maceiras, 'El plan "La escuela al campo": Un logro de la educación en Cuba.' *Educación*, Año 1, No. 3 (Octobre–diciembre 1971) pp. 8–15.

Nelson Amaro Victoria, 'Mass and Class in the Origins of the Cuban Revolution,'

Studies in Comparative International Development, Vol. 4, No. 10 (1968/69) pp. 223–37.

S. Aranda, *Agrarian Revolution in Cuba*, México City: Siglo XXI, 1969, p. 315.

George L. Beckford, *Persistent Poverty: Underdevelopment in Plantation Economies of the Third World* (New York: Oxford University Press, 1972) p. 303.

Belarmino Castilla Mas, Speech delivered at the First National Congress of Education, *Granma Weekly Review* (9 May 1971) p. 2.

Fidel Castro, Speech to the Centennial Youth Column, 12 July 1971. *Granma Weekly Review* (20 July 1971) pp. 1–5.

—. Speech to the Second Congress of the Young Communist League, 4 April 1972. *Granma Weekly Review* (11 April 1972) pp. 1–8.

James D. Cockcroft, Gunder Frank, and Dale R. Johnson, *Dependence and Underdevelopment: Latin America's Political Economy* (Garden City, New York: Anchor Books, 1972) p. 448.

—. Cuba. JUCEPLAN. *Boletín Estadística* 1968, La Habana.

—. Ministerio de Agricultura. Dirección de Enseñanza y Propaganda Agrícolas, *Guía para enseñar a leer, escribir, y contar a los adultos: Ciegos Frente al Sol* (Habana: The Ministry, 1944) p. 97.

—. Ministerio de Educación. *Estadísticas y Planeamiento de la Educación* (Habana: The Ministry, 1969) p. 86.

—. Ministerio de Educación. *Planeamiento de la Escuela Rural* (Habana: The Ministry, 1969) p. 37.

Cuba. National Commission to Unesco. *The Educational Movement: Cuba, 1969–70* (Habana: Instituto del Libro, 1970) p. 139.

—. First National Congress on Education and Culture. *UNESCO Bulletin*, Special Issue (July 1971) p. 32.

—. *Report of Cuba to UNESCO, 1969–70* (Habana, 1971) p. 52.

'Cuba is "Colonizing" Isle with Children in Work-Study Plan,' *New York Times* (14 May 1972) p. 16.

'Cuba: The New Realism,' *Latin America*, Vol. 6, No. 20 (19 May 1972) pp. 154–6.

Fernando G. Dávalos, 'Youth in the Development of Agriculture and Construction Work in the Countryside'. *Granma Weekly Review* (2 April 1972) p. 5.

Matthew Edel, 'An Experiment in Growth and Social Justice: Thoughts on the 1970 Cuban Harvest,' *Economic and Political Weekly*, Vol. 5, Nos. 29–31. Special Number (July 1970) pp. 1–4.

Richard R. Fagen, *The Transformation of Political Culture in Cuba* (Stanford: Stanford University Press, 1969) p. 271.

Ernest Feder, *The Rape of the Peasantry: Latin America's Landholding System* (Garden City, New York: Anchor Books, 1971) p. 304.

Michel Gutelman, 'The Socialization of the Means of Production in Cuba' in *Agrarian Problems and Peasant Movements in Latin America*. Rodolfo Stavenhagen (ed.) (Garden City, New York: Anchor Books, 1970) pp. 347–68.

José S. Hernández 'Brigada Julio Antonio Mella Presente: En Cuba se cambinan de un golpe el estudio y el trabajo como una necesidad de la economia de un pais en desarrollo, y como u na ley de la pedagogía revolucionaria,' *Cuba Internacional*, Vol. 4, No. 33 (May 1972) pp. 40–43.

Frederic Hicks, 'Making a Living During the Dead Season in Sugar-Producing Regions of the Caribbean,' *Human Organization*, Vol. 31, No. 1 (Spring 1972) pp. 73–81.

Leo Huberman, and Paul M. Sweezy, *Socialism in Cuba* (New York: Monthly Review Press, 1969) p. 221.

H. W. Hutchinson, 'Value Orientations and Northeast Brazilian Agro-Industrial Modernization,' *Inter-American Economic Affairs* (Spring 1968) pp. 76–88.

Erich H. Jacoby, 'Cuba: The Real Winner is the Agricultural Worker,' *CERES FAO Review*, Vol. 2, No. 4 (July–August 1969) pp. 29–33.

K. S. Karol, *Guerrillas in Power: The Course of the Cuban Revolution* (New York: Hill and Wang, 1970) p. 624.

Marvin Leiner, 'Day Care in Cuba: Children are the Revolution,' *Saturday Review* (April 1972) pp. 54–8.

Pedro Martinez Pirez, 'Revolución educacional: Escuela en el campo,' *Cuba Internacional*, Año 4, No. 29 (enero 1972) pp. 20–21.

Carmelo Mesa-Lago, 'Ideological, Political, and Economic Factors in the Cuban Controversy on Material versus Moral Incentives,' *Journal of Interamerican Studies and World Affairs*, Vol. 14, No. 1 (February 1972) pp. 49–112.

—. *Revolutionary Change in Cuba* (Pittsburgh: University of Pittsburgh Press, 1971) p. 544.

—. 'Tipología y valor del trabajo no remunerado en Cuba,' *El Trimestre Económico*, 1972, p. 49.

Lowry Nelson, *Rural Cuba*. Second Edition (New York: Octagon Books, 1970) p. 285.

—. 'The School Dropout Problem in Cuba,' *School and Society*, Vol. 99, No. 2333 (April 1971) pp. 234–5.

W. H. Nicholls, *Southern Tradition and Regional Progress* (Chapel Hill: University of North Carolina Press, 1960) p. 202.

James O'Connor, 'Cuba Its Political Economy' in R. E. Bonackea and R. P. Valdés, *Cuba In Revolution* (Garden City: Anchor Book, 1972) pp. 52–81.

Rolland G. Paulston, 'Cambios en la educación cubana,' *Aportes*, No. 21 (July 1971) pp. 60–82.

—. 'Cultural Revitalization and Educational Change in Cuba,' *Comparative Education Review*, Vol. 16, No. 3 (October 1972) pp. 121–44.

—. 'Education', in Carmelo Mesa-Lago (ed.) *Revolutionary Change in Cuba* (Pittsburgh: University of Pittsburgh Press, 1971).

—. 'Planning Non-Formal Educational Alternatives: National Youth Service Organizations in the Less Developed Countries,' *SEADAG Papers on Problems of Development in Southeast Asia* (New York: The Asia Society, April 1972) p. 24.

—. 'Revolutionizing Educational Policy in Cuba,' *School and Society*, Vol. 99, No. 2336 (November 1971), pp. 452–3.

—. 'Some Observations on Adult Education in Latin America and the Cuban Model.' Paper presented at the International Seminar on Life-Long Education, Habana, Cuba, December 1970, p. 14.

Aníbal Quijano, *Nationalism and Capitalism in Perú: A Study in Neo-Imperialism* (New York: Monthly Review Press, 1971) p. 122.

C. Paul Roberts, (ed.) *Cuba, 1968: Supplement to the Statistical Abstract of Latin*

America (Los Angeles: Latin American Center, University of California, 1970) p. 213.

Felix Santié, 'La precolumna Juvenil del Centário: Expresión del sistema paralelo dentro del marco de la educación permanente en nuestro país.' Paper presented at the Interdisciplinary Seminar on Continuing Education, Habana, Cuba, December 1970, p. 22.

Edward H. Spicer, 'Presistent Cultural Systems: A Comparative Study of Identity Systems that can Adapt to Changing Environments,' *Science*, Vol. 174 (November 1971) pp. 795–800.

Rodolfo Stavenhagen (ed.), *Agrarian Problems and Peasant Movements in Latin America* (Garden City: Anchor Books, 1970) p. 583.

Nelson P. Valdés, 'The Radical Transformation of Cuban Education,' in *Cuba in Revolution*, Rolanda E. Bonachea and Nelson P. Valdés (eds.) (Garden City: Anchor Books, 1972) pp. 422–55.

Jacques Vallier, 'L'agriculture, secteur prioritaire de l'économique cubaine,' *Problems économiques* (Paris: Institut National de la Statistique et des Etudes Economiques, 1968) pp. 6–13.

Venceremos Brigade, *Venceremos Brigade: Young Americans Sharing the Life and Work of Revolutionary Cuba* (New York: Simon and Schuster, 1971) p. 412.

Eric R. Wolf, and Sidney W. Mintz. 'Haciendas and Plantations in Middle America and the Antilles.' *Social and Economic Studies*, Vol. 6 (1957) pp. 380–412.

13

Rural Education and Training in Tanzania*

Solomon Odia

Introduction

Probably no country in Africa has made a greater effort than Tanzania to evolve a development strategy that is directly relevant to the practical problems confronting it. The present chapter, which serves to illustrate Tanzania's original approach to these problems, deals with one important prerequisite for rapid development in the rural areas: the adaptation of formal education and other kinds of rural training to the country's employment requirements. This adaptation is already under way; its purpose is to promote a faster growth of production, raise the national income, ease the problems of primary school-leavers and ensure more efficient utilization of the rural labour force. It would not be appropriate here to attempt a general evaluation of the policies adopted, since Tanzania[1] did not begin to make any substantial changes in the educational system inherited from pre-independence days until March 1967, when the guiding principle of 'Education for Self-Reliance' was laid down. Furthermore, while the basic policies have been determined and accepted, the methods of achieving the objectives are still being reviewed and improved in the light of experience and according to need. Before going on to describe these policies, it may be useful to outline the setting in which they have to operate.

Tanzania's population of 12·2 million people (1967 census) is growing at an annual rate of 2·7 per cent (compared with 2·2 per cent before 1960) and is likely to double within twenty-four years. About 50 per cent of the population is under 14 years of age. The strain of such a dependency burden on the economy of a developing country like Tanzania can be best appreciated when one considers that the proportion of children in the same age group in developed Western European countries is between 20 and 25 per cent (23 per cent in the United Kingdom, 22 per cent in Sweden). Average income per head is 400 Tanzanian shillings (TS)[2]

* Reproduced by courtesy of the International Labour Office, Geneva, from *International Labour Review*, Vol. 103, No. 1, January 1971.

per annum, while the average annual economic growth rate was 4·3 per cent during the period 1960/62 to 1969.

The country has tremendous natural potential, most of which has still not been realized. More important, the skilled middle- and high-level manpower required for rapid economic growth still needs to be developed, for over 80 per cent of the population is illiterate; and the proportion of illiterates in rural areas and in the labour force is higher still.

It is not surprising therefore that formal education, the most expensive social service in the country, absorbs almost 20 per cent of the government's revenue. Even so, only 48 per cent of the children reaching 7 years of age in 1970 could attend primary school though, considering the growth of population, this is a tremendous increase compared with 30 per cent in 1960. In 1961 there were 490,000 children attending primary school as against 825,000 in 1967 and 850,000 in 1970. Of those eligible to start school in 1961/62, only 21 per cent received more than four years of primary education, and only 3 per cent entered secondary school.

Introducing the Second Five-Year Development Plan (1969–74)[3], President Nyerere stated that all government activities in the rural areas would be directed towards 'helping the sound, economic development of socialist rural production and socialist living'. In order to make clear the role of education and training in this 'grand design', this chapter will first consider the policies laid down in this field as part of the overall development strategy, and the employment and educational targets the government has set itself. One of these policies, 'Education for Self-Reliance', is described more fully in a second section, which deals particularly with agricultural and non-formal education in the rural areas. A final section is devoted to different types of specifically rural training.

Development Strategy

The expansion of education and training in Tanzania is considered as an integral part of national economic and social development, just as are the achievement of employment targets and the better utilization of available human resources, because it is recognized that development depends, more than anything else, on the efforts of the people. And considering that over 97 per cent of the population lives in rural areas, it is not surprising that rural development is given top priority in the Second Five-Year Development Plan. Hence the importance of rural education and training.

The First Five-Year Development Plan (1964–69) provided a wealth of experience for the preparation of the Second. In the first place, it demonstrated the need for greater realism and for reliance on local resources. Hopes of overseas aid were seriously disappointed and several projects left unimplemented. Secondly, a programme of farm settlement schemes requiring heavy inputs of capital and machinery proved a failure in the sense that it did not provide the basis for widespread change in the rural sector and had to be abandoned. Thirdly, the expansion in the industrial sector during the First Plan period, although impressive, did not generate industrial growth at the rate envisaged and provided employment for only a minute proportion of the increasing labour force.

The Second Plan emphasizes the importance of achieving production targets through cooperation. The cooperative movement is to be encouraged and also radically overhauled to become production-oriented. Consequently, training related to the expansion of the technical skills required for cooperative production has high priority.

Policy Guidelines

There are three policy statements of great political, economic and social importance that serve as the guiding principles for education and trainin the country. These are: (1) the Arusha Declaration;[4] (2) the presidential statement entitled 'Education for Self-Reliance';[5] and (3) the presidential statement entitled 'Socialism and Rural Development'.[6]

The Arusha Declaration is a statement of policies aimed at establishing a 'self-reliant' socialist State.[7] It lays down the policy of the Tanganyika African National Union (TANU)[8] as being to build a socialist state in which exploitation does not exist and incomes do not differ substantially. The major means of production, including banks, insurance, import and export business, land, forests, mineral resources, oil and electricity and large industries (almost all of which have been nationalized) are to be controlled by peasants and workers.

Education for Self-Reliance is discussed in detail later in this chapter. For the present it should suffice to state that this policy aims, in a sense, at eradicating some of the shortcomings in the educational system inherited from pre-independence days. The old educational system has been severely criticized for fostering an elite class and for distorting traditional values, which has led job-seekers to shun manual work in favour of white-collar jobs, thus contributing to the drift to urban centres in search of employment.[9]

Socialism and Rural Development concerns the application of the Arusha Declaration to the practical needs of rural life. The concept of *ujamaa vijijini*[10] was first formulated by President Nyerere in September 1967. It holds that the development of *ujamaa* villages is essential for the transformation of the rural areas and emphasizes their role as the backbone of the country's long-term development strategy.

An *ujamaa* village is based on communal ownership of land and collectivization of production; it is similar in objective and organizational structure to the Israeli kibbutz. Priority is as a rule given to *ujamaa* villages in the provision of educational training, agricultural and other development facilities. Over 65 per cent of the expenditure of the Ministries of Agriculture and Rural Development is earmarked for *ujamaa vijijini* projects. Other ministries have also given these villages top priority, particularly in the provision of schools, water supply and the allocation of regional development funds. While the provision of facilities is one of the main attractions of *ujamaa* villages, actual government intervention is kept to the minimum. The organization of a village is left in the hands of the people, who elect a chairman and set up working committees responsible for the various aspects of the village's activity.

In principle, *ujamaa* villages are voluntarily organized by existing villages with emphasis being placed on self-help and self-reliance. At first the villagers maintain their own plots of land; as the village develops individual activities are reduced in favour of cooperative endeavours. At present, the organization and activities of the villages vary considerably. In some all land is communally owned and cultivated, in others it is still nearly all in private hands. There are a few 'fishing' *ujamaa* villages and some 'cattle' villages, most of the latter simply having communal facilities for cattle owned individually.

In addition to satisfying their own food and other requirements, the villages are supposed to specialize in the production of at least one cash crop. In some well-established villages activities have expanded to include manufacturing. The proceeds from each village are divided among its population according to the number of days devoted to communal production.

From the economic point of view, *ujamaa* villages enjoy some of the advantages accruing to large-scale farming; moreover, agricultural extension services and training can be made available more readily to an *ujamaa* group than to individuals. There is no doubt that properly organized villages of this type could alleviate the considerable under-employment prevailing in the rural areas. While at least 1,000 such villages already exist, with memberships ranging from 40 to 1,000 families, the *ujamaa* policy is still new; in fact, the period covered by the Second Development Plan will see only the beginning of a transition from individual to collective farming.

Employment and Educational Targets

The first and so far the only comprehensive labour force survey in Tanzania, undertaken in 1965,[11] showed that 54 per cent of those covered (32·5 per cent of them females, 21·5 per cent males) had no formal education. Furthermore, eight times as many men had completed primary education (4·3 per cent) as women (0·5 per cent). There was a similar bias in favour of urban areas.

Although the over-all rate of open unemployment was only 4 per cent, the rate of rural underemployment reflected a gross and alarming underutilization of human resources. On the basis of a 40-hour week, about 40 per cent of rural workers were underemployed, or 75 per cent if their meagre earnings were taken as the criterion.

It can be seen that the educational base of the population is narrow and that the majority of the labour force is still unlettered or has had only a minimum of formal education. It follows that there are tremendous opportunities for adult education if the population can be convinced of its importance both in the national interest and for themselves as individuals.

The government's determination to meet the country's educational and training needs is confirmed in its adoption of the following broad objectives: to achieve almost complete self-sufficiency at all skill levels in the economy by 1980; to give every Tanzanian child a basic (primary) education as soon as financial resources permit, which is presently envisaged to be by 1989 (this will involve almost a quadrupling of the present enrolment in primary schools); and to provide additional or further education and training only to the extent justified by the economy's manpower requirements for development.[12]

The plan to give every child a basic education will result in a tremendous improvement in the educational opportunities for girls. The rigid screening imposed after the fourth year of primary schooling will be relaxed gradually and will completely disappear in 1974. This expansion in primary education will of course entail a large expansion of teacher training.

The Second Development Plan also envisages an annual increase of 7 per cent in non-agricultural employment from 250,000 in 1968/69 to 348,000 in 1973/74; no increase above the current level of 109,700 is anticipated in agricultural wage employment. A large number of those employed in the non-agricultural sector will be in the rural areas in jobs requiring from one to three years' training (e.g. teaching, community development, crafts). In pursuance of the Government's commitment to improve the productive capacity and employment opportunities of the rural population, the following action has been taken.

1. In accordance with the recommendations of an ILO mission to Tanzania,[13] constant efforts are made to ensure that the wage structure keeps increases in wages and salaries in line with increases in productivity; that it encourages people to train for skilled work, or for responsible jobs that are essential to the country's economic development; and that it makes employment in the rural areas as remunerative and attractive as in urban areas. The effect of an incomes policy in keeping down the cost of education and training can be substantial, since teachers' salaries

constitute the major part of the recurrent cost of formal education; salary increases have been a major factor in the rising expenditure on education in most African countries.[14]

2. Adult education and various training centres are being reorganized and given official encouragement.

3. The educational system has been transformed in line with the policy of 'Education for Self-Reliance' so that every level of education becomes an integral part of the economic and social development effort. The implications of this policy are described more fully in the section that follows.

Education for Self-Reliance

The principles enunciated in 'Education for Self-Reliance' aim at attaining two objectives. The first is egalitarian: to adjust the educational system to the social goals defined in the Arusha Declaration and 'Socialism and rural development'.[15] Thus, the school is no longer an elite establishment, aloof and detached from the community; it becomes an integral part of the community. Intellectual arrogance is discouraged, the idea of human equality is fostered. The second objective is economic: to prepare pupils for a life of service to the community bearing in mind that their standard of living will depend mainly on the level of productivity they attain in farming.

Formal Education

To achieve the second objective, agricultural education is accorded high priority. Every school has a farm in which pupils acquire practical experience of farming and manual work. The produce of the farm is expected to contribute something towards the school's total cost, but the national education authorities are determined that such activities should not cause any falling-off in academic standards.[16]

The selection and examinations system is a very important, if delicate, subject, particularly in a country aiming to build a socialist and 'classless' society. Established principles of equal opportunity for all are adhered to, but in circumstances where only a few can possibly be provided with full primary education, and even fewer achieve post-primary education, a serious problem obviously arises. The examination and selection system proposed in 'Education for Self-Reliance' is based on a combination of class work and willingness to work for the community and the school. Under the circumstances, the very few selected for post-primary education are expected, even more than others, to dedicate themselves to the service of the nation.[17] According to President Nyerere, 'the only true justification for secondary education (in Tanzania) is that it is needed by the few for service to the many'.[18]

The revision of the school curriculum is an important prerequisite for the successful implementation of 'Education for Self-Reliance'. In Science subjects, for instance, the curriculum is related as much as possible to the rural environment. The animals and plants studied are those to be found in the rural areas and emphasis is placed on the application of science to agriculture, health, nutrition and development in general. The history of Tanzania, and then of Africa, replaces Commonwealth and European history in importance. Civics, which is taught in all schools, emphasizes the pupils' future role in the development of a socialist, self-reliant country, In revising the entire curriculum, the government has run up against two problems, namely the shortage of qualified personnel, and the substantial cost involved in producing the necessary quantity of teaching materials, textbooks and equipment.

A striking and far-reaching change in the educational system is the use of Swahili, the national language, as the medium of instruction in primary schools in place of English.[19] As a result pupils learn more quickly and with greater understanding. They are more willing to participate in class discussions; they ask and answer questions more confidently and with fewer inhibitions. The use of Swahili has also facilitated the rapid expansion of primary education and teacher training.[20] Most important, it has become easier for primary school-leavers to remain literate in an indigenous language and build on the knowledge already acquired. The intention is to extend this policy to higher levels of education and training, but the decision will have to depend on the availability of Swahili textbooks and teaching materials.[21]

In practice, 'Education for Self-Reliance' does not expect schools or pupils to play a leading role in agricultural development directly; instead pupils are, first and foremost, being prepared to face the realities of the sort of life most of them will be leading, either as self-employed persons or as farmers in an *ujamaa* village. Efforts are therefore made to ensure that they develop the right attitude to work and manual labour, and to farming generally – with what success it is still too early to say.

Non-formal Education

'Education for Self-Reliance' will not have much impact on the development of the country if nothing is done to educate and train the substantial majority of the population in rural areas who never had the opportunity of formal education, or those who had only a few years of education but are capable of improving on what they learnt at school. A child with primary school education only cannot be expected to have much influence on his parents or neighbours, in for instance, the application of new methods and techniques in agriculture. A three-pronged effort has therefore been made to (1) integrate the school with the rural community as described above; (2) extend non-formal education and training to as many people as possible in the rural areas; and (3) provide special 'leadership education' to people who are likely to be influential in their communities.[22]

It is not the intention in this section to examine all aspects and types of non-formal education (e.g. correspondence courses, evening classes in general and technical subjects, community development classes, education through mass communication media), but to discuss briefly three types which are either widely used or more directly related to employment and production in the rural areas. These are the adult education programme, work-oriented (functional) literacy training, and education for the members of cooperatives.[23]

Adult Education

In a New Year broadcast message President Nyerere announced the government's decision declaring 1970 'Adult Education Year' and called on everyone to give it very high priority. He added, 'We must educate the adults of Tanzania. We cannot wait until our educated children are grown up before we get economic and social development.'[24]

The aims of the adult education programme in Tanzania are to provide knowledge and skills that will improve productivity and standards of living; to provide further education for primary school-leavers and eradicate illiteracy; and last but not least, to foster a better understanding of the country's policy of socialism and self-reliance.

Following President Nyerere's broadcast, plans have been drawn up to accelerate adult education activities throughout the country (see table) and to tackle two of the major difficulties encountered in the past – sustaining the interest of students and teachers (fewer than 50 per cent of

PLANNED TEACHER-HOURS IN ADULT EDUCATION
CLASSES* AND RECURRENT COST

Year	Teacher–hours	Recurrent cost in TS
1969/70	260,000	1,095,000
1970/71	570,000	2,587,000
1971/72	920,000	3,471,000
1972/73	1,330,000	4,467,000
1973/74	1,810,000	5,606,000

* Classes given by teachers receiving remuneration.

the adults enrolled can at present be regarded as effective students), and finding enough trained personnel. To keep costs down, the fullest possible use is made of existing school premises and teachers. General responsibility for adult education activities in a rural area is vested in the headmaster, who is paid an honorarium of TS20 per month and whose duty it is to select suitable teachers and arrange classes. All educated or qualified persons, particularly civil servants in rural areas, are expected to assist. Teachers are paid TS2 per hour.

Various organizations and bodies are involved in adult education, for instance churches, the YMCA and YWCA, the Tanzania Women's Union, the cooperative movement and TANU. The very important function of encouraging and persuading the rural masses to enrol for adult education classes, as well as undertaking political education, is mainly performed by TANU. The Institute of Adult Education undertakes research into adult education problems and needs, and provides professional training for teachers and assistance to other agencies engaged in adult education.

Functional Literacy

When Unesco launched an experimental World Functional Literacy Programme 'to determine the nature and significance of the links between literacy and development and to make it possible to work out the most efficient and economical approaches, means and methods for the successful conduct of the campaign against illiteracy and, consequently, against underdevelopment',[25] Tanzania was one of twelve countries selected for the programme. A work-oriented literacy pilot project began in January 1968 in the Mwanza area, the objective being to link literacy (in Kiswahili) with vocational skills, particularly in agriculture. Primers have been prepared on community and personal hygiene, nutrition, child care and home economics. There are also primers on cotton-growing and rural construction available for pupils engaged or interested in these activities.

The duration of the courses is nine months with a break of three months during the harvest season. The programme is planned so that after eighteen months of instruction covering two consecutive years participants should be literate and have a good grasp of improving farming techniques. As in adult education generally, the high rate of dropouts and the shortage of qualified personnel remain serious handicaps; nevertheless, steady progress has been achieved. An interesting study of the reasons for dropouts[26] has enabled the programme to be improved in a number of respects. The transfer of the literacy project from the Ministry of Regional Administration and Rural Development to the Ministry of National Education has helped to achieve better coordination with the educational system at the implementation and policy formulation levels;

but the question of providing adequate incentives to part-time teachers is still far from solved.

Educating Members of Cooperatives

With the importance attached to the cooperative movement as a socialist instrument for achieving rapid economic development, it is not surprising that the education of members of cooperatives has received a great deal of encouragement in Tanzania.

Cooperative member education is the responsibility of the Cooperative Union of Tanganyika (CUT), and since a presidential committee of inquiry into the cooperative movement submitted its report in 1966 a national education campaign has been launched. An ILO Adviser on Cooperative Education was appointed in 1963,[27] and a Cooperative Education Centre was established in Moshi with Scandinavian assistance. As a first step in the campaign, priority has been given to the education of certain personnel holding key posts. Accounting staff are in especially short supply. There are frequent courses varying in duration but the most popular are the one-day courses for CUT members. Short-term courses include such topics as income and expenditure, weights and measures, prices and bargaining, and credit or cash trading. Special courses have also been arranged on cooperative principles and practice, agricultural cooperatives, cooperatives and the national economy, etc. Besides, cooperative studies have been included in the subjects taught in schools, adult education and literacy classes, and community development centres.

The problems experienced in launching this campaign are similar to those encountered in other types of non-formal education, aggravated by the fact that the funds available for member education are not commensurate with the importance attached to the programme. Considering the heavy losses incurred in several African cooperative movements due to mistakes, ignorance and wrong attitudes, expenditure on member education may well be the most productive short-term investment that can be made in Tanzania.

Rural Training

It is all too easy, faced with the imperative need for action in the field of education, to overlook the importance of a closely coordinated rural training scheme and the complementary nature of education and training. The reputedly 'unlimited' supplies of labour in rural areas lack the skills necessary to achieve rapid development. Agricultural and other rural techniques have to be improved or changed radically. The demand for craftsmen with new skills has to be met. Training is the answer, of course, but training costs money and presupposes the availability of qualified training staff. Above all, a rational balance must be maintained in the allocation of resources between formal education and training. To do this, it is important to assess the amounts and kinds of training or education most appropriate to the country's employment needs.

In Tanzania the rural training system has been and continues to be scrutinized to determine if the same planned outputs could be produced at less cost and more efficiently. In May 1970 two steps were taken in this direction. First, as proposed in the Second Development Plan,[28] various existing training centres operating under the aegis of three different ministries were amalgamated to form integrated Rural Training Centres (RTCs) in order to facilitate coordination and, by sharing overheads, to reduce the costs of training. The RTCs now come under one ministry, the Ministry of Regional Administration and Rural Development, although the other ministries are still responsible for training within each centre in their respective fields of competence. Rural training committees have been established both at national and regional levels.

Secondly, a mission began work in May 1970, at the request of the government, to evaluate the work of the agricultural research stations and the extent to which information and new findings from them are diffused to the farmers, the training institutes, and the farmer-training sections of the RTCs.[29]

Training priorities in each centre are geared to local rural development needs. Besides providing training in farming, various crafts, rural housing and mothercraft, the centres also assist in the development of *ujamaa* villages. Under the Integrated Rural Training Programme, priority is given to the training of leaders, followed by that of farmers and craftsmen.

The RTCs also give support to self-help projects, particularly the building and improvements of houses in *ujamaa* villages. They help to ensure that locally available materials are used wherever possible and assist in the adaptation of traditional construction methods and the introduction of new but simple techniques. Cinema van units attached to the centres disseminate information and motivate communities towards increasing production, and teach local people various simple skills and ways of improving living conditions. The Mothercraft Training Unit helps to bring the elements of home economics to rural families.

Farmer Training

The overwhelming majority of the rural population are peasant farmers so it is natural that the main emphasis of rural development should be placed on farmer training.[30]

In 1969, for instance, 224 of the 288 courses held at the RTCs were for farmers, the other 64 being for administrators and local leaders. Training courses for farmers are held in the following subjects: general agriculture, farm management, agriculture and politics, dairy cattle animal husbandry, draught animals, poultry, croph usbandry, tractor driving, soil conservation, soils and manures, the use of fertilizers, elements of environmental hygiene and nutrition, rural development, marketing and the use of oxen and newly introduced tools. There are also special courses in the growing and harvesting of particular crops such as rice, maize, cotton, coffee, bananas, tobacco and vegetables. The choice of curriculum is guided by local requirements and ecological conditions, and the need to increase productivity, with the emphasis always on practical training on the RTC farm.

The RTCs collaborate closely with the extension services staff in the selection of trainees (farmers in *ujamaa* villages are given priority) and follow-up on the progress of farmers trained. It is a pity that women, who feature prominently in the rural labour force and play a significant role in farming are, for traditional and family reasons, not in a position to avail themselves of the farmer-training facilities at the centres. Moreover, only 300 to 500 farmers are trained in each of the fifteen RTCs annually. On the other hand, the facilities provided are of a high standard compared with those in many other African countries.

Youth Training

In 1970 it was anticipated that about 250,000 young people aged 15 would join the labour force, of whom about 60,000 would be primary school-leavers. At the same time it was expected that only 11,000 new non-agricultural jobs would be created. The government's long-term answer to this problem is that eventually all young school-leavers should be absorbed into the various rural institutions and trained to become farmers.

But for a few missionary activities,[31] very little has so far been done by way of youth training. Two ILO missions undertaken at the request of the government in December 1967 and 1968 recommended the introduction of pre-vocational training of primary school-leavers, training of polyvalent rural craftsmen and of youth leaders. The cost involved has been the major obstacle to the adoption of these recommendations.

The National Rural Training Committee has made proposals for young farmers' training at Rural Training Centres. Training, according to the committee, should be for two years: the first at a centre and the second at an *ujamaa* village or a special young farmers' village.

It is only from the existing missionary centres that lessons on farmer training for youths can be drawn. A follow-up study, undertaken in 1969, of youths trained at one of these centres showed the following result: at the end of 1967, 118 students had been trained. Of these only 17 are known to have gone back to self-employed farming but even these later abandoned it owing to lack of capital. A few had been quite successful in starting and running *ujamaa* villages. The majority took up wage employment. Youths who had spent two or more years looking for employment without success appeared to have a more genuine interest in farming training and farming, and were therefore given preference in the selection of trainees second only to candidates nominated by *ujamaa* villages.

Apart from the fact that farming has been on the whole less remunerative than wage employment, insufficient encouragement has been given to youngsters who decide to take up farming. The task of clearing a fresh piece of land, the initial cost of up-to-date equipment, the consistent application of the techniques he has been taught – all this can be daunting for a 16 to 20-year-old boy, no matter what his background. Positive assistance and other incentives are absolutely essential during the first few years. Support of this kind, however, is not always possible since it requires substantial sums of money. It may even be considered inequitable to give young farmers advantages that older farmers are denied. Under the circumstances, *ujamaa* villages may be the best place for young farmers. However, the proposal that all primary school-leavers should receive farmer training with a view to joining *ujamaa* villages does not take account of individuals whose aptitudes may lie in a completely different field, of the willingness of youths to join villages (most school-leavers are reluctant to take up farming, and their parents do nothing to encourage them), nor of the actual employment possibilities within *ujamaa* villages. Finally, and most important, it is often forgotten that youth training is not an end in itself, it has to be co-ordinated with youth employment promotion projects and closely tied in with rural construction and over-all capital expenditure programmes.

Training of Craftsmen

On attaining independence, Tanzania inherited an inadequate and completely unsuitable system of craftsmen training.[32] The majority of craftsmen and technicians were Asians, and employers showed little or no concern for the training of Tanzanians. Only two trade schools existed and these were ill-equipped and completely out of gear with the needs of the country's production and construction enterprises. The students followed a three-year course after leaving primary school, but problems were experienced in placing them in the craft for which they had been trained. In December 1959 the two schools had to be closed and the 563 students in them sent down following a strike. The cause of the strike is illustrative of the type of attitude which 'Education for Self-Reliance' aims at eradicating: the students were protesting against having to maintain and clean their own tools and machines, a task which they felt should be performed by 'labourers'.

As from 1965, the government began to take positive action in this field. The responsibility of employers for training skilled workers was stressed, and under the government's policy on the employment of non-citizens, issued in 1966, non-citizens were required to obtain work permits and employers had to prepare training programmes for Tanzanians to replace them within specified periods. This has had a remarkable effect on training in the private sector.

Another major step was taken with the establishment in 1968 of a National Industrial Apprenticeship Scheme[33] and a National Vocational Training Council. The former provides for training and apprenticeship courses in the building, electrical and mechanical trades as well as in auto-mechanics. Mobile units have also been set up to conduct similar courses in the rural areas.

The essentially para-military establishment known as National Service undertakes vocational training in close collaboration with the National Industrial Apprenticeship Scheme. High priority has been given to the role of the National Service in providing technical skills that will help speed up development in *ujamaa* villages.[34]

Conclusion

Emphasis on rural development as the basis for economic growth is new, and while it is certainly no panacea, the bold initiative taken by Tanzania to establish a production-oriented education and training system may well provide some answers to the development problems of other countries. It will be easier to judge the issue in ten years' time.

The strategy for success is twofold. First and foremost, the *ujamaa* villages must succeed and win general acceptance as a national institution. This calls for considerable political education of the people. The existence of efficient *ujamaa* villages in each region, serving as a model, could be more helpful than a proliferation of such villages in achieving a gradual but sound transformation of the entire rural area. Secondly, in order not to reduce standards, the government has the choice between expanding education and training only to the point that locally qualified personnel and other resources permit, and requesting external cooperation to meet planned outputs.

The latter course may appear more expedient in view of the importance and urgency of the educational and training programmes. Yet the extent to which expatriate personnel can participate is limited by various factors. It is almost as difficult to find expatriate personnel from highly developed and 'computerized' societies, capable of understanding local problems and people and communicating with them, as it is to find locally qualified personnel. Furthermore, the presence of expatriates often gives rise to the problem of whose criteria are being met. The most desirable role for foreign personnel is one step removed from the field situation, as for example in the training of trainers, particularly where this training is in new techniques that are adaptable to local conditions. It follows that success in training will continue to depend to a considerable extent on nationals who possess the necessary drive and initiative to hold key positions. This is particularly true of the political education programme and the development of *ujamaa* villages. However, the most important aspect requiring external cooperation, apart from research, is farmer training for youths and adults. To put it mildly, the existing staffs of the extension services and the Rural Training Centres need to be strengthened.

The importance attached to training and non-formal education in the Second Development Plan and elsewhere is not at all matched by the budgeted expenditure in these fields compared with that for formal education. The time may be opportune for a shift of emphasis from formal education to non-formal education and training.

REFERENCES

1. Tanzania refers in this article to mainland Tanzania only.
2. US$1=TS7.14 (approx.); £1 (UK)=TS17.14 (approx.).
3. United Republic of Tanzania: *Tanzania Second Five-Year Plan for Economic and Social Development, 1st July, 1969–30th June, 1974,* Vol. I: *General Analysis* (Dar es Salaam, Government Printer, 1969).
4. *The Arusha Declaration* (Dar es Salaam, Government Printer, 1967).
5. J. K. Nyerere, *Education for Self-Reliance* (Dar es Salaam, Government Printer, 1967).
6. Idem, *Socialism and Rural Development* (Dar es Salaam, Government Printer, 1969).
7. Self-Reliance in this context implies that foreign assistance should play a supplementary rather than a basic role in development plans. It also implies maximum mobilization of domestic resources to achieve development targets.
8. The only political party in Tanganyika.
9. Idrian N. Resnick (ed.), *Tanzania: Revolution by Education* (Longmans of Tanzania, 1968).
10. The Swahili for 'socialism for rural development'.
11. United Republic of Tanzania, Ministry of Economic Affairs and Development

Planning, *Labour Force Survey of Tanzania* (Dar es Salaam, 1966) mimeographed.

12. Idem, *Survey of Manpower Requirements and Resources* (Dar es Salaam, Government Printer, 1965).

13. ILO, *Reports to the Government of the United Republic of Tanzania on Wages, Incomes and Prices Policy*, Government Paper No. 3, 1967 (Dar es Salaam, Government Printer, 1967). Also published by the ILO as mimeographed document ILO/TAP/Tanzania/R.4 (Geneva, 1967).

14. Richard Jolly, 'Costs and confusions in African education: some implications of recent trends', in Richard Jolly (ed.), *Education in Africa* (Nairobi, East African Publishing House, 1969).

15. This aspect is discussed fully by Philip Foster, 'Education for Self-Reliance: a critical evaluation', in *Education in Africa*, op. cit.

16. A. C. Mwingira, *Education for Self-Reliance: the Problems of Implementation* (Dar es Salaam, Government Printer).

17. Post-primary education in Tanzania is free.

18. J. K. Nyerere, *Education for Self-Reliance*, op. cit.

19. A few subjects are already taught in Swahili at the secondary level too, e.g. civics and history. Tanzania is the only newly independent country south of the Sahara that had adopted an indigenous language as the medium of instruction in primary schools.

20. G. E. Perran, *Education Through a Second Language: an African Dilemma* (London, Centre for Information on Language Teaching).

21. An Institute of Swahili Research was established in 1961 with a view to promoting the use of Swahili, particularly in educational and training institutions of all levels.

22. Kivukoni College was established in 1961 to provide leadership education for district political (TANU) leaders, trade union, cooperative and community development leaders, etc.

23. See also Jane King, *The Planning of Non-formal Education and Training in Tanzania* (Paris: Unesco).

24. *Standard of Tanzania*, 1 January, 1970.

25. René Maheu, 'Situation report on the fight against illiteracy', in *Unesco Chronicle* (Paris), Vol. XV, No. 11, November 1969, p. 372.

26. H. S. Bhola, *An Evaluation Report on Training and Performance of Voluntary Literacy Teachers in a Functional Literacy Project in Tanzania* (Paris: Unesco).

27. ILO, *Report to the Government of the United Republic of Tanzania on Cooperative Education and Training* (Geneva, 1969) (mimeographed document ILO/TAP/Tanzania/R.6).

28. Page 24, para. 56.

29. The evaluation survey is being undertaken with the help of the Nordic governments. Another mission under Dr Pettrini is examining sociological factors affecting agriculture.

30. See Jon Moris, 'Farmer training as a strategy of rural development', in James R. Sheffield (ed.), *Education, Employment and Rural Development*. The proceedings of a Conference held at Kericho, Kenya in September 1966 (Nairobi, East African Publishing House, 1967).

31. The Lutheran Church, the YMCA and the Anglican Church each runs a farm school for young people.
32. R. L. Thomas, 'Problems of manpower development', in Resnick, op. cit.
33. Established with cooperation of the ILO under the UNDP/Special Fund programme in collaboration with the Canadian Government.
34. *Standard of Tanzania*, 14 March, 1970.

14

A Comment on Educational Reform and Employment in Africa

Guy Hunter

It seems that, at least in some quarters, an orthodoxy is growing up, to the effect that one major way of tackling the rising menace of unemployment is 'a reform of the educational system'. Exactly what is to be reformed and how is not always stated, but in general it is assumed that it would be 'less literary', 'less academic', 'more suited to the real needs of developing countries', *et hoc genus omne*.

Much of this argument is based on 'If only' propositions – 'if only' developed countries had not introduced to Africa their own models of education; if only the prestige of white collar jobs had not been so high; if only the huge rewards to the educated African around the time of Independence had not established the maxim 'Education means jobs: more education means better jobs: most education means riches, power, and pre-eminence'. Such arguments are not very useful; the present situation is what must be faced. In passing, many of the same 'if only' arguments are applied to the drift to the towns.

The facts about unemployment have been stated again and again, though with some rather startling variations owing to difficulties of definition, mainly felt by those who insist upon applying the categories relevant to modern developed industrial economies. But at least there is unanimity that the problem is serious, growing, hits young people especially hard, and – in some countries – affects those with education worse than those without. This last effect probably mirrors the relatively small size of the modern sector in relation to educational output, and the expectations of the educated (to whatever degree) as to the kind of 'job' they ought by rights to have.

The remedies for unemployment are also now fairly widely agreed – agricultural development, development of small industries, construction, crafts and services of all kinds in the rural areas; minor urbanization and 'growth centres'; lower urban-rural wage differentials; adjustment of exchange rates; less capital intensive technology. In many countries, most of these recommendations are not yet being effectively applied, even if theoretically accepted.

However, many recipes also add 'reform of the educational system' along with the other ingredients. It does not seem at all clear why such a reform should create more jobs except for teachers. We must, charitably, assume that those who put forward this suggestion do not mean 'we must invent an educational system which will reverse the preferences of young people for seeking the more attractive rather than the less attractive chances in life' – for that is what an education extolling the virtues of real present day, African semi-subsistence agriculture would be attempting in many parts of Africa, although not among the best of cash crop farming areas. We must assume them to mean that reform would actually create more jobs. Would it?

There are three possible ways in which, it could be argued, this might happen. The first is that 'better' educated African farmers would be quicker to seize the (alleged) opportunities for farming much better, earning more money, and thus achieving a better life than they could expect in other occupations, particularly in towns. There is not a great deal of evidence that this is so. Such studies as have been done seem to point to two conclusions – that experience outside the village – even as a soldier, or as a migrant worker★ – is more closely correlated with 'progressiveness' among farmers than with higher attainments in formal education; and that, *a fortiori*, those who have succeeded in some non-agricultural walk of life – or, occasionally, those who have been agricultural extension staff – and who bring some financial resources and general *savoir-faire* tend to form a high proportion of the outstandingly successful farmers. Even if this evidence is not conclusive, one must also ask if there *are* real opportunities widely spread throughout the rural economy. To this question, the answer is somewhat uncertain. That there could be opportunities few would deny – provided that adaptive research has been done, physical and financial inputs are available, there is a road to market and a profitable price when you get there – and many other 'ifs'. In fact, the opportunities depend upon multiple factors far outside the educational field – investment, organization, institutions, markets and prices.

The second way in which educational reform might create jobs – or at least better earnings which, when spent, create jobs – is more specialized, and a bit more hopeful. This is through the active training of the adult (and young – postschool) rural community to use real opportunities already engineered for it – 'informal' or 'adult' education, beyond the school system, but still, education.

The third way might be in the stimulation of scientific invention – for certainly inventors eventually create jobs, although in the shortrun they may reduce them. I doubt if this thought is often present in the minds of

---

★ 'Cosmopolitaness' in the Diffusion Theory's terms.

those who advocate educational reform, and it might be that an education designed for this purpose would be Westernized and academic. A parallel argument suggests 'the creation of entrepreneurs'; but the correlation of formal education and entrepreneurship is not very strong. There are cultural difficulties in the conflict between family ethics and business necessities;* and a more serious difficulty that opportunities for entrepreneurship (which are themselves a selection process for entrepreneurial potential) are still scanty in most African countries, and will remain so until the purchasing power of that vast majority of population in the rural areas has been substantially raised.

Finally, there are, of course, quite a large number of expatriates occupying posts in Africa; but it is doubtful if educational *reform* would do much to accelerate localization, since the skills required tend to be the type which the present Westernized educational system produces.

Two major facts stand out. First, the importance of timing. At least in so far as education is felt to be related to 'jobs' – or the process of earning a living – the teaching of skills, manual or intellectual, can be effective only when there is a growing opportunity to use them – when book-keepers and electricians and carpenters are needed in large and growing numbers. Older colonial administrators will remember well the sad tale of excessive output from a few trade schools, or the repeated attempts to create a 'rurally-biased curriculum' which, coming before any real success in agricultural development and rural standards of life, simply infuriated parents who hoped better things for an educated son.

The second fact, closely related but distinguishable, lies in the differential (in its widest sense) between rural and urban (or 'modern') ways of life. Even if there were jobs in the rural area needing a reformed training which present education does not give, they would have to be attractive enough to balance the chances of a better life elsewhere. In so far as urban drift and increasing unemployment in towns reduces the relative pull of urban life, the chances of offering an acceptable alternative in rural areas do slightly increase.

Here particularly the 'if only' arguments must be pushed aside. No doubt, if Africa had been developing in a much earlier century, where the outside world was, indeed, more advanced but still reliant on crafts and fairly simple commerce, the type of economic development in Africa would have been very different, and no doubt would have demanded and used an agricultural/craft/trading type of educational training: shoes would have come from shoemakers and cobblers, not from the Bata Company; clothes from handloom weavers: skills would have passed from father to son: and so on. All this is not so; and the far more subtle

---

* See particularly the work of Peter Marris in Nigeria and Kenya.

problem of adapting both an economy and an educational system to the huge contrasts of the twentieth-century world is what faces developing nations.

Fortunately, education has many other tasks than adaptation to the (narrowly defined) economic system, although a failure there is indeed calamitous. Sir Richard Livingstone's definition of the task of education – to teach young people 'to earn a living, to be a citizen, and to be a man' – contains in its last two clauses a very wide field of action. It may well be that a satisfactory solution to the problem of adaptation to the economy must await, and then closely accompany, the creation of a modern agriculture and a thriving division of labour in the countryside and country towns. But meanwhile there are other valid tasks, as well as the preparation for that future in those limited areas where agriculture *is* modernizing.

When one comes towards positive suggestions, the differences between countries, in budgetary resources, type of economy, and many other ways, becomes increasingly important as the focus narrows to levels of education, curricula, and all the practical tasks which face a Minister of Education and his officials. In general, the narrow economic adaptation obviously weighs less at primary level, where the task of education is so huge and critical – the beginnings of socialization, literacy, physical and mental skills, character, imagination. A 'good' primary system, with all that this involves in teacher training (and rewards), universal if possible, at least widely spread, is probably the most vital target for the general health and energy of a nation.

At the secondary level, 'earning a living' comes nearer, and indeed, according to the economy in being, or closely approaching, here there is room for much more variety of form – not merely 'agricultural secondary' – leading to the usual GCE (General Certificate of Education) or equivalent, but much less literary in emphasis and with more practical experiments in colleges and polytechnics covering far more than agricultural skills. Where the split comes is a technical issue – possibly after the equivalent of Form II in present secondary schools, when the abilities and bent of pupils has had more chance to declare itself. But, once again, the 'practicalness' must bear relation to the actual and *immediately* prospective economy, and change with its changes and, indeed, by location.

If there is to be economy – and there must be economies somewhere in the system – I would believe that, in many countries, it is at university level that they should come, as economies not in quality but in numbers. Higher obstacles, in the form of qualifications, and more contributions by parents or by loan schemes, could at least begin to stabilize the high costs involved – costs which in some countries are already producing unemployed graduates.

Finally, there remains the immensely important field of informal education, in all its many shapes – farmer training, apprenticeship, craft training at simple levels, health and hygiene, self-help, cooperation, youth work, women's work, local 'Service' (why is it always called National Service, with its dangers of centralized 'armies'?), 'adult education' for those who missed formal schooling, and much more. Partly, this is a job of repair work – repair for the missing of opportunities which could not be given in the formal system. Because it is more specifically related to real needs and to locally felt demand, it may well be one of the most flexible and efficient forms of education there is – efficient because it does not (as all schools must do) waste so much effort on pupils who cannot benefit.

Part of it is directly and effectively adapted to the real local economy – to sugar growers or coffee factories or health and housing needs. Of all forms of educational effort, the education of farmers in new technology whereby their incomes, and so their off-farm purchases of goods and services increase, is probably that which will most directly and substantially increase employment. A tremendous amount of local organizing effort is needed for this work – effort which young politicians, and every educated African could slowly learn to give, as the immediacy of the scramble for power is a little slackened in a maturing society. In my own view, this field of action is the most hopeful analogue to the whole economic thrust for rural development which, hopefully, will gain strength in this decade. A tremendous volume of potential energy is running to waste, or even to destructiveness in Africa today. The limitations of a formal educational system, however reformed, prevent such a system from harnessing much of this; schools are so numerous and so expensive, that they lean inevitably to some degree of uniformity which is financially and bureaucratically possible to administer and control. Informal education can be as flexible and varied as African imagination and energy can make it; and if the central government is to aid it financially, it must at all costs be aid without strings, horrifying as this may be to the bureaucratic mind: in those countries where local resources are growing, local aid would be much better.

This contribution is entitled 'A Comment', and it is no more. Readers of this collection will be well able to fill in the evidence and the references. Education is at once a leader and a handmaiden to society. A leader, in that it opens the eyes of children and young people to the horizons of life before them, to their society, to their own physical and mental powers; and on the quality of this opening much of the imagination, energy, and social discipline of a nation depends. But it is also a handmaiden, rather than a leader or a creator of the economy; and it must be content to serve, not some vision of other worlds, but the real, humble, growing tasks of the totality of its society in the present hour.

15

The Formalization of Non-formal Education: Village Polytechnics and Prevocational Youth Training in Kenya

John E. Anderson

Village polytechnics were begun in 1966 as an experimental measure to meet the problem of training young people to play constructive roles in the tasks of rural development. They were created in answer to the recogtion in Kenya, now clear in so many developing countries, that however rapidly the modern industrial commercial sector expands, for some time to come it is the exploitation of the agricultural potential and the improvement of the rural areas that must lie at the base of any effective national development and employment strategy.

The idea of the 'village polytechnic' was first put forward by a special working party of the National Christian Council of Kenya, set up in 1965 to investigate the problem of the rapidly increasing numbers of standard seven leavers unable to find the wage-earning work to which they aspired.[1] The working party was particularly interested in the notion of a youth programme which might be able to link formal schooling and the realities of finding a livelihood more effectively. The term 'village polytechnic' is particularly significant, for the use of 'polytechnic', whilst excluding any direct reference to school or college, provided a modern sounding frame of reference in which to attempt the integration of basic educational skills, agricultural and artisan training, and to develop them in a work-oriented context. The use of 'village' reflected the need for a rationalized communal basis for these new institutions, in which local needs and resources could be taken fully into account and local leadership could play a part.

In particular, it was hoped that the local self-help (*harambee*) movement, which at the time was doing so much to create *harambee* secondary schools, might turn to support the village polytechnics. It was also suggested that once established, village polytechnics would provide the basis for a localized programme of youth service to the community. Thus, within one catchy sounding name, the NCCK working party were able to encapsulate and combine such critical features as relevance, adaptability, communal support and modernity. The purpose of this paper is to look more closely at what has developed in practice.

The Overall Organization of Youth Work in Kenya

At the outset any description of youth work must look at the relationship between youth organizations and the formal education system. In the past a dichotomy between the two was readily accepted and on this basis two long term trends in the development of youth work Kenya can be noted.

First, there was a trend towards providing recreational and educational activities for young people, incidental to their normal occupations in school or employment. Such activities include youth clubs, scouts, the President's Award Scheme, etc. They borrow many of their forms from modern, large scale western nations and tend to be based on the tacit assumption that schooling is available to all and that youth work should supplement this.

The second trend concerns young people who do not go to school and this aims to provide a substitute for schooling. It goes back many years, and during the late 1950s gave rise to the establishment of youth centres. These had a dual purpose, to gather together and control the activities of young people who might otherwise cause trouble, and to provide instruction in simple educational and vocational skills to equip them for adult life in the rural areas.

More recently, as a product of the concern about young people looking for employment, a third, much more widely based trend appears to be developing. This has several growing points; for instance, the National Youth Service (Ministry of Labour) and the Youth Development Foundation (Ministry of Agriculture). It is convenient for the present to place the village polytechnic within this trend and to treat the trend in total as Kenya's contribution to the current move towards non-formal education and alternatives which challenge rather than supplement or complement schooling. This line of thinking will be reconsidered later, but before doing so, it is important to clarify the special relationship which has developed between the youth centres and the village polytechnics.

Youth Centres

Although youth centres were established to offer simple rural-oriented craft training, popular pressure forced them, in general, to copy the primary schools, and as they were denied sufficient resources and staff by the colonial government the result was a poor showing on both fronts, and a steady decline in numbers and enrolments. However, as the number of primary school leavers began to increase some of the more enterprising centre leaders began to develop special craft courses for them and these became known as *senior youth centres*. In a few cases, for instance, Kipterer and Kaitheri, very good craft training courses have been created but these are exceptions, dependent on the personal initiative and commitment of the particular leaders concerned. In general youth centres, both senior and junior, still suffer badly from their colonial origins and in particular from the philosophy that they should parallel formal schools, providing terminally oriented second class training but offering no chance of selection for further education or better wage earning work. Thus they have become widely recognized, particularly in Central Province, as being institutions for the children of the poor or dispossessed. For these reasons, although the NCCK working party considered 'developing Kenya's own youth centres largely as they are . . . to attract leavers to them', it concluded that 'something much more radical (was) needed' with a *new name, a new image and a new status*.[2]

Village Polytechnics

In contrast village polytechnics were developed as a deliberate attempt to break the second class status of rurally oriented craft training. The first polytechnic based on the Anglican mission site at Nambale in Busia, was originally conceived as an improved type of senior youth centre and was initiated before the polytechnic ideas were actually published. The second, at Mucii wa Urata on the Mwea Tbere Rice Scheme, was developed as an arm of an already established NCCK Christian Rural Training Centre. In both cases, the critical factor in their establishment was the resources, both staff and funds, made available by the NCCK and, moreover, attempts to elicit local support were made. Management committees, involving local people, were formed, and interest and help was obtained from local administrative officials and the Department of Community Development. However local involvement remained small and it was outside church support that assured the progress of these two early institutions.

In the development of the later polytechnics, whilst the same general pattern of outside church support was maintained, outside influence began to give way to an increasing element of local initiative. This became especially clear in the Maseno area, where Ndere, Akado and Maseno Depot were set up by local church members, with the help of the then Maseno Diocese Youth Organiser, the Rev. James Mundia. In other areas, for instance Naro Moru, missionary initiative still played a part, but the general tendency has been for the initial moves to come more and more from the local church, and in the cases of Narok and Kevcye, people less directly connected with the church have played key roles in developing an even wider basis of support than that of one particular denomination.

Nevertheless, whilst local initiative and leadership has increased, the protective arm of the NCCK has remained, and through the skilful management of its National Co-ordinating Committee a programme of financial aid, in-service supervision and training has been developed, giving the new polytechnics the type of support and wider vision that the youth centres did not have.

By 1970 18 village polytechnics had been established and several more were in the process of being developed. They were spread over several different areas of the country and had begun the first stages of institutionalizing a new approach to youth training. The forms they took varied considerably, and an interesting range of training experience had begun to emerge which caught the imagination of development planners and educationists, both in Kenya and elsewhere.

The Current Approach to Polytechnic Training

Given the broad context of polytechnic development described above this section looks more closely at the actual form which polytechnic training has begun to take.

Table 1 shows what subjects were being taught at 16 institutions visited during a survey in 1970.[3] Fourteen of these offered formal courses, two others, Karima (Mandeleo ya Vijana) and Soy, did not give formal courses, but carried out extension programmes for young people in their areas, providing facilities for them whilst they worked at occupations of their own. The varying degree of institutionalization of the polytechnics this suggests is discussed in a later section. The focus here is on the actual subjects that were taught to students, and the activities in the polytechnics.

As the table shows, there is a very heavy emphasis so far on the traditional basic skills in the rural areas such as carpentry, masonry, tailoring. Other skills are gradually being considered but the process by which they are developing is very much *ad hoc*. For instance, tinsmithing and bicycle repairing at Naro Moru developed as optional activities offered in the evening, and have come about because a local farmer, who has these skills, offered his services on a voluntary basis. Certainly the most varied programme has been developed at Soy, and this is clearly a product of the work of the director, the Rev. Shadrack Opote who spent three months surveying this area by travelling around talking to people, visiting markets and looking out for exploitable opportunities, before he began offering help to young people. Soy, however, has the special advantage of having a director who not only has a unique vision of his work but who has spent several years as a farm manager and who can turn his hand to showing students how to tackle a wide variety of activities. Most polytechnics lack this type of wide ranging skill, and have to make do as best they can with the interests and skills that arise to support them. Thus the pattern of development in most polytechnics has been to start with basic crafts like carpentry and masonry, because instructors (either Grade 2 or Grade 3 artisans), or local *fundis* (craftsmen) on a part-time basis, can

TABLE 1
Subjects Taught in Kenya Polytechnics, 1970

Carpentry	12
Masonry	7
Tailoring (Male)	7
Tailoring/dressmaking (Female)	2
Domestic Science, including baking and some dressmaking (Female)	5
Typing (Male and Female)	1
Bookkeeping (Male)	4
Bookkeeping (Female)	1
Signwriting	1
Tanning	1
Tractor driving (Special course, 3 months)	1
Poultry keeping (Special course, 3 months)	1
Tinsmithing	1
Tinsmithing/bicycle repairing	1
(Optional in the evening)	1

Agriculture

Agriculture (Male and Female)	10
Animal Husbandry	1

Academic Subjects

English	11
Mathematics	10
Technical Drawing	3
Science	1
Hygiene (Female)	2
Civics	5
Religious Knowledge	7
Swahili	1
Recreational	8

On the Job Learning (Soy and Karima)

Carpentry and Quarrying (at Karima)

Beekeeping
Well digging
Baking
Carpentry/Beehive making
Tinsmithing } all at Soy
Poultry keeping
Agriculture/vegetable growing
Masonry
Rabbit keeping

be found fairly easily. Incidentally, it must be borne in mind that if instructors are so easily found, then their skills are not likely to be so scarce. In addition to these basic trades, support courses in English, mathematics, etc. are generally developed. So far this has been on an *ad hoc* basis, and depends very much on the type of staff available and in this context, overseas volunteers and primary school teachers have been very useful. However, the quality of these academic courses varies greatly: in one or two cases a syllabus related to real needs has been prepared, but in several instances the teaching is done rather unimaginatively, using any textbooks that can be found.

Whilst the availability of staff and equipment accounts for much of the variation in the support subjects one must also consider the actual interpretations of polytechnic training made by the various management committees and directors. These range from teaching skills directly aimed at wage earning employment in the same way that a trade school does, through a series of intermediate stages where polytechnics attempt to supplement such training by adding items like agriculture and business knowledge to the efforts to try to meet the multiple occupational needs of rural life indicated mainly by the work at Soy. In most cases one can identify a general shift in sympathy amongst managers towards providing training for as many aspects of rural life as possible, but this is proving difficult to achieve for several reasons.

First, students expect a specific skill training, and this requirement must be initially met by the polytechnic if it is to gain the interest of students long enough to help them re-interpret their view of finding worthwhile occupations in rural areas, and to improve their preparation for them.

Second, whilst the polytechnics have succeeded in utilizing local resources to a remarkable degree, these resources do not provide sufficient scope in an experimental period for many new ideas to be put into practice. Agricultural innovation requires the help and guidance and initiative of well trained men. The work at Soy, and the efforts of the Dutch volunteer specialists at Withur and Nyangoma, show this. Rural technology requires teachers with a knowledge of modern techniques related to such things as farm mechanics and water, who can think out answers and use locally available materials to meet them. Unfortunately barring the use of volunteer expatriates these are hard to find.

Third, following from the above point, it is not so much new facilities that are required, but rather there is a need for the type of skill and grasp of technology which will provide insight into the way in which modern techniques can help in rural development given limited resources.

In summary then, whilst a considerable diversity in approach to rural youth training has developed, two basic models remain:

1 The Supply Oriented Model

This concentrates on providing some type of training in order to prepare young people to take up or find new opportunities for money making activities, and to improve their capacity to tackle the everyday problems of rural life. It is implicit in this approach that some combination of skill training, farming, hygiene, homecraft, basic academic knowledge, leisure activities should be taught that will enable young people to meet demands for skills, services or goods as yet untapped by present methods of training.

2. The Demand Oriented Model

This is essentially the product of Shadrack Opote's work, but is exemplified by the activities of other institutions too. This approach tackles the whole question of vocational training from the other side, asking 'What are young people doing now?' 'What demands do they recognize in their home areas which they might be prepared to try to meet?' Briefly, Opote's approach is to create an awareness amongst young people in an area, which hopefully results in action. Hence the well-digging programme, bee-keeping, poultry-keeping, the bakery and tinsmithing programmes all of which were developed from a realization of an un-filled demand. All skills are learned 'on the job', and therefore, as Opote points out, there are no leavers and the risk that supply will overwhelm demand, with all that it implies, is minimized.

Thanks largely to Opote, the village polytechnic movement offers a significant contribution to *demand oriented* learning, but unfortunately it is much more significant, given the pressures they face, that the great majority of the polytechnics still derive from the *supply oriented* model.

Management

Initially it was the churches that provided the growth points for village polytechnics, on the one hand attracting financial and technical assistance from the NCCK and on the other stimulating sufficient local interest to provide the necessary foundations; land, labour and the beginnings of management organization. However, unlike most other self-help projects, polytechnic training was a new concept which, in part, ran counter to the commitment of most rural people to get secure wage-earning jobs for their children. Not surprisingly only a relatively small number of people took an interest in the polytechnics and most of these did so because of a Christian concern for the problems facing their communities. Within this general frame the degree to which local commitment was aroused differed markedly, often turning upon one or two key people. This became a very important factor in the development of the more successful polytechnics for it provided the commitment, continuity and initiative on which the NCCK committee could build up working relations. Naturally the organizational ability of the various committees differed considerably but as a general rule the members had little knowledge beyond their own experience of schools on which to rely in creating the new institutions. In fact most of the early initiators had at one time or another been school teachers and naturally they turned to men who had been teachers or instructors to staff the new polytechnics. Thus the latter generally took the organizational shape of schools, often borrowing their ritual even to the extent of prefects and uniforms. The need to counteract the school oriented perspective has increasingly been emphasized by NCCK advisers. However, the problems of achieving a more work-oriented basis place very great demands upon the imagination, initiative and intellectual resources of local managers, particularly if the sympathy of the general public is to be obtained and sustained. At a recent in-service course, instructors agreed that students should get experience in running a shop but argued almost unanimously that school time during the normal weekday session should not be used because students would miss lessons and jeopardize their chances in examinations.

What Happens to Polytechnic Leavers

At first sight the most direct way of evaluating the achievements of the village polytechnic is to ask what has happened to their products. Have they found work or are they still idle? The question seems simple enough but in practice it raises more questions than it answers. In particular, it highlights the need to clarify the 'real objectives' of making education and youth training better related to employment or, to put it another way, what do we mean by work and what do we mean by idleness, and anyway whose definition do we take? For the 1970 report this writer carried out a survey of leavers which was brought up to date for most polytechnics in August 1971.[4] The figures are presented in Tables 2 and 3 but they must be treated with great caution, partly because of the question of definition raised above and partly because of the difficulty of confirming the accuracy of results in a large scale follow-up survey of this type.

Soy presents an interesting problem because according to the policy adopted there are no leavers in the sense of graduates but the following figures are available and refer to boys who are no longer at that polytechnic.

Original Builders:
2 training as mechanics in nearby towns
2 stone crushing for a road making firm
1 working locally as a carpenter
3 at home with no regular work

TABLE 2

Activities of Male Village Polytechnic Leavers in (a) Urban (b) Rural Areas

	Further training	Sec. Sch.	Repeating primary	Employment using skill	Self Employment using skill	Other work	Looking for work	Home	Sick	Unknown	Total
(a) Urban											
Ndere	1	3	0	6	1	3	0	0	0	0	14
Maseno	1	1	0	16	2	6	0	0	0	0	26
Mucii wa Urata	1	0	0	13	1	2	2	0	0	0	19
Mt. Kenya	2	0	0	2	0	5	3	0	0	0	12
Kianjai	0	0	0	1	0	3	0	0	0	0	4
Withur	0	0	0	0	0	0	0	0	0	0	0
Nyangoma	0	0	0	1	0	0	0	0	0	0	1
Keveye (incomplete)	0	0	0	0	0	0	0	0	0	0	0
Nambale (1970) only	12	7	0	3	0	8	3	0	0	0	33
	17	11	0	42	4	27	8	0	0	0	109
(b) Rural											
Ndere	0	0	2	3	9	2	0	13	3	8	40
Maseno	4	1	0	10	16	2	0	6	0	12	51
Mucii wa Urata	1	0	0	24	22	9	0	9	2	24	91
Mt. Kenya	0	0	0	5	7	0	0	12	1	7	32
Kianjai	0	0	0	0	4	1	0	3	0	0	8
Withur	0	0	1	4	0	0	0	5	0	2	11
Nyangome	0	0	0	0	1	0	0	1	0	0	3
Keveye (incomplete)	0	0	0	0	0	0	0	1	0	0	0
Nambale (1970) only	0	0	5	0	5	3	0	14	1	7	35
Rural total	5	1	8	46	64	17	0	64	7	60	272
	(7%)										
Grand total	22 (7%)	12 (3%)	8 (2%)	88 (24%)	68 (17%)	44 (12%)	8 (2%)	64 (16%)	7 (2%)	60 (15%)	381 (100%)

TABLE 3
Activities of Female Village Polytechnic Leavers in (a) Urban (b) Rural Areas

	Further training	Sec. Sch.	Repeating primary	Employment using skill	Self employment using skill	Other work	Looking for work	Home	Sick	Unknown	Total
(a) Urban											
Maseno	0	0	0	4	0	5	0	0	0	0	9
Mucii wa Urata	0	0	0	2	0	2	0	0	0	0	4
Mt Kenya	1	2	0	1	3	3	0	0	0	0	10
Keveye (incomplete)	2	0	0	0	0	0	0	0	0	0	2
Urban total	3	2	0	7	3	10	0	0	0	0	25
(b) Rural											
Maseno	3	0	1	0	4	1	0	19	0	6	34
Mucii wa Urata	0	2	0	0	9	2	0	5	0	16	34
Mt Kenya	0	0	0	2	1	1	0	9	0	1	14
Keveye (incomplete)	0	0	0	0	0	0	1	1	0	0	1
Rural total	3	2	1	2	14	4	0	34	0	23	83
Grand total	6 (5%)	4 (3%)	1 (1%)	9 (8%)	17 (16%)	14 (11%)	0 (0)	34 (33%)	0 (0)	23 (23%)	108 100(%)

Original Carpenters:
1 working as a carpenter at Turbo
1 trading in eggs (not very successfully)

The Bakery Group has now split:
2 moved to start a new bakery near Kakamega
2 still working at the old bakery

Tinsmiths (instructor dismissed):
This group awaits a new instructor. Some members do a little mending, but most of the group are at home.

The tables summarize the most recent information concerning the whereabouts and activities of polytechnic leavers. They suggest that 53 per cent of male leavers and 35 per cent of female leavers are known to be in some form of regular wage-earning employment, and a further 10 per cent of male leavers and 8 per cent of female leavers are in some form of further training. It is also important to note that approximately 30 per cent of all leavers are in urban areas, and almost 37 per cent of the male leavers finding regular wage employment have done so in urban areas. As mentioned above, the tables should be interpreted with considerable caution. Firstly, the figures from some polytechnics are the product of unsystematic knowledge on the part of the managers. The distinction between 'unknown' and 'at home' for instance is not clear, as most managers tend to record those known to have found work. Secondly, the classification of the responses involves a large element of subjective judgement, e.g. in deciding whether or not an acquired skill is being applied in a given job. Nevertheless, taking into account discussions carried out with managers, leavers and employers during this survey the most reasonable explanation for these figures seems to be that the polytechnics are for the present providing a form of training for which there is some demand. At least some primary school leavers who are literate and have some knowledge of tools and simple business techniques, and who, unlike more skilled personnel, are reasonably content to work on a casual basis, picking up a low level of wage (shs 50 – shs 100 per month seems to be the range), can often find an outlet for their skills. When business is bad, wages decline, when it picks up, wages increase, but unlike many 'skilled personnel' polytechnic leavers seem prepared to live with this. They also accept that much of their casual work may well be of the 'clearing up' or labouring kind, and that once a skill is acquired it may mean long periods of routine work such as making chair legs, and doing such 'chores' as walking several miles to buy a bag of nails.

There appears to be considerable advantage to passing a grade test. The breakdown for Maseno, where records are quite well kept, indicates that all with a grade test pass are in work. Hence the pressure for grade tests is likely to increase, and the familiar phenomena of repeating, with some ex-students returning to polytechnics to repeat grade tests, has already been noted.

Some polytechnics have developed cooperative building teams. It is difficult to estimate membership because some members leave to find permanent work and because contracts come in an *ad hoc* way. Thus members may combine to take on a large contract, but otherwise may work on small jobs as individuals. It does seem that structured cooperative efforts so far have been difficult to maintain once initial contracts have been fulfilled. The Ahero Training Institute is an exception, for the Ahero Builders Cooperative was set up by the mission with considerable financial backing, having its own buildings and large scale contracts guaranteed, in some cases well outside the local area (e.g. West Pokot, where a multipurpose training centre is to be erected). But even with this cooperative it seems pertinent to ask what will happen when its members want to get married and establish their own homes.

It is not easy to ascertain to what extent polytechnic leavers are merely replacing primary school leavers without polytechnic training in finding employment, or are really meeting a demand for a type of labour which is at present unmet. But it is important to emphasize that the numbers only refer to a special and relatively small group of potential workers, and also that there is considerable variation between the institutions studied. Even if the figures above do explain the present situation accurately the situation may only be a temporary one, wherein a new low level type of pre-vocational training is filling a demand for a category of labour which, like the demand for administrative skills that occurred immediately after independence, will not occur again at the same level.

Meeting Local Demand

The analysis above has naturally focused on the apparent success of the polytechnic leavers in finding regular wage earning work with the skills they have learnt. But in doing so it reflects the ambiguity facing all concerned with relating education to employment. Naturally, there is widespread urgency about the young finding wage earning work and a sense of institutional pride amongst many of the polytechnic staff and students at their success in their activities. But what of the other, less tangible, but in the long run much more important goals – the seeking out and stimulation of new demands, and the training to meet the opportunities these present. This is much less easy to assess. Of course there are several remarkable individual cases, for instance bakers at Soy, vegetable growers at Thika, and pipe fitters at Kararumo. Each polytechnic could make its claim, but the general pattern of development is diffuse and in each case arguments would depend on the set of particular local circumstances. Clearly a wide range of cases needs to be followed up carefully if they are to be interpreted correctly and fitted into a more general and comprehensive understanding of the employment situation.

However at present some general idea of the opportunities available to village polytechnic leavers can be constructed by taking into account the findings given above, the comments of polytechnic staff and students, and observations made during evaluation visits. In Figure 1 I have attempted to show the major categories of opportunities available in the rural areas and their relationship to each other:

FIGURE 1

	Full Time	Part Time	Casual
(i) Wage Employment	Full time (regular) e.g. market supervisor, hospital orderly, farm labourer, carpenter/ mason	Part time (regular) e.g. shop assistant, farm labourer, carpenter/mason	Casual e.g. farm labourer, carpenter/ mason
(ii) Agricultural Work	Own land, subsistence, cash crops	Family farm, subsistence, cash crops	Work for other land owners, subsistence, cash crops
(iii) Enterprise/ Skill	e.g. setting up own full time business, as individual or member of cooperative or family enterprise etc.	e.g. part-time contracting on same basis as full time	e.g. use of skills on an *ad hoc* basis, like dress making, repairing a house, etc.
(iv) Enterprise/ Trade*	Setting up own trading venture, e.g. shop, marketing agricultural produce, retailing other goods.	Part-time trading in shops or local markets.	Casual trading in local markets.

* In practice too fine a distinction cannot be drawn because trading as such may well be related to production under (ii) or (iii) and/or skills and services under (iii).

This only provides a very rough categorization but it does help to emphasize the need to investigate and support the present pattern of economic activity on a sufficiently localized basis. Equally, it points to the complexity and problematic nature of such a task where economic activities are so diffusely organized and are so liable to fluctuation. In this regard, two fundamental points stand out:

1. For a skilled man or a good farmer, the ability to produce goods and crops, or to offer a service, only pays off to the degree that he has the skill and opportunity to market what he has to offer.

2. In rural areas occupational roles have a multiple nature. If one has land, one farms. If one produces crops, one trades. If one has a skill, one offers it for sale. Each individual thus develops a scale of occupational priorities related to his skills and assets, and the markets available for them. Generally this means emphasizing a skill and where possible obtaining full-time wage earning work through it, even if this means leaving the locality. If full-time work is not available, a skill will tend to be used on a part-time or casual basis, and the remaining time is then used to farm or trade. In this respect a distinction needs to be drawn between farm-managing and farm-labouring, for whilst a successful trader or wage employee nearly always allows himself time to manage a farm, he can usually obtain labour that will follow his directions, either from his family or local people who are prepared to sell their labour on a casual basis.

The National Perspective

The above sections have tended to focus upon the micro situation and to emphasize the locally based perspective which well conceived employment oriented youth training must have. This raises a variety of intriguing questions but one must be careful not to lose the wood for the trees. The experiences discussed above are based upon less than 20 institutions and about 400 polytechnic leavers and they must be considered against the overall picture of what happens to Kenya's youth in general.

As late as 1970 when approximately 350 thousand young people reached the nominal age (14) for leaving school only about 293 thousand of them entered the employment market. This difference is due to the number of students who entered secondary school or continued repeating primary school classes. More important for our purposes, however, is the fact that of the 293 thousand who became available for employment only 37 thousand or 14 per cent found full-time paid wage employment in the modern economic sector. The remainder, including a significant proportion of secondary school graduates, were obliged to seek their livelihood on the land or in a more informal economic milieu. For this group only 2,000 places for some form of continued training were available in all rural youth schemes including Senior Youth Centres and Village Polytechnics. This figure can be contrasted with 45 thousand places available in academic secondary schools at that time.

It was in response to this situation that the government aided pre-vocational youth training programme was created. The programme began in 1972 with the selection of 40 projects, mainly established polytechnics and senior youth centres, but it also aimed to develop new projects, and according to a current policy statement, the programme is planned to include 75 projects in 1973 and 300 by 1975.[6]

The size of the problem gives cause for concern; political anxiety about the school leavers is growing, and any type of training which will help school leavers find employment is not only sought after as a solution to the problem but also as an effort to which politicians can refer when answering awkward questions. But in the short term this does not alter the political reality in which formal education remains the only clear route to the more privileged, secure and interesting jobs in life. As a result the political promise that brings votes in nearly all areas of the country, turns upon the question of increasing formal education, rather than training school leavers for informal employment. Further, the 'self-help' movement reflects this popular ordering of priorities in terms of the massive support it has given to *harambee* secondary schools, and is now directing toward *harambee* technical institutes. By contrast, the support given to village polytechnics, though significant in terms of initiative and commitment, remains minimal in any substantive sense.

It is in this setting that the Department of Social Services has to create its new youth programme. Naturally the officials and advisers concerned seek to give the programme a new and forceful identity, but in doing so they, like the Community Development officials before them, face a lack of response from the general public, a lack of enthusiasm among the politicians, who need votes, a lack of readily available professional expertise. They also have few clearly defined goals of their own, and their activities may tend to conflict with the policies of the more established ministries mentioned earlier. For example, recent relations with the Ministry of Agriculture provide an example of the problems that may arise: while the new pre-vocational youth projects urgently seek agricultural services, Ministry of Agricultural Officials, busy developing their own Youth Development Foundation, argue that their time and skill would be wasted in supporting agricultural activities of a dubious quality outside the control of their own ministry. In the argument both sides have a point. The present Ministry of Agriculture efforts (4K and Young Farmers' Clubs) hardly touch the critical problem of school leavers, for in line with the well known 'extension bias' they are directed towards growing quality crops 'for the show' and interesting more privileged families, while neglecting the fundamental problems facing young people who have to grow subsistence crops on small overworked plots with insufficient capital. But whilst the new youth programme can claim that it is now trying to put this right, there is little evidence of this in practice. The reason is that although a few of the village polytechnics have developd excellent agricultural teaching (Withur and Kararumo for example), these have been developed on an experimental basis, are dependent on exceptional outside resources, and show signs of becoming lost in the rapidly expanding programme. Thus, it is easy for agricultural officials to point to projects where, if agriculture is attempted at all, it is taught very badly, particularly in the senior youth centres. As a result of this and the rapid expansion already noted, it is important to emphasize that while the village polytechnic movement may have caught the imagination of the current crop of rural development-oriented planners, the youth centres provide a much broader institutional base from which any future programme is likely to be developed. Although statistics are none too accurate, there were in 1970 approximately 160 youth centres, about 40 of which had begun to develop some sort of school leaver training, as opposed to only about 25 polytechnics.

The Underlying Dilemma

Put briefly, the present youth administration in Kenya faces a critical dilemma. On the one hand the time appears ripe for rapid expansion in view of the clear need in the rural areas, the volume of government aid, the institutional base of youth centres, and most important of all, the apparent success of the village polytechnics. On the other hand a more critical evaluation of the polytechnic experience suggests that the impact of the polytechnics is more ideological than institutional. They have given a new, positive experimental orientation to employment-oriented youth work but offer no ready-made answers in a field where not only is the process of training open to question, but so are the very occupations toward which that training is aimed.

In these circumstances the officials and advisers responsible for the pre-vocational training programme are attempting to compromise between different lines of thinking, by pushing forward with the expansion mentioned above and at the same time setting up research and training organizations to monitor, guide and support the programme, since evaluation must wait upon the event.[7] The question as to whether such a balance can be maintained and made workable is perhaps a key problem in the field of education and rural development.

This raises a whole range of important sociological questions about the processes of institutionalization that are of critical importance in developing countries. In particular these relate to the efforts being made to create more favourable climates for integrating planning, innovation and imaginative ways of using resources. Put simply, in the field of youth training in Kenya two opposed sets of pressures can be identified, creating a tension between organisational rigidity and operational flexibility. (Figure 2).

Clearly such a list could be developed very much further, but even so it

FIGURE 2

Rigidity	Flexibility
1. Bureaucratic need to establish the programme with full headquarters and provincial staff in the context of inter-ministerial competitiveness.	1. Practical need for flexible cooperation in the field between education, youth work, agriculture, etc.
2. The lack of knowledge and administrative capacity of rural people and their general orientation towards requiring 'government institutions.'	2. The initiative competence and commitment of local groups, and their leaders, e.g. Withur, Ndere, Kipterer and Maseno.
3. The crumbling institutional frame of of youth centres which needs to be saved and utilized.	3. The entirely new concept of demand-oriented training at Soy, which should be followed up as sensitively as possible.
4. The administrative orientation of headquarter's staff and the lack of any ready-made expertise for this type of youth work. This is a worldwide problem, not just Kenya's.	4. The vital bank of experience gradually being built up at the grass roots level, both in Kenya (Soy, Maseno, Kipterer, etc) and countries with similar problems, e.g. Botswana, Nigeria.
5. The supply-oriented concept of training for regular wage earning employment is not only generally much more acceptable but it is far more readily understood than the demand-oriented concept.	5. In the conditions prevailing in Kenya, for the great majority work can only be found by a more thorough understanding of the opportunities in rural life.

is not difficult to understand why much of the evidence at present points to the creation of a series of youth institutions running parallel to secondary schools, but offering expedient training, aimed at low-level craft certificates rather than academic examinations.[8] Such a system may well have its short term successes, as the results quoted above suggest, but set against the wider perspective of the society these successes are seen in terms of gaining formal employment, and thus tend to prevent any major shift in educational thinking towards the diffuse, changeable, less secure occupations in the informal sector.

It is ironic to conclude that despite the first clear signs of interest amongst rural people towards new and broader forms of education, the village polytechnics are, in the final analysis, reinforcing the tradition of second class supply-oriented education they set out to break. But as the present pre-vocational programme takes over the polytechnic activities and expands them rapidly, this is what appears to be happening.

It must be emphasized that this is happening by default rather than by design and that in consequence any attempt to change the situation must take a wider view of education than merely reassessing the youth programme. Of course within the total picture it will be possible to identify new and interesting features such as the work of Shadrack Opote. But if these features are to be utilized effectively they must be recognized for what they are, hopeful but rather isolated and vulnerable prospects which need sensitive support. Further they must not be allowed to cloud the picture of the gradual drift towards formalization and expediency in the system. The reasons for this are easy enough to understand once they are made clear but methods of counteracting such a drift raise very fundamental questions about relating modern bureaucratic institutions to the problems of rapid economic and social development in predominantly rural societies.

However one important effect of the situation in Kenya is to harden the pattern of education and training described in Figure 2 above, so that the general public becomes even more conscious of the separation between the formal school system focusing upon academic examinations, those informal institutions which offer practical skills for lower level wage earning employment and casual on-the-job training for occupations that exists in the rural areas but which is only taken when nothing else can be found. Ironically this is happening just at a point when these rigid distinctions are beginning to be broken down within the formal educational system itself. The reluctance of the present youth administration, the Ministry of Education and other authorities involved in rural development to work towards a unified integrated system is understandable in professional bureaucratic terms, but it spells failure so far as attempts to meet the needs of 80 per cent of the young adults of Kenya are concerned.

REFERENCES

1. *After School What?* A Report of a joint working party of the NCCK and CCEA on the further education, training and employment of primary school leavers. Nairobi, 1966.
2. ibid., p. 60.
3. J. E. Anderson, *The Village Polytechnic Movement*: an evaluation report, IDS, University of Nairobi, 1970.
4. This work was carried out jointly by Edward Wanjal, Wolfgang Mai, David Court and John Anderson.

5. This table is a revised version of a table to be included in the ILO World Employment programme report on Employment in Kenya. This distinction between formal and non-formal employment is elaborated in the report.
6. Youth Development Division, Department of Social Services, Ministry of Co-operatives and Social Service: *Policy Statement* (Fourth Draft) Nairobi, 1971.
7. A central recommendation in J. E. Anderson, op. cit., was the creation of a research, development and in-service organization.
8. David Court refers to the village polytechnic movement as a 'shadow system of education' which provides a safety valve for the marginal losers in the competition for secondary school education. David Court: *Dilemmas of Development* The Village Polytechnic Movement – a Shadow System of Education in Kenya. IDS, Nairobi, Kenya, 1971.

16

Agricultural Education and Training in French-speaking Tropical Africa and Madagascar

André Voisin

This paper examines what is being done in tropical French-speaking Africa and Madagascar to train the technical personnel necessary for the modernization of agriculture. These countries rely almost exclusively on traditional subsistence agriculture. The rural population accounts for 90 per cent of the inhabitants and the main sources of income and exchange and employment possibilities are based on agriculture. Thus improvements in the standard of living depend essentially on the transformation of this traditional agriculture into a market-oriented economy. Moreover, in these countries, very extensive underemployment exists in the rural areas and constitutes an important reserve for development. The poor utilization of this human potential to date calls for an increased awareness of development tasks. It also becomes increasingly important that groups of nationals be found who have received advanced training in the technical and human aspects of modern agriculture: suitable training must be given to these technicians in order that they may, in turn, train farmers and promote development.

A. The Training of Agricultural Personnel at the Higher Level

The system of general education, which is the basis of all technical and vocational education, has been substantially developed in the Francophone countries of Africa, especially since independence, and it is not surprising that it accounts for a large share of their national budgets. This effort in the field of general education resulted in the creation of national elites ready to undergo the scientific and technical training necessary to manage the development organizations. Unfortunately, up to now, the educational system has been too oriented towards industrial values, and this derives from the fact that the leading groups are convinced that the best way toward rapid economic progress is to invest in the urban and industrial areas so that rural communities do not always receive the facilities and incentives necessary for their economic and social evolution. As a result, some trained people who could usefully have contributed to rural development have preferred to become involved in the urban communities where possibilities of promotion seem more rapid and promising.

Before independence, small numbers of agricultural graduates, veterinarians and senior development and rural planning specialists from tropical Africa were trained in Europe. It is therefore easy to understand that these countries, on becoming independent, were obliged to resort to technical assistance from the economically developed countries. This technical assistance, however, is likely to be of a transitory nature; the number of foreign technical assistants is expected to diminish year by year and the developing countries are aware of the desirability of training their own high level technicians locally and to progressively replace the expatriates. Thus in 1961, the National Higher School of Agriculture of Tananarive, Madagascar, was inaugurated to train the Malagasy agriculturists necessary for the rural development of the 'Grand Ile'.

In 1962, the Federal Higher School of Agriculture of Yaoundé was also created, followed in September 1965 by the National Higher School of Agriculture of Abidjan in the Ivory Coast. These two university-level colleges train managerial and higher technical personnel. Yaoundé and Abidjan have very similar programmes of study with an agricultural course lasting five years. Preparation for the competitive admission examination is organized at the university. For this reason, a two-year university diploma of higher studies (DUES – *Diplôme universitaire d'études supérieures*), preparatory to agricultural studies, was created. Only holders of the *baccalauréat*[1] – with specialization in 'experimental sciences' or 'elementary mathematics'– are admitted to this course. Students who have obtained the DUES can compete for entrance into the agricultural faculty. Courses last for three years; the first two are devoted to general scientific and agricultural teaching and lead to a degree in agriculture. The third year is devoted to specialization and is rewarded by a diploma. Apart from theory teaching, it includes practical training periods of varying duration.

The National Higher School of Agriculture of Tananarive was transformed in 1969 into a University Institute of Agricultural Technology and from 1972 has trained intermediate level technicians. Studies last three years after the *baccalauréat*. Actually, this school has always trained technicians of a level equivalent to the French *ingénieurs des travaux*[2] rather than higher technical personnel to the degree level.

The Institute of Veterinary Sciences and Medicine at Dakar has functioned since October 1969 and trains veterinary sciences specialists. It is an inter-state institution on the same lines as the Federal Higher School of Agriculture at Yaoundé or the National Higher School of Agriculture at Abidjan. This institute which at present is a part of Dakar University is due to become a fully fledged faculty. Training lasts for five years: one preparatory year after the *baccalauréat* and four years of special veterinary training. In principle, this institution should satisfy the need for veterinarians in all French-speaking countries south of the Sahara – except Madagascar which does not participate in the running of the Institute.

Regarding water and forests, nothing has yet been created in French-speaking Africa south of the Sahara at the university level. There are, however, plans to establish a division of forestry training within the Federal Higher School of Agriculture at Yaoundé. There are plans also to establish a National Agricultural Higher School at Dakar which could offer agricultural training specifically related to the conditions of the North Guinean and Sahelian zones.

Thus, over a ten-year period, higher agricultural training institutions capable of training rural development specialists have been created in the French-speaking countries of Central and Western Africa and the Malagasy Republic. At the beginning, these educational structures were very much influenced by the French pattern, but they were rapidly adapted to the needs and development conditions of agriculture in tropical countries. African governments have, however, taken care to obtain degree equivalences for agriculturists who want to specialize in the higher schools and universities of Europe. In fact, although certain specializations are possible in a tropical environment, others are possible only in economically developed countries since the number of students likely to specialize in fields such as rural engineering, water and forest management or agricultural industries, does not yet justify the creation of specialized schools at the national level.

Finally, limited financial resources and the limited number of professors available in each country lead to solutions involving several countries of a given region. Higher learning institutions are attached to universities such as the ones at Dakar, Abidjan and Yaoundé, all of which are regional in character. This solves the problem of teachers, gives the basic scientific training in the science faculty and lowers training costs. In addition, these institutions are located close to important research centres. This gives them access to highly specialized part-time personnel, particularly research workers, and enables them to receive technical and logistic help of a very high quality. Nearly all these institutions have three separate training cycles:

1. a preparatory cycle including basic scientific training;
2. a cycle of general agricultural training;
3. a specialization cycle – plant production, animal production, rural economics, extension.

Moreover, agricultural training at the higher level in French-speaking Africa is organized in such a way that it can be easily adjusted to the very different development needs of each country.

Higher Level Technician Training (technical officer below degree level)

Agricultural development in Africa South of the Sahara requires not only managerial and higher technical personnel at university level but also, and in greater numbers, intermediate technical personnel of the level equivalent to *ingénieurs des travaux*. These are trained in the following institutions.

The University Institute of Agricultural Technology at Tananarive which has progressively taken over the functions of the National Higher School of Agriculture has operated since 1969 with a three-year cycle independent of university teaching. It includes one year of common basic courses and two years of specialization. Students are selected through a competitive examination open to holders of the *baccalauréat*. The candidates must undergo selection examinations including a test and a ten-day probationary period on a farm. At the end of their course the students receive a diploma in agricultural technology indicating the subject of the specialization.

The Polytechnic Institute of Katibougou in Mali is a regional institute that succeeded the old technical agricultural college and offers two cycles of training. The first cycle lasts three years and trains agricultural assistants. Enrolment is at the level of the 'diploma of fundamental studies' equivalent to the *Brevet*.[3] The second cycle trains technical officers in the fields of agriculture, forestry and animal husbandry who implement and control rural development programmes under the supervision of university graduates of agriculture or of veterinarians.

Since 1969, the admission of students to the technical officer courses (*ingénieurs des travaux*) has been by selection from among the best diploma students of the first cycle, among the holders of the *baccalauréat* in experimental sciences or by professional competitive examination in which technical assistants (*conducteurs d'agriculture*) or water and forest and animal husbandry assistants who have at least four years of service, can participate. Admission by direct competition is held when there is a sufficient number of candidates who hold a *baccalauréat*. The duration of courses is three years: one year of common courses and two years specialization (agriculture, animal husbandry, water and forests, agricultural engineering, etc.). A diploma of *ingénieur des travaux* indicating the specialization, is given on completion.

The Inter-State School of Rural Equipment Engineers of Ouagadougou in Upper Volta opened in 1969 on the initiative of OCAM (Common African and Malagasy Organization). Candidates are admitted by competitive examinations or by qualifications. The entry examinations correspond to the programmes of DUES and technical assistants in rural engineering can be admitted by professional competition after three years of public service.

A diploma of rural equipment engineer is given on completion. Studies last three years, of which two are spent in the school and one year in practical training. The curriculum covers economic and scientific instruction indispensable for engineers including hydraulics and civil engineering. The practical training can be done in the school itself, in public administration or in an organization accepted by the school.

The National Institute of Forestry Studies of Gabon has two cycles of training; the first produces assistant foresters while the second prepares to the *ingénieurs des travaux* level.

Second cycle students are recruited from among holders of the *baccalauréat* and usually come from French-speaking countries of Central Africa. Courses last three years and are based on forest economics, wood utilization and firm management. Foresters are later employed either in the civil service of their own countries or in private forestry firms.

The University Institute of Agricultural Technology of Baïki, in the Central African Republic will soon start training high level technicians. The importance of the role played by the *ingénieurs de travaux agricoles* in the agricultural development of the countries under consideration does not need to be emphasized. It is at this level that most of the extension personnel and the specialists are found who make it possible to transmit the results of research and technical progress to farmers and to all types of agricultural enterprise. They are responsible for the implementation of plans and policies prepared by agricultural graduates and researchers.

B. Middle-Level Agricultural Education

The Ad Hoc Conference on Middle-Level Agricultural Education in the French-speaking Countries of Central Africa, meeting in Accra in December 1971, stated that the middle-level technician is trained in an agricultural education institution corresponding to the first or second cycles of secondary education. This middle-level technician is responsible for practical work in direct contact with the rural environment and the minimum duration of studies consists of two years of practical and theoretical training. Middle-level personnel play an essential role in the promotion of agricultural development. They are in direct and continuous communication with agricultural producers and the rural community and are therefore active agents in its evolution. Until recently, the training programmes of intermediate-level schools were in general unsuitable to the development needs of agriculture in the tropical countries and were too often inspired by programmes developed by the former colonial powers. They were too theoretical and the intermediate level technician received an encyclopaedic training without being prepared to adapt to the new and different situations that he would meet during his working career.

The Division of Rural Teacher Training of the Federal Higher School of Agriculture of Yaoundé has, in the last two years undertaken the important task of adapting programmes to the needs of the French-speaking countries of Africa and reforming the spirit of teaching and teaching methods.

Students with well-defined tasks are called to serve in the public service or in the private sector and are trained at two levels. The first level prepares technical assistants (*agents techniques*). Admission to this course requires a *Brevet* (lower secondary qualification) and is followed by three years practical and theoretical training. Technical assistants (*adjoints techniques*) are also admitted at the *Brevet* level and are given two or three years of training. Generally, the sequence of the programme follows the effective sequence of field activities on the farm, i.e. the succession of activities during the production cycle. The practical training sessions are, as far as possible, inserted in the course of the teaching programme and coincide with the most important periods in the production cycle. Table 1 indicates the number of middle-level schools in each country.

TABLE 1

Country	For Technical assistants	For Technical Agricultural officers	For Animal Husbandry assistants	For Veterinary assistants
Cameroun	4	2		1
Central African Republic	1	1		1
Chad	1			1
Congo (People's Republic)	1	1		
Dahomey	2	1		
Ivory Coast	3	1		
Madagascar	10*	3		1
Mali	3		1	
Mauritania	1			
Niger	1			1
Senegal	1	1		1
Togo		1		
Upper Volta	1	1		

* Includes one girls' school.

Intermediate-level staff are responsible for the productivity and improvement of rural enterprises and for giving instructions to farmers and they must therefore be trained in the art of communication. They are specially responsible for extension activities in direct contact with the rural community and in the Malagasy Republic in particular, the need to train dynamic extensionists who would be at the same time good teachers, has led the authorities to reform the whole agricultural teaching system which was originally far too academic.

This reform has initially involved the simplification of training programmes with more attention being given to extension work and rural development. Subjects have been regrouped in a different fashion and there are now three main branches of study: plant and animal production, extension and rural development, and rural planning and equipment. Further, a greater knowledge of the rural environment and of the techniques of extension training has been obtained by raising the admission level of students who are now required to have nine rather than seven years of general education. Finally, the addition of a fourth year in the agricultural high schools has permitted students to specialize for two years in either agriculture, animal husbandry, water management, forestry, rural engineering or home economics for girls. Since methods of selection have been improved it is now possible to give more emphasis to training effective agricultural operatives rather than civil servants.

C. Farmers and Youth Training

Several projects have been undertaken in French-speaking Africa to give agricultural training to rural youth. The most important of these have been:

Workshop Schools Camps organized along military lines have been experimented with in several countries. Young people, often unemployed in the urban areas and between the ages of 16 and 18, have been given training in farm management. After training the young people have been settled in cooperative villages which should theoretically be self-supporting. On the whole, these initiatives have not met with success although in some countries there are plans to resume them in the form of national service within a military type organization.

Rural Training Centres and Rural Schools In Senegal in 1967 the Ministry of Education created some experimental classes in rural training in order to absorb primary school leavers who had not gained admission to secondary school. Admission is on the basis of a competitive examination. Courses last three years but the problem of reintegrating these young people into a rural society still remains unsolved.

Rural Schools and Rural Education Centres In Upper Volta the Ministry of Rural Education began to create rural schools or centres for rural education in 1962. There are now about 500 of these schools and they are aimed at children who did not benefit from normal primary school education. Young people aged 13 or 14 years are admitted to a three year course where they receive practical and theoretical teaching and are prepared to be reintegrated into the family group to serve as promoters of modernization.

Two rural teacher training centres have also been created in Upper Volta with courses lasting 10 months. Admission is open to primary school leavers and after the course these rural teachers, who are not civil servants and can be dismissed when they are no longer necessary, are sent back to their own ethnic areas.

Similarly, in Mali, *Centres of Practical Orientation* (COP) have been created whose aim is to give training for farming or other rural skills after the first cycle of general education. Generally, however, these classes of primary rural training centres as presently organized have too academic a slant to be effective and are much too costly to be established more widely.

Rural Training in Private Homes

This French formula for farmer training has been tried with extensive adaptations in several African countries. An attempt is made to integrate the school with the community and the aim is to train youth in their own environment. Trainees have sessions lasting a few days in private homes and then spend a few weeks in villages. During this time they work, observe and reflect on their work following a study plan elaborated during sessions in a Centre. The training aims at making young people capable of understanding and influencing their own environment. Buildings of the centre are simple and inexpensive and are constructed of local materials with the help of villagers with some financial assistance from government.

Training for Adult Farmers

In Senegal, the *Rural Expansion Centres* (CER) are reponsible for extension work. There is a CER in each district which has attached to it an agricultural assistant, an animal husbandry assistant, and a forestry assistant. This integrated staffing system is in direct contact with the farmers at the village level. In addition, the *Rural Animation Centres* (CAR) have the task of inducing rural communities to undertake action concerning rural development through village leaders or *animateurs* and in each province there is a CAR staffed by male and female *animateurs*. One rural vocational training project (Project ILO/SF) undertook the practical training of modern farmers who on returning to their villages would become models through whom progress could be spread.

Moreover, the project undertook the training of the instructors who were to train these farmers. Three specialization centres were created. At present, farmers attend a nine month course which covers the whole production cycle of a year. They then return to their villages where they fully utilize the training they have received and serve as an example to the community.

In the Cameroun rural vocational training started in 1959 and seven centres were created in different parts of the country. Their goal is to give basic training to farmers so that they become more productive and receptive to progress. These farmers become unpaid *animateurs* and are considered as real leaders who make a major contribution to the extension service. Their training is short and only lasts a few weeks.

Conclusion

To sum up, in French-speaking Africa there are two main types of training for young and adult farmers. The first consists in giving short training at a centre to those farmers who are looking for the technical knowledge essential to their work. The second consists in bringing technical information to farmers either at the village or farm level through local leaders who serve as *animateurs* in their own locality and who buttress the extension services. A typical development along these lines occurs in the Malagasy Republic where there are 19 agricultural training centres, eight for men and eleven for women. They aim to give young literate farmers the technical training they lack and they work in close collaboration with local development organizations. After a series of short courses at a centre where he will have upgraded his agricultural skills and learnt to manage a small farm similar to those that exist in his own region, the young farmer is able to become an *animateur* and he will be even more effective in his community since he receives the support of the local extension agency. There are now plans to create 12 new centres, the ideal being to have two training centres in each district, one for males and one for females.

In this way African countries South of the Sahara organize not only to train the staff necessary for rural development but also to provide training adapted to the ecological, economic and social characteristics of individual areas. In the efforts made for the improvement and adaptation of agricultural education programmes, the emphasis is not so much on the inclusion of new elements in the curriculum, but rather on the constant development of new teaching methods and their adaptation for training the staff necessary for developing agriculture in an emerging economic system.

REFERENCES

1. Secondary school leaving examination.
2. Two or three years technical training after completion of secondary education.
3. *Brevet de fin d'études du premier cycle* (BEPC) obtained after four years of secondary education (subsequent to five years of primary schooling).

17

Education for Agriculture*

Gelia T. Castillo

In our quest for a magic formula which would open the horizons for development, agriculture looms large as an inevitable possibility. If agriculture were only a matter of hoe, seed, stick, and mud, it would be relatively simple but the basic biological process involves a whole network of human relationships, the transformation of which is bound to be difficult and seldom immediately rewarding. The instrument often called upon to enable actual and potential manpower to meet the task of modernization in agriculture is – education and 'educational' activities. This chapter, in an attempt to examine educational experiences in the Philippines relating to agriculture, includes the following:

(a) A survey of the agricultural education scene
(b) An analysis of the different facets of agriculture and their educational implications, and
(c) Some educationally unorthodox approaches to education for agriculture.

I. *A Survey of the Agricultural Education Scene*

If Philippine agriculture has not developed farther than it has, lack of agricultural schools can never be blamed for it. As of 1965, there were 90 government-supported institutions operating agricultural and rural high schools. A count in 1970 showed 18 more private schools operating collegiate programmes in agriculture besides the 52 already identified agricultural colleges (public and private). The expected output of these new institutions would increase the estimated 1,600 or so graduates produced annually in the early 1960s. From the vocational agriculture schools, an average of about 4,000 graduates are produced annually. Figures for 1957 to 1968 show that there are at least 10,683 college graduates in agriculture. In the year 1968–69 there were 33,633 students enrolled in agricultural high schools which constituted 30 per cent of the total 105,831 students in all vocational schools.[1] Originally, agricultural

* We are grateful to the Editorial Board of the *Malayan Economic Review* for permission to reproduce this article which first appeared in XVI No. 2 (October 1971).

high schools were established and operated with the controlling purpose of meeting the needs of persons of 14 years or older who had entered upon, or who were preparing to enter the farm or the farm home.[2] In recent years these high schools have served the twin aims of preparation for college in addition to the original intent of terminal education for future farmers. This dual-purpose trend has been labelled a *waste* by the Chairman of the Committee on Education of the House of Representatives. According to him:

> Roughly 20,000 of the 79,455 students enrolled in vocational secondary schools in the school year 1967–68 enrolled for the purpose of using these schools as stepping stones to college education. For this reason, it was not necessary to have admitted them to vocational schools and to have spent ₱500 for each of them or ₱10 million for all these 20,000 students. The amount of ₱140, to include tuition would have sufficed for each student; for all 20,000 students this would have come to ₱2.8 million. Here we see ₱7.2 million going to waste. Approximately 55 per cent of the curriculum in vocational secondary schools consist of general education subjects which could have been taken as well in general secondary schools, say for the first two or three years. Result: Of the remaining 60,000 students (these exclude the 20,000 who enrolled for general secondary education), those enrolled in the first, second, and third years could have attended general secondary schools and spent less. With these first, second, and third year students numbering about 45,000 the cost could have been ₱6.3 million at ₱140 per student as against ₱22.5 million at ₱500 per student in vocational schools. Here again we see another ₱16.2 million going to waste. Total loss in school year 1967–68 for vocational secondary schools therefore came to approximately ₱23.4 million.[3]

A study done by Contado in 1964 on the occupational choice of the vo-ag senior found the following: reasons for enrolling in the agricultural school were mainly to prepare themselves for farming and for college studies but when asked what they would do upon graduation, only 26 per cent chose farming, 50 per cent chose college studies, and 24 per cent, wage employment. Furthermore, key positions held in school organizations are associated with the choice of college education over farming and wage employment after graduation. But very revealing of parental aspirations is the fact that about one-half of the parents wanted their sons to go to college. Only 14 per cent wanted them to become farmers in spite of the fact that 81 per cent of the parents were farmers.[4] A more recent study of vo-ag high school students reinforces the earlier findings. They believe that preparation for a college education had 'much influence' on their enrolment in the agricultural high school. The second most frequently mentioned reason was the lower cost of studying in an agricultural high school. To get established and be progressive in farming and to prepare themselves for jobs related to farming had 'little influence' on their desire to enrol in an agricultural high school. Parental reasons for enrolling their children were almost the same as those given by the children, and preparing the children for farming had little influence on their choice of the agricultural school. What is even more interesting is that school administrators, teachers, students and parents have different opinions on the importance of the objectives which they want their schools to pursue. Administrators want their schools to give more emphasis to applied aspects which would contribute to increased production. Teachers want their schools to include an emphasis on preparation for college education in agriculture aside from increased production. Students and parents want their schools to be more than vocational education in agriculture so that the curriculum should include courses preparing the students for any field of higher education.[5] For an idea as to where the vocational-agriculture students actually went after graduation, Table 1 shows that about a third went to farming and another third pursued college studies; 19 per cent were engaged in work related to agriculture, and the rest were in non-agricultural occupations. It will be noted that among those who graduated from high schools which are part of state colleges and universities, the proportion of those pursuing further studies is double (60 per cent) that of the graduates from schools under the Bureau of Vocational Education and correspondingly the proportion going to farming is lower (20 per cent) than for the other group (33 per cent).[6] The attraction of college studies in the former group is built into the situation because college level programmes are the major concern of state colleges and universities.

In search of explanations for this pattern of choice of occupations, Contado et al.[7] investigated several factors. One of the most frequently mentioned reasons for vo-ag students' failure to engage in farming after graduation is the fact that they are very young. Data from the study showed some support for this contention because the younger students (age 20 and below) tended to choose college studies while those 21 years and older were more inclined to go immediately into farming and gainful wage employment. Regarding what is considered the right age for farming it is interesting to note that the young students prescribed higher age levels than their actual ages and those who were older prescribed lower age levels. In other words, they were either too young or too old to immediately go into farming. Of those who thought they were of the right age, only 40 per cent chose farming.

The amount of influence parents have on their sons is manifested in the observation that almost two-thirds of the boys studied indicated that the decision to enrol in the agricultural school was made jointly with their parents or by their parents alone. When the parents' aspirations were for college studies, the sons tended to make the same choice. Among farmers children, almost half preferred college studies to farming immediately after graduation. High achievement in school as measured by general average grades in agriculture and related subjects is associated with choice of college studies. Actually, it is the 'low achievers' who were more inclined to choose farming. Unavailability of resources for farming is another argument frequently advanced for failure of vo–ag graduates to go into farming. Results of the study show that those who own bigger areas of land were no more inclined to take up farming than those who had smaller areas to cultivate. Among those who said they could secure capital without much difficulty, 51 per cent expressed a desire to go to college and only 31 per cent planned to farm.

TABLE 1

PLACEMENT OF VO–AG HIGH SCHOOL GRADUATES (1964–65) AS REPORTED BY ADMINISTRATORS

	Twenty-two Schools under the Bureau of Vocational Education		Four State Colleges and Universities		Total	
	No. of graduates	per cent	No. of graduates	per cent	No.	per cent
Farming	2,144	33	100	20	2,244	33
Educational work in agriculture	329	5	33	7	362	5
Technical work in agriculture	166	3	10	2	176	3
Occupations related to agriculture	775	12	9	2	784	11
Occupations not related to agriculture	1,002	16	42	9	1,044	14
Pursuing further studies	1,980	31	296	60	2,276	34
TOTAL	6,396	100	490	100	6,886	100

SOURCE OF DATA: S. R. Santos, Jr., B. R. Sumayao, M. V. Jarmin. *Training in Agriculture at the College, High School and Elementary Levels in the Philippines,* UPCA and ACAP, 1970, p. 70.

Because ownership of land and availability of capital did not seem sufficiently inviting to lure students into farming the vo–ag seniors were asked what area of land and what amount of capital they considered adequate for full-time farming operations. The group inclined toward college studies tended to prescribe a bigger area of land and a larger sum of money for profitable full-time farming operations than the group planning to farm after graduation. Apparently those who aspire for a college degree also think 'big' in terms of farming. But more realistic and significant is the finding that only 23 per cent of the vo-ag seniors studied indicated that there were jobs ready for them. Seventy-seven per cent were not aware of any specific employment opportunities despite the fact that graduation from high school was only within a month.

Finally, there are those who protest and argue: 'What's wrong with vo-ag graduates going to college especially if they plan to pursue further studies in agriculture? Wouldn't they be better prepared for a college career in agriculture?' So far, studies on scholastic performance in college of graduates from vo-ag schools and those from general academic schools showed no distinct advantage of the former over the latter even in agricultural subjects.[8]

At the college level, the University of the Philippines, College of Agriculture functions as the mother institution to the Association of Colleges of Agriculture in the Philippines (ACAP) and it is also the Southeast Asian Regional Center for Agriculture (SEARA). In enunciating the mission of the college, the former Director of Instruction stated:

> Higher education in agriculture provides training to persons for positions of leadership in the gigantic agricultural-industrial business sector of the economy, advances knowledge and techniques in agricultural science and technology and finds solutions to problems in agricultural development with emphasis on today's challenges and takes responsibility for the transmission and utilization of such training, knowledge, and techniques for the Filipinos' purposes and welfare and hopefully for those of our Asian neighbors. The missions of training, acquisition, transmission, and utilization of knowledge and techniques correspond to the U.P. College of Agriculture's trilogy of functions – instruction, research and extension. These functions are not exclusive of each other, rather they are interrelated and interdependent and they are held in proper balance.

Obviously, this is a take-off from the American land-grant concept minus its underpinnings. The philosophy of instruction is stated summarily as follows: 'for teaching and learning to be effective and viable, the teacher must constantly infuse his subject matter with new findings from his research and his judgment must always be guided by the feedback he gets from his experience in extension work.' To meet the main objective of producing effective leaders in the field of agriculture, the four-year curriculum was revised to a five-year one. The new curriculum integrates a general education programme with the sciences emphasizing mathematics, the physical, biological, and social sciences including the humanities. The instructional programme is directed towards the promotion of a rounded and well-balanced education. One special feature of the new curriculum (as yet unimplemented) is the option for students to undertake a semester of major practice in selected private or government agricultural enterprises to imbue them with the intricacies of agricultural production under actual conditions.[9] Although this contemplated practicum is quite attractive, mechanics for its implementation have yet to be devised and it is unlikely to be easy. The rationale for the new five-year curriculum which is now in its third year is as follows:

(a) To accommodate the demands of a growing and complex society.
(b) To accommodate the rapid advances in science and technology.
(c) To produce graduates with professional status as engineers, pharmacists, chemists, etc. who are graduates of five-year programmes; and
(d) To overcome some of the shortcomings of the lower levels of instruction.

Because the ACAP colleges always look up to the UPCA (University of the Philippines, College of Agriculture) as a model, their alumni were surveyed regarding the adequacy of their four-year training to determine whether they should follow suit. Sixty-three per cent of the 364 alumni studied felt that their undergraduate training prepared them for most of the work they do in their jobs and yet only 20 per cent of them thought that four years was adequate for the BSA degree and 52 per cent felt it was inadequate. Eighty-one per cent of them said five years was needed. When asked to suggest the objectives of a possible five-year curriculum, 74 per cent of the responses focused on the following objectives: 'To produce quality students by providing for a more thorough training and preparation especially in the field of specialization.'[10] This is in contrast to the aim of providing a well-balanced general education emphasized in the new five-year curriculum. Furthermore, the 1963 UPCA Alumni Survey also revealed that graduates under the 'old' curriculum felt more adequately prepared, followed by those of the 'honours' and then by those of the 'general' curriculum. The first two curricula provided for some degree concentration in a major field. The latter did not have a major field. Those who belonged to the 'old' and 'honours' curricula also had a greater liking for their job than those who had the 'general' course.[11] Furthermore in a study of Technical Manpower Needs in Agriculture, data suggest that manpower needs in agriculture are getting more and more specialized. Employment opportunities available among prospective employers are oriented to specialized training.[12]

Placement of Agricultural College Graduates

Because colleges and universities turn out high-level trained manpower at a considerable cost not only to parents but also to government, the use eventually made of them is of no small consequence. The eventual placement of the graduates produced by institutions offering higher education in agriculture is an important indicator of the extent to which its objectives are being met. The 1962 UPCA (University of the Philippines, College of Agriculture) Alumni Survey showed that 26 per cent were in teaching; 29 per cent in research; 21 per cent in extension; 17 per cent in administration; 6 per cent in sales promotion and only 2 per cent were self-employed. Eighty-nine per cent were government servants.[13] A more recent study of placement of graduates from other colleges in 1965 shows a higher percentage who went into farming (Table 2).

TABLE 2
PLACEMENT OF AGRICULTURE COLLEGE GRADUATES, 1965

	Graduates From	
	Three agricultural Colleges under the Bureau of Vocational Education	Six State Colleges and Universities
	per cent	per cent
Farming	15	16·27
Educational work in agriculture	33	55·14
Technical work in agriculture	3	24·40
Occupations related to agriculture	5	2·29
Occupations not related to agriculture	13	1·12
Pursuing further studies	31	0·78
TOTAL	100	100·00
TOTAL NEEDED	509	2,053

SOURCE OF DATA: S. R. Santos, et al. *Training in Agriculture at the College, High School, and Elementary Levels in the Philippines*, UPCA and ACAP, 1970.

A striking observation in the preceding set of figures is the fact that one-third of the graduates from three agricultural colleges under the Bureau of Vocational Education are pursuing further studies after their BS degrees. It should be borne in mind that these schools were originally vocational agricultural high schools which had recently acquired collegiate departments or had just been converted to colleges. Perhaps these particular graduates felt inadequate with their BS or else they pursued further studies while awaiting employment. Although the percentage engaged in farming (16) was higher than that reported for the UPCA graduates, the proportions found in educational work were considerably higher (33 and 55 per cent). An earlier UPCA study in 1957 showed only 8 per cent engaged in farming.[14] A later and more comprehensive survey revealed only 1·3 per cent engaged in private farming or business.[15] The rest were engaged in jobs readily classifiable as white-collar. This phenomenon of minimal engagement in the basic function of production was labelled *white-collarization* of the agriculture degree by Jamias and he relates its development to what he calls *verbal culture*, the basic concern of which is 'the manipulation not of the objects of production but rather the symbolic components of the agricultural enterprise,' which distinguishes the social system with a traditional state of agriculture from that with a modern one. He regards the components of the verbal culture, namely, education, research, and extension, as the tactical processes of innovation and change which are needed for progress. In the Philippines where the expected impact of a developed verbal culture on agricultural development is yet to be more extensively evidenced, it is impossible to claim that this lack of far-ranging impact is due to the underdeveloped state of our verbal culture. There is a proliferation of agricultural schools, colleges, government and private agencies engaged in teaching, research, and extension in agriculture. For example, the Agricultural Productivity Commission whose main function is to accelerate progressive improvement in the productivity and the advancement of farmers had a total of 4,586 extension officers (1964–65) including 2,858 agricultural extension officers, 975 home extension officers, 800 rural club officers, 151 fibre extension agents, and 102 farm cooperative officers.[16] At present under the unified concept of the Land Reform Programme, the plethora of agencies involved in agricultural development has an even much larger complement of agriculturally trained personnel, all of whom are college graduates. The gap between the verbal culture or the symbolic component of agriculture and the first level production problem is illustrated in Montecillo's study of *Uses and Effects of Interposed Agricultural Communications*.[17] The study showed that press releases and radio farm news are effective channels of communication in so far as the person-mediators, such as extension and community development workers, are concerned. The first step flow which traces the link between the mass media and the person-mediators was empirically supported. The findings mean that the person-mediators not only use the press releases and radio farm news but are also affected by them, i.e. they gain knowledge, develop comprehension, and undergo behaviour change. However, there was no second-step flow which concerns the passing of information from the person-mediators to the farmers. Mass media with the exception of radio have practically no use for nor any effect on farmers. Printed materials can be used effectively with person-mediators but they do not seem to be of much use to farmers. The absence of the second-step flow of information and influence reaching the farmer could very well represent the distance between verbal culture and the practical world of realities in agricultural production.

The *white-collarization* of the agriculture degree is closely related to the fact that a great majority of the graduates are employed by government agencies. The few alumni employed in private industry expressed feelings about the greater inadequacy of their undergraduate training and lower job satisfaction than those in the school system and in the government agencies. As Leonor observed, 'the job qualifications of the graduates seem to be highly oriented toward jobs in the government service. A constriction of hiring by the public sector (government agencies), the

TABLE 3

CURRENT AND ANTICIPATED NEEDS FOR AGRICULTURAL GRADUATES AS REPORTED
BY DIFFERENT EMPLOYER GROUPS

	Current and Anticipated Needs for		
	BSA	MS	PhD
	Per cent	Per cent	Per cent
Government Agencies			
Agricultural Productivity Commission	30·33	3·67	0·52
Department of Agriculture and Natural Resources	7·34	5·21	7·14
Others	1·00	2·13	10·20
School System			
Bureau of Public Schools	43·58	7·10	—
Bureau of Vocational Education	4·39	36·33	8·16
Bureau of Private Schools	0·75	9·23	6·12
State Universities and Colleges	1·70	26·39	67·86
Private Firms			
Crop/livestock	1·57	3·55	—
Food Processing and Sugar Mills	1·24	1·18	—
Ag. Chemicals/fertilizers	5·08	2·37	—
Ag. Machinery	0·68	0·95	—
Livestock Feed	0·37	—	—
Veterinary Suppliers	0·18	—	—
Rural Banks and other private banks	0·59	0·47	—
Others	1·20	1·42	—
TOTAL	100·00	100·00	100·00
TOTAL NEEDED	13,549	845	196

SOURCE OF DATA: M. D. Leonor, Jr., *High Level Manpower Needs in Agriculture as Reported by Employers*, unpublished PhD thesis, UP College of Agriculture, 1969.

largest employer of agriculture college graduates, would terribly dislocate (as it did) the employment of the graduates. There would be a very keen competition for jobs in the private sector for which most of the graduates seem not too well qualified. Practical experience, technical competence and managerial capabilities are qualifications demanded by the private sector; these qualities appear to be very difficult to find among the graduates. Several top-paying positions advertised remained unfilled.'[18]

Data for the five-year period 1963–64 to 1967–68 show a total of 6,101 BSA graduates from only 24 institutions. The yearly average output was 1,220. Classified according to major subject-matter areas, 19·08 per cent were in the plant sciences (agronomy, botany, plant pathology); 10·73 per cent in the animal sciences (animal husbandry and entomology); 7·51 in the physical sciences (agriculture, engineering, soils, agricultural chemistry, food technology, applied mathematics); 24·78 in the general curriculum and 37·90 in the social sciences (agricultural education, agricultural extension, agricultural economics, agricultural administration, communications and home technology). Obviously even in agriculture the majority of graduates tend to specialize in education-oriented fields, all of which are directed toward *teaching* both in and out of school. What, therefore, are the prospects for the future? The Leonor study found that of the needs reported by employers only about 48 out of every 100 could be met by the 1967–68 supply from schools. However, the actual supply as of that year in certain areas of training was far greater than what the employers wanted while in other areas acute shortages existed. The study also found that MS and PhD graduates were in short supply. Based on the employers' reports on anticipated needs and on an estimate of the potential supply within the next five years, only about 72 out of every 100 of the anticipated needs could be met. However, if the rate of increase in manpower stock for the two-year data analysed is used as basis for effective hiring for the next few years, the employers could absorb only as many as 46 out of every 100 in the total supply.[19]

For an indication of the needs reported by employers, Table 3 very clearly shows that again it is the school system and government agencies which expressed the highest incidence of need. Much of the need in the Bureau of Public Schools is for teachers of elementary gardening. Only about 11 per cent of the reported need for the BSA and only 5 per cent for the MS is in private firms which anticipate no need at all for PhDs. Apparently only the school system, and to a limited extent the government agencies, find any need for the MS and PhDs.

Table 4 shows the nature of agriculture college seniors'[20] preferences for employment. The educational system is still perceived as the greatest potential employer, followed by government agencies. Private industry

TABLE 4

AGRICULTURAL COLLEGE STUDENT PREFERENCES FOR EMPLOYMENT

	Per cent	Rank
Educational system	36·69	1
Government office/agency	30·30	2
Private industry	16·52	3
Create own enterprise	6·62	4
Remain unemployed for some time	4·30	5
Pursue further studies	4·22	6
Other	1·34	7

comes a poor third and wanting to be an independent entrepreneur remains a rarity. What is more intriguing is the finding that students from lower-income families tend to seek salaried jobs; students in the social sciences have their sights on the schools; lower scholastic ability groups tend to choose private industry or would like to set up their own enterprise while the high-ability groups prefer to get into the school system. Considering that there are already 70 public and private schools (as of 1970) operating collegiate programmes in agriculture and the limitations of employment opportunities, placement of the output of college graduates in agriculture becomes very problematical indeed.

Peculiar Problems of Agricultural Education in the Philippines

As has been said, the quantity of 'trained' secondary and high level man-power in agriculture is not the critical bottleneck in agricultural development except in the sense that a large quantity of so-called 'trained' man-power poses almost as much of a problem as its shortage. Aggravating this condition is the situation of surplus in quantity accompanied by shortages in certain 'qualities' strategic for bringing about development in agriculture. The quantity exists not only for graduates but also for schools. Accompanying the latter, however, is a pervasive problem of inadequacy from the elementary to college levels. In the Santos, et al. study, about 90 per cent of the problems encountered in teaching agriculture dealt with inadequate funds, laboratory facilities, classrooms, farm tools, textbooks, reference materials, housing, equipment, work animals, supplies, and instructional materials.[21] The 1968–69 Annual Report of the Bureau of Vocational Education also mentions lack of qualified personnel both in the administrative, supervisory, and instructional level. Noticeably the report focused on the dearth of qualified personnel. It did not simply say lack of personnel because the needed numbers are in fact, available.

Closely related to the major problem of shortages in financial, material and qualified human resource in agricultural education is the so-called 'unwarranted conversion of vocational schools' pointed out in the report. 'Schools were organized through legislative enactment without the endorsement of the bureau with only partisan interest as the main consideration. Since not enough funds were allotted to such schools they were forced to operate with substandard facilities and without adequate personnel.'[22] Under this system, a high school acquires a collegiate department; eventually the high school 'grows' into a college and the Principal becomes a Dean. At the next level, a Dean graduates into a President when the college is subsequently converted into a university. To the cynical observer of such a practice, it is only the label of the school, the title of its head and his annual salary which changes. Despite the weaknesses of the educational system one wonders why the system has not only survived but has managed to expand vigorously without too much difficulty. The answer perhaps lies in the fact that a college degree serves a very important social function – that of conferring social status on the individual and his family. Education – particularly higher education – is an upward social leveller. It is the one social device by which a poor man can face a rich man with a sense of 'equality'. A person with a college education is almost never classified as 'lower-class'. On the other hand, suddenly-found wealth takes time, finesse, etc. before its possessor truly makes it to the upper class. Hence despite criticisms of an educational system which leaves much to be desired in terms of providing functional manpower for development goals, a college degree is still a passport to upward social mobility. In a society where inequalities in income distribution are pronounced, a degree is a badge which brings forth some respect if not from other people at least for oneself. As long as there is enough evidence of college graduates making their way up, higher education will remain a source of hope for a better future.

Issues in Agricultural Education

Implicit in the disappointment about the small proportion of agricultural high school and college graduates who go into farming in the Philippines is the expectation (warranted or unwarranted) that agricultural schools will produce farmers. What should be noted is that countries like Japan, Taiwan, and Korea report that more of their agriculture graduates are engaged in farming than those in the Philippines, Thailand, and Indonesia.[23] Ironically, schools in these latter countries have all the inadequacies in terms of resources, and facilities which are essential for learning the 'hows' and 'whys' of modern, profitable and scientific farming and hopefully, for enticing students to choose farming after graduation. At any rate to attribute non-engagement in farming to the curriculum and type of school is to attribute too much to the role of the school. This phenomenon is as much a product of the nature of farming and the stage of agricultural development in the country, or motivations for going to school in the first place and is only partly due to the school system itself. Where subsistence farming still predominates how many parents would want a future for their children under the same circumstances? In such a country, therefore, going to school opens the only way out of a difficult life. It is the only alternative to an otherwise 'no choice but farming' situation. The question therefore is: if many students do not go into farming anyway, why should they be in vocational agriculture schools which cost a lot more to operate than general high schools? But there is something seductive about the idea of a school which prepares 'youth from the poor masses of rural people' for a career in farming. When the seduction is pursued by a politician, the birth of a school can only be fostered, seldom prevented; for being against such a school is like being against humanity. It can only be nurtured, even kept half alive but it can very rarely be killed after the moment it is allowed to be born. There are those who argue that even at the lower primary level the curriculum should relate to the kind of rural life students will live after they leave school, especially if there is such a high dropout rate. This means inculcating the values of practical work in school gardening or on small farms as much if not more than equipping the children with the basic academic tools of reading, writing, and arithmetic. Julius Nyerere of Tanzania advocates that 'every school should also be a farm'.[24] It has likewise been proposed that 'rural schools should have a special curriculum based on the needs of rural life and taught by a specially trained cadre of rural teachers'.[25] One response to this idea is the argument that such a proposal ignores what parents want from the schools which they regard as 'a means of escape for their children from the hardships and privations of rural life'. Therefore to establish special schools for rural children where the curriculum deliberately attempts to keep them on the land is to thwart their hopes and ambitions for their children and for their own old age.[26] Quite apart from what parents want is the possible limiting and narrowing effects of a rural based school, a rural life-oriented curriculum taught by rural teachers. It is an established fact that a modernizing agriculture thrives on a relationship of interdependence rather than independence from the outside world. Unless the farming envisioned for these students is subsistence-oriented, an extremely rural focus could be abortive rather than facilitative of modern agriculture. Politically, of course it may be a stabilizing factor to keep the rural, rural. Perhaps all these controversies are premised on the educator's bias that schools are the overwhelming determinants of what happens or does not happen in development. A contrary view is that 'the problems of agricultural education are not primarily educational; they are intimately bound up with the solution of economic, technical and social problems over which Ministry of Education has no control – systems of land tenure, improved land use, finance and marketing, research and development, traditions and tribal customs, being among them'.[27]

II.   *Different Facets of Agriculture*

In attempting to define education which will be facilitative for agricultural development, it may be more strategic to start looking at the problems of agriculture before examining the problems of education. The latter usually involves matters of curriculum, teaching methods, school administration, course content, etc. but it is entirely possible for an educational system to be excellent within itself and yet be irrelevant as far as development needs in agriculture are concerned. For this purpose, at least five facets of agriculture which are not mutually exclusive will be examined.

(a) *Agriculture as a Subsistence-oriented Way of Life*

Dotting the countryside across the length and breadth of the Philippines are millions of cultivators who manage to derive an existence from the soil. As of 1967 agriculture and the related industries of forestry, fishing and hunting provided full time or part-time employment for 6·3 million workers, or 58 per cent of the total employed. The highest median grade completed for persons in the rural labour force is Grade IV but 15·2 per cent of the rural population have not had any formal schooling and those in farming and related occupations have the lowest educational attainment among the different occupational groups.[28] Although no doubt many of those who belong to this category are above the subsistence level, it is a fact that the production process in agriculture is largely in the hands of these farmer producers who have low educational attainment. Any assessment therefore of education for agriculture cannot ignore this fact especially in a developing country like the Philippines. Whatever basic tools for learning about modern farming might have been contributed by the educational system, the most likely contributor would be the primary school. Needless to say, there is tradition, experience, and the school of 'hard knocks'. Since the transition from traditional to modern agriculture must take place in this sector if we are to speak truly of agricultural development, and if issues of equity and welfare are to be tackled, the greatest challenge to creativity and serious effort in education for agriculture lies in this particular facet of agriculture. The problem is made doubly difficult by the realization that these farmer producers are not a captive group who can be or would even be amenable to being herded back to school. Any application of new learning for them is bound to be a case of risk-taking unlike that of a child whose learning is regarded as preparation for life. Fortunately, recent events in the so-called 'green revolution' have shown that these farmers are neither ignorant nor reluctant to adopt new agricultural technology if opportunities and alternatives are present so that their problem is often not that of ignorance or resistance but one of making options available to them in a manner which makes for viable choices. For example, the use of high-yielding rice seed does not become a viable alternative unless the farmer realizes what it is, how it is used, and how he can actually obtain it.

In transforming agriculture, the subsistence farmer is only one of the decision makers. Several layers of policy makers (large and small) have to make decisions which affect farmers directly or indirectly. Therefore the process requires concomitant changes in the bureaucracies, in the change agents themselves, in politics, in the landlords, in the politicians, etc. if facilitative rather than frustrative actions are to be taken. The 'education' of these decision makers and actors is therefore as crucial to agricultural development as that of the farmers themselves.

(b) *Agriculture as an Instrument of Development*

If development is defined in terms of reducing poverty, unemployment, and inequality,[29] to what extent is the existing agricultural education system contributing to agriculture as an instrument of development? There is no doubt that agriculture is a source of subsistence, a producer of raw materials for industrialization, a tool for enhancing purchasing power in the countryside if made profitable, and to the extent that agriculture is dependent on institutions outside the farm for inputs, markets, policies, etc. then it is a vehicle for forging interdependent links between different sectors of society. This particular facet is closely related to the first because at least rhetorically, strategies to increase productivity are purportedly aimed at subsistence farmers. Whether or not they become the actual beneficiaries of the intent is another matter. How does one therefore 'educate' for thought and action in agriculture which will be contributory not only to reduction of poverty but also to job creation and greater equality?

(c) *Agriculture as Subject Matter to be Taught and/or Learned*

Academically, agriculture is divided into disciplines known as agronomy, animal husbandry, agricultural economics, plant pathology, entomology, etc. or some other variation of this taxonomy. Formal education in agriculture constitutes a combination of these different subject matter areas in certain quantities (hours or credits) taken in a particular sequence. One who completes such requirements is entitled to a degree or certificate of some kind. As far as this facet of agriculture is concerned, the

Philippine agricultural education system has achieved a relatively high level of sophistication and quantitative proliferation of these subject matters which form the core of degree programmes in the numerous agricultural institutions all over the country. This widespread offering of the different academic disciplines in agriculture does not automatically imply increased ability to cope with real-life agricultural programmes for this involves a translation from the 'verbal culture' to the dynamics of applying knowledge and skills to the production process or to the fact of getting things done. Incidentally, the 'verbal culture' is an 'English verbal culture' a command of which is indispensable for scholastic performance but which often aggravates the gap between academia and the world of action, especially at the farm level.

To cite another irony, in any agricultural education curriculum there is a *general education* component of language, physical, biological and social sciences, Eastern and Western thought, etc. but agriculture, agricultural development or its equivalent is never a component of general education in non-agriculture curricula. One facetious illustration of this irony is the case of a Filipino agriculture student who could not graduate because he lacked *Western thought* but one can hardly find a law, political science or liberal arts student in the same predicament because he failed to pass a course on agricultural development or its equivalent. And yet agriculture is a major fabric in our economic, social, and political life. It is also a fact that many decisions relevant to agriculture are made by people from outside agriculture. This means that agricultural education is only a fraction of the effective education for agricultural development which goes broader and deeper than agronomy, animal husbandry, etc.

(d) Agriculture as a Science

In the pursuit of agricultural development science and technology, as one of the most important ingredients, has received considerable attention in the Philippines (relative to the other facets of agriculture), judging from the number of research projects, publications and agricultural scientists. There have also been notable achievements in the development of science-based agricultural technology by way of high yielding varieties of crops, improved breeds and livestock management practices, better control of diseases, weeds, insects, etc. There is also a growing pool of scientific manpower in agriculture. What remains to be explored more intensively is the problem of getting results of science and technology which pass the test of physical, economic and social feasibility 'on the ground' so that they become actual rather than simply potential ingredients in the transformation process. Having accomplished that, one has to examine the impact of new agricultural techniques on the environment, both physico-biological and socio-cultural. A further challenge lies in how to 'educate' for science and the scientific approach to problem-solving in traditional agriculture so that it might be part of the daily decision-making process. Finally, the people problem in agriculture has presented considerable bottlenecks in agriculture but has not received as much scientific scrutiny as the biology of agriculture.

To illustrate the nature and magnitude of the problem cited, the national average yield for corn is 14·5 cavans per hectare (1 cavan=2·13 bushels) the average yield in applied research plots in farmers' fields is 43 and the average yield in experimental plots is 65. Although scientists have produced high yielding varieties and improved cultivation practices, a study of farmers in predominantly corn-growing areas reported 'very low physical productivity. Pest and disease control problems were aggravated by the little impact of functional extension services, assistance or information on corn production at the farm level. The farmers possessed negligible expertise to cope with technological problems'. As a matter of fact, about 75 per cent of 200 farmers interviewed confessed ignorance of innovative farm practices.[30] On the other hand, another study showed a significant relationship between frequency of contact with corn expertise and the adoption of recommended production practices.[31] Obviously, there is a series of keys which open new doors toward greater actualization of potentials. How does one, therefore, 'educate' to open new doors?

(e) Agriculture as a Business
Despite the enunciated mission of higher education in agriculture as that of 'providing training to persons for positions of leadership in the gigantic agricultural-industrial business sector of the economy,' previously cited, information on actual and anticipated placement or manpower needs expressed by employers, indicates that the private agri-business sector has not been and is not likely to be a big employer of agricultural college graduates. Neither have they provided the entrepreneurship for agro-industrial ventures. The Leonor study, for example, showed that sugar haciendas did not feel a strong need for agriculturists in their employ; poultry and livestock farms said they could generate their own staff to handle technical jobs; almost all owner-operators of poultry and pig farms were not agriculture graduates and neither did they manifest a wish to employ trained agriculturists; food processing firms employed chemists instead of food science graduates to perform the routine work of quality control; agricultural chemical firms, agricultural machinery firms, feed mills and feed distributors and veterinary drug suppliers expressed needs for sales promotion, marketing and distribution services rather than for research and production jobs. As a further constriction to employment opportunities, there is evidence of substitutability of skills

in some subject matter areas of training such as chemists and pharmacists for food technologists and sugar technologists; mechanical and hydraulic engineers for agricultural engineers even in farm machinery firms.[32]

These findings are reinforced by Arcega's more intensive study of agricultural entrepreneurs. Out of 34 enterprises only 15 employed agriculture graduates and even these had disconcerting thoughts in hiring them because the 'graduates were so well-versed in theories but could not apply them in practice and their knowledge is not adaptable to the situation.' Only 6 out of 35 entrepreneurs had any academic preparation in agriculture. When asked about the origin of the idea for the enterprise, the answers ranged from: force of circumstances, perception of opportunities provided by the environment, contacts with and influence of other businessmen, friends and relatives, travel, on-the-job experience and formal education. Among the experiences regarded most useful for the enterprise were job experience, exposure to family business or similar enterprises, travel and observation tours, training other than in school, association with people in the same business and formal education. It should be noted here that non-school associations, exposure and experiences are significantly mentioned. However, this does not mean absence of agriculture expertise in the conduct of the business, for these non-agriculture trained entrepreneurs know how to use technical expertise through the personal advice of experts, conferences, technical journals, etc. but not necessarily through the full time employment of such experts. They are usually paid on a consultative basis.[33]

The prospects for drawing substantial entrepreneurial-managerial talents from the premier college of agriculture in the country are not very bright if for no other reason than even at the post BS level, the graduate degrees are designed to 'develop the students' ability for critical inquiry and independent research for the advancement of the frontiers of knowledge and to develop the students' competence in the exercise of professional leadership.' This is basically a research and professional agriculturist orientation. Quite a contrast to this, is the Asian Institute of Management's Statement of Purpose which is not the enhancement of knowledge but the development of administrative skill and which regards management not as an intellectual but an administrative pursuit.

> It does not attempt to stuff students full of more theories, concepts, tools, and techniques but . . . it helps people to become decision-makers, to think constructively about the problems of business, to see the alternatives present in a business situation, to evaluate the pros and cons of any one course of action, to select from among those courses of action that which, in view of the facts, seems to be the least risky and the most productive and then to determine how that particular course of action is to be implemented by whom and when.[34]

The major pedagogical device which is the case method and the problem-solving technique exposes students to descriptions of real business situations in which executives take corresponding courses of action and are accountable for results.[35] Just as important as the curriculum and the teaching method is the arena for personal contacts with the business world which is offered by such an institute because its students are drawn from many existing business enterprises. But lest one gets carried away by the infallibility of such an institute, further notes on the non-role of schools in entrepreneurship are provided by Papanek who observes that, 'Since books on development are usually written by teachers, it is not surprising that many stress the importance of formal education. If Pakistan's entrepreneurs do not follow the script, it may be in part because some of them cannot read it. Many of Pakistan's industrialists obtained most of their education from their business-oriented families, not the school system.'[36] Regarding the development of African entrepreneurship, Maris mentions the first need as that of 'finding and developing points of contact, so that the opportunities of a wide-ranging economic interdependence can be realized through a corresponding network of social familiarity.' He cites the importance of European and African businessmen gaining familiarity with each other and each other's societies and establishing personal relationships.[37]

III. *Some Educationally Unorthodox Approaches to Education for Agriculture*

Although education has always been considered as an important means of enhancing an individual's susceptibility to change, the educational system itself is far from being avant-garde. As a matter of fact, it functions as an active preserver of the *status quo*. Vested interests are well-entrenched, particularly in the Philippines where the educational system is the largest bureaucracy whose domain stretches to the village level. But even in the premier university in the country which is supposed to be the centre of intellectual ferment, it takes at least a year and quite often longer than that, just to change course numbers or titles, let alone course content, curriculum and structure. For example, in order to institute a sugar technology curriculum which would meet the high-level technical manpower needs of the booming sugar industry, it took more than two years to get the curriculum through the 'bureaucratic' mill of the university. It is entirely possible that the sugar industry will be on its downward trend before the first graduates are produced. But a more appropriate illustration is the response of the educator-bureaucrats to the report of the *Presidential Commission to Survey Philippine Education* on the restructuring of the educational system. The mood of the Philippine Association of School

Superintendents is to do away with the major recommendations of the Commission because they think the task of introducing meaningful changes in education should be undertaken by the constitutional convention and it was also felt that the report concentrated too much on structural reforms and not on more important aspects of curriculum content. They assailed the proposed dissolution of the bureaux of private and vocational schools and preferred the *status quo* to the proposed revamp of state colleges and universities which would centralize their operations.[38] But of far greater significance is the response of the President of the Philippine Association of State Universities and Colleges who believes the Commission's Report placed too much emphasis on the country's manpower needs and neglected the more glaring anomalies in the educational system. He said that education geared principally to manpower development is 'wrong and irrelevant education' for 'manpower development through the schools is and should be a secondary objective, not its whole philosophy, much less the rationale for restructuring the entire educational system.' For him, 'education has a higher, nobler purpose, that of developing to the fullest the individual's talents and potentialities'.[39]

In the light of such resistance, the one ray of hope is to experiment with a series of unorthodox 'educational' approaches partly within but mostly outside the existing formal educational system. The intent of such 'experiments' or 'pilot' undertakings is to develop imaginativeness in dealing with the critical bottlenecks in agriculture rather than to develop a standard strategy for general application. Local heterogeneity as a special feature of agriculture militates against standard operating procedures applied everywhere. The following examples of 'educational' type activities aimed at the *links* in the implementation process in agriculture illustrate a focus on problems of agriculture rather than on problems of education.

1. The Philippine Press Institute seminar series on reporting agricultural research, population, economic and other issues has an important role in bringing agricultural science to the public. As Roces points out: 'the government's decision to adopt an official family planning programme would not have been possible if the press had not studied and popularized data gathered by the University of the Philippines Population Institute, and whatever faults the press may have committed, the high yielding varieties spread faster because the press wrote of miracle rice.' The purpose of their seminars is to improve the media's ability to report information accurately and to interpret them perceptively to the readers who must make the final political decisions on policies for development.[40] Anyone who is familiar with the Philippine press will not fail to appreciate the significance of such a role.

2. The Federation of Free Farmers (FFF) has a very dynamic response to the urgency for group action among farmers. Their Leadership Formation Course which is a rich blend of ideology and tools for action includes such topics as: man and society, the state and politics, the constitution, the Philippine government, basic principles of economics, role of farmers in the Philippine economy, nationalism and culture, the agricultural land reform code, the programme and functions of different government agencies relevant to the farmer, principles of leadership and organization, problems in connexion with court cases (what a farmer should do given different circumstances in court), practical examples and discussion of problems in court cases, public speaking, argumentation and debate, public demonstration, etc.[41] Since the FFF is an operating, acting association, its training programme is intimately tied to the real problems faced by its leaders and members rather than a theoretical discussion of principles for action. It is not training for training's sake – but rather a process of equipping farmer leaders with skills in dealing with actual problem situations.

3. In its educational programme for the development of the fertilizer market, a private company in the Philippines tried to broaden the farmers' 'board of advisers' to include agro-salesmen and dealers. The latter were required to complete a training programme conducted in their communities. The idea was to have dealers who were qualified to advise farmers on the proper use of fertilizer, agricultural chemicals and other improved practices. The agro-salesmen also served as business advisers to dealers suggesting improvements in market development and business operations.[42] Since the dealer is in direct contact with the farmers in the sale of chemical inputs for the farm, he is in a strategic position when the farmers need to make decisions about kind, amount and use of such inputs.

4. In the programme to introduce the new high yielding rice varieties, two new strategies were employed by the International Rice Research Institute:

(a) *Changing the change agent*, a system whereby extension workers were asked to go through the entire procedure in the rice production process from land preparation to harvesting. This not only provided them with the necessary knowledge and skills and the self-confidence needed to enable them to face experienced farmers but it also helped to develop a new reference group in terms of work norms.

(b) *Applied research plots* in farmers' fields introduced the experimental approach to the farmer while reducing the extension worker's risk of making the wrong recommendation as to which combination of seeds, fertilizers, etc. would work best in the farmers' particular situations.

5. Village-level action-research projects in agricultural development engaged in by the Farm and Home Development Office of the University of the Philippines, College of Agriculture provide academia with actual development experiences without which their credibility as trainers would be suspect.

6. A study of the sociological aspects of irrigation showed the unique and central position of the irrigation personnel, particularly, the ditch-tender with respect to the day-to-day activities of tending water. He was the person most farmers went to when they had irrigation problems. He lived with the farmers and many of them preferred to deal with the ditch-tender given a choice of other personnel.[43] Considering the position which he occupies, if the ditch-tender were given training in rice production, his impact on productivity would be immediate for he lives where decisions on production are made.

Another example of more direct influence on a decision maker is the seminar for landlords who were reluctant to share in the cost of producing the new high yielding varieties and therefore prevented the tenants from planting them.

7. An excellent example of the partnership between scientists and implementers is the Intensified Corn Production Programme of the University of the Philippines' College of Agriculture and the National Food and Agriculture Council which in 1970 was expanded to include sorghum and soybeans to supplement the Feed Grains Programme. This programme includes the following:

(a) First phase – training of production technicians, research workers, corn specialists, and selected farmer leaders on corn and related crops production.
(b) Second phase – adaptability tests and fertility trials.
(c) Third phase – encouragement of seed production at the municipality level in order to insure the supply of certified or good seed.
(d) Fourth phase – Since 'research for research' sake is not enough unless the results of research are adopted, the college introduced the publication of informational materials on all new technology.[44]

The one feature which makes this programme unique is the fact that the researchers themselves who developed the technology serve as project leaders. The training is not just training but is associated with definite actions with respect to corn production. The training is a built-in component of implementation.

Many more such 'educational' activities could be cited but the few examples given should suffice to illustrate creative measures designed to facilitate the development process. The essence of these measures is their relatively non-institutionalized character and the *ad hoc* nature of implementation which permits experimentation but allows for abandonment if results are unfavourable.

Conclusion

Looking at the stage of general and agricultural education in the Philippines and the facets of agriculture discussed above, one can say that our agricultural education system's greatest contributions may be found in the areas of *agriculture as a science* and in *agriculture as the subject matter content of education*. The latter is in many ways a case of *agricultural education for agricultural education* and it is a system that feeds on itself in the sense that agricultural education prepares graduates for agricultural education and only incidentally functions as education for agriculture. Furthermore, the educational system is a substantial consumer of agricultural education products and therefore it is a self-reinforcing, almost self-contained, circular system with only a marginal relationship to agriculture. It has had a minimal impact on the managerial, entrepreneurial and business aspects of agriculture except through the technology which comes as a by-product of agriculture as a science. In agriculture as an instrument of development via the transformation of traditional agriculture, the creative and effective mobilization of agriculture graduates employed in various government agencies providing agricultural services remains to be realized.

An agricultural education system made up of a plethora of schools producing graduates who work for the school system itself in order to train more people who will train even more, and graduates employed in government agencies which have difficulties in 'getting agriculture moving', is a very expensive model to emulate except in the sense that it is possible to point to the only country in Asia where all agricultural extension and other government personnel involved in agricultural services are college graduates. Incidentally, the dysfunctions of 'overeducation' present themselves also in the use of traditional academic means for upgrading personnel. Through one academic programme for professional growth, for example, a development agency's most talented personnel moved out of the agency into academic life so that now they only teach about development and do not have to do it. Therefore, in choosing routes to personnel growth, an MS or PhD may be inimical to development goals.

The state of underdevelopment in Philippine agriculture relative to the large number of training institutions in agriculture and the equally sizeable number of high school and college graduates they have produced, leads us to suspect that if education is to serve agriculture, one should start from agricultural development planning rather than from educational planning. Then perhaps we will arrive at the conclusion that the traditional type educational institution is not the answer to our agricultural problems. Further investment in education for agriculture might receive its biggest pay-off in the area of experimental, even *ad hoc* and unorthodox 'educational' approaches. One would hope eventually that such imaginativeness and unorthodoxy would undermine the traditional educational institutions to a point of functional impotence, and final obsolescence.

REFERENCES

1. Martin V. Jarmin, 'Whither Agricultural Education?' (paper prepared as Executive Secretary of the Association of Colleges of Agriculture in the Philippines) (College, Laguna: 1965), typescript; M. D. Leonor, Jr., Project: *Occupational Information and Placement Service, Summary Status Report as of December 31, 1970* (College, Laguna: University of the Philippines, College of Agriculture, 1970); S. R. Santos, Jr. *et al.*, *Training in Agriculture at the College, High School and Elementary Levels in the Philippines* (College, Laguna: U.P. College of Agriculture and ACAP, 1970); Bureau of Vocational Education, *Annual Report of the Director of Vocational Education, Vocational-Technical Education in the Manpower Development Program 1968–69* (Manila: Bureau of Vocational Education, Department of Education, 1969).

2. Board of National Education, *General Educational Policies: A Report of the Board of National Education* (Manila: Phoenix Press Inc., 1955–57), p. 306.

3. Aguedo F. Agbayani, 'We are wasting about ₱25 million a year for vocational secondary schools!,' *Congressional Economic Bulletin* Vol. 1, No. 9 (May 25, 1970).

4. Tito E. Contado, 'Some Factors Associated with the Occupational Choice of the Philippine Vo-Ag Seniors' (MS thesis, University of the Philippines, College of Agriculture, 1964).

5. R. E. Ulep, and S. R. Santos, Jr., 'Concepts of Administrators, Teachers, Students, and Parents on the Objectives of Vo-Ag Education in Agricultural Schools in the Philippines,' *Department of Agricultural Education, UPCA Mimeographed Publication* No. 1 Series (April, 1970).

6. S. R. Santos, *et al.*, *Training in Agriculture at the College, High Schools and Elementary Levels in the Philippines* (College, Laguna: U.P. College of Agriculture and ACAP, 1970).

7. T. E. Contado, G. T. Castillo and M. V. Jarmin, 'A Search for Trained Young Men in Farming: A Study of Vo-Ag Seniors' Choice of Occupations', *Agricultural and Industrial Life*, Vol. 27, No. 6 (June, 1965), pp. 8, 49–50.

8. F. A. Battad, 'A Comparative Study of College Students' Scholastic Performance at the Mindanao Institute of Technology (MS thesis, University of the Philippines, College of Agriculture, 1962) and H. A. Ables, G. T. Castillo and G. F. Saguiguit, 'Scholastic Performance of Freshmen in the U.P. College

of Agriculture During the Academic Year 1960–61,' *Philippine Agriculturist*, Vol. 46 No. 5 (September, 1962), pp. 198–214.

9. F. B. Calora, 'Towards More Effective Teaching-Learning in Agricultural Science,' in *1968 Faculty Conference*, Paulina F. Bautista (ed.) (Quezon City: University of the Philippines), pp. 190–203.

10. S. R. Santos, Jr. and B. R. Sumayao, *Alumni Survey on Adequacy of Training at the Four-Year Bachelor's Level* (College, Laguna: UPCA and ACAP, 1970), mimeographed.

11. G. T. Castillo, *et al.*, 'The UP Agriculture Graduate Looks at His Job,' *Philippine Agriculturist*, Vol. 49, Nos. 6–7 (November–December, 1965), pp. 540–554.

12. M. D. Leonor, *et al.*, *Technical Manpower Needs in Agriculture as Reported by Employers* (paper read in a Seminar on the Present Situation and Outlook of Manpower in the Country, National Science Development Board, Manila, 3–5 February 1969).

13. G. T. Castillo, *et al.*, 'The UP Agriculture Graduate Looks at His Job,' op. cit., pp. 540–554.

14. M. V. Jarmin and A. O. Gagni, *Occupations of Recent Graduates of the UP College of Agriculture* (1950–57) (College, Laguna: UPCA), mimeographed.

15. C. M. Montecillo and S. W. Mariano, *Employment Statistics of UP College of Agriculture Graduates* 1911–62 (College, Laguna: UPCA).

16. Juan F. Jamias, 'The Verbal Culture and the Problems of Agricultural Development in the Philippines,' *Philippine Journal of Psychology*, Vol. 1, No. 1, (1968), pp. 2–6.

17. Catalina M. Montecillo, 'The Uses and Effects of Interposed Agricultural Communications' (MS thesis: University of the Philippines, College of Agriculture, 1970).

18. M. D. Leonor, Jr., Project: *Occupational Information and Placement Service, Summary Report as of 31 December 1970* (College, Laguna: University of the Philippines, College of Agriculture, 1970).

19. M. D. Leonor, Jr., 'High Level Manpower Needs in Agriculture as Reported by Employers' (PhD dissertation: University of the Philippines, College of Agriculture, 1969).

20. ibid.

21. S. R. Santos, Jr., *et al.*, Training in Agriculture at the College, High School, and Elementary Levels in the Philippines (College, Laguna: University of the Philippines, College of Agriculture and ACAP, 1970).

22. Bureau of Vocational Education, *Annual Report of the Director of Vocational Education in the Manpower Development Program 1968–69* (Manila: Bureau of Vocational Education, Department of Education 1969).

23. A. O. Gagni, D. P. Barile, and H. R. Cushman, *Innovative Agricultural Educational Secondary School Programs in Southeast Asia* (College, Laguna: Department of Agricultural Education, UPCA, 1970), and *Agricultural Education in Some Asian Countries*, College, Laguna.

24. Julius Nyerere, 'Education for Self-Reliance,' *Development Digest*, Vol. 8, No. 4 (October 1970), pp. 3–13.

25. Nongyao Karnchanachari, 'The Challenge of Agricultural Innovation to

Education and Manpower Development,' in *Agricultural Revolution in Southeast Asia: Consequences for Development*, Vol. II (New York: The Asia Society, 1970), pp. 55–56.

26. V. L. Griffiths, 'The Problem of Rural Education,' *Development Digest*, Vol. 8, No. 4 (October 1970), pp. 14–26

27. ibid.

28. *Bureau of Census and Statistics Special Release*, 'Employment by Industry and by Occupation for the Philippines, Urban and Rural, October, 1967,' No. 77 (November, Series of 1968).

29. Dudley Seers, 'The Meaning of Development,' *A/D/C Reprint*, The Agricultural Development Council, Inc. (September 1970).

30. R. R. Huelgas and D. B. Antiporta, 'Corn Production and Marketing in Cotabato and Bukidnon' (paper read at the Second Annual Conference on Intensified Corn Production Program, College, Laguna, 26 March 1971).

31. Nerelito P. Pascual, *Adoption of Corn Production Practices Among Leyte Corn Farmers* (MS thesis, University of the Philippines, College of Agriculture, 1971).

32. M. D. Leonor, Jr., *High-Level Manpower Needs in Agriculture as Reported by Employers*, op. cit., passim.

33. Victoria M. Arcega, *An Exploratory Study of Filipino Agricultural Entrepreneurs* (MS thesis, University of the Philippines, College of Agriculture, 1971).

34. Stephen H. Fuller, 'A Statement of Purpose, Asian Institute of Management,' *Special Report of Manila Chronicle* (February, 1971) p. 4.

35. Rafael V. de Guzman, 'A Business School for Asia,' *Special Report of Manila Chronicle* (February, 1971), pp. 5–6

36. Gustav F. Papanek, 'The Industrial Entrepreneurs of Pakistan,' *Development Digest*, Vol. 8 No. 3 (July 1970), pp. 30–41.

37. Peter Maris, 'Social Barriers to African Entrepreneurship,' *Development Digest*, Vol. 8, No. 3 (July 1970), pp. 3–11.

38. Roz Galang, 'Politics-free Educational System Urged,' *Manila Times* (13 May 1971), pp. 1 and 26.

39. Carolina Montilla, 'Proposals of Education Survey Body Disputed', *Manila Chronicle*, 14 May 1971.

40. Joaquin P. Roces, *Science and the Media* (paper delivered at the 35th Initiation and Induction Ceremonies of the Society for the Advancement of Research, University of the Philippines, College of Agriculture, 4 March 1970).

41. Syllabi of Subjects, FFF Leadership Formation Course. (Mimeographed, 13 p.)

42. ESFAC, Philippines, *Fertilizer: Its Importance in the Development of Philippine Agriculture*, ESSO Standard Fertilizer and Agricultural Chemical Co., Inc.

43. Gekee Wickham, *Sociological Aspects of Irrigation* (MS thesis, University of the Philippines, College of Agriculture, 1970).

44. *Upland Crops Newsletter*, Vol. 1, No. 1 (January 1971), College, Laguna.

18

Rural Education for Development: Burma and Malaysia, a Contrast in Cultural Meaning and Structural Relations*

Manning Nash

The role of education in promoting and inhibiting social change is at once problematical and challenging, but when the social change aimed at or sought lies in the general area of social, economic, political and cultural modernization the connexions of education to the process of change become so convoluted that almost none of the empirical statements in the vast literature can bear serious scrutiny. This less than happy state comes not so much from a dearth of careful, empirical, and often quantitative studies on education and change, but from the analytical opacity of disarray of the frameworks of interpretation. It has taken much work and research energy to overcome the seductive simplicity of the manpower planning model with its restrictive notions of educational demand and educational supply meeting in some smooth equilibrium state where the marginal rates of return to educational investment follow rational capital budgeting rules while the labour force absorptive capacity minimizes unemployment and underemployment of educated persons.

While this model has lost its vogue, other models of change, modernization and the educational variables compete for analytical dominance. A recent suggestion (Aran, Eisenstadt, and Adler, 1972) moves in fruitful directions by introducing some notions from macro-sociological analysis, chiefly the notions of a society with a centre and a periphery; structured modes of participation in the central institutions; and the conditions of productive participation in the centre of a society as they relate to role autonomy. All of this I believe is in the right direction and conduces to the stipulation of empirically testable hypotheses about educational inputs into other social areas and the feedbacks of other institutional spheres on the educational area itself.

* The research in Burma 1960–61 was financed by an NSF grant and fieldwork in Malaya, 1964, 1966, and 1968 was also supported by NSF.

What is further needed is the cultural meaning of education in given societies, and the structural position of education within the whole social system. In this chapter I undertake the first part of that task for parts of Malaysia and of Upper Burma. I shall describe the meanings attached to various kinds of education in those cultures, compare the meanings, and attempt to assess the probable effects of those meanings on rural education aimed at economic development.

In contemporary anthropology, the concept of culture is usually taken to mean a set of symbols in the minds of actors. This symbol set defines the world, gives cognitive categories, and interprets experience for the actors. At this level of abstraction a culture is a set of meanings, more or less organized or integrated, to be discovered in the activities and artifacts of a society. Part of the meanings embodied in the symbol set can be gotten directly from informants, but much of it must be constructed by the anthropological observer. The analogy to linguistics is particularly apt: every speaker of a language uses and manifests a code of which he is only partially aware, but by analysis the linguist can construct the code governing the meanings of utterances. The major difference between pure linguistic analysis and cultural analysis is that semantics tends to be purely structural in linguistics, while in anthropology cultural semantics is necessarily a mixture of content and of structure. The meaning in anthropology of a symbol is more than its relation to other symbols and the rules of that relationship; it necessarily implicates a particular content, a specific definition of reality, and a given orientation to social action. It is this accent on content that makes comparison among cultures so difficult, so nearly an act of aesthetic performance, that few significant cross-cultural generalizations about culture can bear scrutiny.

Aspects of Schools in Malaysia

On the Malay peninsula in the State of Kelantan, district of Pasir Mas, the whole range of educational institutions, below the university level, can be observed in a Malay cultural and social setting. In Pasir Mas are the *pondok* religious schools, the national schools using both Malay and English as mediums of instruction, the Arabic schools (*madrasah*), and the Chinese schools. The town of Pasir Mas itself is the hub of an educational industry in which more than 4,500 students are enrolled.

There are seven religious boarding schools (*pondok*), in and around Pasir Mas town. These seven schools are historically the oldest form of education in this part of Malaya, and while deeply Islamic they probably pre-date the coming of Islam to Kelantan. Each *pondok* is centred about a particular *guru* who has achieved a reputation for Islamic knowledge. The students are resident around the *guru*'s house (and in some a *surau* or chapel) in huts or barrack-like dwellings. The students are either self-supporting or the community provides them with food. They or their families often give gifts to the *guru*, but there is no tuition required. There is also no fixed amount of time a student must stay, or a fixed period after which he must leave. The curriculum at a *pondok* is entirely religious – the study of monotheism, the study of Islamic law, the study of the Koran and Hadith (the non-Koranic sayings and customs of the Prophet Mohammad), and the study of Arabic.

In these *pondok* the meaning of religious education can be found, and since some of that meaning leaks into the Arabic and national schools (but of course not the Chinese schools), it is the template for the cultural meanings of education in this peasant, Malay, Muslim society. The ultimate aim of all the *guru-murid* relationship with its religious subject matter is to attain *makrifat*. *Makrifat* is the subjection of the self to *ilmu* (religious knowledge). What is taught, therefore, is *ilmu* in the strict sense of religious knowledge leading to an understanding of Allah's design for the world and man. The discipline of study is guided by the notion of *ijtihad*, the striving to attain truth by reasoning (*akal*). *Akal* alone is not enough to attain *ilmu*, *akal* must be guided by *iman*, faith or the spirit of religion. Ultimately a student who applies himself under a learned *guru* will find the *kunchi*, the key to *ilmu*, and hence to the proper life and a full understanding of what subjection of the self to truth and Allah means.

From these meanings of religious education stem a style of teaching and learning, an image of the educated man, and the methods of adding to knowledge. The *guru-murid* relationship is initially hierarchical, the superordination based on superior grasp of *ilmu* by the *guru*. Deference, respect, awe and gratitude are expected from the student. The *guru* should avoid arrogance, for *ilmu* is without end, and exhibit *halus*, or refined, gentle behaviour. The teaching is largely rote, with students memorizing texts and accepting the *guru*'s glosses on law, theology, the Koran, correct *chilafiah* (religious practice) and *aqidah* (religious doctrine). Logic and legalistic reasoning are the chief tools employed in the transmission of the heritage. The appeal to authority is frequent in setting out the right interpretations and *taqlid* (reliance on religious authority) is in some tension with the avowal of the use of *akal* as the final element in approaching truth.

Like all religious training based on scripture, dedicated to reason, embracing master pupil relationships, engaged in rote learning, and encrusted with authority and legalistic paradigms, there is a tendency for the content, method and style of religious education to ossify, to become rigid, repetitive and sterile. There are two sources, historically, which have prevented the embalming of Islamic religious thought and education. First there is the integral capacity for gifted *gurus* to challenge received tradition and learning on the basis of superior use of *akal*, offering a new and pristine interpretation of text and law, often after residence at a foreign Islamic centre of learning. Also within the religious tradition is the mystic strain of the *tarekat*, the path of direct religious knowledge, by-passing the legalistic worldly surface of *ilmu* for the personal experience of Allah's message to man.

Religions exist in the world, and the world affects them profoundly. Islam faces competition as the legitimate definer of the world from the inputs of modernization including the political processes of representative government and the co-existence of large communal, non-Muslim groups. Both the internal pressure to keep Islam proper and relevant and the external pressures to show the excellence of Islam in a modern setting keep Malay Muslims in some tension and their version of Islam from being a fully settled and stagnant belief system. But even if Islam in this setting is dynamic and changing, its educational relevance to economic development in the countryside is problematic. It does not seem to have the orientation toward the application of tested knowledge to the processes of production which is the keynote of an education effective in economic development. But Islamic education in the *pondok* of Kelantan is concerned with proper social life, proper religious conduct, and proper religious precept, and while only a small part of the population is actually involved in this education, it may play a role in providing the kind of social and cultural setting in which economic motivations and the drive toward *kemajuan* (progress) may take on the energy and devotion harnessed by religious institutions.

The Arabic schools are a state supported, regularized and differentiated version of the *pondok*. To the religious subjects are added many secular subjects approximating what is given in the national type schools. The meanings attached to education are like those of the *pondok*, but the Arabic school is not necessarily a terminus, as the *pondok* tends to be. The output of the Arabic school is likely to be teachers for other similar schools, or boys and girls who will return to the *kampong* (the rural rice growing village or hamlet) and bask in the honour of being a possible *lebai* (pious and learned). The *pondok* and the Arabic schools reflect the deepest levels of Malay consent on what education is, and ideally should be for. The teachers, the students, and the community which supports them all subscribe to the *pondok* and Arabic school meanings of education.

Language Medium

What is striking, however, is that the bulk of school enrolled children attend the national type schools which use either Malay or English as the medium of instruction. Now what education means in this system is more difficult to decide because at least four groups are involved in it and their cognitive mapping of education is not isomorphic. The first group is the national education bureaucracy, from the minister of education through the teacher training colleges and the federal budget expenditures on education. Taken at face value the documents produced by the bureaucracy give a clear picture of what education is about: the building of a Malaysian national consciousness and the inculcation of skills and knowledges required to run a modernizing economy. This reflects the two chief problem areas as the political elite see them – the overcoming of communal tensions among Malays, Chinese and Indians, and the diversification of the export economy away from near total dependence on rubber and tin. The heavy federal expenditures on education stem from the belief that a Malaysian identity can be built, and built by the school system as the chief architect, and there is also the notion that an educated population will be somehow economically more productive. Both of these beliefs are, of course, para-empirical, stemming from cultural axioms, not inductions from Malay or anyone else's experience. They are para-empirical because it is unclear just what effects a common education will have on common identity, when most other contexts of identity are compartmentalized and bounded by communal markers. The belief of the elite is not anti-empirical because students who make it to the secondary school level do in fact seem to have values and attitudes somewhat transcending parochial and communal identities (Nash, 1972). The elite notions of education are also para-empirical because economic opportunities do not match the flow of the educated, and soon a large, young, educated and idle population may swamp the backwaters of Northeastern Malaya.

A second group in the education complex are the teachers. Most of the teachers aim to implement the stated ends of the national programme, and thus may be said to subscribe to the meanings and values of the elite. But many of the teachers in the district are from the more prosperous and modernized West Coast of the peninsula and many of them are either non-Muslim or do not match the fundamentalist piety of the bulk of the peasantry of Pasir Mas district. Hence many of the teachers are time servers, waiting until their stretch of exile on the East Coast is over so they can return to the more congenial and sophisticated West Coast. Over time more and more Kelantanese will be trained as teachers and presumably they will be more content to stay in Kelantan. But at the time of writing the teaching cadre is a frail reed for the enthusiastic prosecution of the aims they and the elite share.

The third group in the national complex are the families of Pasir Mas who send their children to the national schools. The fact that more than 90 per cent of eligible school children are in fact in schools reflects the value placed on education. Part of that high regard comes, of course, from the *pondok*-Arabic notions of the role of education in the living of the proper life, in the proper society, according to Allah's proprieties. But there are other meanings and expectations, otherwise the *pondok* and Arabic enrolments would exceed, as they do not, the national type school enrolments. One expectation is that education be conducive to social mobility. In the colonial era those who moved from peasant to salaried bureaucrat did so by successfully moving through a series of school hurdles, and the earliest Malays to get Western education were the sons and daughters of the aristocracy. So the colonial legacy was that education meant white collar positions and a style of life based on the town and the aristocratic style. There is a species of *halus* behaviour that goes with all educated persons, and this refinement, secular or religious, is much desired. In addition to the social mobility aspirations from *kampong* to town or from farmer to clerk are communal goals: Pasir Mas residents expect the education of their children to promote pride and competence in Malay culture and language. The whole national controversy over the language question of the gradual easing out of English as a medium of instruction in part reflects the blocked mobility of Malay-only language users and in part echoes the low status of Malay among the elite and as a symbol of sophistication. Parents see the use of Malay exclusively or predominately by those at the centre of the society as an upgrading of Malay culture, *kampong* ideology, and even casting luminescence on the humble way of the peasant. Schools, then, are expected to teach Malay history, Malay geography, Malay literature, and Malay language. In Kelantan, thought to be a bastion of Malay values, the reinvigoration of Malay culture is something the parents expect the schools to be an agency of. The hopes of parents include increases in the understanding of Islam and in the depth of their children's piety in Islam. To this end the national schools include courses in Islamic history, theology, and philosophy.

The bundle of hopes in the parental group is a contradictory and confusing one. Like parents everywhere in the modernizing nations they recognize the duality of education; the symbolic stress on the cultural heritage coupled with the pragmatic pulls of social mobility and occupational diversification, often coupled with urban residence (which again either erodes or makes impossible the practice and observance of the cherished style of Malay life).

The students in the educational institutions have yet another set of notions about what they are doing in school and what schooling is for. From a sample of 661 students in secondary school a value profile was constructed (Nash 1972). The list of hopes, reasons, and attitudes was elicited by a modification of the Cantril self-anchoring scale. An important finding was that students tend to work out a set of values more congruent with those thought to be central to a modern or modernizing society. Schooling to the secondary level does give symbols and values transcending the parochial, the communal, and the traditional. At least at the level of motivation, secondary schools promote national identity, values of individualism, and status and acquisitive drives.

Taking the range of educational activities, their differing social loci and their partially overlapping cultural categories, some interesting characterizations of the complex and its role in economic development are worth formulating. First, little of the education is directly aimed at economic development in the vocational sense or the technological sense. Some of the education is indifferent to or contemptuous of ideas like economic development. Secondly, the high place of the educated man, both in the secular and the religious idiom, is the driving force for educational demand by the peasantry of Kelantan. Educational supply comes partly from the Westernized elite's understanding of modernization and partly from the hope to achieve that modernization.

Although there is little direct effort to teach 'useful arts' or to tailor education to the social and cultural settings of the *kampong*, there are by-products of the educational complex useful and crucial to the continuing economic development of Malaya. The religious education provides a set of symbols which makes economic striving and increased production the means to the just and proper society envisioned in Islam. It provides a set of ends for which economic activity can strive, ennobling that activity by linking it to the eventual fashioning of a moral community, an *ummat* based on divine writ.

Secular education, beside providing literacy as a useful input in development, appears to promote consensus on values emanating from the centre. Since the secular schools are effectively tied to the central institutions they manage to enhance ideas of civility, national identity, and rational economic activity, values strong in the elite.

In the most general sense, schooling inculcates the commitment to the reason-governed social matrix, and this matrix is often declared as important to continued economic development. More precisely the schools promote the value commitments to a reason governed social matrix, but they do not create it. How orderly that social setting is depends largely on the political and economic organizations competing in it. The competition in political and economic arenas is but tangentially related to amount, kind, or level of education, and is obviously affected by factors largely beyond the control of educational programmes and policies. Nonetheless rural education for development as a separate category in Kelantan barely exists. And whether it should is a moot question. The rural population is getting educated in a variety of contexts and on balance the educational contexts do the most important things education can do for development. They provide attitudes, motivations, values, and symbols generally germane to the process of modernization.

The road to further modernization is fraught with many pitfalls – communal strife, the breakdown of parliamentary procedure, the capricious shifts in the international markets, the possibilities of war and subversion, and the inequities and hostilities inevitable in skewed wealth distributions. But the educational complex of Malaya, as seen in Kelantan, will not be singled out for abuse if the path to further development is tortuous and painful.

Implicit in the above description of education in Pasir Mas are several assumptions about rural education. First is that local schools must be socially and culturally detached, in great part, from the local societies in which they are embedded if they are to be effective agents for the sort of change conducive to modernization. The national schools march largely to the drums of the central elite and their values in Kelantan, while the religious schools are tied to the Islamic centres of learning which are ever sending fresh pulses upsetting the complacency and rigidity of local interpretation. Second, the notions of the meaning of education, the image of the educated man, and modes and styles of teaching need little congruence with local cultural values for they receive their legitimacy from traditions or structures transcending the local, rural culture and society.

The Position in Upper Burma

These assumptions were in part given empirical underwriting by looking at village schools in Upper Burma, and I shall give just enough data here to make them plausible if not convincing.

In Upper Burma the peasant heartland of Burmese society and culture, as that has been modified by occupation, warfare, revolution, independence, and military government, still is vigorous and persisting (Nash, 1965). Upper Burma has not reached the level of structural differentiation that characterizes Malaya, but Kelantan is somewhat comparable to the region south and west of Mandalay, the Sagaing district. The village in this part of Burma is analogous to the *kampong* in the Kelantan delta, and a town like Monywa is similar enough to Pasir Mas town. But my comparison here introduces a disjunction: I compare the village schools of Burma to the educational complex of the town of Pasir Mas, so the comparison is not point for point. That does not vitiate it, for I believe that the contrast underwrites the assumptions earlier spelled out and underlines the ways in which education in a rural area affects social and cultural changes.

In the village itself there are no public buildings, only the pile houses of the cultivators, the buildings for grain storage and cattle pens. About a mile or so outside of the village are two *phongyi kyaung*, housing the resident monks who serve the village. The *phongyi kyaung* is where villagers gather for the duty days of Buddhism, to visit and consult with the monks, and to perform special religious devotions. The spatial fact that the *phongyi kyaung* must be far enough from the wells of the village so that the monks 'cannot hear the voices of women washing' is a clue to one of the major meanings of education, for all the village formal schooling, secular and religious, takes place in the two *phongyi kyaungs*. Education, avoiding the anagogic level which villagers and village monks do not attain, is primarily for literacy. The literacy is primarily for reading the *tipitika*, the canon of Theravada Buddhism. The point of having famili- arity with the major *sutta* (verses) in the canon is to be able to follow *dhamma*, the law of the universe as expounded by the Buddha who apprehended it in his moment of enlightenment under the Bo tree. The point of following *dhamma* is to accumulate merit, and the point of increasing moral merit is to better the moral nucleus of an individual, his *kan*. The point of purifying one's *kan* is to secure a more moral rebirth via the process of metempsychosis. The point of morally better rebirth is to attain detachment from the world of change, suffering, and self-illusion. And finally the point of detachment is the attainment of *neikban*, the final extinguishing of desire, of self, of dependence on the phenomenal world.

I have stated the everyday world view of the peasant and his *phongyi* as though it almost were a catechism of hierarchically arranged symbolic assertions. This stretches the orderliness in most villagers' view, but does not belie the content, and most anthropologists have elicited similar meanings for Burmese Buddhism (Spiro, 1970; Nash, 1966). Buddhism does not exhaust the world view of the Burmese (any more than Islam does for the Kelantanese, or Christianity for Europeans) for there are other cultural systems like the *nat* cults, divination and predictive systems, witchcraft, and alchemy. Buddhism, like Islam, is the master artifice through which reality is apprehended, constructed, interpreted, under- stood, and elaborated (these verbs being the functional consequences of symbol sets in any culture).

In the *phongyi kyaung* schools, one a federal school with secular teachers, the other a lower school with *phongyi* instructors, there is some divergence in content. The state primary school teaches reading and writing, some history, arithmetic, geography, and general science. The *phongyis* teach only reading and writing, a bit of Pali (the language of the Buddhist scriptures), and bits of Buddhist cosmology and parts of the life of the Buddha. The only point of friction between the curricula lies in geo- graphy. The state school teaches about the globe and uses mercator maps. The *kyaung* imparts the traditional four island, many levelled world of Hindu cosmology. The children learn both and believe but one, the Buddhist.

So dominant is the Buddhist derived idea of education, that its influence swamps the marginal differences in curricula to give both the *phonghi kyaung* and the state primary school the same ethos, style, and tone. In traditional Buddhist belief the things most worthy of honour are the Buddha, the *Sangha* (the monkhood), the *Dhamma* (the teaching), the parents and the teacher. The teacher's role is thus one of great respect, and the gap between him and student is not only generational and status, it is also a moral gulf. At many ceremonials the five honourable entities are recalled, and children frequently are made aware of the debt they owe the teacher.

The teacher, the *phongyi* explicitly and the lay teacher a bit less so, is a repository of knowledge. There is no knowledge in books alone, nor can one learn auto-didactically. Learning takes place in the presence of the learned whose knowledge allows them to explicate, expound, and exemplify truth. The teacher knows and he leads the student forward into knowledge. Students used to, and in *phongyi* schools still do, perform many personal services for the teacher. He carries the teacher's parcels and books, brings him tea and refreshments, performs odd jobs, and brings problems of deep personal concern to the teacher for advice and counsel. The linguistic expression of pupil teacher distance is marked by the formal address to teachers *hsaya* (master) or *hsayagiyi* (great master) and its reciprocal *ma* (for a woman) and *maung* (for a man) both indicating junior status.

The knowledge that a teacher conveys is conceived of as a fixed, finite corpus of relatively unchanging meaning. Differences between student and teacher, and master teacher and ordinary teacher is not that they know different things, or have better or worse means for discovering knowledge; it is rather the depth of penetration into the inner meanings of the knowledge. This view of knowledge conduces to a sort of stultification of exploration and inquiry. There are, for example, almost no theological differences among Burmese monks, and the sects are split over minute points of interpretation of the rules of monastic deportment.

This leads to a mechanical teaching process. The teacher writes something on the blackboard. The students read it aloud in unison. Their job is to get it letter perfect. Questions are asked of them, asking them only to repeat what the teacher has given. The only questions students ask are questions of clarification of the material, if they do not understand it or hear correctly. They would never challenge it, or say anything they have heard or seen outside the classroom that raises doubt, or that they think or know differently from what the *hsaya* teaches. For a Burmese pupil to question his teacher is nearly unthinkable. The definition of education virtually precludes a questioning, restless curiosity from the process of learning. The purpose of education is to train the memory, to stuff the mind with received wisdom, and to fix a respect for what is known and those who know it. Students are rewarded for feats of memory, not flights of imagination; for long letter perfect recitations, not poetic variations; for knowing standard answers to standard questions, not for reformulation.

Even on the evidence given here the education in village schools is aimed and suited for the ends of social continuity and stability. Education is exclusively a means of cultural transmission, contributing in some measure to maintenance of the significant meanings etched by Buddhism. The school is too embedded in the local institutions to be a force for innovation or a locus for rural education aimed at development.

There is another extreme in the countryside of Burma which adds weight to the contentions offered about village schools and their roles in social change. This is the extreme of the totally disembedded school for upgrading the skills and knowledges of selected farmers in the hope that the knowledge they get will be diffused among their fellow villagers. As an example, the rural development branch of the agricultural department decided to inaugurate an intensive training session for farmers from 31 villages in the Mandalay-Sagaing region. Each village was supposed to send two or more delegates to the school to be held in a village called Nayakan. With the request for trainees to village headmen came a list of topics to be covered in the week long session: agriculture, Burma's constitution, village libraries, suppression of crime, maintenance of irrigation canals, animal husbandry, the economics of cooperatives, the meaning of social welfare, and the uses of cooperation. This potpourri of topics obviously evolved in some planner's office was laced with the then current internationally generated panaceas for overcoming the supposed lethargy of supposedly traditional peasants. The topics were of no interest to villagers, but delegates were sent. From the villages I knew, the delegates were selected by the headman and since busy farmers had no time to spare for schooling, young and unemployed men were chosen.

From the earlier sketch of Burmese cultural meanings of education and the place of education in the village social system, the futility of this is readily apparent. Knowledge flows from older to younger. It is presumptuous for a junior to instruct senior members of society, and it is contrary to village notions of wisdom and knowledge as fixed entities, absorption of which increases over time. What the delegate learned stayed with him, it did not become part of village knowledge or practice. Elders controlled most of the land, and the delegate had none to put into practice, even if he so desired, what he had learned.

Conclusion

The conclusions of this chapter can be drawn together on two levels, and a policy implication adumbrated on a third. First, the educational process besides being an organizational, economic, political and social pheno-menon, is also cultural. Cultural in the sense that a skein of meanings exists which defines, organizes, and gives cognitive reality to the observed enterprise of education. This cultural variable is important, for it is a crucial input to understanding what the economic aspect is attempting to maximize, what the political process is struggling about, and what the social arrangements are attempting to form. The first level of conclusion then, is that cultural meanings of education are a variable on the same level of potency as economic, political and social, and that the understanding of education needs the long neglected dimension of the meaning template for action in the heads of actors summarized in the symbolic content of a given culture.

At this stage of development in cultural analysis, the major strength is the elucidation of a particular set of master symbols for a culture. The means of cross cultural comparison are yet elusive, and the analytical links descending from culture to social structure to individual and group activity not yet fashioned. Important as cultural analysis is, at this point in time it is a diagnostic tool for a specific set of circumstances, not a vehicle of broad comparative use.

Descending from the level of symbols to the level of empirical generali-zation leads to statements about relations, not content. It is not meaningful, at present, in my opinion, to contrast the role of Buddhism versus Islam in economic development. For the contrast in content, in symbolic state-ment, in reality mapping between them does not necessarily lead to different empirical activities. And of course the stipulation of the modes of institutionalization, the values, the groups who carry them, and the circumstances and opportunities facing socially differentially situated groups, make the role of the symbols moot as socially consequential.

Despite these reservations, some empirically based connexions between culture and education may be hazarded. Systems of cultural meaning, when closely integrated, like village Buddhism in Burma, are likely to be less innovative than systems of meaning which have dynamics at their core, like the interplay between local understanding of Islam and the meanings issuing from world centres of Islamic learning, as found in Kelantan. Educational systems receive their ethos, their style, and their meaning from the larger cultural themes. A tension between the expres-sion in the educational system and in their larger culture is productive of change when the semantic distance between education and the larger culture still allows ambiguous communication, as the interaction between elite and local values in Kelantan, but not conducive to productive change when the semantic universe is so diverse that no communications take place, as in the special school in Upper Burma and the farmers who attended it.

Which, if any, policy implication stems from the foregoing description and analysis? First, it is fairly clear that educating directly in the school system for rural development is difficult to envision, plan and execute. For development as envisioned by the planners may or may not be development as envisioned by the students. Furthermore, the cultural meaning of development may not be amenable to school presentation. And finally, the school may only be (beyond literacy) a minor engine of development, important because it subserves a host of other culturally relevant ends.

From observation and experience in the Asian scene, rural development takes place largely beyond and without the intervention of formalized schooling. The so-called 'green revolution' is the chief case in point. When significant technological breakthroughs are made economically feasible, the peasants of Asia eagerly exploit them. What education contributes to development is much more subtle than skills, information, or ability to calculate economic advantage. Education produces or inhibits a generalized receptivity to novelty; a sense, or its lack, of civility; a transcending or narrowing of the bonds of social identification; an enhancement of meaningful goals or a diminution of them. It is these aspects of education that make it important in development, whether that education is in the countryside for rural dwellers, or in the exploding cities of Asia for the newly urbanized.

REFERENCES

1. L. Aran, S. N. Eisenstadt, and C. Adler, 'The Effectiveness of Education Systems in the Processes of Modernization', *Comparative Education Review*, Vol. 16, No. 1, 30–42, 1972.
2. Manning Nash *et al.*, *Anthropological Studies in Theravada Buddhism* (New Haven: Yale University Press, 1966).
3. Manning Nash, 'Ethnicity, Centrality and Education in Kelantan', *Comparative Education Review*, Vol. 16, No. 1, 1972.
4. Manning Nash, *The Golden Road to Modernity. Village Life in Contemporary Burma* (New York: John Wiley, 1965).
5. M. E. Spiro, *Buddhism and Society: A Great Tradition and Its Burmese Vicissitudes* (New York: Harper & Row, 1970).

19

The Contribution of Schooling to Agricultural Modernization: An Empirical Analysis

Bruce R. Harker

The prospects for economic growth in the less developed nations have attracted much attention, both scholarly and political, and how these prospects might be enhanced through expenditures on schooling has been a particular focus for research and policy. Perforce, economic development in these nations cannot be separated from the drive to increase agricultural production. For that reason, the contribution of education to agricultural development and especially the relative contributions of general schooling in literacy or in communication skills and of agriculturally-specific schooling have become a much debated issue. Public support of agricultural training at the various levels of schooling and in such non-formal educational settings as extension lectures is the common translation into public policy of the belief that education will lead to dramatic increases in agricultural production. In most countries, formal agricultural schooling is aimed at affecting potential farmers during the secondary-school years in a traditional agricultural school curriculum, which is linked to a more or less developed system of agricultural extension and experimental farms.[1]

Efforts to turn policy into practice confront a complex set of realities. Schooling at the primary level, literacy and numeracy training, is an expensive undertaking, especially in a democratic state committed to concepts of equity and equality of opportunity, and plans for the provision of secondary training must rest upon the earlier accumulation of primary school graduates. The costs to the public treasury of both levels of schooling are only a portion of the total cost of providing such training wherever the children must forego work time in order to attend classes. This is, of course, the case in much of the less developed world. In addition, irregular attendance and high dropout rates make educational expenditure per school graduate soar when compared with that which was initially budgeted.

Whether schooling of an agriculturally-specific nature, typically at the secondary level, results in a satisfactory improvement in agricultural output is unclear. The recent experience of Korea is a case in point. With a strong and elaborate system of agricultural high schools dating from the years of Japanese occupation, Korea is faced with a perplexing problem. An overwhelming percentage of the graduates of agricultural schools has been found to leave farming – paralleling the movement of graduates of other high school curricula into urban labour pools. Furthermore, it is the most capable students of agriculture who are most likely to find non-agricultural employment. Fully 52 per cent of the highest ranking graduates of Korean agricultural high schools for the years 1953 to 1962 were employed in explicitly non-agricultural service occupations in 1964.[2] The same pattern is found among students engaged in 4-H programmes in Korea: those 4-H members rated the highest in overall promise as future farmers are those most likely to leave farming for non-agricultural employment.[3]

Such selective migration patterns make the matter even more frustrating for planners of education and of economic development. High rates of migration out of rural areas and into urban employment on the part of the more educated and the more capable serve to reduce the stock of trained manpower in the rural areas. Although some of this manpower finds its way even in the urban setting into agricultural and agriculturally-related employment, the pattern is one of depletion of newly formed cohorts of persons who were trained presumably to become farmers.

Irregular attendance, high dropout rates, and emigration of the better trained must be balanced against the evidence of higher incomes, greater productivity, and more modern attitudes of those agricultural school graduates who remain in agriculture when compared with evidence for less educated farmers. Indeed, data from studies of farmers in Korea and Taiwan show that, in terms of gross agricultural output, output per acre, and use of new farming practices, farmers who are graduates of agricultural schools (even though they may be as a group the scholastically poorer graduates of such schools), are more successful and more modern farmers as compared with farmers without such training.[4]

As with most of the evidence presently available regarding the contributions of farmers' education to agricultural development, the evidence cited here is only suggestive. Precise quantification of such interrelated factors as inherited wealth, farm size, parental schooling, farmer's schooling, farm output, and use of modernized practices is necessary before any firm conclusions can be drawn regarding the actual contribution of schooling to agricultural development. It is unclear even for the history of development in the economically advanced countries whether schooling is a lead or a lag variable when measuring economic development. There is also a lack of solid evidence that schooling of prospective farmers either in general classroom literacy skills or even in specifically agricultural knowledge and skills is effective preparation for efficiency and innovation in farming. These questions continue to confound decisions of policy regarding alternative investments of public funds with the end in view of stimulating agricultural development.

This paper explores in empirical analysis evidence from India and Japan as it pertains to investment in education for agricultural development. Especial attention is given to the contributions of farmer literacy as well as of further schooling to the acquisition of new farming information and to the adoption of new farming practices. The use of information sources such as the mass media and agricultural extension services is also examined to learn how they may complement or substitute for different amounts and kinds of schooling in the process of agricultural modernization.

Two Schools of Research

Roughly grouped, previous research on these problems is of two types. The first is generated predominantly by economists who adopt a Cobb-Douglas type of production function. Standard factors or inputs to agricultural production (land, labour, rain, fertilizer) and some measure of schooling are evaluated statistically to reveal their marginal contributions to the total picture of income production on the farm.[5] The second type of research, most often represented by rural sociologists in the United States, has measured the influence of numerous social and psychological characteristics of farm operators upon the adoption of changes in farming practices.[6]

In 1966 two economists, Nelson and Phelps, suggested a way in which education might affect productivity (though not specifically agricultural productivity) and diffusion of technology when they pointed to the likelihood that at any given time there will exist a 'gap' between the technology available and the portion of that technology actually in use. They suggested that if education enlarges the ability of an individual to adjust to changing conditions, then the contribution of education to productivity would be related to the *rate* of technological change and to the size of the 'technological gap'.[7]

Later, another economist, Finis Welch, echoed the hypothesis of Nelson and Phelps in a specifically agricultural context:

> If educated persons are more adept at critically evaluating new and reportedly improved input varieties, if they can distinguish more quickly between the systematic and random elements of productivity responses, then in a dynamical context educated persons will be more productive. Furthermore, the *extent* of the productivity differentials between skill levels will be directly related to the rate of flow of new inputs into agriculture.[8]

Welch further suggested that education contributes to a farmer's productivity in two distinct ways: (1) through a 'worker effect', which is 'the marginal product of education as marginal product is normally defined; that is, it is the increased output per change in education, holding other factor quantities constant'; and (2) through an 'allocative effect', which increases the cultivator's 'ability to acquire and decode information about costs and productive characteristics of other inputs', thereby changing the selection and allocation of inputs to producton.[9]

For many years rural sociologists have studied differences among farmers in their adaptation to changing conditions in farming. These studies have concentrated by and large upon the different sources used by farmers in the search for new information and upon the relationship between use of different sources of information and measures of adoption of new farming practices. A systematic attempt has been made to specify the stages through which farmers pass from their first awareness of new ideas to the adoption of new practices and to discover the media through which farmers at each stage find information.[10] While most such studies have not undertaken to identify the influence of a farmer's education upon his search for information or upon his adoption of new practices, some studies have contained an education variable. Coughenour reports that the more educated farmers in his study tend to rely more on magazines and other printed matter and less on agricultural extension agents than do the less educated farmers.[11] Other evidence from multivariate analysis with United States farmers also suggests that contact with agricultural schools or with agricultural extension agents as sources of information is related positively to adoption of new practices.[12]

However, in a little recognized study published in 1932, Wilcox, Boss and Pond reported that other factors such as age, general intelligence, and ambition were more important than formal schooling in determining differences in financial returns in farming for farmers in the United States. Wilcox and his associates found that there was no appreciable difference in financial returns between farmers who had completed only eight years of schooling and those who had twelve years of schooling. Agricultural knowledge independent of age, of scale of the farm, and of formal schooling was found to be a positive correlate of greater financial returns in farming.[13]

A Model: The 'Allocative Effect' of Education

It helps to put these results in perspective if one considers them in the context of developing a causal model. Figure 1 shows the causal relationships among educational attainment (E), technological adoption (A), and farm product (P) as implied in Welch's exposition of education's effects upon product. (A set of variables such as age, location of the farm, education of parents, family size, farm size and other relevant background characteristics also might be controlled in multivariate analysis. The lines connecting background variables to A and to P are dotted to indicate that for purposes of this discussion the effects of background are omitted.) Values expressed in either partial correlations or standardized regression coefficients can be calculated by multivariate analysis and be given to each line in the diagram.[14]

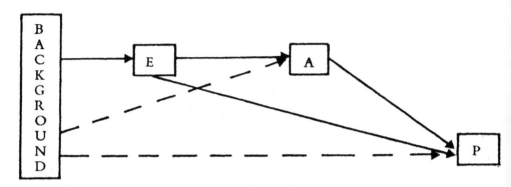

Figure 1.—A causal diagram of the relationships of educational attainment (E), technological adoption (A), and farm product (P)

An hypothesis of this and earlier studies is that educational attainment affects the adoption of new agricultural technology by modifying a farmer's communication behaviour. The diagram in Figure 2 incorporates this hypothesis by including communication behaviour (C) and in this way now incorporates both the allocative effects of education in production as suggested by Welch and the information search and adoption scheme hypothesized by rural sociologists.

Hypothesized 'worker effects' of E directly upon P (unmediated by C and A) are shown in both Figures 1 and 2. The value of this correlation in Figure 2 is expected to be lower than in Figure 1 due to the explanation by C of a portion of the direct effects of education upon production. Likewise, the correlation of E with A is expected to be lower in Figure 2 than in Figure 1. If a correlation of C with P is revealed (whatever the effect on the correlation of A with P), it theoretically would be composed, as is the correlation of education with farm product, of a 'worker' and of an 'allocative' effect.

The worker effect of educational attainment upon farm product (E–P) as shown in Figure 2 may be a function of differences in what was taught in school. Accordingly, the scheme in Figure 2 may be adjusted by the addition of a matrix $(E_{L \cdot T})$ as shown in Figure 3. This matrix represents both educational level and curriculum in order to make explicit the possible contribution to farm product of any differences in the content of schooling (particularly as regards agricultural secondary schooling).

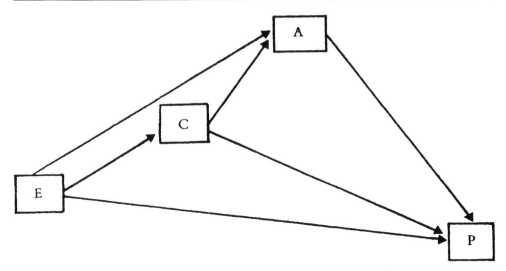

Figure 2.—A causal diagram of the relationships of educational attainment (E), communication behaviour (C), technological adoption (A), and farm product (P)

The matrix formulation also allows more precision in assessing the effects of schooling upon communication behaviour and technological adoption.

The relationships among variables as specified so far are not unaffected by prior income levels. Prior income is an important factor in determining present levels of education, communication, adoption, or farm output. Thus, the model would include substantial unspecified interaction effects of a common antecedent variable unless a measure of previous income (I) is introduced in the left-hand side of the diagram. Since in most cases it is not possible in social science research to include time series data, it is often necessary, as it is in this paper, to use a variable such as farm size or income from the same year as a proxy for prior income. Prediction of income from factors of production could not be undertaken meaningfully if a good measure of prior income were included in the prediction equation since that variable alone, as a function of the high year-to-year correlation of incomes, would be so strong as to preclude any measure of the effects of other factor quantities. However, if the purpose is to explain the communication and adoption behaviour of farmers, the *a priori* expectation is that correlations with the independent variable, income will not be nearly so great as when income itself (from another year) is the dependent variable; thus the influence of other independent variables (schooling for example) may be more apparent statistically.

Two issues of central concern can be considered by application of this model to empirical data. The first is that of the lead or lag character of education in agricultural production. This issue can be resolved statistically by following the scheme of the model in Figure 3. A measure of income or,

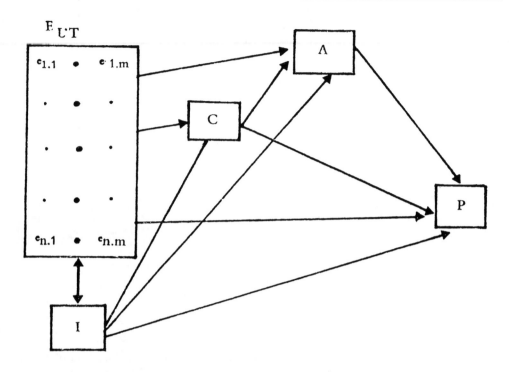

Figure 3.—A diagram of the causal relationships of educational level and curriculum type ($E_{L \cdot T}$), communication behaviour (C), technological adoption (A), and farm product (P) with a variable for income (I)

where that is unavailable, of the scale of the operation (farm size) introduced statistically in such a way as to permit it to dominate the explanation of variance wherever it is capable produces an underestimate of the effects of all variables entered later into the equations. If education is found to be a significant factor under these conditions, then its influence upon agricultural modernization can be accepted with some degree of assurance.

The second issue dealt with by this model is the specification and measurement of the amount and type of schooling that are important to agricultural modernization. The influence of literacy, of agricultural training, and of other types of schooling beyond the primary years can be evaluated by means of regression equations with dummy variables representing each of the different levels and types of training commonly reported (as is schematically indicated by the matrix, $E_{L \cdot T}$).

Economic and Educational Setting of the Analysis

The two countries from which the present data come are greatly different in size, population, climate, historical and cultural experience, and level of economic and educational development. Japan ranks among the richest industrial nations of the world in GNP and in per capita income and has one of the most highly educated populations in the world. In 1960, only 2·9 per cent of all Japanese 25 or more years old had not completed elementary school. (The corresponding figure for the United States was 8·3 per cent.) Japan ranks second, behind the United States, in the percentage of pupils continuing their study beyond the compulsory school age and in the percentage enrolled in upper-secondary schooling.[15]

India, on the other hand, while not among the very poorest nations economically, is still predominantly an agricultural country with approximately one-half of her national income deriving from the agricultural sector and with between two-thirds and three-fourths of her population dependent upon agriculture for livelihood.[16] In contrast to Japan's high completion rates for elementary schooling, during the 1960s approximately 60 per cent of boys and 70 per cent of girls who were enrolled in elementary schools in India failed to complete the first four years. Thirty-nine per cent of all males and 18 per cent of all females are literate as of the 1971 census. These figures are from one-sixth to one-third lower in rural areas.[17]

Each of these two countries has a recent history of important changes in agricultural production. India has experienced an increase in the production of wheat of approximately 70 per cent since 1960 – a result of the introduction of dwarf varieties originally produced in Mexico, but a result which rested upon the adoption of the complementary inputs of fertilizer, pesticides, herbicides, and seed treatment chemicals. Furthermore, the research efforts of Indian agronomists quickly followed the Mexican wheat with indigenously bred new varieties, thus sustaining the rapid pace of change in wheat culture and expanding the new information and practices to be considered by Indian farmers. (To a lesser extent, the same was true of rice.)

In Japan, which as recently as 20 years ago experienced 'more rice' demonstrations, rice is now a surplus commodity that is converted into animal fodder. The surplus is in large part the result of yield-increasing changes in seed, fertilizer, farming practices, and mechanization. In addition to the changes in rice growing, Japanese agriculture has shown a trend toward increased animal husbandry and wheat production owing to a growing consumption of meat, bread, and milk by the Japanese as their incomes have risen.

Each of these countries offers a dynamic agricultural context in which the more educated farmers would be expected to have an advantage in efforts to bring their farms nearer to the point of maximization of their profit potentials. The low incidence of literacy or of completed primary schooling in India makes it possible to look at the effects of literacy upon communication and adoption behaviour. The influence of agricultural schooling in India cannot be assessed with the data available. By contrast, the very high base level of schooling in Japan, though making it difficult to measure the effects of increments in education over most of the first six to eight years of schooling, does permit the assumption of widespread, well-developed literacy and numeracy skills against which to contrast the influence of secondary schooling and specifically agricultural schooling upon farming behaviour.

Income and Farm Modernization

Comparison of the results of factor analyses of variables in three studies of modernization of farming exemplifies the difficulties encountered when deciding how to treat farm income in statistical analysis. Table 1 lists in order of statistical prominence the variables predicted by the first factor produced in two studies of Indian farming and in one study of Japanese farming.

The association of education with indicators of relative social and economic modernity and with agricultural success is evident both for farm communities and for individual farmers. In the remainder of the factor analysis for Indian villages, another factor (the fourth generated) was a somewhat better indicator of low income communities; in the study of Japanese farm communities, no other factor (eight factors were generated) predicted community income. In the factor analysis for Indian farmers (the third column in Table 1) the second factor generated was actually a better identifier of high income individuals and showed no association with measures of education. Two of these three analyses indicate that with some reservations it could be assumed that income and education are independent of each other. However, the reason for caution in declaring the independence of these two variables is shown by the pattern of correlations in the table.

Zero–order correlations calculated from factor loadings in these studies also indicate that such caution is appropriate. Gross farm sales and agricultural education are correlated at 0·50 among Japanese communities (implying some contribution of agricultural schooling to income in light of the low prestige of the agriculture curriculum relative to other high school curricula in Japan). Income and education have only a 0·10 correlation for Indian villages; however, among Indian farmers the size of owned holding and the index of assets of farm families are correlated with farmer's education level at 0·62 and 0·64 respectively. (Other measures of education in column three of Table 1 show only slightly lower correlations with these two indicators of relative income.) Comparable correlations between the number of years of schooling for Japanese farmers and their farm size and gross farm sales are 0·12 and 0·24, respectively.

Among individual farmers, correlations of education with income range from a negligible 0·12 for the number of years of schooling for

TABLE 1
VARIABLES PREDICTED BY THE FIRST FACTOR IN EACH OF THREE FACTOR ANALYSES OF FARM MODERNIZATION

30 Japanese Farm Communities*		108 Indian Villages**		270 Indian Farmers†	
Load-ing	Variable	Load-ing	Variable	Load-ing	Variable
(0·92)	Farm Mechanization	(0·71)	Level of Agricultural Technology	(0·95)	Family Literacy
(0·70)	Gross Farm Sales			(0·92)	Age
(0·64)	Gross Sales per Acre	(0·70)	Population	(0·91)	Socio-economic Status
(0·50)	Proportion of Men in Community with Agricultural Schooling	(0·66)	Commercialization	(0·90)	Size of Cultivated Holding
		(0·60)	Transport and Location	(0·89)	Index of Adoption
		(0·54)	Awareness of National Social Legislation	(0·80)	Education Level of Farmer
(0·50)	Recent Adoption of Mechanized Farm Implements	(0·52)	Education‡	(0·76)	Level of Schooling in Family
(0·40)	Rice Yield per Acre	(0·40)	Income	(0·76)	Extension Contact
				(0·48)	Size of Owned Holding
				(0·48)	Index of Assets

* SOURCE: Bruce R. Harker, 'Education, Communication, and Agricultural Change: A Study of Japanese Farmers', unpublished PhD dissertation, University of Chicago, 1971, p. 110.

** SOURCE: Irma Adelman and George Dalton, 'A Factor Analysis of Modernization in Village India,' *The Economic Journal*, LXXXXI, No. 323 (1971), 569.

† SOURCE: V. M. Rao and N. S. Shetty, 'A Principle-Components Study of Technological Progressiveness of Farmers – Illustration of an Approach Evaluation,' *The Econometric Annual, Indian Economic Journal*, LV, No. 4 (1968), 486.

‡ Education is a composite variable including measured enrolment rates, male literacy rates, and educational facilities available to the village.

Japanese farmers to 0·64 for the educational level completed by Indian farmers. It is not surprising that where education is compulsory and is commonly available at public expense, the number of years of schooling is a poorer correlate of income than where education is costly and extremely uncommon. Nevertheless, the interpretation of this relationship can and should be inverted in order to call attention to the likelihood that where education, especially literacy, is rare relative to other inputs, it is a highly important factor in agricultural modernization.[18]

Literacy as a Factor in Agricultural Development

Evidence from a number of studies of Indian farming confirms the correlation of schooling with adoption of modern farm practices. In his doctoral dissertation, A. S. Murthy reports a zero-order correlation of 0·36 between the number of years of schooling completed and the adoption of new practices among 180 Indian farmers in West Godavary, a district in the coastal region of Andhra Pradesh.[19] Prodipto Roy and his associates report the same correlation (0·36) for 680 Indian farmers from villages chosen to represent all of India; however, they also found that when 'level of living' was used as a control, it was a stronger indicator of adoption and, in fact, caused education to drop to a negligible partial correlation.[20]

V. S. Sanharan Potti in a study of 222 farmers from three villages in the Union Territory of Delhi found that if the three villages were ranked according to aggregate adoption scores, the ranking was the same as that based upon the distribution of schooling within each village. The village with the lowest proportion of illiterate farmers and the highest proportions of farmers with primary or higher schooling was the most adoptive of new practices. The least adoptive village also had the highest percentage of illiterates and the lowest percentage of farmers with schooling above the primary level. This relationship was statistically significant at the 0·01 level in a chi-square test.[21]

Questionnaires collected and first analysed by Shiva Nath Singh in 1969 provide the data for the following application of the causal model.[22] These data were collected from 90 Indian farmers from six villages in the Union Territory of Delhi. All six villages were involved in the High Yielding Varieties Programme for the diffusion of new varieties of wheat, and all of the farmers chosen for this analysis had, in fact, introduced new wheat seed. Singh's test of adoptive behaviour was whether other complementary inputs to wheat production – fertilizer, seed treatment, and herbicides – were also used. These inputs were readily available at low cost and were recommended by extension experts as essential to the full realization of the potential of the new wheat variety. Adoption of each of these inputs was given a weight commensurate with its ease of adoption.

Thus, the seed itself was weighted 1, fertilizer 2, seed treatment 3, and herbicides 4; the maximum possible score was ten points if all complementary factors were adopted.

Singh calculated education scores on a straight 0–6 scale for farmers and also as a mean of all members of their families; illiteracy was scored 0, reading alone 1, reading and writing 2, and for each of four levels of schooling completed one point was added. (The mean of this scale for individual farmers was 2·2 in an initial sample of 936 cultivators.) Communications behaviour was scored as frequency of use on a 0 to 3 scale for seven media including, among others, radio, cinema, magazines, bulletins, and posters. The scores were combined to form one index with a range of 0 to 21. Knowledge of the practices being examined was scored in personal interviews in which farmers were questioned regarding their awareness of each practice and their recognition of its relevance to their own situation.

TABLE 2

ZERO-ORDER CORRELATIONS OF SELECTED VARIABLES WITH AGRICULTURAL
ADOPTION AMONG 90 INDIAN FARMERS*

	Media Use	Knowledge	Farm size	Adoption
Education of Family	0·63	0·41	0·28	0·64
Use of Mass Media	—	0·53	0·29	0·63
Knowledge of New Practices		—	0·32	0·56
Farm Size			—	0·64

* Singh, 'Adoption and Investment,' p. 116.

While Singh did not attempt to speak to the exact problem being examined here, it is possible in most cases (through reanalyses involving mathematical conversion of his data to standardized coefficients) to fit his data into the causal model. In Table 2 the zero-order correlations among the variables are shown; it can be seen that all of the relationships are strong. Education is represented by the family index of schooling, which showed a greater correlation with adoption than did the schooling of the cultivator (0·64 as compared with 0·22). The hypothesized order of causation is from education to media use to knowledge of new practices and finally to adoption. It is, of course, not a closed system since some sources of information used commonly by farmers – their neighbours, the farm co-operative, or the extension agent – are not included in the measure of media use. Also, a direct measure of prior income is lacking. A proxy for prior income, farm size, is available as a control for the scale of the farm and is highly correlated with the final dependent variable, adoption – much more so than with any of the independent variables. Farm size was used as a control variable in this analysis, but it had no substantial effect upon the relationships among the variables of the causal sequence and is, therefore, omitted from this presentation. The relationships reported are taken to be those directly resulting from the interactions of the variables themselves and not from some uncontrolled effects of differences in the scale of the farm.

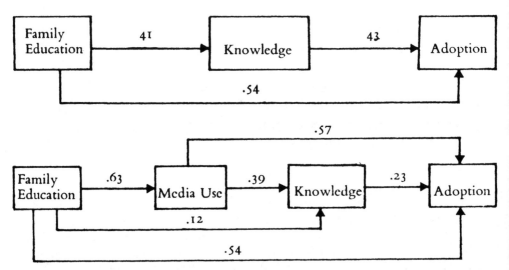

Figure 4.—Causal diagrams with standardized coefficients for the relationships among education, communication, knowledge of new practices, and adoption for a sample of 90 Indian farmers.

The causal diagrams in Figure 4 show the multivariate relationship among the variables in standardized regression coefficients wherever possible and otherwise in partial correlations. (Because these calculations are of a second-hand character, no precise statement of variance explained can be made. However, a regression equation approximating the content of the second diagram produced the R^2 of 0.73 in Singh's original analysis.) Comparison of the coefficients in the first diagram with the zero-order correlations reveals the expected decrease in the correlation of education with adoption upon the inclusion of the knowledge variable. The decrease is not great, but neither is it negligible. It should be noted that the results reported by Wilcox for United States farmers with eight and twelve years of schooling are not confirmed when the amount of education being considered is literacy or a few years of primary schooling. As Wilcox reported, knowledge of the practice in question is strongly related to adoption; however, in a reanalysis of Singh's data, education not only remains strong in multivariate analysis but also reduces the coefficient of the knowledge variable by a proportionally greater amount than it is itself reduced.

The second diagram of Figure 4 shows the complete causal sequence.

Media use is introduced as intermediate between education and knowledge of new practices as well as operating as a determinant of adoption. All co-efficients shown in Figure 4, with the exception of that of the relationship between education and knowledge of new practices in the second diagram (0·12), are statistically significant at or beyond the 0·01 level of significance for a two-tailed *t*-test. The results are striking and confirm the expectation of an information-search component of the allocative effect of education as a reality. The coefficients demonstrate that education's positive relation-ship to knowledge of new practices is almost exclusively a function of media use.

As predicted, the coefficient of the relationship between education and adoption is reduced by the introduction of media use and knowledge of new practices; nevertheless, education is a very strong determinant of adoption. In these diagrams education is second only to media use in its positive influence upon adoption, and in the one case where control of farm size makes a difference in the observed relationships, education is a stronger predictor of adoption than is media use when farm size is con-trolled. Some reduction of education's unmediated influence upon adop-tion might be produced if the use of extension agents (which had a zero-order correlation with adoption of 0·39) could have been included. Unfortunately, that step was not possible as a result of limitations of the reported data. The results shown in Figure 4 demonstrate that mere knowledge of a set of highly recommended and profitable new practices is not as strong a determinant of adoption of those practices as are family education and use of the mass media.

This analysis quite clearly indicates a strong influence of literacy upon agricultural modernization and, by reasonable inference, upon agri-cultural production also. Moreover, the level of family schooling is a more salient factor than the cultivator's own schooling.

Education's positive influence upon knowledge of new practices operates almost entirely through the measure of media use. Both education and the mass media have strong positive and independent influences upon adoption of new farming practices. Moreover, the magnitude of the partial correlation between family education and adoption even after the effects of media use have been removed, suggests that there may be an attitudinal dimension associated with schooling which has important implications for technological change.

Effects of Education upon Farming in Japan

The data for this analysis of the effects of educational attainment and of agriculturally-specific education upon communication behaviour, agri-cultural adoption, and farm income in Japan are taken from a question-naire survey of 971 middle-aged farmers from locations representative of farming in Central and Southern Honshu, in most of Shikoku, and in the Fukuoku area of Kyushu. These are areas of predominantly rice cultivation and ones which have undergone extensive changes in agricultural technology since the close of World War II.

At the time of this survey in 1966, the greatest impact of the adoption of new rice varieties (adopted in previous years by all but laggard farmers) was already being reflected in increased rice yields, and probably the most marked indicator of differences in agricultural innovativeness was the degree of mechanization of rice cultivation.[23] Mechanization in the form of ownership of power implements such as thresher, cultivator, sprayer, cutter, huller, or even possibly a three-wheeled truck is considered to have been among the most influential contributors to increases in agricultural productivity and output in Japan.[24] This measure of adoption is one which undeniably is related to the scale of the farm, but with proper inclusion of a measure for farm size or gross farm sales in the multivariate analysis, this problem is statistically resolved, producing an *underestimate* of the relationships between mechanization and measures of education and communication behaviour. When the final dependent variable in the analysis is gross sales, a control for farm size greatly reduces the circular nature of the statistical association between sales and owership of power equipment and permits focus upon the causative influence of mechanization upon farm sales. The measure of mechanization chosen for this analysis is a cumulative index of power implements owned. (This choice is based on a careful study of patterns of multiple ownership of power implements as compared with national records of ownership. The general pattern is that ownership of some implements, for example, cutters or hullers, implies the ownership of others, such as a thresher or a cultivator, the two most commonly owned power implements.)

Education is represented by a variable for the number of years of schooling completed and by a set of dummy variables representing each level and type of schooling commonly available in Japan. Communication behaviour is represented by an index composed of use of agricultural magazines, of extension agents, and of agricultural broadcasts on the radio. Based on findings of previous research, the use of magazines, the most cosmopolitan of the three sources, scored higher than the use of extension agents or radio broadcasts, and the use of extension agents was scored higher than the use of radio broadcasts.

As was done for the Indian data, initial analyses examined the effect of income upon education and its relationships to the other variables in the analysis. Farmers gross sales have only a low zero-order correlation (0·14) with the number of years of schooling farmers had completed. The number of years of schooling completed by the farmers is more highly related to the schooling of their fathers (zero-order correlation of 0·31).

Agricultural schooling has a correlation of 0·18 with gross sales (a much lower correlation than is found when aggregate values for communities are correlated) and of 0·21 with father's schooling. When gross sales is the dependent variable, farm size (which has almost the same correlation with the number of years of schooling completed by the farmer, 0·12, as does gross sales) and father's education are used as independent variables to control for differences of income among farms that should more properly be explained in terms of differences in past generations than by reference to the allocative decisions of the present cultivators. Father's education, but not farm size, is a control variable when communication and adoption are the dependent variables. Relative urban or rural location of the farm and the age of the farmer are used as control variables in all equations.

Figure 5 shows the standardized regression coefficients of the main variables of this analysis along with the form and multiple R^2 for each regression equation of the sequence.

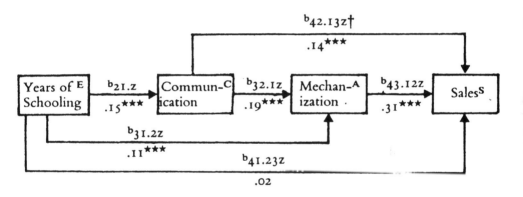

1. $C = b_{21.z}E + Z_1 + e_1$ $\qquad R^2 = .086$

2. $A = b_{31.2z}E + b_{32.1z}C + Z_2 + e_2$ $\qquad R^2 = .102$

3. $S = b_{41.23z}E + b_{42.13z}C + b_{43.12z}A + Z_3 + e_3$ $\qquad R^2 = .378$

† z is the set of background variables for father's education, location of the farm, and farmer's age; when gross sales is the dependent variable, farm size is also a contol variable. e is a random error term.

★★★ significant at the .001 level in a two-tailed t-test.

Figure 5.—Causal diagram of regression analysis with gross farm sales as the final dependent variable for a sample of 971 Japanese farmers.

The fundamental hypothesis embodied in the causal model is that for any correlation between education (especially as measured by the number of years of schooling) and gross sales, a portion of that correlation may be attributed to an allocative effect. The extent of the allocative effect becomes evident when measures of communication behaviour and of agricultural adoption are introduced to the analysis. Statistically, the effects of introducing each intermediate variable in the causal sequence are recorded in changes in the partial coefficients.

Each link in the causal chain is a stronger predictor of the next link than was the previous link, and with the introduction of each successive link the earlier correlations are reduced. The partial coefficient of the number of years of schooling regressed on farm sales is a statistically significant 0·13; that partial coefficient is reduced to 0·09 with the addition to the equation of the communication variable and is further reduced to a negligible 0.02 with the addition of the adoption variable. If mechanization instead of farm sales is taken as the dependent variable, an initial coefficient of 0·16 for number of years of schooling is reduced to 0·11 by the introduction of communication behaviour. A correlation of 0·26 between communication and farm sales with the number of years of schooling controlled is reduced to 0·14 when farm mechanization takes its intermediate position.

The coefficients in the analysis of the Japanese data are smaller in size than those for the Indian data. In pattern and in statistical significance, however, the partial coefficients at each successive stage of the causal model are very much the same. One major difference is evident: in the Japanese case there is no measure of agricultural knowledge. Thus, no comparable statement can be made regarding the influence of schooling and of communication independent of agricultural knowledge.

Agricultural school graduates are distinctly different from other Japanese farmers in their farm-related communication behaviour. Agricultural school graduates and, to a slightly less extent, the sons of agricultural school graduates make more frequent use of agricultural extension agents than do men with any other level or type of schooling. While any form of post-primary schooling is associated positively with the use of more cosmopolitan sources of information and with a higher score on the communication index, men with agricultural schooling have the highest score of all. Nevertheless, it is a finding of this study that in Japan agricultural school graduates are no different from other secondary school graduates in their farm sales, degree of mechanization, earliness of adoption of important new practices, or in their yield of rice per acre. This finding contrasts sharply with that reported for Korea by Lee, who found that as compared with all other farmers having post-primary education, including farmers with more than 12 years of schooling, agricultural school graduates had a higher average farm income, higher income per acre, and higher income per man.[25]

A parallel study of Japanese farming communities from which the factor analysis presented earlier is taken, confirms the findings among individual farmers. A high initial correlation between the proportion of men in a community with agricultural schooling and the gross farm sales of the community (0·50) is greatly eroded when controls are added for the average farm size, the rurality of the community, and the proportion of men in the previous generation who had only primary schooling or less. When average gross sales in 1966 is the dependent variable, low education in the previous generation has the largest and most significant coefficient ($-0·51$), and average farm size and the proximity of the community to large urban centres have significant positive coefficients (0·34 and ·032, respectively). In the same equation, which had an R^2 of 0·812, the proportion of farmers with agricultural schooling is of no statistical importance. On the other hand, of all the variables mentioned only average gross sales has a significant coefficient when the dependent variable is the proportion of men with agricultural schooling. The coefficient of average gross sales is positive, but the R^2 for the equation is only 0·208. The pattern of results from these cross-sectional data is one in which a greater average number of years of schooling in the past has contributed to present gross sales more than has present education, even though present sales is the best predictor of present proportions of men with agricultural schooling. Although approximately twenty years have passed since the majority of the active farmers in these communities completed agricultural schooling, the effect of their education upon communication behaviour and gross sales is still eclipsed by the influence of education in their fathers' generation.

Conclusion

The evidence from this study clearly supports two important propositions. (1) In so far as schooling contributes to the development of general communication skills, including an awareness of the modern sector of society, it can make an important contribution to agricultural modernization. (2) An equally great contribution can be made by the mass media and by a system of agricultural extension services. These two factors, schooling and a strong infrastructure of sources of farming information, while mutually supportive, are also capable of independently providing a stimulus to agricultural change.

Agricultural secondary school graduates make more use of agricultural extension agents than do men with other forms of schooling. Otherwise, agricultural secondary schooling appears to add very little to farmers' allocative behaviour or to their earning potentials when compared with other schooling at the same level.

REFERENCES

1. The unpublished data on India appearing in this paper were made available through the support and cooperation of Dr Kissin Kanungo, Dean of the Graduate School, and of Dr K. N. Singh, Chairman of the Faculty of Agricultural Extension, at the Indian Agricultural Research Institute, New Delhi, India.

2. Central Education Research Institute, *Follow-up Study of Vocational Agriculture High School and College Graduates and an Examination of Schools to Determine the Extent of their Long-term Contribution to Agricultural Production: Agricultural Education Survey of Korea* (Seoul: Central Education Research Institute, 1964).

3. Office of Rural Development, *Economic Value of 4-H Members' Farming Activities – Their Earnings and Productivity: A Korean Case Study* (Suwon, Korea: Office of Rural Development, March, 1971).

4. Jil-Hyun Lee, 'Economic Value of Korean Farmers' Education,' *Journal of Korean Agricultural Education*, No. 1 (1970), 69–89; and O. Donald Meaders, 'Contributions of Senior Middle School Graduates to Taiwan Agricultural Development,' a preliminary report, Michigan State University, 1968.

5. See Theodore W. Schultz, *Transforming Traditional Agriculture*, Studies in Comparative Economics, Vol. 3 (New Haven, Connecticut, and London: Yale University Press, 1964); and Zvi Griliches, 'The Sources of Measured Productivity Growth: U.S. Agriculture, 1940–60,' *Journal of Political Economy*, LXXI (August, 1963), 331–46.

6. A recent book by Everett M. Rogers is a good general summary of this type of research as it pertains to development, *Modernization Among Peasants: The Impact of Communication* (New York: Holt, Rinehart and Winston, Inc., 1969).

7. R. R. Nelson and E. S. Phelps, 'Investment in Humans, Technological Diffusion, and Economic Growth,' *American Economic Review*, LVI, No. 2 (1966), 69–76.

8. Finis Welch, 'Education in Production,' *Journal of Political Economy*, LXXVIII, No. 1 (1970), 47.

9. Welch, 'Education in Production,' p. 42.

10. See James R. Findley, 'Adoption: A Predictive Model,' *Rural Sociology*, XXX, No. 1 (1968), 1–18; and Everett M. Rogers, *Diffusion of Innovations* (New York: The Free Press of Glencoe, 1962).

11. Charles Milton Coughenour, 'The Functioning of Farmer's Characteristics in Relation to Contact with Media and Practice Adoption,' *Rural Sociology*, XXV, No. 3 (1960), 293–4.

12. Frederick C. Fliegel, 'A Multiple Correlation Analysis of Factors Associated with Adoption of Farm Practices,' *Rural Sociology*, XXI (1956), 284–92.

13. Walter W. Wilcox, Andrew Boss, and George A. Pond, *Relation of Variations in the Human Factor to Financial Returns in Farming*, University of Minnesota Agricultural Experiment Station, Bulletin 288 (St. Paul, Minnesota: University Farm, 1932).

14. For the statistical justification for choosing standardized regression coefficients rather than partial correlations, see Charles E. Werts and Donivan J. Watley, 'Analyzing College Effects: Correlation vs. Regression,' *American Educational Research Journal*, V, No. 4 (1968), 585–98.

15. Ministry of Education, *Educational Standards in Japan: The 1964 'White Paper on Education'* (Tokyo: Government of Japan, 1965), 13, 14, 31.

16. Perspective Planning Division, Planning Commission, *Perspective for Agriculture in India 1968-69 to 1985-86* (New Delhi: Government of India, July 1971).

17. R. C. Sharma and C. L. Sapra, *Wastage and Stagnation in Primary and Middle Schools in India* (New Delhi: National Council of Education Research and Training, January 1969); and *Census of India 1971, Paper 1 of 1971 - Supplement Provisional Population Totals* (New Delhi: Government of India, March 1971).

18. The study of Japanese farmers was first reported in the author's doctoral dissertation, 'Education, Communication, and Agricultural Change: A Study of Japanese Farmers' (University of Chicago, 1971).

19. A. S. Murthy, 'Social and Psychological Correlates in Predicting Communication Behavior of Farmers' (unpublished PhD dissertation, Indian Agricultural Research Institute, New Delhi, 1969).

20. Prodipto Roy, Frederick C. Fliegel, Joseph E. Kilvin, and Lalit K. Sen, *Agricultural Innovation Among Indian Farmers* (Hyderabad, India: National Institute of Community Development, 1968), 96.

21. V. S. Sankaran Potti, 'A Study of Differential Adoption of Improved Farm Practices in Relation to Reference Group Influence and Community Norms' (unpublished PhD dissertation, Indian Agricultural Research Institute, New Delhi, 1966).

22. Shiva Nath Singh, 'A Study on Adoption of High Yielding Varieties and Investment Pattern of Additional Income by Farmers of Delhi Territory' (unpublished PhD dissertation, Indian Agricultural Research Institute, New Delhi, 1969). (Hereinafter referred to as 'Adoption and Investment'.)

23. See Prue Dempster, *Japan Advances: A Geographical Study* (London: Methuen & Co Ltd, 1967); Bruce F. Johnston, *Agriculture and Economic Development: The Relevance of the Japanese Experience* (Stanford, California: Food Research Institute, 1966), reprinted from *Food Research Institute Studies*, VI, No. 3 (1966) 251-312; Masanobu Kuwahara, 'The Development of Agricultural Prodiction Since the War,' *Rural Economic Problems*, I, No. 1 (1964), 1-24; and T. Sarma Mallampally, 'An Analysis of Factors Influencing Increases in Rice Yields within Japan' (unpublished PhD dissertation, University of Chicago, 1966).

24. Hiromitsu Kaneda, 'The Sources and Rates of Productivity Gains in Japanese Agriculture, as Compared with the U.S. Experience,' *Journal of Farm Economics*, XLIX, No. 5 (1967), 1449-50. Also see Robert B. Hall, Jr., 'Hand Tractors in Japanese Paddy Fields,' *Economic Geography*, XXXIV (1958), 312-30; and Keizo Tsuchiya, 'Land Improvement Schemes and Innovations in Agricultural Technology,' *Rural Economic Problems*, I, No. 1 (1964), 45-60.

25. Lee, 'Korean Farmers' Education,' p. 76.

BIBLIOGRAPHY

Census of India 1971, Paper 1 of 1971 – Supplement: Provisional Population Totals. New Delhi: Government of India, March 1971.

Central Education Research Institute. *Follow-up Study of Vocational Agriculture High School and College Graduates and an Examination of Schools to Determine the Extent of their Long-term Contribution to Agricultural Production: Agricultural Education Survey of Korea.* Seoul: Central Education Research Institute, 1964.

Charles Milton Coughenour, 'The Functioning of Farmer's Characteristics in Relation to Contact with Media and Practice Adoption,' *Rural Sociology,* XXV, No. 3 (1960), 283–97.

Prue Dempster, *Japan Advances: A Geographical Study.* London: Methuen & Co Ltd, 1967.

Frederick C. Fliegel, 'A Multiple Correlation Analysis of Factors Associated with Adoption of Farm Practices.' *Rural Sociology,* XXI (1956), 284–92.

Zvi Griliches, 'The Sources of Measured Productivity Growth: U.S. Agriculture, 1940–60.' *Journal of Political Economy,* LXXI (August, 1963), 331–46.

Robert B. Hall Jr. 'Hand Tractors in Japanese Paddy Fields.' *Economic Geography,* XXXIV (1958), 312–20.

Bruce R. Harker, 'Education, Communication, and Agricultural Change: A Study of Japanese Farmers.' Unpublished PhD dissertation, University of Chicago, 1971.

Bruce F. Johnston, *Agriculture and Economic Development: The Relevance of the Japanese Experience.* Stanford, California: Food Research Institute, 1966. Reprinted from *Food Research Institute Studies,* VI, No. 3 (1966), 251–312.

Hiromitsu Kaneda, 'The Sources and Rates of Productivity Gains in Japanese Agriculture, as Compared with the U.S. Experience,' *Journal of Farm Economics,* XLIX, No. 5 (1967), 1443–51.

Masanobu Kuwahara, 'The Development of Agricultural Production Since the War,' *Rural Economic Problems,* I, No. 1 (1964), 1–24.

Jil-Hyun Lee, 'Economic Value of Korean Farmers' Education,' *Journal of Korean Agricultural Education,* No. 1 (1970), 69–89.

T. Sarma Mallampally, 'An Analysis of Factors Influencing Increases in Rice Yields within Japan.' Unpublished PhD dissertation, University of Chicago, 1966.

O. Donald Meaders, 'Contributions of Senior Middle School Graduates to Taiwan Agricultural Development.' A preliminary report, Michigan State University, 1968.

Ministry of Education. *Educational Standards in Japan: The 1964 'White Paper on Education.'* Tokyo: Government of Japan, 1965.

A. S. Murthy, 'Social and Psychological Correlates in Predicting Communication Behavior of Farmers.' Unpublished PhD dissertation, Indian Agricultural Research Institute, New Delhi, 1969.

R. R. Nelson and E. S. Phelps, 'Investment in Humans, Technological Diffusion, and Economic Growth,' *American Economic Review,* LVI, No. 2 (1966), 69–76.

Office of Rural Development. *Economic Value of 4-H Members' Farming Activities –*

Their Earnings and Productivity: A Korean Case Study. Suwon, Korea: Office of Rural Development, March, 1971.

Perspective Planning Division, Planning Commission. *Perspective for Agriculture in India 1968–69 to 1985–86.* New Delhi: Government of India July, 1971.

V. S. Sankaran Potti, 'A Study of Differential Adoption of Improved Farm Practices in Relation to Reference Group Influence and Community Norms.' Unpublished PhD dissertation, Indian Agricultural Research Institute, New Delhi, 1969.

Everett M. Rogers, *Diffusion of Innovations.* New York: The Free Press of Glencoe, 1962.

—*Modernization Among Peasants: The Impact of Communication.* New York: Holt, Rinehart and Winston, Inc., 1969.

Prodipto Roy, Frederick C. Fliegel, Joseph E. Kilvin, and Lalit K. Sen, *Agricultural Innovation Among Indian Farmers.* Hyderabad, India: National Institute of Community Development, 1968.

Theodore W. Schultz, *Transforming Traditional Agriculture.* Studies in Comparative Economics, Vol. 3. New Haven, Connecticut, and London: Yale University Press, 1964.

R. C. Sharma and C. L. Sapra, *Wastage and Stagnation in Primary and Middle Schools in India.* New Delhi: National Council of Education Research and Training, January 1969.

Shiva Nath Singh, 'A Study on Adoption of High Yielding Varieties and Investment Pattern of Additional Income by Farmers of Delhi Territory.' Unpublished PhD dissertation, Indian Agricultural Research Institute, New Delhi, 1969.

Keizo Tsuchiya, 'Land Improvement Schemes and Innovations in Agricultural Technology.' *Rural Economic Problems,* I, No. 1 (1964), 45–60.

Finis Welch, 'Education in Production.' *Journal of Political Economy,* LXXVIII, No. 1 (1970), 35–59.

Charles E. Werts and Donivan J. Watley, 'Analyzing College Effects: Correlation vs. Regression.' *American Educational Research Journal,* V, No. 4 (1968), 585–98.

Walter W. Wilcox, Andrew Boss, and George A. Pond. *Relation of Variations in the Human Factor to Financial Returns in Farming.* University of Minnesota Agricultural Experiment Station, Bulletin 288. St. Paul, Minnesota: University Farm, 1932.

20

Rural Education and Agricultural Development – some Empirical Results from Indian Agriculture

D. P. Chaudhri

The role of education has been examined in some recent studies on economic growth.[1] However, the evidence cited has been almost exclusively from advanced countries. The precise relationship between education and productivity has not been analysed much in the context of under-developed countries. This chapter is a modest attempt to examine this question in the light of available recent evidence, particularly from Indian agriculture.

II

Historical evidence from present day developed countries is at best suggestive. Studies relating to growth accounting indicate that a large part of growth remains unexplained when we try to attribute growth to conventional economic factors.[2] Solow calls the unexplained part 'technical progress' while Balogh and Streeten [1963] prefer to call it the 'co-efficient of ignorance'. Griliches [1963], Welch [1966], and Hoffman [1964] attempt to explain a part of this residue through what they call 'human capital' of which formal schooling or education is considered a major component.[3] These studies are indicative of the fact that economic growth (including that in the agricultural sector) in the present day developed economies was accompanied by substantial improvements in the educational level of the labour force. The causal relationship is hypothesized. In spite of very careful and detailed and highly plausible explanations on the part of these authors the statistical problem of identification is not solved to the satisfaction of the profession, largely due to the lack of required detailed time-series data.

Studies by Tang [1963] and Johnston [1970] relating to Japan do

* In this chapter I report some of the results from my doctoral dissertation 'Education and Agricultural Productivity in India,' Delhi University, April 1968 (mimeographed). I owe my interest in the subject to Professor Amartya K. Sen and am deeply indebted to him for comments and helpful suggestions. Thanks are also due to T. W. Schultz, A. L. Nagar, M. D. Chaudhry, Ashok Rudra and K. L. Krishna for helpful suggestions. Responsibility for the views expressed and the remaining deficiencies is entirely mine.

emphasize the crucial role of education and its recognition by the policy makers of that time, e.g. Johnston [1970, p. 60] quotes Kikuchi [1909] 'Every man only after learning diligently according to his capacity would be able to increase his property and prosper in his business. Hence knowledge may be regarded as the Capital for raising one's self; who then can do without learning?'

The cross-section studies, e.g. Griliches [1964], Welch [1970], relating to present day agriculture in the developed countries clearly support the historical evidence that education of the rural labour force, level of productivity and agricultural wages move together. The causal relationship is still not conclusively established because identification problems in the strict sense still remain. Simultaneous equation models might solve the problem, but the required detailed data are not available.

In any case the experience of the advanced countries, historical and present day, is not strictly relevant to present day developing countries. At best it is suggestive, in view of the fact that the developing countries are trying to achieve in a few decades what became feasible for the advanced countries over more than a century. Moreover, the land-man ratio in the advanced western countries has never been as low as in the present day developing economies of Asia. Japanese experience seems more relevant in this context.

III

Why should farmers' education be important in agricultural modernization? Schultz [1962], [1963], [1964], [1968] provides detailed and cogent reasons; Wharton [1965], Chaudhri [1967], [1969], Welch [1970], Griliches [1968], Nelson and Phelps [1966] emphasize aspects of these reasons; Chaudhri [1968], and Harker [1971] in addition to examining these reasons carry out detailed statistical tests for Indian and Japanese agricultural sectors respectively.

A farmer's education could be relevant because it enables him to acquire:

(a) the ability to decode new information – know what, why, where, when and how;

(b) the ability to evaluate costs and benefits of alternative sources of economically useful information;

(c) the ability to establish quick access to newly available economically useful information;

(d) the ability to choose optimum combinations of crops, new inputs and agricultural practices with the least number of trials;

(e) the ability to perform agricultural operations more effectively in the economic sense, i.e. the ability to produce more from a given amount of inputs.

Conceptually, we can think of the education impact, if any, comprising the following components:[4]

(i) the innovative effect – this would consist of (a), (b) and (c) described above;

(ii) the allocative effect – according to above descriptions (d) would belong here. This can be seen to consist of two parts, namely (1) business activity (2) production activity;

(iii) the worker effect – quality of labour as described in (e) above;

(iv) externality – neighbouring farmers and other producers in the vicinity who are in direct contact with educated farmers would be able informally to consult and to copy educated leaders in adopting successful new crop and input combinations and in related production and business techniques.[5]

Figure 1 depicts various components of the educational impact.

In the situation of traditional agriculture as defined by Schultz [1964] when there are no additional economic overheads, no additional research results becoming available and no institutional changes being induced by development planners, farmers find themselves in a state of long term equilibrium. The only two sources of disturbance are (1) natural factors and (2) market factors, as is clear from Figure 1. Since small subsistence farmers and large market-oriented farmers are economically rational their response to this situation will be different. The small subsistence farmers choose cropping patterns which give them not necessarily a maximum yield in any particular year but an assured yield each year, e.g. the mixture of wheat and grain sown by small farmers in North India. Being illiterate and thus handicapped in decoding market information, they find it economically profitable not to participate in the sale of outputs and the purchase of inputs. They diversify their cropping pattern so as to produce mainly for self consumption, thus minimizing the twin risks of natural and market uncertainties. Large, market-oriented, farmers on the other hand, diversify their cropping pattern to the extent necessary to safeguard against vagaries of weather but find it necessary and useful to acquire market information decoding ability.[6] Thus economic dualism as described by Sen [1966] emerges. We get a set of subsistence farmers, economically rational, but having a different objective function (maximization of utility), and a set of market-oriented large farmers, maximizing profit.

Functional literacy or education in a situation of long run equilibrium in traditional agriculture would be of very little economic value to small, utility-maximizing farmers, but would be an important economic input for farmers largely participating in the market system.

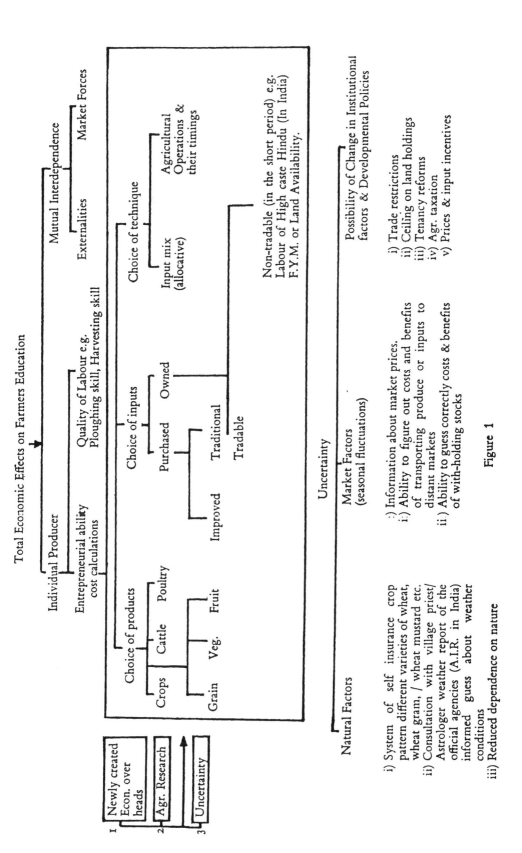

Figure 1

Now let agents of change appear on the scene in the form of state authorities wanting to provide:

(a) Economic overheads.
(b) Market regulations in terms of economic incentives/restrictions.
(c) Changes in the institutional structure, such as provision of agricultural credit through co-operatives in an attempt to replace high-cost money lenders.
(d) Agricultural research information about high-yielding varieties of seed and new inputs through extension agents, radio and printed leaflets.[7]

The sources of information of the two sets of farmers would be different. Small, utility-maximizing, subsistence farmers would be passive, involuntary recipients of information through local sources – other farmers and occasionally extension agents or a radio, if they have equal access to the latter two sources in the village. The market-oriented large farmers would have more cosmopolitan sources of information, including printed leaflets.

The use of extension agents is obviously inconvenient and inefficient when compared to the potential of printed media.[8] Unless the administrators of development strategy specifically take corrective steps, one would inevitably find that farmers with greater access to economically useful information and the ability to decode it (education), and greater access to required capital, would be early adopters of the new technology and thus be regarded as innovators.[9]

If they can overcome the handicap of limited access to capital markets, the smaller farmers will ultimately be found adapting to change with a lag; this response is a beneficial 'externality' caused by the demonstration effect of the educated and market-oriented large farmers. But the pace of diffusion of the new practices will depend on the number of better educated farmers who can quickly decode new information for themselves and who serve as examples and as transmitters of information to their neighbours. We shall examine some empirical evidence in this connexion in the next section.

The information-decoding ability of the farmer is also crucial in establishing a two-way process of communication between researchers and farmers, without which the research results may not be directly relevant to immediate practical problems. Education provides this ability, among its other benefits. In principle, it is always possible to think of alternatives to formal education of farmers – for example the use of television. But these alternatives have to be evaluated in terms of their relative costs and effectiveness.

IV

Empirical evidence from the Indian agricultural sector is very interesting and highly suggestive of the correctness of our conceptual distinctions.

We examine the role of farmers' education[10] in the choice of modern inputs and level of agricultural productivity in Indian agriculture during 1960–61. Data have been analysed at various levels of aggregation taking as units of observation 13 Indian states, each of 256 districts of India, and individual households. Two main hypotheses tested were:[11]

(a) that the level of agricultural output is positively related to the level of education of farm workers;
(b) that the pattern of agricultural inputs and adoption of new practices and inputs is positively related to the level of education of farm workers.

Three types of equations are used at each level of aggregation to examine educational impact:

(a) A gross measure of educational impact which postulates the simple relationship

$$\text{Output} = f\ (\text{Education})$$

This probably errs on the high side because of the association of education with other factors that may in turn have independent association with outputs.

(b) Measurement of educational impact by estimating a production function of an unrestricted Cobb-Douglas variety with the following specification

$$\text{Output} = f\ (\text{Land, Irrigation, Chemical Fertilizer, Labour, Education})$$

with a control-of-weather variable. This would be erring on the low side in a causal interpretation, since those inputs (e.g. fertilizers, irrigation) which farmers have chosen precisely because of education would capture their effects directly; the coefficients on education then give a minimal measure of educational impact. Actual educational impact would be greater than this lower estimate but less than the gross measure.

(c) Choice of modern inputs is related to education directly, as:

$$\text{Modern Input} = f\ (\text{Education}).$$

These relationships are examined at various levels of aggregation to take account of mutual inter-dependence which, as explained earlier, takes the form of 'externalities'. If we examine inter-household data from the same region, the externality is almost completely ignored. It gets internalized to a successively greater extent at village, district and state levels. Thus the same equation applied at the household level would show a much lower impact of education in accounting for variance than at the district, state or country level.[12] Only the state and district analyses are reported here.

V

Statistical Results

Education and Productivity: Educational Impact

Taking the logarithm of gross value of yield per acre as the dependent variable in zero order regressions on education variables also expressed in logarithmic form gave the results shown in Tables 1 and 2, using observations by districts and by states respectively.

These results are in the expected direction, although the regression coefficients estimated from the district-leval data differ from those obtained with state-level data. Interestingly enough, the coefficients with district data are consistently somewhat lower.

One explanation may be that the externalities of education which were completely internalized at the state-level aggregation, get excluded to some extent when we deal with inter-district data. This may partly account for lower regression-coefficients in the latter case.

On the basis of these results, it is difficult to decide which measure of education best explains the variation in outputs, particularly in view of the fact that the education measures are inter-correlated and the results are statistically significant with each of the four measures. With state-level data, literacy, secondary education and years of schooling (each of them individually) explain 65 to 70 per cent of variation; with district-level data they explain 34 to 36 per cent of variation. Efficiency of primary education in this respect is lower with both state-level data and district-level data.

As proposed in section IV, we attempted a statistical estimation of the parameters of a log-linear production function, using ordinary least squares, on the 256 district-level observations for the country as a whole. As in Tables 1 and 2, the regression coefficients are therefore elasticities of outputs with respect to each of the independent variables. Results are summarized in Table 3. The statistical fit in all the four cases is good, all parameters except labour are well estimated, and the multi-collinearity problem does not seem to be too serious in this set of data (as is clear from the zero order correlation matrix, Table 4).

The correlation table not only reassures us that multi-collinearity is not a serious problem with this set of data, but supports many of the familiar conjectures about various input-output correlations. For example, fertilizer use goes with labour intensive methods of cultivation; rainfall and

TABLE 1

REGRESSION OF LOGARITHM OF VALUE OF YIELD PER ACRE ON LOGARITHMS OF
EDUCATION (E); OBSERVATIONS BY DISTRICTS (N=256)

Measure of Education	Constant	Regression Coefficients (elasticities)	R^2
Log E_1 Literate	2·5462 (0·0392)	0·3660★ (0·0321)	0·3381
Log E_2 Elem	2·4590 (0·0395)	0·1824★ (0·0200)	0·2453
Log E_3 10+	2·7470 (0·0533)	0·2071★ (0·0171)	0·3646
Log E_4 Yrs. Educ.	2·4139 (0·0275)	0·3256★ (0·0278)	0·3491

★ Significant at 1% level.

TABLE 2

REGRESSION OF LOGARITHMS OF VALUE OF YIELD PER ACRE ON LOGARITHMS OF
EDUCATION (E); OBSERVATIONS BY STATES (N=13)

Regression No.	Independent Variable	Constant	Regression Coefficients (elasticities)	R^2
1	Log E_1	2·6618 (0·1039)	0·4550★ (0·0899)	0·6995
2	Log E_2	2·6510 (0·1675)	0·2797★ (0·0921)	0·4557
3	Log E_3	3·0060 (0·1906)	0·2917★ (0·0645)	0·6498
4	Log E_4	2·5238 (0·0825)	0·4365★ (0·0914)	0·6743

★ Significant at 1% level.

irrigation are independent of each other but there is a positive association between irrigation and fertilizer use; and irrigation is associated with the use of labour. The zero order correlations of education (each of the four measures) with irrigation, fertilizers and yield are particularly noteworthy.

The coefficients of land and rainfall display the highest elasticities, as could be expected in present day Indian agriculture.[13] The coefficients on education are higher than the labour coefficients, which are insignificant (subject to high standard error). These results for labour presumably reflect the poor measure of labour; in the absence of labour input data in man–hours or man–days, we were forced to define agricultural workers as

TABLE 3

Estimated Parameters of the Log-Linear Production Function; Observation by Districts ($N = 256$)

Measure of Education	N	Constant	R'fall.	Irr.	Fert.	Land	Educ.	N-Lab.	Sum of Coefficients	R^2
E_1	256	2·4651	0·3733★ (0·051)	0·1356★ (0·015)	0·0891★ (0·015)	0·6058† (0·044)	0·0735† (0·038)	−0·0482 (0·047)	1·2292	0·7911
E_2	256	2·5162	0·3700 (0·051)	0·1392★ (0·015)	0·0813★ (0·016)	0·5950★ (0·044)	0·0500★ (0·019)	−0·0165 (0·046)	1·2192	0·7933
E_3	256	2·5104	0·3935★ (0·048)	0·1179★ (0·015)	0·0783★ (0·014)	0·6161★ (0·042)	0·0819★ (0·018)	−0·0378 (0·047)	1·2500	0·8031
E_4	256	2·4256	0·3637★ (0·051)	0·1343★ (0·015)	0·0767★ (0·016)	0·5851★ (0·043)	0·0823★ (0·032)	−0·0189 (0·028)	1·2232	0·7941

Figures in brackets indicate standard errors
All variables appear in the logarithmic form.
★ Significant at 1% level.
† Significant at 5% level.

TABLE 4
MATRIX OF ZERO ORDER CORRELATIONS BETWEEN VARIABLES;
OBSERVATIONS BY DISTRICTS (N = 256)

Vari-ables	I	F	L	N	Y	E_1	E_2	E_3	E_4
R	− 0·029	0·080	− 0·196	0·184	0·159	0·224	0·187	0·063	0·189
I		0·573	0·084	0·515	0·571	0·535	0·389	0·622	0·501
F			0·228	0·476	0·644	0·672	0·675	0·654	0·724
L				0·549	0·617	0·451	0·384	0·239	0·437
N					0·685	0·684	0·495	0·538	0·215
Y						0·731	0·651	0·650	0·732

those workers who were reported as cultivators and agricultural labourers at the time of the 1961 census. This definition implies 'workers' in the sense of dependents on agriculture directly for their livelihood rather than specific quantity of labour input in agricultural production.

Education and Modernization: Use of Chemical Fertilizers

As discussed earlier we examined the dependence of the use of chemical fertilizers on the level of education. We fitted ordinary linear regression equations to the 13 state observations and to the 256 district observations taking the quantity of chemical fertilizer used as the dependent variable and education as the only independent variable. The results are presented in Tables 5 and 6. Regression coefficients in this case are slopes, not elasticities, since we did not use logarithmic transformations.

All coefficients are highly significant: it seems clear that better educated populations do on the average use larger amounts of chemical fertilizers,[14] and the association between education and agricultural productivity which we observed earlier is unlikely to be a statistical illusion.[15] There seems to be a presumption in favour of the proposition that the application of chemical fertilizers in different states of India is influenced by education of the farm workers in these states.[16] However, there are large inter-state variations in rainfall, availability of irrigation facilities, and other factors that may be independently associated with both use of chemical fertilizers and the level of education (measured in any one of the four alternative ways). In inter-district data, this problem is considerably reduced.

VI

Conclusions

Our analysis in the preceding sections lends support to the possibility that the level of agricultural productivity is significantly related to the level

TABLE 5
REGRESSION OF PER ACRE CHEMICAL FERTILIZER USE ON EDUCATION (E); STATE OBESRVATIONS (N=13)

Regression Number	Measure of Education	Constant	Regression Coefficients	R^2
1	E_1	−0·00054 (0·002)	0·0179★ (0·002)	0·869
2	E_2	−0·00054 (0·0001)	0·0754★ (0·013)	0·754
3	E_3	−0·0001 (0·0002)	0·6226★ (0·069)	0·880
4	E_4	−0·0006 (0·0002)	0·0103★ (0·001)	0·983

★ Significant at 1% level.

TABLE 6
REGRESSION OF FERTILIZER USE ON EDUCATION; DISTRICT OBSERVATIONS (N=256)

Measure of Education	Constant	Regression Coefficients	R^2
E_1	−0·00012	0·0107★ (0·0011)	0·514
E_2	0·00015	0·0285★ (0·0020)	0·512
E_3	0·00031	0·2622★ (0·0360)	0·415
E_4	0·00015	0·0059★ (0·0005)	0·575

★ Significant at 1% level.

NOTE: We measured fertilizer use in terms of tons for the estimation of the Cobb–Douglas production function (in that case the unit did not matter). In the above simple linear equation also we continue to measure chemical fertilizer use in tons.

of education. Furthermore, the relation is strong with each of the four alternative measures of the education of the farm workers. These relationships are likely to be much stronger in a more dynamic agricultural setting. e.g. the post-green-revolution situation in Asian agriculture. This underlines the importance of literacy as well as *sustained school education*. The set of results seem to have considerable relevance for development planning in the less developed countries with conditions similar to those of India.

REFERENCES

1. See in particular, Schultz (1964), (1968), Millikan (1962), Millikan and Hapgood (1967), Wharton (1965).
2. Solow (1957), OECD (1964), Denison (1962).
3. This has led to very interesting studies on the vehicle–of–technical progress, embodiment hypothesis. In this connection see, in particular, Jorgenson (1966), Jorgenson and Griliches (1967), Arrow (1962), Sen (1966). For a detailed discussion on Education and Human Capital formation see Schultz (1963), Becker (1965).
4. Originally proposed in Chaudhri (1968).
5. The industrial sector innovations are patented and thus can be copied only at a price through market inter–dependence, but in agriculture, with the exception of some latifundias in Latin America who employ their own botanists and plant breeders, this takes the form of externality.
6. This probably explains why the ability to read and write is highly respected in these communities, and it is acquired by large farmers only. Apart from having higher ability to pay, its economic utility also seems to be higher for the large farmers in traditional agriculture.
7. Assume that all this information about the new technology is scale–neutral and the developmental authorities are benevolent (and not short-period, production-results conscious) and want to help small farmers as much as large farmers.
8. See Wharton (1965, pp. 208–211).
9. See Rogers (1962).
10. We define education in four alternative ways and carry out statistical tests with each of them with a view to finding out, if possible, the level of education which is most relevant in the Indian setting. The definitions of education are: (i) number of literate farm workers (E_1): (ii) number of farm workers who have successfully completed at least lower elementary education (E_2): (iii) number of farm workers who have at least 10 years of successful schooling (E_3), and (iv) total number of years of schooling of the farming family workers (E_4).
11. The aggregate data relate to an average of three years (1958–61) and are compiled from the published and unpublished records of the Ministry of Food and Agriculture, Government of India.
12. One can even get statistical results with inter-household data which indicate no significant impact of education. This does not immediately imply no educational impact, but only indicates that the question needs further examination. One of the possibilities could be that there is really no impact, it is also possible that externality is large and therefore the impact at individual level is not captured in the measurement.
13. Less than 20 per cent of the area cultivated has irrigation facilities in Indian agriculture.
14. In this case identification of the causal chain does not create too much difficulty. Education of the workers can influence the use of fertilizers, but current demand for fertilizers cannot affect the stock of education at the same point of time. Interaction, if any, will be via productivity.

15. Note that the regression coefficient is highest for E_3. This is as expected, since E_3 is a measure of the number of people with at least 10 years of schooling, while E_1 (say) measures the number of all literates.
16. National Council of Applied Economic Research, New Delhi, in one of its studies states similar conclusions. See NCAER (1964).

BIBLIOGRAPHY

Agricultural Economics Research Centre, *Elementary Rural Education in India – Participation and Wastage*, Delhi University (mimeographed, 1968), (New Delhi: Tata-McGraw-Hill Publishing Company) (in press).

K. J. Arrow, 'The Economic Implications of Learning by Doing', *RES*, Vol. 29 (1962).

Thomas Balogh, P. A. Streeten, 'Co-efficient of Ignorance', *BOIES*, May, 1963.

G. S. Becker, *Human Capital: A Theoretical and Empirical Analysis with Special Reference to Education* (Princeton: Princeton University Press, 1965).

Mark Blaug, 'Economic Implications of Literacy Programmes', *School Review*, 1966.

D. P. Chaudhri, 'Education and Agricultural Productivity – Some Preliminary Results from Indian Agriculture', *Education Quarterly*, New Delhi, 1967.

D. P. Chaudhri, *Education and Agricultural Productivity in India*, PhD thesis, University of Delhi, April 1968 (New Delhi: Tata-McGraw-Hill Publishing Co.) (in press).

D. P. Chaudhri, 'Education of Farmers and Productivity', in *Measurement of Cost, Productivity and Efficiency of Education* (H. N. Pandit (ed.)), NCERT, New Delhi, 1969.

E. F. Denison, *The Sources of Economic Growth in US and Alternatives Before Us.* Committee of Economic Development, 1962.

Zvi Griliches, 'The Sources of Measured Productivity Growth: United States Agriculture 1940–60', *JPE*, LXXI, August, 1963.

Zvi Griliches, 'Research Expenditure, Education and Aggregate Agricultural Production Functions', *AER*, LIV, December, 1964.

Zvi Griliches, 'Education in Production and Growth Accounting', paper presented to NBER Conference on Education and Income, at Wisconsin University, Madison, November, 1968.

B. R. Harker, *Education, Communication and Agricultural Change: A Study of Japanese Farmers*, unpublished PhD thesis, University of Chicago, June, 1971.

W. F. Hoffman, 'Expenditure on Education and Research in the process of Economic Growth', *German Economic Review*, 1964, 2(2), pp. 97–110.

International Labour Office, *Towards Full Employment*, A programme for Colombia prepared by an inter-agency team, ILO Geneva, 1970.

Bruce F. Johnston, 'Japanese "Model" of Agricultural Development: Its Relevance to Developing Nations', in *Agricultural and Economic Growth: Japanese Experience*, Kazushi Ohkawa, Bruce Johnston and Hiromitsu Kaneda (eds.) (Princeton: Princeton University Press, 1970).

Dale W. Jorgenson, 'The Embodiment Hypothesis', *JPE*, LXXIV, February, 1966.

Dale W. Jorgenson and Zvi Griliches, 'The Explanation of Productivity Change', *RES*, XXXIV (3), no. 99, 1967.

Baron Kikuchi, *Japanese Education*, London, 1909.

J. E. Kivlin, Roy Prodipto, F. C. Fliegel, and L. K. Sen, *Communication in India – Experiments in Introducing Change*, National Institute of Community Development, Hydrabad, 1968.

Max Millikan, 'Education for Innovation', in *Restless Nations, A Study of Tensions and Development*, written under the auspices of the Council on World Tensions (Dodd, Mead and Co. Inc., 1962).

Max Millikan, and David Hapgood, *No Easy Harvest – The Dilemma of Agriculture in Under-developed Countries* (Boston: Little, Brown and Co., 1967).

R. R. Nelson, E. S. Phelps, 'Investment in Humans, Technological Diffusion, and Economic Growth', *AER*, LVI, No. 2, 1966.

OECD, *Residual Factors in Economic Growth*, Paris, OECD, 1964.

E. M. Rogers. *Diffusion of Innovations* (New York: The Free Press of Glencoe, 1962).

G. R. Saini, 'Technological Change and its Diffusion in Agriculture', Agr. Econ. Research Centre, Delhi University (mimeo), 1966.

T. W. Schultz, 'Reflections on Investment in Man', *JPE* Supplement, October, 1962.

T. W. Schultz, *Economic Value of Education* (New York: Colombia University Press, 1963).

T. W. Schultz, *Transforming Traditional Agriculture* (New Haven: Yale University Press, 1964).

T. W. Schultz, *Economic Growth and Agriculture* (New York: McGraw-Hill, 1968).

A. K. Sen, 'Education, Vintage and Learning by Doing', *Journal of Human Resources*, Vol. 1, No. 2 (Fall, 1966).

A. K. Sen, 'Peasants and Dualisms – with and without Surplus Labour', *JPE*, 1966.

A. K. Sen, 'Crisis in Indian Education', Lal Bhadur Shastri Memorial Lecture, February, 1970, Delhi School of Economics, Delhi (mimeo).

A. K. Singh, 'Hindu Culture and Economic Development of India', *Conspectus*, 1967.

Robert M. Solow, 'Technical Progress, Capital Formation and Economic Growth', *AER*, Vol. 52, 1957.

A. M. Tang, 'Research and Education in Japanese Agricultural Development, 1880–1938', *Economic Studies Quarterly*, XIII, February and May, 1963.

Erik Thorbecke and Irma Adelman, *The Theory and Design of Economic Development* (Baltimore: Johns Hopkins, 1966).

Erik Thorbecke (ed.), *The Role of Agriculture in Economic Development*, New York: National Bureau of Economic Research, 1969.

U.P. Agricultural University, *Changing Agriculture in Two Regions or Uttar Pradesh in 1969-70*, U.P. Ag. University, Pantnagar, India (mimeo), 1970.

Finis Welch, 'Determinants of Returns to Schooling', unpublished PhD thesis, University of Chicago, 1966.

Finis Welch, 'Education in Production', *JPE*, January, 1970.

C. R. Wharton, Jr., 'The Role of Education in Early Stage Agriculture', *Education and Economic Development*, C. Arnold Anderson and Mary Jean Bowman (eds.) (Chicago: Aldine Publishing Co., 1965).

The World Year Book of Education: A Postscript

Brian Holmes

When the *Year Book of Education* was founded in 1932 by the Chairman of Evans Brothers, Sir Robert Evans, its Editor-in-Chief for the first four years (1932–35) was Lord Eustace Percy, formerly President of the Board of Education. Both these men of vision wanted the *Year Book* to be more than a volume of academic interest. They hoped it would be of value to politicians, administrators and educationists. Articles should help governments to formulate policy and inform a wide lay audience about contemporary education issues. Percy himself persistently advocated the reform of secondary education and the expansion of technical education. The early volumes reflect these and other concerns. Throughout its life the range of issues explored has been wide and it has never been the intention of the publishers, the editorial boards or the editors to publish articles which would simply or principally appeal to and satisfy the needs of research workers and scholars. They have always wanted the *Year Book of Education* to be a forum for discussions about pressing educational problems. It is against this vision that the volumes published between 1932 and 1940 and then between 1948, when it was revived after the Second World War, and 1973 should be judged.

· For many years of this second period of its life, in fact from 1953 to 1971, I was closely associated with the *Year Book of Education* (renamed the *World Year Book of Education* in 1965) through all its stages of preparation and with those unashamed pioneers of comparative education who in making major contributions to their chosen field helped to fashion the *World Year Book*. Nicholas Hans played a major role in its evolution during the late thirties and was Joint Editor of the first six postwar volumes. Joseph Lauwerys played a leading part in its revival after the war (Minutes of a meeting held 24 April 1946 to consider reviving the *Year Book of Education*). From its reappearance in 1948 until he retired from his professorship in Comparative Education in the University of London in 1970 Lauwerys was Joint Editor, first with Hans, then from 1953 with an American counterpart nominated by Teachers College, Columbia University, when it became formally associated with the University of London Institute of Education. The first Joint Editor in New York was Robert

King Hall; the second was George Z. F. Bereday who succeeded him as Professor of Comparative Education at Teachers College; and David G. Scanlon was Joint Editor from 1968 to 1971. The contributions of Hans, Lauwerys, King Hall and Bereday to the study of education and the development of comparative education need no documentation here. They are well known. Certainly Hans, Lauwerys and King Hall helped to fashion my approach to comparative education and convinced me that in spite of the difficulties it was a subject well worth studying. Consequently my brief account of the birth, life and untimely death of the *World Year Book of Education*, written at the request of the London editorial board, is the testimony of an interested party. In wider perspective, however, this account inevitably touches on the development of comparative education over the last forty years, and places the role of the University of London Institute of Education into some kind of perspective. Not surprisingly this review calls more heavily on personal experience and judgment than on carefully validated evidence. Moreover, it is London-centred for reasons which should be apparent as the story unfolds. It offers three impressions on which readers may wish to reflect.

The first of these is that the *World Year Book of Education* achieved the original purposes intended for it by its publisher-founder and its first Editor-in-Chief. These were to popularize educational literature, to involve more people in the study of education policy, and to provide a forum for the discussion of educational issues in the United Kingdom, the British Commonwealth and elsewhere. Secondly, Mr H. Lionel Elvin, Director of the London Institute, was correct when he wrote in the 1970 volume in his appreciation of Lauwerys' contribution to the *World Year Book* that 'these volumes have made a substantial contribution to the development of Comparative Education' (WYBE 1970). This assessment should be seen in the light of the hope expressed by Dr. G. B. Jeffery, then Director of the Institute, in the 1949 volume that a study of the same fundamental problems in different countries would 'promote the true study of Comparative Education' (YBE 1949). Lauwerys' own comments may serve as a third hypothesis. He writes: 'Il est intéressant de noter que c'est ainsi que, avec la publication des *World Year Books* de 1954 et 1956 – qui traitaient des études comparées dans le domaine de l'éducation –, naquirent deux nouvelles sciences; l'économie de l'éducation et la planification en matière d'éducation' (M. Debesse, G. Mialaret (eds.) *Traité des sciences pédagogiques; 3 Pédagogie Comparée*, Presses Universitaires de France, Paris, 1972, p. 26). Acknowledging their earlier origins, Lauwerys nevertheless suggests that the present position of importance enjoyed by these two disciplines in the study of education owes much to the initiative of comparative educationists and the pioneering work of the *World Year Book*.

A forum for informed debate, a standard work in the development of comparative education, and a source of inspiration of important educational sciences are descriptions used at one time or another of the *World Year Book* by persons closely connected with it. It is not for me to assess the validity of these claims. I shall however attempt to show in the two periods of its history – from 1932 to 1940 and then from 1948 to 1973 – how policies evolved, what considerations were taken into account when changes were made, and how, at least in the second period, volumes were prepared. Evidence has been culled from the minutes of the London editorial board since 1946, from plans (in their numerous stages) on which volumes were based. Reference will be made to reviews received by the British publishers, Evans Brothers, and to the place given to seminal articles in other scholarly publications. In the final analysis, however, the volumes must speak for themselves and readers must judge for themselves whether the *World Year Book of Education* has achieved what its founders and those who have prepared and published it hoped for. It is a matter of speculation how far the London editorial board was wise at its meeting on 8 February 1972 in deciding to terminate its publication on the grounds that 'in its present form (it) no longer provided the outlet for which it was designed . . .' (Minutes, Editorial Board, 8 February 1972). If it is indeed to have no future, it is against the changing circumstance in the field of educational studies during the thirties, the fifties, and the sixties that the contribution made by the *World Year Book of Education* has need to be assessed.

A Forum for Discussion

First, perhaps some explanation is needed of the title, *Year Book of Education*, and the fact that it never followed the normal format of an annual publication. Each volume did more than update information collected and presented in a previous volume. The decision to make it lively and stimulating by including expressions of opinion on contemporary subjects was deliberate, and it is interesting that the decision was justified by Donald Maclean of the Board of Education in his foreword to the first volume. He outlined two possible approaches:

> In compiling a yearbook two alternatives at any rate are possible. One may be content with the safe but somewhat unambitious course of compiling a volume of the principal facts and figures relating to education; or, on the other hand, one may go further and adopt the more venturesome and interesting alternative of endeavouring to bring these facts and figures into some sort of perspective and to suggest underlying principles and lines of development (1932, Foreword written 1931).

The bolder course was chosen. As a yearbook it was not merely to be a 'repository of facts to be kept up to date' but was to 'open up new ground'

(YBE 1933, Introduction) and thus challenge the authorities to think more closely of future needs. Moreover it was not simply to reflect official thinking. Contributors were (and always have been) free to express radical opinions on controversial matters. Certainly the *World Year Book* has frequently been ahead of established opinion. In Percy's day many chapters were written by 'high officials' who remained anonymous, suggesting that their views were not necessarily those of the government or Board of Education. Subsequently most of the authors were research workers and academics. This conception was admirable, many articles were lively and anticipated future needs, but perhaps the choice of this 'bolder' course made it difficult for the *World Year Book* in the long run to receive substantial official support from national or international sources. Certainly its mode of production precluded any form of official censorship (however mild), and thus encouraged writers from virtually every country in the world to contribute.

But as a challenge to official thinking the *World Year Book* has always been an English publication. Originally the educational needs of England and Wales were given priority. Over the years this was broadened to include the English-speaking nations of the world. A second feature is that it has always had a comparative frame of reference. From the start it was decided to review problems in English education in an international context. They were to be studied in the light of common British traditions, which meant that articles on aspects of education in the Commonwealth and Empire were included. Percy had the vision to go further. He saw the need to extend the scope of the *Year Book* beyond a survey of the whole Empire. He wrote:

> If the common features of British education at home and overseas are to be intelligently observed, it is also necessary to study British education against the background of the educational systems of other nations (1932 Introduction, p. xiv).

Throughout the pre-Second World War period and well into the second period of its history special attention was paid to educational problems in Britain, the Dominions and the colonial territories. It is not, therefore, the fault of a succession of editors if educationists in England in general remained parochial and unwilling to learn from continental Europe and the USA. Certainly some reviews in the *Times Educational Supplement* of the early postwar volumes suggest that there was in certain quarters a 'general hostility to the whole idea behind the *Year Book*' (Minutes, 20 February 1952).

In order to challenge the authorities to think about the future and help them formulate policy it was originally thought necessary to provide them with facts and figures. Percy intended the methods of enquiry on which they were based to be 'strictly empirical'. It was soon obvious that methods of collecting comparative data had to be improved. Taxonomies were needed on the basis of which, in the light of useful indicators, educational data could be classified and statistical information compared. One of the early contributions made by the *World Year Book* to the development of comparative education was in the gathering of statistics.

The starting point from which a classificatory system emerged was the central place given to statistical information about education in the United Kingdom and especially in England and Wales. In the first volume (1932) Part I included information about Great Britain and Northern Ireland under the following headings: 1. administration and finance, 2. the school system, 3. further education, 4. the universities, 5. the health services, 6. special schools and 7. legal notes. Much of this material was given in detailed statistical tables. In Part II of this volume education in the British Commonwealth was described and in Part III there were chapters on France, Germany, Italy, USA, Sweden, Czechoslovakia, Russia, the Argentine, China, Turkey, and Egypt.

The indicators on which statistics and narrative were based were retained with some modifications throughout this prewar period, when it was hoped to summarize and keep up to date the facts of education. The 1937 and 1938 volumes indicate what was being attempted. In Part I of the 1937 volume (prepared by Hans and Harley V. Usill, then General Editor) twenty-six statistical tables showed the number of institutions and pupils and teachers in them in the schools (public, grant-aided, and Headmasters' Conference), teacher training colleges and universities in England and Wales. Summary tables pictured education in Scotland, Northern Ireland, Canada, Australia, South Africa, New Zealand, and the Irish Free State. Statistics of educational systems not derived from British origins were even briefer. They were not tabulated and under each of the mentioned indicators, administration, school system, etc. was given a short description.

Some of the problems were evident. In their introduction to a comparative survey of Commonwealth systems, Hans and Usill recognized the difficulties of standardizing methods of collecting material. Commonwealth cooperation among ministries and local authorities had enabled them to reach some measure of standardization and 'to present this year a few comparative tables of the British Commonwealth of Nations' (YBE 1937, p. 80). Graphs and block diagrams of enrolments at various levels of education were introduced to facilitate comparisons, thus anticipating Unesco presentations. Hans and Usill thought that their next task was to standardize statistics for foreign countries.

In this they proposed to tackle a perennial problem in comparative education. The nineteenth century pioneers had recognized it, and William

Torrey Harris warned that statistics should be collected on the basis of unambiguous and acceptable concepts. Nevertheless a succession of Commissioners at the US Bureau of Education, e.g. Henry Barnard, John Eaton and Harris himself, had collected a vast amount of statistical data for the USA and foreign countries. International agencies such as the International Bureau of Education had also done some work and Hans and Usill suggested that if they were to succeed they would need the cooperation of such an international agency. Of course, after its establishment Unesco undertook as one of its tasks the establishment of indicators and the accumulation of statistics on a worldwide basis. It was in a far better position than any other body to do this. The need for intellectual rigour and a depth knowledge of comparative education in compiling them is apparent when these figures are scrutinized carefully. It is evident that statistics collected for national purposes may not fit into an international framework and that indicators developed for one country may not be suitable when international statistical data are being gathered. Philip J. Idenburg, formerly Director General of Statistics in the Netherlands, pointed to major difficulties in collecting statistical information in comparative education (see 'Die Bedeutung der Statistik für die Vergleichende Erziehungswissenschaft' in *I R E* Hamburg Vol. V, 1959, No 3). So did Sir Fred Clarke in his article in the 1933 volume. He wrote: 'The real objection to a statistical method, from the present point of view, is that it must fail to exhibit those differences and resemblances that are truly *significant*' (YBE 1935). Perhaps his influence resulted in the lessened emphasis on statistical material and comparisons based upon it. The statistical problems which arose in the postwar period when it was decided to treat in each volume a general theme were insurmountable and after 1952 the section on statistics was abolished. Clearly, the difficulties of standardizing data should not lead to the abandonment of attempts to overcome them. But they demand for success the resources of well-financed and well-staffed organizations. Without the help of major national and international agencies, the *World Year Book* was not in a position to tackle successfully a task recognized as important by Hans in the thirties.

Systematic and Continuous Research

Associated in the early volumes of the *Year Book* with summary statements about education was a catalogue of 'events of the year' in the English-speaking nations. Some of these were discussed, commended or criticized and policies were recommended. White papers, handbooks and so on published by the Government were treated in this way. Examples of particular policies advocated are the reform of secondary education and the expansion of technical education. The historical chapters contributed by Hans in 1938 and 1939 and several other *Year Book* articles anticipated the report of the Consultative Committee (the Spens Report) which dealt with these issues and helped to clarify and amplify many of the conclusions reached by that Committee.

Among the events so recorded was one which transformed the *Year Book*. In 1933 Percy identified as the most significant event of the year the transfer of the London Day Training College to the University of London (YBE 1933, Introduction). Of its future he wrote:

> It may be a dream, but it is at least significant that London, which those nations are not ashamed to regard as the centre of the British Commonwealth has at last provided itself with a University Institute of Education . . . (which) can, perhaps, legitimately aspire to be a centre of research and a focus for the culture of that Commonwealth (YBE 1933).

He cited an article in this volume by (Sir) Fred Clarke (writing from McGill) in which he made a plea for an Imperial Institute of Education (op. cit.). In 1935 it was argued that the Institute of Education had been created to discharge in education the functions of a university, namely systematic and continuous research and discussion. Percy (YBE 1933) maintained that the comparisons made by Clarke of South Africa and Canada in the previously mentioned article was the 'kind of comparative research which should occupy the attention of the new Institute of Education'. Clarke evidently agreed and when he became Director of the Institute and Chairman of the Editorial Board of the *Year Book* he did much to develop comparative education in the Institute and to give it a sociological flavour.

The new university Institute under Director Sir Percy Nunn, apparently quickly appreciated the possibilities of using the *Year Book* as a way of presenting the fruits of systematic and continuous research including those produced by members of its own staff. The Institute wished to associate itself with the editorship and approached the publishers and Percy with this in mind. A long period of cordial and productive collaboration was initiated. A joint editorial Board of Lord Eustace Percy, Sir Percy Nunn and Professor Dover Wilson of King's College, London, was established. When Percy resigned, Harley V. Usill took over as General Editor and the Joint Editorial Board in 1936 and 1937 comprised Nunn, Wilson, Professor H. R. Hamley (Institute of Education), Fred Clarke (Institute of Education) and G. Winthrop Young (King's College, London). When Nunn was succeeded by Clarke, Professor F. A. Cavanagh (King's College, London) and Professor I. L. Kandel (Columbia University, New York) were brought onto the Board in 1938, 1939 and 1940. The active interest of the publishers in editorial policy was reflected in the inclusion of Sir Robert

Evans in the 1940 editorial board when Dr F. H. Spencer took over as General Editor.

One consequence of the Institute's involvement was immediately apparent. In the 1935 volume research themes were presented. Articles appeared on 'Psychological Aspects of Child Development' by Susan Isaacs and on 'The Testing of Intelligence' by H. R. Hamley, R. Rusk, E. J. Schonell, P. E. Vernon and R. A. C. Oliver. A comparative study of native dependencies was made by W. Bryant Mumford of the Institute's Department of Colonial Education. A report by Sir Philip Hartog dealt with the International Institute's examinations enquiry. There were chapters on the relationships between education and juvenile unemployment and juvenile delinquency. This heterogeneous survey of research appeared in a volume which had as its theme the question: Has the reform of education been based upon confusion about the characteristics of social change? In spite of its lack of unity many of the topics have a contemporary air about them.

The idea that through its links with the Institute, the fruits of 'continuous original research into specific problems of Education' should have a permanent place in the *Year Book* was well received. Current research, for example, was reviewed by Cavanagh in the 1939 volume. Under *Philosophies of Education* appeared an illuminating and provocative justification of the National Socialist Movement, the Adolf Hitler Schools and the Hitler Youth written by a German supporter of the Nazi regime. In 1940 research articles on the costs of higher education, on some problems associated with simplified English, and on the social and educational problems of housing estates, illustrate the extent to which contributors, in their research, were anticipating future needs.

As a research volume however the *Year Book* increasingly acquired a comparative education flavour. A number of articles by Hans and Reinhold Schairer were truly comparative. They reflected the particular interests of these scholars in relationships between education and other aspects of social life. The analyses by Hans of the religious traditions which influence education were brilliant. Schairer's article in 1937 showed the relevance of the continental educational crisis to England and would appeal to present day deschoolers and those who feel, as Britain enters the European Economic Community, that 'So far no great continental movement has had any direct repercussion in England'. Hans and Schairer were undoubtedly in outlook 'European' but the *Year Book* retained far stronger ties with the English speaking world, principally with the Commonwealth and to some extent with the USA when Kandel (an outstanding pioneer of comparative education at Teachers College, Columbia University), became a member of the editorial board in 1938.

Thus by 1940 the stage on which postwar growth took place was set.

The future of the *Year Book* was inextricably linked with the future of the University of London Institute of Education as a university Institute committed to systematic and continuous research and as a Commonwealth centre for educational studies. It had been oriented by Percy to a comparative approach and this commitment had been re-enforced by Clarke as Director of the Institute. He clearly favoured non-statistical comparative studies with a sociological bias of the kind developed so well by Hans. Inevitably the *Year Book's* future became linked with the development of comparative education as a university study. Institutionally its future in the postwar period was dependent on the support it received from the Comparative Education and the Education in Tropical Areas departments of the London Institute of Education. In the event it offered the Comparative Education department an outlet for its work, but in so doing the *Year Book* became less English and Commonwealth centred. But the editorial board was never overtly in favour of going into Europe. The *Year Book's* success in the postwar period was bound up with the support it could attract from one or all three sources: the Commonwealth, the USA and Europe. As in the realm of national politics, its London editorial board attempted to establish a special relationship with the USA, Commonwealth ties were weakened and Europe as a source of institutional support was really never considered.

Postwar Volumes

Thus under Clarke's chairmanship the *Year Book* became the major publication of the London Institute in which a wide range of research was reported. It had become a standard work on comparative education and was used as a forum for discussion by Commonwealth contributors. Under the circumstances of the thirties the pressures from outside the Institute to revise the formula were not strong. Certainly some major questions of policy had not been resolved before the Second World War forced a suspension of publication.

One issue turned on the need to give each volume coherence and the means of achieving it. Percy had maintained that the *Year Book* 'must be written by many hands' and had agreed that as a result it would lack unity. His own proposed solution was for himself to write a number of linking chapters. Before he could attempt this he relinquished the editorship. Thereafter editors had to pay more attention to editorial board opinion. So when Sir Percy Nunn as Director of the London Institute became chairman of a joint editorial board, he proposed that each *Year Book* should be given more unity by a gradual reduction in size (it ran to 1,000 pages) by making the contents less varied and by concentrating 'more specifically on certain selected fields of current interest' (YBE 1936, Introduction). Any loss would be compensated for by an 'enhanced concentration and unity of theme and interest'. Nunn's successor Clarke agreed that the bulk of the volume should be reduced. He did not accept that unity should be achieved at the expense of failing to meet the needs of a very wide audience which should include not only members of the profession but politicians and the lay public. He opposed the restriction of each volume to a general theme.

On a second, and related issue, clear guide lines were not established. Should the *Year Book* be principally a popularizing or a research publication? Clarke had reservations about so-called 'research'. He wrote, 'Much of it, no doubt, is of little value and the validity of a good deal more may be called into question' (YBE 1937, p. 9). He had in mind comparative studies based upon insights and judgments which would get behind quantitative evidence to what was truly significant. At the same time the idea that education was becoming a 'specialized technique of modern life' prevented Clarke from dismissing research studies entirely, but he wanted education to be seen as 'an essential and sensitive aspect of government'. The *Year Book* was still to be a popularizer, a book in which the fruits of research were presented and an aid to policy formulation.

After 1946 a succession of editorial board meetings failed to reach a clear decision about priorities of purpose for the revived *Year Book*. Perhaps it was because Sir Robert Evans, Sir Fred Clarke and Dr Nicholas Hans, who had in their respective ways influenced its evolution, remained on the board. In any case several prewar policies were reaffirmed. The *Year Book* was to be an English publication, international in scope but principally addressed to the English-speaking world. Facts and trends were to be summarized in a statistical section. Opinion should be free and should not simply reflect official thinking. Contributors should not be censored but should take responsibility for the views they expressed.

Not all these decisions were reached without considerable debate. Indeed the board minutes from 1946 to 1952 reflect by implication the kind of choices Britain faced in a postwar world of shifting and debated political alliances. At first it was hoped that relationships with the Soviet Union could be established and maintained. Correspondence was not found easy and it was reported in 1950 that there was evidence of a definite unwillingness to collaborate. It was argued that the Germans and Slavs had always thought that the *Year Book* represented the views of the British Government (Minutes, 24 April 1946). Nevertheless for many years the *World Year Book* was the major source of information in English on Soviet education by Soviet writers. On the other hand hopes were entertained that official statements about the postwar education situation could be obtained from Spain and Portugal, while making clear these were 'not necessarily the official views of the *Year Book*' (Minutes, 3 December 1946). At one time it was suggested that to invite an American to serve on the editorial board might not be appropriate (Minutes, 24 April 1946). In the event Kandel was invited to be a member and served for some years. Paradoxically, yet for obvious reasons, the first postwar volume (1946) emphasized postwar educational reconstruction in Western Europe. Proposals to establish closer working links with Unesco were not received with any marked enthusiasm (Minutes, 4 December 1947 and 18 January 1949). Academic contacts with many parts of the world were developed and strengthened but it was not until 1952 that an attempt was made to obtain the institutional support of another organization. Then the special relationship with the USA was formalized and strengthened.

Until this major change of policy Commonwealth links had been strengthened by inviting the Directors of recognized research bodies in Scotland and the Dominions to act as an Advisory Council. Later the Directors of the National Foundation for Educational Research in England and Wales and the Chairman of the American Council for Education were invited to join the advisers. It was held to be 'inadvisable to ask representatives of other countries' to serve. One consequence of this move was that the Directors themselves frequently contributed to the *Year Book* from their knowledge of research in the Dominions. World cover was attempted however. The first two volumes were devoted to the effects of war on education. Countries were grouped on a 'geographical, and not ideological, basis'. The 1948 volume dealt, as stated, with Europe; the 1949 volume with countries outside Europe. The arrangement of chapters caused little difficulty and the editorial board spent most of its time proposing and approving the names of persons who might contribute. Not surprisingly outside the Commonwealth they were, for the most part, scholars known personally to Lauwerys and Hans. The former's work with the Conference of Allied Ministers of Education during the war placed him in a good position to invite prominent officials to write.

It was evident, of course, that the effects of war had differed profoundly from one country to another. Consequently these volumes, although better than those of the thirties, lacked unity. Authors as before tended to comment rather freely on a wide range of problems. On the other hand the statistical summaries were much less full. And members of the editorial board seemed to sense that the centre of interest was moving away from Britain and the Dominions (Minutes, 20 June 1947). The drift was towards a major decision on whether the *Year Book* 'should consist mainly of articles contributed from different countries describing changes and trends of policy, or whether one or several themes should be followed through' from among issues which were alive in many countries (Minutes, 4 December 1947). Virtually the whole board was in favour of continuing to ask contributors from selected countries, since world coverage was impossible, to write on their 'live' problems (Minutes, 18 January 1949).

The joint editors, Lauwerys and Hans, disagreed and their view prevailed. The decisive argument was that existing international agencies, Unesco and the International Bureau of Education in Geneva, were getting annual reports from Ministries of Education of member states. Unesco was moreover going to publish a statistical yearbook. It was evident that these international agencies were in a better position to prepare summary accounts of education throughout the world than the *Year Book* whose only advantage was that its contributors were independent experts with personal opinions to express. The policy that each year a general theme should be selected for special treatment was accepted and by the middle of 1949 the editorial board was discussing its choice of theme and the appropriateness of questions related to it. At the same time its view remained that the coverage in each volume should be as worldwide as possible.

These decisions had repercussions. Attempts had, as we saw, been made in the early postwar volumes to provide a section on statistics. This had not appeared regularly and Jeffery as Chairman of the Board maintained that the 'value of statistics was their regular appearance' (Minutes, 22 February 1951). Hans disagreed. But once it had been decided to treat a general theme each year, the problems of gathering the relevant statistics on a large scale were found to be insurmountable. For example, as the Ministry's representative stated on one occasion, statistics on the finances of the non-state schools in England and Wales could not be produced (Minutes, 5 May 1950). Hans, who was largely responsible for this section, admitted that frequently vital figures on a chosen theme were not available. Only major research would enable them to be provided. The board agreed in 1952 to abandon the section on statistics.

The decision was wise. Novel themes demand new empirical data. Indicators have to be selected, and appropriate questions have then to be asked so that the information may be collected. Personnel are needed to do this and to tabulate it. These are considerable tasks and cannot be done on a large scale quickly. There were simply not the resources to tackle what would have been a valuable addition to a series of studies of successive themes. Fortunately over the years other agencies were accumulating a mass of data which can now be used in comparative studies. In contrast, during the fifties the indicators were crude, frequently inappropriate to the theme under discussion and not sufficiently standardized to allow valid international comparisons to be made. Special data had to be collected and this task was undertaken by OECD, IEA and so on.

It was thus in a sense the very absence of quantitative data during this decade which made it possible for the *Year Book* to perform a pioneering role in the development of comparative education and some other educational sciences by its choice of themes and by the manner in which they were studied.

The Fifties

Themes during the fifties reflect the forward thinking of the editorial boards and the editors. A succession of topics were taken up at a time when the literature on them was limited. Parenthetically it should be said that more often than not the amount of available American literature was greater than from any other source. For example when in 1950 the theme of selection and differentiation through education was tackled there was already a good deal of research information from the USA on the social determinants of educational opportunity. But elsewhere the situation was different. In a seminal article Jean Floud made the point that on the topic of educational opportunity and social mobility in Britain there was very little literature (YBE 1950, p. 117), but went on to analyse the social and occupational selective functions of the school system. In this undeveloped field, the editors prepared for this volume a comparative study of the social origins of students in the universities of six countries. Much of the information was statistical. Subsequently the volume of sociological literature on these topics grew enormously.

It was not so easy to give to the next volume, on education and morals, the same methodological focus. An anthropologist, a medical doctor, a communist lawyer and a sociologist were invited to analyse the problems in this relationship. Again in treating the 1952 theme dealing with the reform and reconstruction of education since the war, the editors were not able to avail themselves of a ready-made conceptual framework. They saw the reform of education taking place under the influence of two forces – the demand by individuals for more education as a human right and the demand for education in terms of manpower needs. Again this volume anticipated a spate of research based on this kind of analysis. In 1953 the social and economic status of teachers was reviewed in the light of its sociological determinants, the psychological traits of teachers and the position of teachers in tribal societies and the status of women teachers in Europe.

In these four volumes the plan was simple. Special studies by well-known or rising social scientists and educationists were followed by national studies classified on a regional basis. The British Isles took precedence, then the Dominions and the USA, Europe, the colonial territories and then Asia. After 1953 attempts were made to move away from this scheme and to adopt each time an analysis based upon the problem approach. It resulted in more coherent volumes without the loss of world coverage.

The first of the volumes to be tackled in this way was the 1954 volume which dealt with the role of education in the technological development of economically underdeveloped countries. It was an admirable example of the problem approach. In the first section the political, economic and moral aspects of technological development were analysed in the light of its various aims. Section II dealt with the sources of these problems through an analysis of cultural change in a number of case studies. Planning and Education was the title of Section III in which regional (TVA, Zuiderzee), national (India, Iran) and international (UN, US Point 4, Colombo) planning was exemplified. Section IV examined the more specific techniques and methods adopted as solutions to the problems of development and in Section V were described some of the agencies of administration involved. Finally, and significantly, in Section VI an assessment of the impact of Western culture on these territories was made. Articles by David H. Blelloch and T. L. Green raised many of the doubts and questions which have perplexed planners ever since. The literature which addresses itself to these and other problems now constitutes the science of educational planning.

At this point I should mention the influence of Robert King Hall, the first American joint editor. When Teachers' College, Columbia entered into a formal agreement to share editorial responsibility with the London Institute King Hall, who had succeeded Kandel, helped to give rigour and precision to the comparative approach which had been accepted by Lauwerys for some time. King Hall presented a paper to a conference of comparative educationists in New York in which he outlined in detail the way in which the problem approach could be used in comparative studies ('The improvement of the teaching of Comparative Education' in New York Conference on Comparative Education 1955; see also 'Comparative Method' in *Comparative Education*, Unesco, Hamburg 1955). The influence of his thinking was apparent in the outline prepared for the guidance of contributors. One consequence of this initiative was that the formula adopted in previous volumes – a few special studies followed by national responses to a series of questions – was abandoned. Whenever possible an attempt was made (1) to analyse the constituents of a major problem, (2) illustrate them in specific contexts, (3) describe proposed solutions and agencies of implementation and (4) anticipate some of the outcomes of policy. It was not always possible to include all the ingredients of the problem approach. Much depended upon the availability of suitable theoretical models and empirical data. Yet most of the volumes anticipated further research.

The 1956 volume which dealt with education and economics is a case in point. Its preparation illustrates how topics were selected and analysed, how advice was sought and how contributors were chosen. The editorial board was discussing articles on the relationships between education and economic change as early as 1948 (Minutes, 7 June 1948) but the first preliminary draft for discussion prepared when the 1956 volume was being planned suggested that it should be restricted to 'problems connected with the finance of education' (First Draft YBE 1956). After discussion among educationists the emphasis changed to the 'question of the material support given to education – that is in the problem of which the "financing of education" is a particular aspect' (Second Draft). Further meetings to discuss this draft included economists who proposed a radically different approach based upon problems as they saw them. Advisers in the USA were working on similar lines and the final draft was a merger of outlines based upon the advice of advisory committees in the USA and UK. It directed attention to the problem of allocating real resources in economies where competing demands cannot be fully satisfied. Education competes with publicly maintained services – defence, communications and health – and with private organizations for personnel, capital and equipment. Within education universities may compete with nursery schools and with vocational education for scarce resources. At the same time it was recognized that education is part of the production-mechanism of a community and could be considered as an economic investment (Final Draft). The volume dealt with the creation of a demand for education – a social demand and a demand for technically trained personnel. Section II examined how resources are acquired and distributed in the light of competing claims on resources. The problems of fiscal management, the provision of services through private agencies and the paying of teachers were reviewed in Section III. In the final Section IV some socio-economic consequences and determinants were discussed, including the return on educational investment in an article by Harold F. Clark of Columbia University. The availability of theoretical models from economics made it possible to give this volume considerable unity. Parenthetically it was not well received by some educationist reviewers who claimed that it was 'improper' to regard education as economic investment.

Theoretical models were not available when in 1957 the editorial board decided to investigate the relationship between thought and action in a volume with the theme *Philosophy and Education*. In an analysis of the perplexing problems of the day-to-day implementation of aims and principles in actual institutions the main question was: How do novel ideas get institutionalized? Reviews show that this was one of the least well understood *Year Book* of the fifties. It is not unreasonable to suggest that a spate of studies in the sixties dealing with innovation theory and strategy dealt more thoroughly with problems similar to those surveyed in the 1957 volume. In much the same way the editors made tentative steps towards conceptual models which would facilitate the study of curriculum determinants (YBE 1958), and the problems of policy in the modern world created by university institutional autonomy and the academic freedom of individual faculty members (YBE 1959). The decade ended with themes which looked at gifted children from psychological (YBE 1960) and sociological frames of reference (YBE 1961).

In summary it might be said that outside the USA it was still possible in the fifties to conduct educational research without expending vast resources. The absence of research studies on the problems investigated made it easier in those years for the *Year Book* to make a research contribution in the field of comparative education and to the development of the sciences of education than it was able to make in the sixties.

A survey of reviews of the volumes published during the fifties reveals that most reviewers saw the *Year Book* as a reference 'book' or 'symposium' offering a 'mass of information' and articles revealing 'range, depth and variety'. Some reviewers were uncertain of the audience for which it was intended. One claimed that some of the expert articles were well nigh incomprehensible to laymen. In contrast, another maintained that too few of the contributors were experts. Inevitably, few reviewers failed to observe that the quality of the articles was uneven and that many of them seemed mere descriptions of the situation in a particular country rather than analyses of the problem under consideration. Some reviewers hoped that depth of treatment would come to replace breadth and that the number of thoughtful original articles in each would be increased. Most reviewers implied that they would prefer to find in a mine of information what they wanted without digging for it.

Nevertheless there is strong evidence to suggest that the *Year Book* was recognized as breaking new ground. In the 1956 volume the editors complained that in the economics of education 'unfortunately we soon discovered a quite appalling shortage of factual enquiries. It appeared that far too little work had been done to make it possible for us to realize our plans with complete success'. Relatively soon after its appearance F. Edding quoted approvingly a further editorial comment:

> The studies and papers presented in this Year Book are, in many cases, little more than tentative explorations of almost virgin land. There is here an almost unlimited field for educational research of high significance at this period of technological change; research which would provide a solid base for the planning of the educational statesman (F. Edding, *Internationale Tendenzen in der Entwicklung der Ausgaben für Schulen und Hochschulen*, Kiel, 1958).

The *Year Books*, including editorial introductions and outstanding articles, soon got into the literature about selection and social patterns (Floud, the editors, Hans), the status and role of teachers (T. H. Marshall, Vernon, Hans, Tropp), educational planning (Singer, Evans, Leach, Lebkicher, Blelloch), the economics of education (Harris, Peacock and Wiseman, Clark, Floud and Halsey, Ginzberg), curriculum innovation (Miles,

McLuhan) and the reform of higher education (Anderson, Morris, Vaizey). Moreover authors such as M. Liebermann in *Education as a Profession*, J. Vaizey in the *Costs of Education* and F. Edding in *Ökonomie des Bildungswesens*, made early reference in their pioneering works to particular volumes.

Finally during this period many reviewers commented on the lack of prominence given in the English edition to the theme and to the editors' names. The USA edition, published by World Book Company, gave more prominence on the title page and spine to these particulars. Indeed the anonymity of authors was to some extent preserved by placing signatures at the end of articles and by identifying editorial contributions under the signature of *The Editors*. These decisions were felt to be largely for the publisher and owner to take. It meant that until the early sixties readers could not easily recognize the theme of any volume or its editors. After 1962 this policy was changed.

George Bereday, King Hall's successor at Teachers College and joint editor from 1957 to 1967, was influential in persuading the publishers and editorial boards to print the theme and the names of the editors on the spine. Both appeared there after 1965. He also initiated the change of title to the more appropriate *World Year Book of Education*. These apparently minor changes in policy were in fact significant. Had they occurred earlier the impact of particular volumes might have been greater. Certainly it would have reflected, under American influence, the thematic approach to comparative studies. As for the problem approach it must be said that on the evidence of Bereday's own book, *Comparative Method in Education*, he was far less committed to it than either Lauwerys or King Hall. Nevertheless during this period of transatlantic cooperation Bereday successfully mobilized considerable American support for the *World Year Book* and retained a personal commitment to a thematic approach and worldwide cover.

The collaboration between the two institutions which had been initiated at one level by Lauwerys and King Hall and at another level by Jeffery, as Director of the London Institute and Dr. William F. Russell as President of Teachers College, New York, in 1953, was consequently maintained. Both the London and New York editorial boards were enlarged to include an appropriate range of academic and administrative interests within the Institute and King's College, on one side of the Atlantic and within Teachers College on the other. No major change of policy was proposed when the agreement was reached but it was recognized that the *Year Book* would 'have available far greater resources for the implementation of its policy than it had in the past' (YBE 1953, Introduction, p. xi). Moreover the arrangement was regarded as 'an outward and visible sign of a collaboration between educationists on the two sides of the Atlantic' (ibid.).

This basis for collaboration was at the time founded on two departments which in the field of Comparative Education were outstanding in the world. Since then other university departments have developed, some with lines of approach different from those pursued in London and New York. Nevertheless the *World Year Book of Education* continued to be supported by leading American comparative educationists, notably in the earlier days by Robert J. Havighurst and during the sixties by C. Arnold Anderson and Mary Jean Bowman, all of Chicago University, and others. The late Saul B. Robinsohn while at the Unesco Institute for Education in Hamburg and then as a Director in the Max-Planck-Institut für Bildungsforschung in Berlin was always willing to help by advising the editorial staff and writing. Philip J. Idenburg, too, and Martin J. Langeveld from the Netherlands over the years took a personal interest in the preparation of several volumes by commenting on draft outlines, suggesting contributors and on occasions writing stimulating articles. The editors moreover, could always call on Masunori Hiratsuka or one of his colleagues for an article on Japan. These are but a few of the names which spring to mind when surveying the personal support given to the *World Year Book* by comparativists outside London and New York. These advisers, from practically every part of the world, ensured that, in terms of cover, the volumes were authoritative without necessarily reflecting official outlooks. They had more cohesion than those of the thirties and they were treating topics of concern to national governments.

The Sixties

During the sixties, therefore, the same major policies were followed with little debate in spite of the fact the *World Year Book* was facing stronger competition in the fields of comparative education research and specialized educational studies. Each year a theme was chosen by the two editorial boards which never met. It was then analysed by the joint editors and their advisers. Care was taken by the boards and by the editors to look for and invite the best qualified contributors from all parts of the world. Authors were paid a nominal sum as an honorarium and consequently the editors had to rely on the goodwill of scholars throughout the world and the intrinsic interest they found in preparing articles outlined in some detail for them by the editorial staff. It says much for the reputation of the editors and the prestige of the sponsoring institutions, namely the London Institute and New York Teachers College, and the name of the publishers, that so many distinguished scholars wrote for the *World Year Book*. Nevertheless it was not always easy to maintain in each volume the quality and the kind of balance that was desired by the editorial boards. As a working rule it was hoped that each year one third of the articles would come from Britain and the Commonwealth, one third from the USA and one third from the rest of the world. This policy was pursued in the interests of viewing problems in worldwide perspective. It had its advantages and disadvantages. It resulted in descriptive rather than analytical studies from countries in which research on a given theme had yet to develop. It also meant that on some topics national case studies seemed to do less than justice to the range and depth of available research. From one viewpoint it might have been wise to limit the number of authors and choice of area. From another viewpoint had this been done the *World Year Book* would have been misnamed and one of its distinguishing characteristics would have been lost.

In the event themes were taken up in the sixties which reflected the interests emphasized in the fifties. In 1961 and 1962 the psychological and sociological aspects of the selection and education of gifted children were reviewed. In 1963, in a follow-up to the 1953 volume, the role and status of teachers was treated sociologically. In 1964 church-state relationships were analysed, whereas religious traditions had been the theme of the 1951 volume. The 1967 volume on planning, carried further the pioneering approaches of the 1954 and 1956 volumes. The volume on examinations (1969) looked in greater detail at some topics of curriculum reform examined in 1958. The 1959, 1971/72 and 1972/73 volumes dealt with higher education, the first of these in a manner which subsequently received considerable attention from other authors. New ground was broken in the *Education Explosion* volume (1965) for which there was a great deal of available statistical data on which authors could base their analyses. In rather different ways the volumes on *Education within Industry* (1968) and *Education in Cities* (1970) surveyed virgin territory. In the first of these volumes, in the absence of a clear conceptual model, policies throughout the world were reviewed. In the second of these volumes models of analysis, drawn mainly from American sociological sources, helped to place case studies of cities throughout the world into some kind of perspective.

All of these volumes included some articles of considerable originality. The standards of the fifties were maintained. Reviewers praised the same features and criticized similar weaknesses. But in the sixties the contribution of the *World Year Book* had to be seen against the explosion of educational literature. Without major financial support it was perhaps a vain hope that it could break new ground, maintain its position of pre-eminence in the field of comparative education research, and give rise to new educational sciences. What might have been attempted with success would have been to collect each year a relatively small number of high quality, previously published articles on a worldwide problem. Nobody was prepared to allow the *World Year Book of Education* to become a textbook of readings however scholarly. Yet in one sense one of its major contributions has been to provide teachers and students of comparative education with sound data and insights about education throughout the world. Selected volumes enable the development of major issues in education to be reviewed, e.g. higher education, teacher training, curriculum and examinations. By the same token collections of articles dealing with particular countries, notably France, the USSR, Japan and India provide useful national non-official area studies. In these ways a contribution was made to the informed teaching of comparative education in universities and colleges of education.

In terms of approach by the early sixties the *World Year Book of Education* was no longer unique. Among the developments which helped to change its position in the world of comparative education were the studies carried out by OECD, the International Educational Achievement workers, Unesco, the World Bank, the International Institute for Educational Planning, the Council of Europe and the European Cultural Foundation. Moreover a host of research units funded by national and philanthropic agencies were carrying out comparative studies. In addition, an important development was the growth in numbers of research units at the University Institute of Education of London, and the range of topics studied. These units had sufficient funds to provide for adequate research assistance and secretarial help. Their work could be spread over several years of endeavour. The editors of the *World Year Book* were never able to command such resources.

These developments placed the *World Year Book* at a disadvantage. It had to meet criteria of scholarship based upon an explosion of research and literature. Even during the fifties to impress American educationists and social scientists the volumes had to be seen as making a real contribution to American literature. They could rarely add substantially to the body of knowledge about US education. Consequently to succeed in America the *World Year Book* had to be seen as a contribution to comparative, international, and development education. An earlier consensus of outlook in these areas had already been fragmented. Moreover the focus of interest in these fields in the USA had become the Third World in which British and USA interests were sometimes more in conflict than in harmony. Perhaps the original intention of giving a central place to educational problems in England and Wales in the light of British traditions persisted into the period of US collaboration and the overt widening of scope. Consequently American readers perhaps found the contents of some volumes of marginal relevance to their studies in comparative and development education. In volumes in which problems common to Britain and the USA were analysed, as for example in 1954, 1956, 1957, 1967 and 1970, the reception given to the *World Year Book* in the USA was more favourable than when it appeared to treat pressing American problems and solutions rather superficially.

In practice, however, British and Commonwealth interests received less attention in the postwar volumes. For example, the Advisory Council whose members were the directors of national educational research councils in England and Wales, Scotland, Australia, New Zealand, and South Africa was dissolved after the London–New York links had been formalized. Again the Comparative Education Department rather than the Department of Education in Tropical Areas at the London Institute played a major role in editing the *World Year Book*. This meant that close links with Europe were maintained in spite of the ambivalence in outlook among British people about entry into the European Economic Community. At the same time the amount of research, from particular viewpoints, about education in Britain and a growing familiarity with continental developments made it impossible for the *World Year Book* to perform in Britain the unique dissemination-of-research role that it had played in the thirties and to some extent in the fifties.

The most important changed feature of the sixties was the growth in the number of well-financed projects undertaken by world and regional organizations. They could command resources which enabled them to follow, develop and extend techniques of research enquiry in comparative education initiated by the editorial staff of the *World Year Book*. Typically staff members of the international organization discuss and formulate topics with national representatives and advisers. Having drawn up a draft outline they frequently circulate it for critical comment by experts in the field before bringing together potential research workers at a conference or workshop to work out theoretical models and to discuss research techniques in the light of agreed questions and the kind of data needed. Research workers subsequently either collate already published material, or collect new information and check out their findings by conducting field studies. Background documentation is provided and the raw reports are then edited by staff members and again sent out for critical and constructive comment to experts. Final drafts may well have to be cleared by a representative of the governments of countries involved in the enquiry. Only after these careful and costly procedures have been carried out is a final general report prepared and published. At each stage it is usually possible to pay participants a professional fee. Staff members of the international organization are frequently supported throughout by expert consultants.

The resources needed to mount such comparative research were never available to the editorial staff of the *World Year Book of Education*. Prior to 1953 the joint editors worked virtually unaided on the editorial side. From then on they had the help of a London Assistant Editor but an arrangement in the late sixties to meet the burden of work by associating all members of the growing Department of Comparative Education at the London Institute was short-lived. In the event the editorial staff were invariably preparing three volumes: one in the final stages of publication, a second in the throes of inviting, receiving and editing articles, and a third in the initial stages of planning. As mentioned earlier care was taken to obtain the best expert advice available in formulating a theme and analysing it. But it was never possible to convene a planning conference, to hold joint editorial board meetings or to arrange for the editors to meet on a regular basis. Pressure to publish annually meant that it was rarely possible to grant contributors the kind of time needed to prepare original research studies unless they were on sabbatical or had financial support from other sources. The editors were heavily dependent on the goodwill and expert depth knowledge of colleagues throughout the world.

A further problem was created by the fact that each year a different theme was taken up so that it was not possible to follow up over a period of years a specific research topic. The success of the 1967 volume on *Planning* was perhaps due to the fact that it included so much of the fruits of research in the economics of education stimulated by the 1956 volume. In general, however, against systematic continuing research supported by considerable funds and personnel the research role of the *World Year Book* in the sixties must be seen in perspective. It was bound to be limited by lack of resources. It had a complementary rather than, as previously, an innovative task to perform. It did this perhaps by generating novel hypotheses and providing, as always, non-official accounts of education problems in most countries of the world.

In considering its future the editorial boards had to take into account the problem of providing the kind of support required if the scope and purposes of the *World Year Book* were not to be changed radically. There seemed little likelihood that these would be forthcoming under existing arrangements. The London board considered the possibilities of reducing or omitting the comparative element but no other Department showed a desire to take it on either on a yearly or permanent basis. Certainly to encourage any Department to shoulder the burden of preparing an annual publication unless it was regarded as a major departmental research contribution was unrealistic. There was little support for a policy of limiting the number of authors invited to contribute as a long term solution. Certainly the possibility of transforming it into a textbook by collecting together each year some new and some already published articles on a particular theme did not appeal. Several alternatives were considered by the London board together with proposals from the New York board. The London board was not able to recommend any of them to the publishers, hence the decision to terminate its publication.

In Retrospect

Looking back I think the *World Year Book of Education* has achieved on the international stage the kind of aims its founder, Sir Robert Evans, and its first Editor-in-Chief envisaged. It was to provide a forum for the discussion of pressing educational issues, in the first instance in the United Kingdom but viewed in a world context. Subsequently with the collaboration of a university Institute which became the Commonwealth centre of educational research and which helped to pioneer the study of comparative education, it disseminated the fruits of educational research. In the post war era it was the first publication to deal regularly and systematically with problems arising from the relationships education has with other aspects of society from a comparative point of view. Finally, it was an example of collaboration, extending over twenty years, between educationists on the two sides of the Atlantic which won the goodwill and support of educationists from all parts of the world.

These achievements were possible only as a result of the close and happy partnership established between the owners and publishers, Evans Brothers of London, and the University of London Institute of Education. Throughout this period of association the publishers have always taken a keen interest in the professional success of the *World Year Book*. In my experience they never placed constraints on the editorial staff and always put academic before commercial considerations in their contribution to policy debates and decisions. As members of the Editorial Board in London Sir Robert Evans, Mr Noel Evans, Mr Quinn-Young and Mr Robin Hyman brought to its meetings an expertise in educational publishing and a wide and deep understanding of educational problems at home and abroad. On the American side Mr William Ferguson of World Book Company took a personal interest. In the day-to-day work of preparing the *World Year Books* the editors were fortunate to have the conscientious and devoted help of Miss Barbara Hall who since 1953 as a member of the staff of Evans Brothers participated in every aspect of the work first as secretary to the editors and the editorial board, and then after 1970 as Assistant Editor.

Without this very real support from the publishers editorial responsibility could not have been discharged in a way which enabled the *World Year Book of Education* to make its contribution to the literature of education and in particular to the development of comparative education. It will be missed, I suspect, by those who believe with Clarke (in spite of the very real advances made in it) that the statistical method, from some points of view 'fails to exhibit those differences and resemblances that are truly *significant*' (YBE 1937, p. 9) and who have looked in the past to the *World Year Book* to point up some of these comparisons. It will also be missed by teachers of comparative education who could turn to it for reasonably up to date non-official information and interpretations of education throughout the world.

For my part, I am proud to have been associated with the *World Year Book of Education* for so long.

Appendix

The World Year Book of Education 1932 to 1974

Themes

1932–40 Discussion of educational issues in the United Kingdom, the British Commonwealth and elsewhere; statistical information

1941–47 not published

1948 The effects of the war on education; Europe and the English-speaking countries

1949 The effects of the war on education: other countries and a survey of the growth of nationalism, plural communities, language, industrialization

1950 Selection and social patterns

1951 Education and morals

1952 The reform of education

1953 The economic and social status of teachers

1954 Education and the technological development of underdeveloped countries

1955 Education and guidance

1956 The economic bases of education

1957 Education and philosophy

1958 Curriculum and the secondary school

1959 Higher education

1960 Communication media and the school

1961 Concepts of excellence

1962 The gifted child

1963 The education and training of teachers

1964 International understanding

1965 The education explosion

1966 Church and state in education

1967 Educational planning

1968 Education within industry

1969 Examinations

1970 Education in cities

1971/72 Higher education in a changing world

1972/73 Universities facing the future

1974 Education and rural development

Editors

1932–35 Editor-in-Chief: Lord Eustace Percy

1936–39 General Editor: Harley V. Usill

1940 General Editor: F. H. Spencer

1941–47 not published

1948–52 Joint Editors: Nicholas Hans (UK), Joseph A. Lauwerys (UK)

1953 Joint Editors: Nicholas Hans (UK), Joseph A. Lauwerys (UK), Robert King Hall (USA)

1954–55 Joint Editors: Nicholas Hans (UK), Joseph A. Lauwerys (UK), Robert King Hall (USA)
Assistant Editor: Brian Holmes (UK)

1956 Joint Editors: Joseph A. Lauwerys (UK), Robert King Hall (USA)
Assistant Editor: Brian Holmes (UK)

1957–59 Joint Editors: Joseph A. Lauwerys (UK), George Z. F. Bereday (USA)
        Assistant Editor: Brian Holmes (UK)

1960   Joint Editors: Joseph A. Lauwerys (UK), George Z. F. Bereday (USA)
        Assistant Editor: Brian Holmes (UK), with the assistance of C. R. E. Gillett

1961   Joint Editors: Joseph A. Lauwerys (UK), George Z. F. Bereday (USA)
        Assistant Editor: Claude Russell (UK)

1962–65 Joint Editors: Joseph A. Lauwerys (UK), George Z. F. Bereday (USA)
        Assistant Editor: Richard F. Goodings (UK)

1966   Joint Editors: Joseph A. Lauwerys (UK), George Z. F. Bereday (USA)
        Assistant Editors: Richard F. Goodings (UK), Barbara M. Hall (UK)

1967   Joint Editors: Joseph A. Lauwerys (UK), George Z. F. Bereday (USA)
        Special Consulting Editor: Mark Blaug (UK)

1968   Joint Editors: Joseph A. Lauwerys (UK), David G. Scanlon (USA)
        Assistant Editor: Laura Goodman Howe (UK)

1969   Joint Editors: Joseph A. Lauwerys (UK), David G. Scanlon (USA)
        Assistant Editor: Amy Lou Brown (UK)

1970   Joint Editors: Joseph A. Lauwerys (UK), David G. Scanlon (USA)
        Assistant Editor: Barbara M. Hall (UK)

1971/72 Joint Editors: Brian Holmes (UK), David G. Scanlon (USA)
        Associate Joint Editor: W. Roy Niblett (UK)
        Assistant Editor: Barbara M. Hall (UK)

1972/73 Joint Editors: W. Roy Niblett (UK), R. Freeman Butts (USA)
        Associate Joint Editor: Brian Holmes (UK)
        Assistant Editor: Barbara M. Hall (UK)

1974   Joint Editors: Philip Foster (UK), James R. Sheffield (USA)
        Assistant Editor: Barbara M. Hall (UK)

Index

For Product Safety Concerns and Information please contact our EU
representative GPSR@taylorandfrancis.com Taylor & Francis Verlag GmbH,
Kaufingerstraße 24, 80331 München, Germany

Printed and bound by CPI Group (UK) Ltd, Croydon, CR0 4YY
11/04/2025
01844005-0002